PIMLICO

660

ROME '44

Raleigh Trevelyan was born in 1923 in the
Andaman Islands. The son of an Indian
Army officer, he spent much of his child-
hood in Kashmir. As a young officer in the
Rifle Brigade and seconded to the Green
Howards, he landed at Anzio and within
the next four months was twice wounded.
He remained in Italy until 1946 when he
returned to England, first to work in a mer-
chant bank and then to become a publisher.
His previous books include *The Fortress*,
Princes Under the Volcano, *A Hermit Disclosed*,
The Big Tomato, *The Shadow of Vesuvius* and
A Pre-Raphaelite Circle.

ROME '44

The Battle for the Eternal City

———

RALEIGH TREVELYAN

PIMLICO

Published by Pimlico 2004

2 4 6 8 10 9 7 5 3 1

First published in Great Britain by Martin Secker & Warburg Limited 1981

Pimlico edition 2004

Pimlico
Random House, 20 Vauxhall Bridge Road,
London SW1V 2SA

Random House Australia (Pty) Limited
20 Alfred Street, Milsons Point, Sydney,
New South Wales 2061, Australia

Random House New Zealand Limited
18 Poland Road, Glenfield,
Auckland 10, New Zealand

Random House South Africa (Pty) Limited
Endulini, 5A Jubilee Road, Parktown 2193, South Africa

Random House UK Limited Reg. No. 954009

A CIP catalogue record for this book is available from the British Library

ISBN 1-8441-3546-2

Printed and bound in Great Britain by Bookmarque Ltd, Croydon, Surrey

ONCE AGAIN IN MEMORY OF THE FOUR

We were 20,000 feet over Rome.

The voice of the bombardier in the nacelle sounded calm.

'Bomb doors open!'

'OK,' said the captain.

'Bombs away!' came the bombardier's answer.

That was all.

I could not see the bombs drop. But I saw them tumble in clusters from the other Forts ahead ...

As we switched towards the sea, I could see the white ribbon of the Tiber, flowing past the Vatican, whose spirals rose in the clear sunlight far from the inferno of smoke and bomb-bursts.

From 'Twenty Angels over Rome' by Richard McMillan,
London, 1944

Look back across the Tiber at the city spread beneath our feet in all its mellow tints of white, and red, and brown, broken here and there by masses of dark green pine and cypress, and by shining cupolas raised to the sun. There it all lies beneath us, the heart of Europe and the living chronicle of man's long march to civilization: for there, we know, are the well-proportioned piazzas with their ancient columns and their fountains splashing in shade and shine around the sculptured water-gods of the Renaissance; the Forum won back by the spade; and the first monuments of the Christian Conquest. There rise the naked hulks of giant ruins stripped long ago by hungry generations of Papal architects; and there, on the outskirts of the town, is the Pyramid that keeps watch over the graves.

From 'Garibaldi's Defence of the Roman Republic'
by G. M. Trevelyan, London, 1907

We do not want Germans or Americans. Let us weep in peace.

Written on a wall in Trastevere, Rome, January 1944

'Otto, Otto! Ich sterbe, Otto!'

A cry from no-man's land, Anzio Beachhead, February 1944

CONTENTS

MARCH

APRIL–JUNE

List of Illustrations, Maps and Cartoons

Dramatis Personae – January–June 1944

The following is a list of some central figures affecting or affected by the city's destiny, and in relation to this book.

THE VATICAN

Pope Pius XII (Eugenio Pacelli)
Cardinal Luigi Maglione: Secretary of State
Monsignor Domenico Tardini: Secretary of the Congregation of Extraordinary Ecclesiastical Affairs
Monsignor Giovanni Battista Montini: *Sostituto* or Substitute Secretary of State, later Pope Paul VI
Monsignor Amleto Cicognani: Apostolic Delegate in Washington
Padre Pancrazio Pfeiffer: Superior-General of the Salvatorian Order; liaison with German authorities
Sir D'Arcy Osborne: British Minister to the Holy See
Harold H. Tittmann Jr: United States Chargé d'Affaires to the Holy See
Baron Ernst von Weizsaecker: German Ambassador to the Holy See

THE 'NAZIFASCISTI'

Lieutenant-General Kurt Maeltzer: German Commandant in Rome
Colonel Eugen Dollmann: Waffen SS liaison officer for General Wolff, head of SS in Italy
Lieutenant-Colonel Herbert Kappler: head of Gestapo
Pietro Caruso: Fascist Chief of Police
Pietro Koch: head of Fascist political police squad

THE ROMAN UNDERGROUND

MILITARY FRONT ('BADOGLIANI')
Colonel Giuseppe Cordero Lanza di Montezemolo: Commander to 5 January
General Quirino Armellini: Commander 5 January to 24 March
General Roberto Bencivegna: Commander 24 March onwards
General Filippo Caruso: Commander of Carabinieri
Ettore Basevi (Centro X, Intelligence)

COMMITTEE OF NATIONAL LIBERATION (CLN)
Ivanoe Bonomi: head of CLN, Labour Democrat
Conte Alessandro Casati: Liberal
Alcide De Gasperi: Christian Democrat
Ugo La Malfa: Action Party
Pietro Nenni: Socialist
Meuccio Ruini: Labour Democrat (Democrazia di Lavoro)
Mauro Scoccimarro: Communist
Giorgio Amendola: Communist, Military Junta, Commander of 'Gaps' throughout central Italy
Riccardo Bauer: Action Party, Military Junta
Sandro Pertini: Socialist, Military Junta

THE ROMAN 'GAPS' (GRUPPI DI AZIONE PATRIOTTICA)
Antonello Trombadori: Commander to 2 February
Carlo Salinari: Commander from 2 February

JEWISH ASSISTANCE
Padre Benedetto (Benôit-Marie de Bourg): Capuchin monk, head of Delasem, organization for assistance to foreign Jews

THE ROME ESCAPE ORGANIZATION

Monsignor Hugh O'Flaherty: Irish, at the Congregation of the Holy Office, Vatican; initiator of organization 'Council of Three'
John May: butler to D'Arcy Osborne; one of original 'Council'
Conte Sarsfield Salazar: at Swiss Legation, one of original 'Council'
Major Sam Derry: senior military officer in charge from December 1943
Mrs Henrietta Chevalier: Maltese, first to supply accommodation for escaped POWs

OSS (OFFICE OF STRATEGIC SERVICES) SPY NETWORK

Peter Tompkins: Fifth Army intelligence
Major Maurizio Giglio ('Cervo'): operator of clandestine radio
Barone Franco Malfatti: Socialist underground
'Coniglio': member of SIM, Italian Army military intelligence

POLITICIANS IN THE SOUTH

Marshal Pietro Badoglio: Prime Minister
Benedetto Croce: Liberal, philosopher and historian
Conte Carlo Sforza: Independent, pre-Fascist Foreign Secretary and
    diplomat
Palmiro Togliatti ('Ercole Ercoli'): head of Communist party in Italy;
    arrived from USSR in March
Harold Macmillan: British High Commissioner, member Allied
    Advisory Council to April
Robert D. Murphy: US member of Advisory Council, ambassadorial
    rank
René Massigli: French member of Advisory Council
Andrei Vyshinsky: Soviet member of Advisory Council to March
Alexander Bogomolov: Soviet member of Advisory Council from
    March
Sir Noel Charles: British member Advisory Council from April 1944,
    ambassadorial rank
Alexander C. Kirk: US member Advisory Council from April 1944,
    ambassadorial rank
Major-General Sir Noel Mason-MacFarlane: Chief Commissioner,
    Allied Control Commission
Harold Caccia: British Vice-President, political section Control
    Commission
Samuel Reber: US Vice-President, political section Control Commission

ALLIED COMMANDERS AT ANZIO

General the Hon. Sir Harold R. L. G. Alexander: Allied Armies in Italy
Lieutenant-General Mark W. Clark: Fifth Army
Major-General John P. Lucas: US VI Corps to 23 February
Major-General Lucian K. Truscott Jr: 3rd US Infantry Division to 17
    February, VI Corps from 23 February

Major-General V. Evelegh: British Deputy Commander VI Corps from 17 February

Brigadier-General John W. O'Daniel: 3rd US Infantry Division from 17 February

Major-General Ernest W. Harmon: 1st US Armored Division

Major-General W. R. C. Penney: 1st British Infantry Division

REINFORCEMENTS TO APRIL

Major-General William W. Eagles: 45th US Infantry Division

Major-General G. W. R. Templer: 56th Infantry Division

Brigadier-General Robert T. Frederick: 1st US–Canadian Special Service Force

Major-General P. G. S. Gregson-Ellis: 5th British Infantry Division

REINFORCEMENTS IN MAY

Major-General Charles W. Ryder: 34th US Infantry Division

Major-General Fred. L. Walker: 36th US Infantry Division

GERMAN COMMANDERS AT ANZIO

Field-Marshal Albert Kesselring: Commander-in-Chief South-West and Army Group C

Lieutenant-General Ernst Schlemmer: Commander Rome Area, responsible local commander until 23 January

Colonel-General Eberhard von Mackensen: Fourteenth Army

General Alfred Schlemm: I Parachute Corps

General Traugott Herr: LXXVI Panzer Corps

Major-General Paul Conrath: Hermann Goering Panzer Division

Major-General Helmuth Pfeifer: 65th Division

Major-General Heinz Trettner: 4th Parachute Division (promoted during campaign from Colonel)

Major-General Wilhelm Raapke: 71st Infantry Division

Major-General Hans-Georg Hildebrandt: 715th Infantry Division

Lieutenant-General Smilo von Luettwitz: 26th Panzer Division

Lieutenant-General Walther Fries: 29th Panzer Grenadier Division

Lieutenant-General Fritz-Hubert Graeser: 3rd Panzer Grenadier Division

Lieutenant-General Karl Eglseer: 114th Jaeger Division

Lieutenant-General Heinz Greiner: 362nd Infantry Division

Allied Forces at Anzio: January to April
VI Corps, US Fifth Army

BRITISH
1st Infantry Division
  24th Guards Brigade
    5th Battalion Grenadier Guards
    1st Battalion Irish Guards
    1st Battalion Scots Guards
  2nd Infantry Brigade
    6th Battalion The Gordon
      Highlanders
    1st Battalion The Loyal Regiment
    2nd Battalion The North Staffordshire
      Regiment
  3rd Infantry Brigade
    1st Battalion The Duke of
      Wellington's Regiment
    1st Battalion The King's Shropshire
      Light Infantry
    2nd Battalion The Sherwood Foresters
  2nd, 19th, 67th, 24th Field Regiments
    RA
  80th Medium Regiment RA (The
    Scottish Horse)
  90th Light AA Regiment RA
  23rd, 238th, 248th Field Companies RE
  1st Reconnaissance Regiment
  2nd/7th Battalion The Middlesex
    Regiment (MG)
  46th Royal Tank Regiment
  3rd Beach Group (54th The Durham
    Light Infantry, 70th The Queen's
    Own Royal West Kent Regiment)
  2nd Special Service Brigade
    9th, 43rd Royal Marine Commandos
    (40th in April)
56th Infantry Division
  18th Infantry Brigade
    1st Battalion The Buffs
    9th Battalion The King's Own
      Yorkshire Light Infantry
    14th Battalion The Sherwood
      Foresters
    167th Infantry Brigade
      7th Battalion The Oxfordshire and
        Buckinghamshire Light Infantry
      8th and 9th Battalions The Royal
        Fusiliers
    168th Infantry Brigade
      1st Battalion The London Irish Rifles
      1st Battalion The London Scottish

    10th Battalion The Royal Berkshire
      Regiment
  169th Infantry Brigade
    2nd/5th, 2nd/6th, 2nd/7th Battalions
      The Queen's Royal Regiment
5th Infantry Division
  13th Infantry Brigade
    2nd Battalion The Cameronians
    2nd Battalion The Royal Inniskilling
      Fusiliers
    2nd Battalion The Wiltshire
      Regiment
  15th Infantry Brigade
    1st Battalion The Green Howards
    1st Battalion The King's Own
      Yorkshire Light Infantry
    1st Battalion The York and Lancaster
      Regiment
  17th Infantry Brigade
    2nd Battalion The Northamptonshire
      Regiment
    2nd Battalion The Royal Scots
      Fusiliers
    6th Battalion The Seaforth
      Highlanders
    5th Reconnaissance Regiment
    7th Battalion The Cheshire Regiment
      (MG)
AMERICAN
1st US Armored Division (less Combat
  Command 'B' until end April)
  1st Armored Regiment
  6th Armored Infantry Regiment
3rd US Infantry Division
  7th, 15th, 30th Infantry Regiments
  504th Parachute Infantry Regiment
  509th Parachute Infantry Battalion
  1st, 3rd, 4th Ranger Infantry Battalions
  751st Tank Battalion
45th US Infantry Division
  157th, 179th, 180th Infantry Regiments
  158th, 160th, 171st, 189th Field Artillery
    Battalions
  645th Tank Destroyer Battalion
1st Special Service Force (Canadian–
  American)
36th, 540th Engineer Combat
  Regiments
1st Naval Beach Battalion

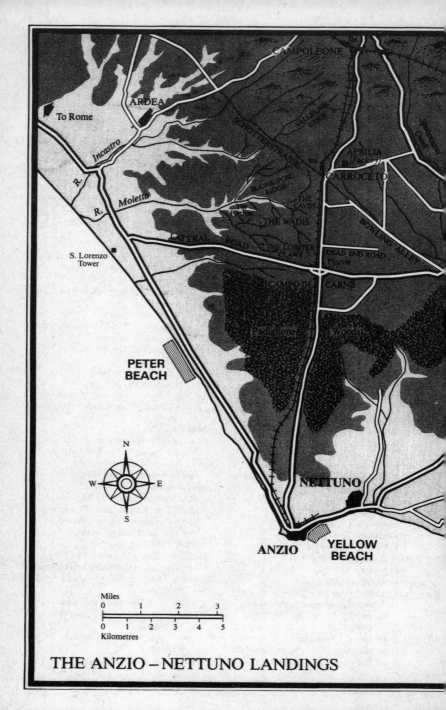

THE ANZIO – NETTUNO LANDINGS

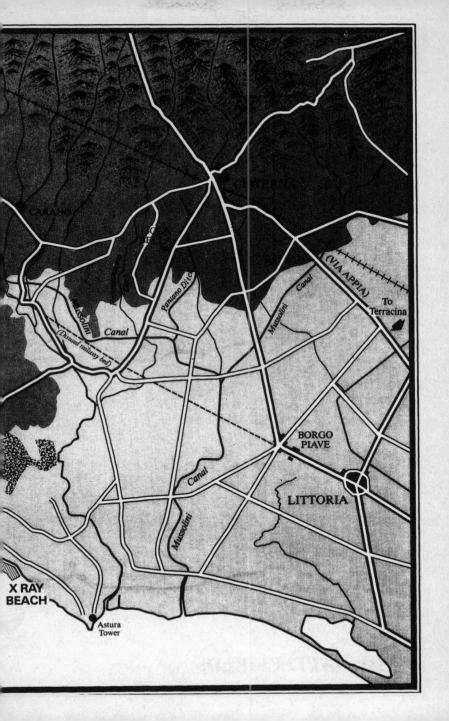

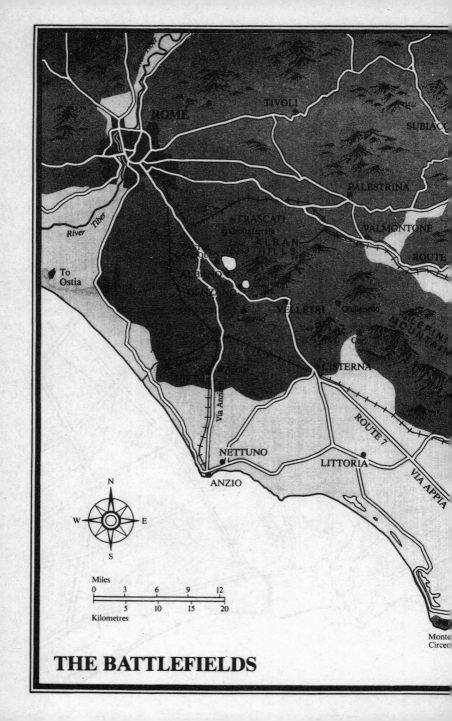

THE BATTLEFIELDS

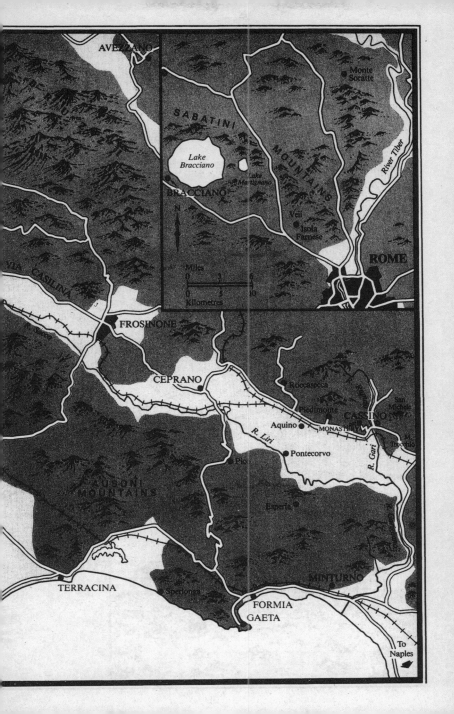

AVEZZANO

Monte
Soratte

SABATINI

Lake
Bracciano

Lake
Martignano

MOUNTAINS

River Tiber

BRACCIANO

N

Veii

Isola
Farnese

ROME

Miles

Kilometres

VIA CASILINA

FROSINONE

CEPRANO

Roccasecca

Piedimonte

San
Michele

CASSINO

Aquino

MONASTERY

M.
Trocchio

R. Liri

Pontecorvo

R. Gari

Pico

AUSONI
MOUNTAINS

Esperia

MINTURNO

TERRACINA

Sperlonga

FORMIA
GAETA

To
Naples

THE STRUGGLE FOR MONTE CASSINO

MONTE CASTELLONE

VILLA SANTA LUCIA

ALBANETA

VIA CASILINA ROUTE 6

THE MONASTERY (MONTE CASSINO)

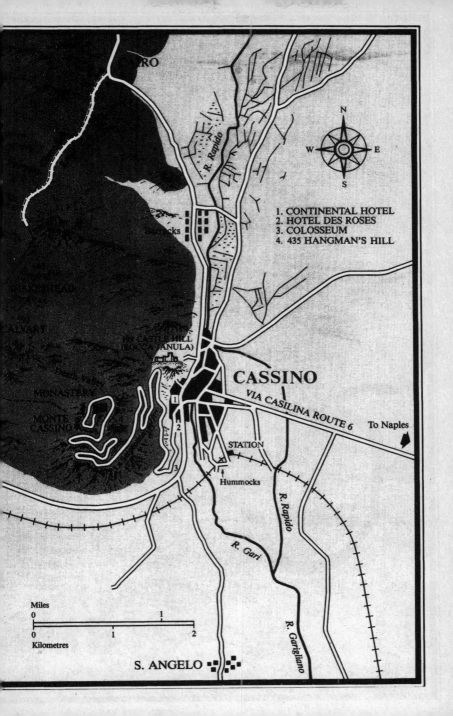

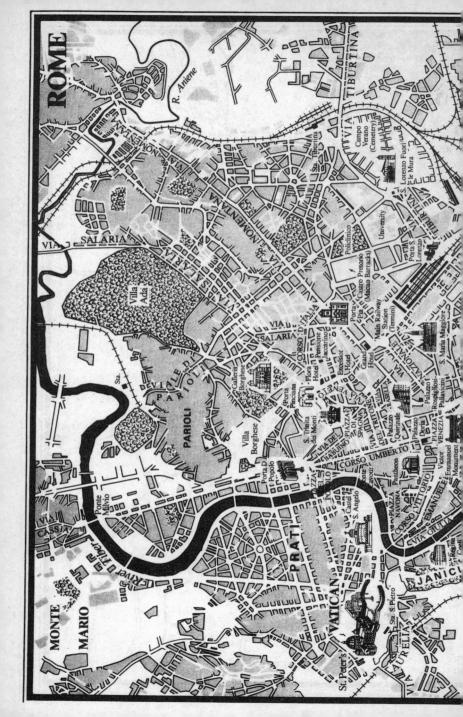

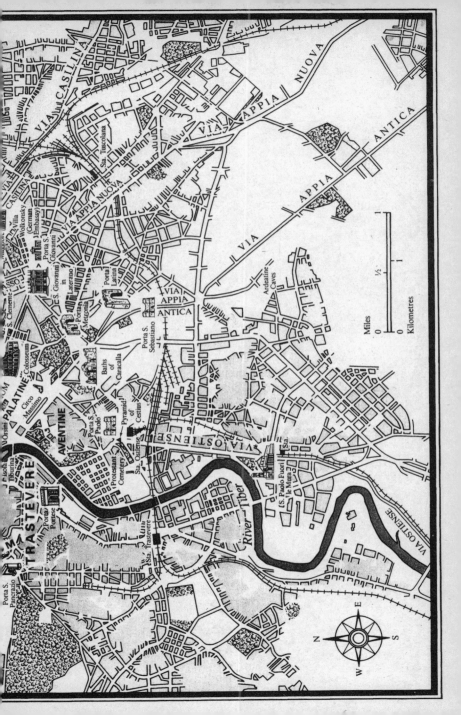

Prologue

I first went to Rome in October 1944, and stayed there on and off for the next couple of years. Having spent, earlier on, nearly three months in the slit-trenches and dugouts of Anzio, I was glad to have a base job with a peculiar Anglo-American organization called MMIA, the Military Mission to the Italian Army, known to the Italians as Mamma Mia.

'Why did you Allies stay so long at Anzio?' Romans sometimes asked in a semi-teasing way. I only began to learn some of the answers a long while afterwards when I read books about the campaign. At Anzio I had been a platoon commander, aged twenty, and like others around me had to believe that the discomforts and the deaths had a point, and that those in charge of our destinies knew what they were doing and never made mistakes, and that they were never affected by fatigue, vanity, jealousy or megalomania.

I wrote a book about some of my experiences at Anzio, and as a result of that met a German who had fought opposite me. We became friends, a favourite joke being that we used to throw grenades at one another. I think we both had the same sort of feelings in the front line. One goes on fighting, killing, simply because one has to; there is a strange compulsion in battle, but it is usually a matter of self-preservation.

I never thought I would want to return to Anzio, or to Cassino, but fate has drawn me back there several times. Anzio is now a large cheerful holiday resort, with some of the best fish restaurants I have known. The monastery of Monte Cassino, on the other hand, is still to me a sombre place; the Polish cemetery beneath it is beautiful, but haunting and painful.

Coming to Rome was the realization of a dream. In the trenches it had always seemed the great inaccessible. I was soon to learn something about my Roman friends' ordeals, but on the whole they preferred not to discuss them, just as I preferred to forget my own recent experiences. Time has changed all that, and it even helps to remember. Several of the people I mention here are friends of mine – Italian, British, American, German. Several more have told me their stories, which were indispensable as background for the period but, unfortunately, had to be left out for reasons of length.

This book covers controversial episodes which can still arouse passions. Within reason I have tried to be objective when describing them, though being English I cannot help having a bias occasionally. In writing about battles I have avoided meticulous details of military operations. I have aimed to show what it was like to have lived through those months in the first half of 1944 from both sides of the fence, within the context of higher command, and in this way I have tried to be subjective. Some evil deeds have had to be recorded here, but I think it is important to emphasize from the beginning that they do not indict a race or nation.

Why did the Allies stay on so long at the Anzio Beachhead? Why indeed?

*   *   *   *

The landings took place on 22 January 1944, so this date is the starting point for my book. At the end I have given a list of some main events in 1943, followed – for reference if need be – by another list of events in the first half of 1944, mostly to do with Rome and the Italian campaign.

By January 1944, although stalemate had been reached in Italy, the tide of the war was beginning to turn in the Allies' favour. It was known that the Japanese were about to launch a crucial offensive in the Arakan in Burma; however the Americans, with great boldness, were preparing to land forty thousand troops in the heart of the Marshall Islands in the Pacific. The Russians were sweeping forward. On 20 January the ancient city of Novgorod was recaptured. The blockade of Leningrad was about to be lifted, the Ukraine had been entered and the Crimea cut off.

The success of the campaign in Sicily had led to the fall of Mussolini on 25 July 1943. On 3 September the British Eighth Army had crossed the Straits of Messina unopposed, and on 9 September the US Fifth Army had landed at Salerno with very different results, though ultimately successful. In the meantime there had been secret negotiations for an armistice between the Allies and the Italian government headed by Marshal Badoglio. The announcement of the armistice on 8 September by General Eisenhower came prematurely from the Italian point of view, and resulted in the flight of Badoglio and the royal family from Rome to Brindisi, soon to be safely occupied by the Allies, who also entered Naples on 1 October after four days' popular uprising. On 3 October the Germans finally evacuated Sardinia and Corsica.

The armistice resulted in fierce German reprisals against Italian troops in Yugoslavia; the Italian fleet sailed to Malta. In Rome an anti-Badoglio coalition of left and right patriots, known as the CLN, was set up, but all resistance was soon crushed by the Germans, and on 9 September the occupation of the city began. The CLN went underground. A rival pro-Badoglio organization, the Military Front, under Colonel Montezemolo, was in due course also secretly formed. The Badoglio government remained under Allied control in Brindisi.

On 12 September there was the famous rescue of Mussolini by Skorzeny from the Gran Sasso in the Abruzzi mountains. Mussolini was flown to Munich, and soon afterwards set up a puppet republican government at Salò on Lake Garda.

The Allied advance northwards to what Churchill had called the 'soft underbelly' of Europe was slowing down. This was partly due to mountainous country, the exceptionally bad weather and swollen rivers. Hitler had also determined that no more ground in Italy should be lost. The other important factors were the Americans' insistence that preparations for Overlord in 1944 must be given overriding priority and their anxiety to bring the war in the Pacific to a quick end; Washington was not therefore anxious to be committed to an expensive and exhausting campaign in southern Europe.

On 13 November the British were forced to evacuate islands in the eastern Aegean, partly through lack of American support. This was a great disappointment to Churchill, who had thought that their successful occupation might encourage Turkey to join the Allies, and that this in turn might ensure British–American, or at any rate British, predominance in the Balkans before the arrival of the Russians.

On 22 November the first Cairo Conference, between Churchill and Roosevelt, opened, followed by the Teheran Conference with Stalin on 28 November. Churchill did not succeed in gaining support for his ideas about stronger efforts in the Mediterranean, though it was agreed that the winter offensive in Italy would continue. It was re-emphasized that all priority must be given to Overlord, with its ancillary operation Anvil – a landing in the South of France – about which Churchill was unenthusiastic. At the second Cairo Conference, beginning on 4 December, Roosevelt and Churchill agreed that Eisenhower should return to Britain to take charge of Overlord, and that there now should be a British Commander-in-Chief in the Mediterranean. In the event Turkey did not come into the war. Churchill, left on his own and on a sick-bed, continued to brood on more dramatic ventures in Italy, 'to finish off the Rome job' as he put it. Hence Anzio ...

*   *   *   *

Since this book is mainly concerned with the experiences of individuals whose destinies were largely governed by other people's decisions, I have relied a great deal on notes and tape-recordings of interviews, as well as diaries, letters and unpublished reminiscences. I have also used regimental accounts and books of memoirs, many published soon after the war; fitting them together was something of a jigsaw, as I balanced one against the other, correcting facts on occasions, adding bits from conversations with the authors themselves, or with people who knew the authors and took part in the events described, and from my own knowledge. My first book, *The Fortress*, much shorter and entirely personal, was based on the diary I kept at Anzio, and I have therefore avoided using the same material, when I appear in this story, and instead have quoted from letters I wrote at the time or other extracts from my diary. A list of people whom I have interviewed or who have helped me is at the end of the book.

I have been particularly fortunate in having access to the diaries of Nick Mansell, Sir D'Arcy Osborne and Harold H. Tittmann 3rd. As the diary of Tina Whitaker was also in part the basis of another book of mine, though again quite different, I have concentrated on unpublished extracts. The diary of Mother Mary St Luke was published in 1954 under the pseudonym of Jane Scrivener; her nephew, Robert L. Hoguet, has kindly provided me with additional material. Major-General Walther Gericke generously made his Anzio war diary and maps available to me. Wilhelm Velten, who himself is the author of a book on the 65th Division, has – also generously – supplied me with a quantity of diaries and re- miniscences, all unpublished, by his comrades, as well as a transcription of the Fourteenth Army War Diary and the account by Schmitz of the bombing of Cassino. Much of this German material has been put on to tapes in English for me by Joachim Liebschner, often I fear in more detail than I have been able to use; I count myself lucky in having such a friend.

Father Robert A. Graham SJ and Monsignor Elio Venier have guided me to many important documents and people concerned with Church matters in Rome; the official Vatican documents for the period, in a volume partly edited by Father Graham, were made public just before I completed this book. Gianni Bisiac arranged a special showing of his excellent television documentary *Testimoni Oculari* (1979), which in- cluded interviews with Dollmann, Kappler and Amendola. Marisa Musu was instrumental in my being able to interview several key figures in the Gaps. I am also grateful to Emanuele Pacifici for providing me with much material on the Jews of Rome, including the 'Black Panther'.

The two official volumes on the US Army in World War II by Martin Blumenson and Ernest F. Fisher are of course prime sources for the campaign, as is the British equivalent edited by Brigadier C. J. C. Molony and others. Blumenson and Fisher have included in their books some extracts from General Mark Clark's diary, now at the Citadel, Charleston, South Carolina; some of these I have used, supplemented by

General Clark's own autobiography, *Calculated Risk*, and his interviews with Sidney T. Mathews (1948) and Colonel Forest S. Rittgers (1972), transcripts of which are at the US Military History Institute, Carlisle Barracks, Pennsylvania. I was able to study not only the whole of General Lucas' Anzio diary but several interviews with US officers who were at the Beachhead, all sent from Carlisle Barracks. I have also had much assistance from various departments at the Center of Military History, the National Archives, Washington, DC, and am in particular grateful for many transcripts of recorded comments on the conduct and strategy of the war in Italy by Kesselring and German generals.

The sad death of Brigadier Molony has meant that the official British history of the campaign after 31 March 1944 has yet to be completed. Nevertheless, the release of documents at the Public Record Office, Kew, under the thirty-year rule has to some small extent compensated for this. Of particular importance have been Churchill's memoranda and cables, the trials of Kesselring, Maeltzer and Mackensen, and the files containing cables to and from D'Arcy Osborne. Wynford Vaughan-Thomas, author of the first major British book on Anzio (1961), has provided me with personal anecdotes and directed me to transcripts of original BBC broadcasts by himself and Denis Johnston.

I am also indebted to Lady Tuker, who has deposited her late husband's papers at the Imperial War Museum. Indeed the library at the Imperial War Museum has been indispensable in my researches, not only in the way of books and magazines, but in giving me access to original MSS, such as the diary of Lieutenant Peter Royle at Cassino.

I must thank Mrs Joan L. Haybittle for her great help in the various stages of typing this book, and Marianna Traub for advice and assistance with some Italian tape-recordings. Nina Taylor translated Polish documents given me by Colonel M. Mlotek, who has my sincere thanks — again I have not been able to use everything provided. Miriam Benkovitz kindly sifted through papers at the Franklin D. Roosevelt Library, Hyde Park, and Lieutenant-Colonel G. A. Shepperd, author of a standard work on the Italian campaign, has also given me much useful advice. Ranger James J. Altieri has supplied me with essential details about his brave comrades. Ennio Silvestri's hospitality at Anzio has been not only Lucullan but has enabled me to lay many ghosts. Finally, my special thanks go to Janet Venn-Brown for research in Rome, to Donald E. Spencer in Washington, to Laszlo M. Alfoldi at Carlisle Barracks, and as always to Raul Balin, who has helped me with research and advice, not to mention encouragement at every stage.

In a book like this it is not possible to mention every regiment that fought at Anzio, or at Cassino. On p. xvii I have listed units (less medical etc.) which took part in the first months of the Beachhead fighting.

JANUARY

Rome

'Your aunt is ill and about to die.'

This curt sentence was received with delight by scores of people in Rome during the small hours of 22 January 1944. For it was a message code, and meant that the Allies had, at last, landed somewhere near the city.

'The news electrifies. Our liberation approaches!' wrote a future Prime Minister of Italy in his diary. The Germans were showing signs of alarm and packing up ready to leave. Would there now be a mass uprising like the Four Days in Naples at the end of September?

22 January 1944. For a start, take thirteen people living in the city of cities.

First, an American nun, born Jessie Lynch in Brooklyn, now known as Mother Mary St Luke and working for the Vatican information bureau. Her convent was off Via Veneto, near the fashionable hotels requisitioned by the Germans. Nobody was as yet certain where exactly the landings had been – somewhere to the south, evidently. The BBC was deliberately vague, and Rome Radio mentioned them not at all. But the news was like a cloud lifting, she wrote. And indeed it was a perfect Rome morning, with the sun on the cupolas and the fountains, and the sky a bird's egg blue. That night she found it difficult to sleep, because of the swish of cars passing continually along the streets. 'Bliss,' she wrote the next day, 'to think the Germans are leaving.'

Mother Mary was a woman of spirit, humorous, once a champion squash-player. She belonged to the Society of the Holy Child Jesus. The convent was a large building of the turn of the century, with a garden full of wistaria, plumbago and bougainvillea. In the seventeenth century this area of Rome had belonged to Cardinal Ludovisi, nephew of Pope Gregory XV, and the great wall of Marcus Aurelius was a few hundred yards away. The Byzantine General Belisarius had entered through the gate, now known as Porta Pinciana. Belisarius was often referred to in the

papers nowadays. A warning had been sent to Churchill by the Vatican
newspaper *L'Osservatore Romano*, after some sinister threats by the BBC
about the possibility of yet more bombings: 'Rome belongs to all
mankind, not to Italy alone. In AD 544 Belisarius dissuaded Totila from
destroying it with the plea that Rome was the property of the whole
world, and that whoever destroyed it would be destroying not the city of
another country, but his own city.' Now, of course, there was worse
danger than from mere bombings. If the Germans eventually decided not
to evacuate Rome, it could well turn into another Stalingrad.

The Germans had pretended to acknowledge Rome as an 'open city',
but that was hokum. They had a Transport Command, for instance, in
Via Sistina, which was so full of troops that the American nuns called it
Brighter Berlin. The main German headquarters was just over the wall, in
Corso d'Italia. This as a result had become a magnet for partisan activity,
and at night-time one often heard rifle shots and grenade explosions.
Barbed-wire barricades and machine-gun posts had appeared after the
Flora Hotel bomb on 10 December – apparently Kesselring had been there
the very morning of the incident, when some Germans had been killed. In
Mother Mary's street there were also notices forbidding the use of
bicycles, because of what she called 'cycle murders'; anyone who
disobeyed would be shot on sight. It was typical of the resourceful
Romans that they should use tricycles instead.

Fascist police kept an eye on the convent, just in case escaped prisoners
of war or Jews might take refuge there. Not, in theory, that they ought to
do anything about it if such a thing did happen, as the convent was extra-
territorial property and therefore supposed to be inviolate. However, just
before Christmas there had been the alarming raid on the Collegio
Lombardo, Vatican property, with the consequent arrest of various left-
wing refugees concealed there. Officially there was a death penalty for
hiding or helping prisoners of war, just as there was for owning a radio
transmitter. Hiding Jews would mean being sent to labour camps. It was a
law now that a list of the names of all inhabitants of a building had to be
posted downstairs in the entrance hall.

The only 'guests' at Mother Mary's convent were four Sicilian
refugees. Another convent of the Holy Child, up on Monte Mario, had
been sheltering thirteen Jews ever since the October deportations. As for
escaped prisoners of war, there were supposed to be scores of them, chiefly
British, hidden all over Rome. There was also a handful in the Vatican
itself.

'Surely,' Mother Mary wrote, 'the Allies must take Rome soon. I
wonder if they know how, for us, every minute makes a difference.'

Peppino Zamboni, aged eleven, an orphan, was as quick as a weasel. He lived on the other side of the Tiber, in a crumbling Trastevere tenement, with his aunt, Zia Luisa, Roman of the Romans, enormous and voluble, in normal times a dealer in olive oil and wine.

Zia Luisa was not at all delighted by the news of the landing and started to wail, saying that Rome was going to be bombed again and they would all die. For her sister, Peppino's mother, had been among the several hundred killed during the terrible Allied air-raid on 19 July 1943; she had been a flower-seller at the Verano cemetery. During that raid the basilica of San Lorenzo had been badly damaged, and the Holy Father, Pius XII, had gone there at once, alone with Monsignor Montini, and had moved among the crowd of the bereaved and homeless, blessing them. He had actually laid a hand on Peppino's head and this was one of the main reasons why Zia had taken in the boy. Peppino's younger sisters had not been so lucky. They had been sent to Frascati, to another relative who sold wine, and had not been heard of since the big raid on 8 September, the day before Marshal Badoglio and the royal family had fled from Rome and the Germans had moved in.

Peppino was an *orfano di guerra*, because his father had also died, from typhoid in Kenya whilst a prisoner of war, and was thus entitled to wear a mourning band with two stars on it. He was very excited about the landings. Perhaps above all he looked forward to not being hungry any more. He and some other boys had formed themselves into a group that they called the 'Aviatori', specializing in the dangerous and not always successful task of letting out air from the tyres of German vehicles. Their great dream was that one day they could plant a bomb somewhere. Yet Peppino had a good friend who was a German sergeant called Leo, and who gave him lifts to Civitavecchia, forty-five miles north of Rome; he went in search of food, but the trips were often nightmarish as Civitavecchia was bombed almost every day. Zia Luisa was quite fond of Leo too and invited him upstairs sometimes; she seemed not to worry about sending Peppino on these dangerous journeys. Once, after a heavy raid, he and some women and girls had had to stay the night in a barn. A German officer and his platoon wanted to shelter there too. The farmer had offered to turn the Italians out, but the officer insisted that they should remain; the Italians could sleep at one end, the Germans at another. The Germans never made any attempt to interfere with the women: something that Peppino was to remember many months later when he became accustomed to the behaviour of American troops.

The Duchess of Sermoneta had heard the news from a German diplomat at a smart luncheon party, and had tried not to look too pleased about it. After a telephone call the man had rushed off, 'presumably to see to his packing', as she said. Soon there was every sort of rumour: the Germans were fleeing; no, they would defend Rome house by house; the Communists were preparing to take over the Capitol; political prisoners were to be shot; an American armoured car had been seen on the old Appian Way. During the night she clearly heard artillery fire to the south, like 'roars of angry tigers'.

Once beautiful, still striking, Vittoria Sermoneta was a leading figure in international society. Having been born a Colonna, she was a member of the 'black' or Papal aristocracy. She was also partly English. Her critics said that she was arrogant and worldly, and that she liked collecting famous people. As Colonel Dollmann of the SS said: 'All the best known film stars of the day, particularly those of the masculine gender, had drunk very dry Martinis among her centuries' old art treasures.' She was a lady-in-waiting to the queen, who had fled ignominiously with the king, the crown prince and the Prime Minister Badoglio on 9 September, following the declaration of the Armistice with the Allies.

Vittoria lived in Palazzo Orsini, built within the Theatre of Marcellus, nephew of Augustus, between the Tarpeian Rock and the Tiber: a fantastic construction that more than almost anything gives reality to the hackneyed phrase 'Eternal City'. She and her friends indulged in reckless anti-German propaganda. As a result some of the great ladies, like Virginia Agnelli, half American and daughter-in-law of the Fiat boss, had ended up in a temporary prison in the convent of San Gregorio. These ladies' princeling sons, who had been in hiding, for greater safety now applied for posts in the Palatine Guard at the Vatican. Vittoria was becoming nervous, especially as she had two men, one an Army deserter, concealed in her apartment. Her greatest worry, in view of the rumours about Nazis being ready to shoot prisoners, was for the inmates of San Gregorio.

She was to write later: 'In our ignorance we said: "It will not be long, the Allies will be here in a few days."' Within a week she herself was arrested, and the Allies had not arrived.

Eugen Dollmann was a colonel in the Waffen SS, a liaison officer between Himmler's chief of staff in Italy, General Wolff, and Field-Marshal Kesselring, and between Kesselring and the Vatican. The SS had 'honorary' members and Waffen (fighting) members. The former were non-combatant and regarded as the élite of the Nazi party, a 'moral bulwark' and not concerned with arrests and deportations. The Waffen SS were crack assault or shock troops. The honorary SS were often confused with yet another branch of the SS, comprising the SD (*Sicherheitsdienst*) or intelligence service, and the Gestapo, or political police, which after a while were more or less merged. In Rome the head of the Gestapo-SD was Colonel Herbert Kappler.

Lean, good-looking, Bavarian, a bachelor, Dollmann loved Rome 'with every fibre of my being'. He also had a weakness for Roman high society, and it was generally but probably wrongly assumed by Romans that he passed on information to Kappler which resulted in arrests. Vittoria Sermoneta ignored him, and for this reason he hated her more than she realized. By a coincidence, the wife of one of the men she was hiding in Palazzo Orsini lived in the same pension as Dollmann, above the Spanish Steps.

Dollmann had been roused from sleep within an hour of the landings and summoned to Kesselring's headquarters. There he learnt that the Allies were at the seaside towns of Anzio and Nettuno, only thirty-five miles from Rome. Exactly how big a force had landed was not as yet known, but it could have been three divisions. The Field-Marshal had been caught unawares and had only just sent his two spare divisions to the Cassino front, sixty miles further south; there were no reserves left in Central Italy. He was afraid of an uprising in the city, but Dollmann, always cynical, told him he need not worry – he knew the Romans too well. Dollmann remembered the pathetic sight of soldiers' abandoned weapons and even uniforms littering the streets and fields on 8–9 September, after poor old Badoglio had announced the Armistice and then bolted, as if the Italians had thought the war was now over. A few civilian fools had fired shots and got killed in the area of the Pyramid of Cestius, but the Romans had learnt well enough how to get their own way without resorting to revolt and insurrection, 'first under the Caesars, and then under the Popes'. Vittoria Sermoneta's informant at the pension, on the other hand, maintained that Dollmann was 'nervous and agitated', and preparing to leave.

Dollmann's knowledge of the Italian language and way of life had made him an ideal interpreter at top-level conferences, including those between Hitler and Mussolini. He saw himself in the rôle of a subtle worker for the saving of his beloved city, and had been responsible for the closing down of a torture-house run by Italian Fascists at Palazzo Braschi. He must have known of the equally dreadful things that happened in the Gestapo interrogation centre at Via Tasso, run by Kappler, the real terror of Rome. Kappler disliked Dollmann, whom he regarded as a drawing-room soldier, with nebulous duties that were 'clear neither to himself nor to anybody else'.

Sunday 23 January was as calm as Dollmann predicted. Somebody had scrawled 'VV gli inglesi liberatori' in Via Condotti. He decided to be brave and drive with his dog down the road towards Anzio. He was surprised not to encounter (just as well, no doubt) any Allied columns racing across that ancient landscape of the Campagna, dotted with its umbrella pines, ruined towers and crumbled aqueducts. All he noticed was a hastily improvised contingent of German soldiers, hauled out before time from the VD hospital in Rome and being formed up to march south.

There was nothing to prevent the Allies from driving straight to St Peter's.

Celeste Di Porto was aged eighteen, a Jewish prostitute. She was black-haired, black-eyed, with high cheekbones. As a child she had been known as 'Stella', or star, because of her vivacity and beauty. Her nickname now was the 'Black Panther'.

Being of limited intelligence, she perhaps – on that morning of 22 January – looked forward to fresh conquests when the Anglo-Americans arrived. All the same, she could scarcely expect much mercy at the Liberation. For she made a living out of denouncing fellow-Jews to the Gestapo, at five to fifty thousand *lire* a head, and was not averse to betraying her own relatives.

The Ghetto began just behind Palazzo Orsini, near the remaining columns of the Temple of Apollo. Some of its inhabitants claimed direct descent from the Jews brought by the Emperor Titus to help in the building of the Colosseum, and many more from those expelled from Spain in 1492. Not all Jews lived in the Ghetto, however. Kappler had captured the Chief Rabbi's list of addresses, so the great round-up of 16 October had spread to Trastevere and even to hotels. Pregnant women, children and invalids had been included among the thousand-odd people trundled into cattle trucks on that day and sent north to the gas chambers.

It was said that the Black Panther would accompany male suspects to the Gestapo headquarters and delight in pulling down their trousers to prove that they were circumcised. Not that she was alone in this game of betrayal. The Roman police were accustomed to receiving letters from anonymous Aryans about Jews in hiding. Mother Mary had written: 'It is nameless horror. People you know and esteem, brave, kind, upright people, just because they have Jewish blood . . .'

Ivanoe Bonomi was an elder statesman from pre-Mussolini days; he had once been a Socialist deputy and was now head of the small right-wing Labour Democratic party. After the Armistice, when Rome had been left without government, the clandestine Committee of National Liberation, or CLN, had been formed under his leadership. Bonomi, with his white-pointed beard, was a well-known figure in Rome, so he and his wife (both, as it happened, non-believers) were in hiding in the huge Seminario building at the rear of the basilica of St John Lateran. Yet on occasions he managed to slip out to meetings in other parts of Rome.

The CLN consisted of six parties. The most powerful and best organized was the Communist. Its head was the almost legendary figure of 'Ercoli', alias Palmiro Togliatti, still in exile in Moscow, and it was distrusted and feared by the Vatican. The small Party of Action was primarily an intellectuals' party, taking its origin from an old anti-Fascist movement, 'Justice and Liberty'. Its leaders had suffered persecution and imprisonment, and saw the Resistance in terms of a new Risorgimento, a recreation of Italy, spiritually and economically; it had a well defined programme of redistribution of wealth, agrarian reforms etc., but was non-Marxist and did not want any allegiance to Moscow. The Socialist party, led by the considerable figure of Pietro Nenni, harked back to original Socialist principles before Mussolini's march on Rome. Bonomi's Labour Democrats were right of centre, not so violently anti-monarchist as the three leftist parties, but opposed to King Victor Emmanuel and the Badoglio government, now established in Brindisi. The Christian Democrat party, led by Alcide De Gasperi, representing Conservative and Catholic opinion, was the most powerful in terms of popular support throughout Italy, while the Liberals, further to the right, owed their inspiration to the ideals of the Neapolitan philosopher Benedetto Croce. The Christian Democrats and Liberals also opposed Victor Emmanuel and Badoglio. On the whole they supported Croce's view that the king should abdicate in favour of his grandson.

Other CLNs had been formed in industrial cities of the North, where as the year proceeded partisan resistance tended to become fiercer and unrelenting, more than in Rome perhaps because to a great extent it was a bourgeois city. But in Rome the CLN had its rival, the Military Front, founded by Colonel Giuseppe Montezemolo, supporting the monarchy and Badoglio, and in this lay deep danger of quite another sort.

About eight hundred people were sheltering in the Seminario, including Nenni, De Gasperi, some ex-Army officers and Jews. In effect, because of Bonomi's presence, the Seminario was the headquarters of the CLN, which had its own radio contacts with the South (though not in the building). The Germans could not fail to know that it was such a hotbed. Indeed they had machine-guns posted a few hundred yards away near the Scala Santa, the Holy Staircase, in theory to protect the Porta San Giovanni, one of the main entrances to Rome, but also able to be trained on the great façade of the basilica, dominated by its fifteen colossal statues. As St John Lateran was the Cathedral of Rome, its refugee residents felt safer there than in most other Papal extra-territorial buildings, though there were plenty of alarms about possible 'invasions'.

The Military Front considered itself the true representative of Italy's government and opponent to Mussolini's puppet organization at Salò in northern Italy. Because Montezemolo had only the rank of colonel, Badoglio had recently nominated General Armellini (who had a Canadian-born wife) as head of his armed forces in the city, with instructions to be ready to take over key points in Rome on the departure of the Germans, such as bridges, ministries and newspaper offices. He had sent Bonomi a peremptory message, demanding that the CLN should abstain from any political activity on the Allies' arrival. Bonomi, on 18 January, had called a meeting of the leaders of the six parties at a house off Piazza di Spagna: a very dangerous undertaking, as it meant passing through crowded main streets in daylight. Needless to say Badoglio's proposal was rejected, and in any case Armellini was considered 'tainted'. Then came 22 January. To Bonomi's alarm it soon was apparent that the left-wing parties of the CLN were determined to prevent the Military Front from gaining supremacy in Rome and that elements were preparing to occupy crucial buildings. Bonomi now feared armed *conflitti*, clashes, within the city and sent out a message saying that he would not accept any responsibility for such disorders. 'Let us give the Allies the spectacle of national strength, rising above these inevitable political disagreements.'

Major Sam Derry of the Royal Artillery was 'incarcerated' in the Vatican flat of the British Minister to the Holy See, Sir D'Arcy Osborne, a descendant of the first Duke of Marlborough and himself later to be Duke of Leeds. Derry was a central figure in the organization for helping Allied escaped prisoners of war, of whom there were over two thousand at large in Italy and some eighty in Rome. Over six feet, athletic and unmistakably a military man, he had fought bravely in the Western Desert, where he had been captured. In October 1943 he had himself escaped from a German prison train and had made his way to Rome.

January had been a black month for the organization. The Gestapo had intensified its house-to-house searches, looking for Jews, Communists and young men for sending to labour camps in central Europe, and as a result had caught several escaped prisoners, including an American Air Force sergeant and one of Derry's main assistants. Most of them had been sent to the dreaded Regina Coeli gaol, on the west bank of the Tiber. The originator of the Rome organization was an Irish monsignor from Killarney, Father Hugh O'Flaherty, a magnetic character, fanatically keen on golf, tall, a considerable joker, with a thick brogue and blue eyes behind round steel-rimmed spectacles – a Scarlet Pimpernel maybe, but no Baroness Orczy hero in appearance, in spite of cloak, sash and wide-rimmed black hat. O'Flaherty lived in – of all places – the Collegio Teutonicum, or German College, between the old palace of the Inquisition and the Vatican. It was from here that for the past months, since the Armistice, he had plotted and planned, arranging disguises and false identity cards, finding accommodation for prisoners in Rome and supplying them with cash. He also arranged for prisoners' messages to their families to be sent by the Vatican radio, and through a secret transmitter had for a while connections with No 1 Special Force, the branch in Italy of British intelligence, SOE, Special Operations Executive.

Sam Derry had been one of the first British officers to reach Rome. His abilities were obvious, and soon he too was invited to live at the Collegio Teutonicum under a pseudonym. It was a weird experience for him to be waited on at meals by German nuns saying *Bitte* and *Dankeschoen*. Through No 1 Special Force, Derry was able to arrange for supplies to be dropped to escaped prisoners in remoter parts of Italy, sometimes arms as well if they were working with partisans, and he also was in touch about escape routes through the front line or by sea.

Various Irish and Maltese priests, not to mention theological students, were now helping the organization. Derry, however, tried not to involve them in intelligence work. The operator of the secret transmitter was arrested (and eventually shot), so now a subdivision of Montezemolo's Military Front, known as Centro X, came to be of particular use. This Centro X was mainly run by civilians and dealt not only with the circulation of newssheets and the sending out of radio messages to the Allies on German troop movements, minefields and ammunition dumps, and details of arrest, but with the fabrication of false identity and ration cards. The radio messages were supplementary to those sent by agents specially trained by No 1 Special Force or the American OSS, Office of Strategic Services, who worked separately in complete secrecy and anonymity. For a while the Centro X transmitter was in Palazzo Rospigliosi-Pallavicini, one of the great houses of Rome, but the Gestapo had traced it there; the young Princess Pallavicini jumped from a window just in time, hurting her leg, and also made her way to the Collegio Teutonicum.

Derry was, in effect, the organization's chief of staff. After the arrests of his colleagues he was told by O'Flaherty that the German Rector had said he must leave the College, even though it was Papal extra-territorial property. Indeed O'Flaherty himself would now be in danger of arrest if seen in the streets of Rome. As one of O'Flaherty's original helpers, before Derry's arrival, was Sir D'Arcy Osborne's manservant, John May, it was quickly arranged that Derry should be moved into the Minister's own apartment within the Vatican.

The British, French and Polish diplomatic 'guests' of the Vatican – an area of about one hundred acres, half being gardens – lived in the Hospice of Santa Marta, a five-storeyed stucco building used before the war to accommodate pilgrims, and the Americans and Yugoslavs were in a *palazzina* opposite. South American and Chinese diplomats were accommodated in the mustard-coloured Palazzo del Tribunale. Visitors to any of these had to cross St Peter's Square, marked by a white line over which the German sentries were not allowed to pass; they then mounted the steps and entered the Vatican precincts at the end of the Bernini colonnade to the left of St Peter's. Although they would be watched by the Germans through field-glasses, they usually had no difficulties with the Swiss Guards, in traditional blue and yellow uniforms – unless they were Allied prisoners inadequately disguised. One passed through the graceful archways of the baroque Sacristy, and the diplomats' buildings were in a large square, where there was also the convent of the Sisters of St Vincent de Paul who, in their wide-winged coifs, prepared meals for various ecclesiastics and diplomats. Derry had been smuggled in dressed in one of O'Flaherty's soutanes. For the next months this square and the Vatican gardens, dominated by the magnificent architecture of St Peter's, would be the limit of his world: an embalmed kingdom, with its feeling of ageless peace and non-violence, disturbed only by the clangour of the great bells.

D'Arcy Osborne in theory knew nothing about the organization, though in practice he kept it supplied with cash, as did – to a lesser extent – the American Chargé d'Affaires, Harold Tittmann, who at first seemed to regard the organization simply as a British intelligence operation. Other money came to O'Flaherty from the eminent anti-Fascist, Prince Filippo Doria, who was in hiding in Trastevere. The number of escaped American prisoners in Italy was at first few, as the United States had entered the war only some months before the fighting had ended in North Africa – most of the British prisoners having been originally captured in the Western Desert. In general, most of the Americans were pilots who had bailed out. A handful of British prisoners had managed to take refuge in the Papal Gendarmerie barracks within the Vatican, but the Secretariat had vetoed the admission of any more. Thus the remainder had to be hidden either in extra-territorial buildings or in well-wishers' houses in Rome, to their hosts' considerable danger. There were also similar organizations, though necessarily smaller, run by French, Greeks and Yugoslavs; these also had to be assisted financially by Derry, as were some escaped Russians and Arabs.

Derry heard of the landings within the first hour or two, and he was able to see some flashes of gunfire from the roof of the Hospice. The problem was whether to advise the prisoners 'to sit tight or crack off'. First he decided to get Blon Kiernan, the pretty daughter of the Irish Minister, to call on her friend the first secretary at the German Embassy. She came back with the news that the Germans did expect to withdraw from Rome. So Derry decided that it would be best to advise everybody to remain in their billets until the Allies arrived.

Marisa Musu was aged seventeen. She was a small, ardent, dark-skinned Sardinian, a member of the Communist combat group in the GAP (*Gruppi di Azione Patriottica*).

The military head of the Communist party in Rome was Giorgio Amendola, the son of a great Liberal leader who had been assassinated by the Fascists. He had been in part responsible for forming these GAPs on the model of the French maquis. The Gapists were, in effect, terrorists. Their job was to 'eliminate' the invaders, spies from Mussolini's puppet government at Salò in the North and anything connected with them. Nearly every day there were attacks with grenades or machine-guns, causing casualties. The Gapists had been responsible for the bomb at the Hotel Flora and a big explosion with many dead and wounded at the Barberini cinema, where German soldiers had been to a film show in their honour before leaving for the front. On 18 December a grenade was thrown as the Germans were changing guard outside the Regina Coeli prison; eight Germans were killed and others wounded. At present, however, the Germans had not yet been goaded into drastic reprisals.

Marisa lived in the Prati district, behind Castel Sant' Angelo: a newish quarter of apartment buildings which in that period was mostly inhabited by the professional classes. She was the daughter of Bastianina Musu, one of the founders of the Party of Action. In spite of Badoglio's order to Bonomi, immediately after the Allied landings there had been radio messages from the South telling Resistance workers to be prepared for a general rising. Marisa was now tensely waiting for that signal. She and other Gapists had their weapons ready, while other Communist groups would cut telephone wires, put down spikes along German lines of retreat, and carry out other forms of sabotage. Then there were the strongpoints to be occupied.

It was through her boyfriend, Valentino Gerratana, one of the main Communist leaders, that Marisa had got to know of the Gaps. One day, in a café in the Piazza del Popolo, she had dared to approach Amendola about joining. At first he had just laughed and had told her to concentrate on darning Valentino's socks. But she had persisted, and he had soon recognized that an extraordinary flame of idealism burned inside the girl.

Most of the Gapists were very young, and several women were among them. Their political and moral training was intense, and there were meetings to discuss the theory and practice of Communism. They were selfless people, full of fervour; they were not even told each other's real names – Marisa was known as Rosa, and she had the rank of captain. There were other Gapist groups throughout occupied Italy, including the province of Lazio surrounding Rome and the Alban Hills to the south. Occasionally Party of Action men joined in a particular 'incident', such as on 20 December when a German railway convoy taking petrol to Cassino was blown up, damaging two locomotives, destroying several trucks and killing and wounding soldiers. As it happened, this particular incident was thanks to Colonel Montezemolo of the Military Front; he had given the information to Amendola about the precise time of the train's passing. 'I never would have believed that I would have collaborated with a Communist,' he had said. Other political parties controlled partisan bands; in the case of the Christian Democrats, sabotage was confined to outside the city for fear of reprisals.

One occasion must have convinced Amendola of Marisa's courage. She was returning by bicycle with Valentino from the outskirts of Rome, where she had been to collect some mortar-bombs, to be converted into hand-grenades. Valentino carried a despatch case with papers in it, but Marisa had all the bombs in a cloth shopping bag attached to the front of her bicycle. They came to a road-block, and Valentino was the first to be checked and questioned by the soldiers, Italian Fascists. Then the soldiers turned to Marisa. '*Che cosa hai li dentro?* What have you in there?' Marisa knew that there was an order to shoot anybody on the spot if caught carrying arms. 'Ha ha,' she said. 'Be careful. It's full of bombs.' '*Fai la spiritosa.* You're the funny one,' said a soldier contemptuously, and waved her on. For once Marisa was not carrying a gun, for which she was grateful. If she had had a gun, her first instinct would have been to shoot her way out.

As a result of the landings, some Resistance workers became careless about security. The Gaps also obtained new recruits. There was no point in lagging with the work of sabotage and elimination. In particular, road-blocks were created, forming bottlenecks of German vehicles which were machine-gunned by Allied aircraft.

The Communists had their newspaper *L'Unità* ready, with its headline '*Roma insorge*, Rome rises up.'

General Simone Simoni was aged sixty-four. Born near Frosinone, between Anzio and Cassino, he began his military career as a sergeant. A true hero, upright, loyal, devoutly religious, he had been awarded seven medals for bravery in the Great War, in which he had been badly wounded.

Simoni in the past had spoken out against Italy's alliance with Germany. He was one of the officers who had rallied round Montezemolo and the Military Front, and like Montezemolo was careless about personal security. Both were tall, conspicuous figures, and people said that some day they would be recognized in the streets and arrested. It was also said that Simoni's particular hatred of the Fascists was due to the circumstances surrounding the death of his only son. He was distressed by the feud between the Military Front and the CLN, and held several meetings between representatives of the two in his house off Via Nomentana – on a spot, as it happened, where there were catacombs associated with another persecution, that of Domitian.

If many Germans were preparing to evacuate Rome on 22 January, the minions of Colonel Herbert Kappler, the Gestapo chief, were not relaxing in their work of rounding up suspects and tracing Resistance workers. On that very day they broke into Simoni's house and took him to 155 Via Tasso, the Gestapo interrogation centre, prison and barracks.

It was ironic that the name of one of Italy's greatest poets, Torquato Tasso, the author of *La Gerusalemme liberata*, should become associated with a mean building in a dreary street that had become a byword for all the horror and misery associated with the occupation. It was ironic too that the house – a typically gimcrack Fascist construction – should be so close to St John Lateran, where so many potential detainees for 155 Via Tasso were in hiding. As always in Rome no street is devoid of historical interest; at the top of Via Tasso are the remains of Nero's walls, and at the back of No 155 is Villa Massimo, also then requisitioned by the Germans, with some important pictures of the nineteenth-century Nazarene School. Across the way was a castellated building which was a monastery of the Frati di Sant'Antonio, patron saint of lost things.

Kappler, suave, booted, with a great scar across his face, came to see Simoni immediately after his arrest. He was well pleased. 'At last we have the honour to welcome you here,' he said. That entire night Simoni was tortured, for Kappler particularly wanted to find Montezemolo. He was whipped and beaten with spiked mallets. The soles of his feet were burnt with gas jets. He fainted three times, but never spoke until it was all over when he said, 'I am sorry not to be younger or I would have been able to have done more.' In another room a colleague, the Carabiniere Colonel Giovanni Frignani, was being beaten up under the eyes of his wife, who was pretending that they were strangers. They too managed to keep silent, although Frignani's face, hands and feet were swollen into black bleeding lumps. Simoni was taken to a windowless cell, some twelve feet by six. Here he was to remain indefinitely. Scratches, still visible on the wall, show that he shared it for a while with two British soldiers – '5882820 SSM J. Lloyd, British Army' and 'M. Phillips, 318889, Worthing, Sussex'. The general himself drew a cross on the wall and below it wrote: 'Jesus Christus parce nobis'. Another inmate of the cell, an Italian, was to say: 'He used to prepare us mentally for our interrogation, and when we were brought back from torture, he was able so to inspire us with his words that the pain seemed lessened.'

Peter Tompkins, of the American OSS, had been educated partly in

England, and for some years before the war had lived in Rome as a correspondent for the New York *Herald Tribune*.

He had been landed on 21 January by torpedo-boat from Corsica at a point some hundred miles north of the city. By early morning on the 22nd he found himself disguised as a Fascist auxiliary policeman and, moreover, roaring up the Corso on the back of a motorcycle. 'Naturally my heart was in my mouth, though it amused me to think that the people we passed had no idea an American agent – however frightened – was riding up the main street of their capital.' As yet he did not know whether the Allied landings had taken place. His mission was to make contact with OSS agents, especially the operator of the clandestine Radio Vittoria, and to act as intelligence officer for the Fifth Army in Rome; he would arrange for sabotage measures to be taken to coincide with the landings.

'A little mad but very nice' was a verdict by one of Tompkins' Italian colleagues; an 'intellectual and literary roughneck' an American colleague has said. He had been at the Salerno landings, and then with Malcolm Munthe, the British son of the author of *The Story of San Michele*, had been among the first Allies to set foot on Capri. In Naples he had been responsible for training Italian agents to send behind the lines. Italians sometimes said that they preferred to work with the OSS rather than the SOE, since Americans of Italian extraction tended to be used in the former while many British in key positions at SOE and No 1 Special Force could not even speak Italian – 'a kind of *coquetterie*', insisting on being so very very British. However there were also Italians who despised the Italo-Americans, especially those originating from Sicily; and with reason, for a number of these ex-Sicilians turned out to be connected with the Mafia. A point much in No 1 Special Force's favour at this time was that it was a good deal more experienced, and therefore professional, than OSS, which had become Washington's dumping ground, so they said, for 'bourbon whiskey colonels' and playboys – which was why the unconventional OSS chief, General Donovan, welcomed eccentrics instead, such as Peter Tompkins.

Relations between the higher ranks of OSS and SOE were good, though less so lower down where they have been described as a 'snakepit'. There was friction over the British support of the Italian monarchy, and some Americans considered that they were being used as a means of perpetuating the British Empire. Thus OSS and No 1 SF acted almost entirely separately, with different sets of agents, not only in Rome but throughout northern Italy; and sometimes these agents would send out conflicting radio reports. The OSS operated from Caserta and Naples, while No 1 SF was based at Monopoli near Bari, with an advance unit under Malcolm Munthe on the island of Ischia. General Mark Clark of the American Fifth Army was interested in the possibilities of the OSS, which was no doubt why the British were 'squeezed out' of smuggling a representative of their own into Rome at the time of the landings. However, both No 1 SF and OSS were to send contact men – including Munthe – to Anzio and Nettuno soon after the landings.

Tompkins had volunteered for the job. He had boldly brought false documents that purported to identify him as a prince in the Caetani family. He was understandably nervous on arriving in Rome. A very social person, he had many Roman friends and could easily have been spotted. His first meeting was to have been in Via Sistina, but he discovered that the house was opposite the Hotel de la Ville, where German troops were billeted. So he made his way to an old palazzo near the Tiber in Via Giulia, a long street full of ancient houses and artisans' shops. There he had been welcomed by the porter and his wife, who had been his family's servants. The unfortunate people were desperate about their son, who had been in hiding for months – the boy did not dare go out of doors for fear of being caught in a *retata* or round-up for forced labour in Germany. 'You can't stay in this building. Too many people could recognize you. Are you sure you weren't seen coming in?' Finally Tompkins had been able to spend the night in the house of an OSS agent codenamed Cervo, or Stag, the very man who was operating Vittoria. And this Cervo, otherwise Maurizio Giglio, worked as an auxiliary Fascist policeman, hence Tompkins' early morning ride on the motorcycle.

The other main OSS agent was Coniglio, or Rabbit, also originating from the Neapolitan Resistance. Tompkins on meeting them was appalled to discover the extent of the rift between the CLN and the Military Front. The whole city was tense, waiting for developments but remembering only too well the bitter and crushing experience of the Germans' entry into Rome in September. If some hotheads came out too soon, they could be wiped out by the *tedeschi*. To delay, on the other hand, might mean being too late, and that would be a disaster. Some catalyst, Tompkins felt, was needed, some major and spectacular event which would cause an instantaneous flare-up in the city, so that every man and woman, irrespective of party, would be compelled to act at once, without choosing their own moment. The only catalyst Tompkins could think of was a landing of Allied paratroopers in the heart of Rome itself – and where better than in the Borghese Gardens? Anti-tank weapons would be essential too ... He prepared to relay this message to Fifth Army Headquarters.

Monsignor Giovanni Battista Montini was *Sostituto* or Substitute Secretary of State at the Vatican, under Cardinal Luigi Maglione. Born near Brescia in 1897, he was a dark, slim, quiet and self-effacing man, the son of a lawyer. To the British Minister D'Arcy Osborne he was 'a man with vision, courage and a nice dry wit'; 'how he can work as hard and unceasingly I cannot imagine.' He lived in apartments that had originally belonged to Clement VII, the Pope who had refused to sanction Henry VIII's divorce from Catherine of Aragon. In 1963 Montini was to become Pope Paul VI.

By and large Vatican foreign policy was in the hands of Maglione. Montini dealt more with the running of domestic and specifically Italian affairs. In the earlier part of the war, for instance, he had been concerned with the fate and treatment of Italians who were prisoners in Allied hands, and in due course with Allied prisoners in camps in Italy. When in September 1943 two British naval officers took refuge in St Peter's, it was to him that Osborne naturally appealed for assistance; and it was he who agreed that the men could be housed in the Papal Gendarmerie barracks.

The German ambassador to the Vatican, Baron Ernst von Weizsaecker, admired Montini greatly and thought him the 'busiest of bees'. 'I was often embarrassed,' he wrote, 'to have to trouble this overworked priest with my trivial affairs.' Montini was indeed well suited to be under Pope Pius XII, who hardly ever allowed himself to relax and would not even spend a holiday at the Papal villa at the town of Castel Gandolfo in the Alban Hills.

It was the director of the Papal villa, Bonomelli, who brought a first-hand account of the Allies' landings to Montini and others assembled for a meeting at the Apostolic Nunciature on 22 January. The bare details had been announced on the Allied radio, but now Bonomelli was able to describe the Allied fleet, literally hundreds of vessels, easily visible through binoculars from Castel Gandolfo, with aeroplanes circling overhead like protective birds, sometimes darting inland to blast or machine-gun German vehicles and troops arriving from all directions. There had been little artillery fire so far. It would seem inevitable that the Allies would aim to occupy Castel Gandolfo and other towns in the Alban Hills as soon as possible. With the memory of the destruction at Frascati, the situation was without doubt extremely serious. On the other hand there were clear signs that the Germans were preparing to flee from Rome, which presumably meant that the Allies were expected to push northwards – hopefully bypassing the Alban Hills.

Montini had reason enough to be alarmed by the bombing policy of the Allies, seeing that they had not even recognized Rome's 'open city' status. It was generally felt that the British had never forgotten Mussolini's request to Hitler to participate in the raids on London. On 20 January 1943 Anthony Eden had said in the House of Commons that the British had 'as much right to bomb Rome as the Italians had to bomb London . . . We should not hesitate to do so with the best of our ability and as heavily as possible if the course of the war should render such bombing convenient and helpful.' Were Christian sanctuaries, it was asked, less worthy of consideration if situated in Great Britain rather than in Italy? Earlier still the British had threatened to retaliate against Rome if the Italians dared to bomb Athens or Cairo – as a result of which Mussolini denounced the British as a race of brigands who had 'brutalized a quarter of the human race'. The saturation bombing of northern Italian towns, with tremendous civilian casualties, was another grisly warning. Frequent appeals to spare Rome were sent directly by the Pope to Churchill and Roosevelt, with the usual ambiguous replies. Not long after the President had said military objectives in and around Rome 'could not be ignored' there had been the bombing of the San Lorenzo district – the attack on the nearby railway marshalling yards having gone awry.

As the Pope had himself pointed out, it was in any case virtually impossible, on Rome's 'sacred soil', to avoid 'devastation of revered buildings', whatever precautionary measures were taken. It was realized at the Vatican that the United States, because of its large Catholic population, was likely to be more lenient in its policy than Britain, even if Montini found Osborne 'very accommodating on the subject'. A plain fact was that the Germans, in spite of having indicated that they recognized the 'open city', had by no means withdrawn their military installations. Indeed if only for geographical reasons and because of the railway system, it was difficult for them to do so. There was also the question of the safety of the great Benedictine monastery of Monte Cassino, which was now right in the front line. The Germans, realizing that it could be endangered, had already persuaded its Abbot to let them remove some of the treasures to safety. Weizsaecker became irritated by Montini's repeated requests for an assurance that the Monastery was not being used by the German military, and Kesselring had taken it upon himself to assure the Vatican that German troops would refrain from entering the building. On 8 January the American Chargé d'Affaires Harold Tittmann cabled to Washington that Montini had been told that 'insofar as the German military authority are concerned everything possible is being done to preserve the Monastery of Monte Cassino from war damage at the present and in the future'. Unfortunately the Allies seemed unconvinced. On the 13th a shell landed in the famous Bramante cloisters.

During January there had been further Allied air-raids in the vicinity of Rome. A Vatican food convoy had also been machine-gunned, in spite of the distinctive yellow and white markings on the vehicles. The fact that the Pope was also Bishop of Rome was reason enough for him to feel a responsibility to save the city – with a population now swollen by the rush of refugees to nearly three million – from almost certain starvation, and it had been decided by Montini and the Secretariat to risk sending out a fleet of trucks in search of flour and other foodstuffs in Umbria, Tuscany and the Marche.

So much now would depend on the Romans themselves. The Germans had often indicated that they would defend Rome street by street. Even the appearance of an Allied patrol on the outskirts might be spark enough for a general rising, as in Naples. And then, again as in Naples, there would be the inevitable retaliation . . .

Padre Benedetto's real name was Benôit-Marie de Bourg, and he came from Marseilles. The Germans by now were beginning to realize that this small brown-robed Capuchin monk with the round spectacles and long black beard was as dangerous as Monsignor O'Flaherty. For Padre Benedetto was the head of Delasem, the organization in Rome for assistance to foreign Jews; indeed few individuals in Rome were to do more by way of helping and hiding Jews during the period of the Occupation. It was reckoned in the end that four thousand people received aid from the Capuchin monastery in Via Boncompagni – very close to Mother Mary St Luke's house and, as it happened, from February onwards to an infamous Fascist interrogation centre and torture-house, where many partisans died or were crippled for life.

Refugees, especially French and including some Jewish escaped prisoners of war, would come to the monastery asking for the 'Père des Juifs'. One of Padre Benedetto's brother monks became alarmed about this and spoke to the Superior. 'Do not worry,' was the reply, 'if anyone goes to prison with Padre Benedetto it will be I not you.' After the fall of France Padre Benedetto had worked with Jewish relief organizations in Marseilles, Cannes and Nice. He had come to Rome in 1943 and had an audience with the Pope on 16 July, on behalf of fifty thousand French Jews who had been deported to Germany. He also had a plan for transferring some of the remaining Jews to Italy and thence to North Africa. The Pope, on hearing of the behaviour of the French Vichy police, is said to have exclaimed: 'I could never have believed that of France!' Four ships were even found, but the whole, probably forlorn, plan collapsed at the Armistice.

The mysterious 'silences' of Pius XII concerning the massacre of European Jewry will remain one of the great and bitter controversies of World War II, and indeed a crucial point in the matter of whether or not he should be canonized. Montini, on the very day he became Pope Paul VI, had a letter published on the subject in the British Roman Catholic paper The Tablet, in which he said: 'To take up an attitude of protest or condemnation would not only have been futile but harmful; and this is the whole truth of the matter.' In other words, Pius XII and his Curia believed that to speak out 'in fury' would only have made the whole situation of persecution in Europe very much worse. After all, one was dealing with Hitler, a quasi-psychopath who only too easily could fly into an uncontrolled rage. Other Vatican spokesmen have since insisted that the Pope's main concern was for victims of the war, and that he never wished to boost his own prestige or power through human suffering, preferring to proceed silently and secretly at the risk of appearing inactive or indifferent.

There is no doubt whatsoever that by 1943 the Vatican knew the substantial truth about the horrors that were being committed by the Nazis. The Pope's general policy was to let individual bishops speak out if they felt it advisable, but when this happened it had always resulted in savage reprisals. Tittmann had also been specifically told by the Pope that he could not condemn the Nazis by name unless he also condemned the atrocities perpetuated by the Bolsheviks, and this no doubt – the Pope said – 'would not please' Russia's Western allies. On 30 April 1943, for example, the Pope had written to Bishop von Preysing in Berlin about the Jewish question: 'Unhappily, in the present state of affairs, We can bring them no help other than Our prayers.' The Pope had been Papal Nuncio in Munich during World War I and had an affection for the German people, with 'a very accurate knowledge of German affairs' as the ambassador Weizsaecker said, but this did not mean that he had to condone Nazism. It was believed that he felt that if he spoke out against concentration camp practices there would be a reaction against German Catholics. In any case, he would be acting against the Concordat of 1933 with Germany.

Even after the deportation of Roman Jews in October the Pope decided against a public protest, again presumably for fear of even more vicious reprisals against the remainder; he simply allowed the publication of a rather tortuous communiqué in L'Osservatore Romano, emphasizing his 'fatherly care for all people, regardless of nationality, religion or race [underlined]' – on the very day, though he did not know it, that several of these unfortunate Italian Jews were being gassed at Auschwitz. By that time, it is true, there was a strong (and justified) rumour that Hitler was preparing to abduct the Pope, the Curia, and the 'whole swinish pack', as he called it, of the diplomatic corps which had taken refuge in the Vatican, not to mention its art treasures, to Lichtenstein. If provoked, Hitler would certainly have accelerated these plans. The Cardinal Secretary of State did make a personal protest to Weizsaecker immediately after the arrests on 16 October, as a result of which some of the non-Italian Jews were released. From then onwards the Jewish population of Rome went into hiding, and at least four thousand were taken into monasteries, convents and other extra-territorial sanctuaries – the Pope having sent letters by hand to the bishops instructing them to allow this to be done. The Chief Rabbi, Israel Zolli, 'disappeared' into the Vatican itself, having been smuggled in disguised as a bricklayer – but the Jewish community thereby had been left without a leader.

Jewish refugees continued to reach Rome from abroad. Padre Benedetto informed Monsignor Montini on 5 November that 499 had arrived from France, mostly Poles and Yugoslavs, and the Vatican supplied them with money and food. There was alarm when it was discovered that Padre Benedetto was also forging identity documents, but Montini decided that the blind eye was the best policy. Some money for the Padre was provided by Osborne; Tittmann also received the equivalent of $120,000 from a private fund in a New York bank for the relief of Jews; these sums would be passed to Monsignor Hérissé, who like the diplomats lived in the Hospice of Santa Marta, and he would give them to Padre Benedetto.

At the time of the Anzio landings Padre Benedetto had a near escape. Forty of his Jews had been lodged in a pension in Piazza Independenza, a somewhat nondescript area of Rome developed in the 1890s, near what had been Sejanus' camp of the Pretorian Guard. He was with them when suddenly the pension was surrounded by German police. Fortunately there was a courtyard at the back, and all the Jews managed to escape over a wall. The Padre stayed behind with the pension's staff, and was only released after three hours' questioning.

Finally, there was the strange predicament of a wealthy Englishwoman, Tina Whitaker, a widow, aged eighty-five, who lived with her two middle-aged daughters, Delia and Norina, the latter an invalid, in the Parioli quarter to the north of the Borghese Gardens.

The Whitaker family had made a fortune in the last century out of Marsala wine and was accustomed to living in an aristocratic style. As they were near the so-called Croatian Embassy, the household was never without electricity. Every night Mrs Whitaker and her daughters listened to the BBC, and Delia would stand to attention when 'God Save the King' was played. Yet Norina's nurse was a German, a simple and loyal woman though frequently meeting and talking to German soldiers in the city.

Mrs Whitaker was too frail to leave the villa much. In her diary she wrote about the *cacce all'uomo*, the man-hunts, and how there had nearly been a riot in the Post Office square when the Germans had confiscated bicycles. Police dogs were being used in searches for Jews. Princess Mafalda, the king of Italy's daughter, had been sent to the Buchenwald concentration camp in Germany. The big Roman hotels were said to be dynamited in case of a German withdrawal. By Christmas butter had cost

250 *lire* a kilo and sugar 90 *lire*; three weeks later butter was 350 and sugar 200. Hunger was 'staring Rome in the face'.

There were stories of German deserters asking to be taken into convents where Jews were hiding. The Whitaker gardener had been terrified when a German officer had forced him into a dark corner and told him to strip. The German had then taken off his own clothes, put on the gardener's and disappeared. Schwester Weisskopf, the German nurse, had gone to Ostia for the day, only to be told by a compatriot that an Allied landing was expected there – the beaches had been mined and all Italians evacuated. After the bomb at the Hotel Flora resulting in guns being mounted in Via Veneto, very near the Whitakers' dentist, Delia was at least able to make a joke: she was now afraid of having her teeth machine-gunned, she said. Any day Mrs Whitaker expected a knock on the door, and she, Delia and Norina would be bundled off in a cattle truck in the wake of Princess Mafalda.

Delia was listening to *Swiss Family Robinson* on the BBC, when the programme was interrupted with the thrilling news about the landings. She climbed the villa's tower. Nothing in the direction of Ostia, but spirals of smoke kept rising from the Alban Hills. By the next day everyone knew that the Allies were at Anzio and Nettuno. There were sirens 'every other minute', and German tanks and lorries full of troops were 'grinding' incessantly down the Corso. Schwester Weisskopf had been summoned by the German command to take a turn of duty at the railway station, to be ready to receive the gravely wounded. She had been crying because she thought she was going to be shot by partisans. Young men were 'openly proclaiming' themselves to be Communists; 'after twenty-two years of silence people are now discussing their political views freely on the streets.'

Meanwhile it seemed, as Tina Whitaker's friend Admiral Frank Maugeri sarcastically was to say, as if the 'proud warriors of the Master Race' had overnight turned into Flying Dutchmen. The scenes in the foyers of hotels looked like 'poorly directed mob scenes in provincial operas'.

Algiers

I heard about the landings in Italy when I was at La Pérouse, an Army rest-camp on the Bay of Algiers. From my tent, over a hedge of prickly pears, I could see the tiled roofs and minarets of the village, and then far away a blue range of hills above Algiers in the shape of a sleeping woman. I was awoken by someone ripping open the tent-flaps and telling me the tremendous news. After all the stories of stalemate in the Italian campaign, and of our troops being bogged down in the mud of an exceptionally bad winter, it seemed like the greatest moment in the war – a splendid and spectacular act of bravado. Rome would surely soon be ours, the first Axis capital to fall, the first European capital to be liberated from the Nazis: Rome, which all my life I had longed to see.

We learnt shortly afterwards that the landings had been at Anzio and Nettuno, but within a week everyone was referring to the Anzio Beachhead, and Nettuno was hardly mentioned except in American bulletins. I was a lieutenant, recovering from jaundice, and having a lazy time in this ideal spot, much warmer than in Italy. Some weeks before, several members of my regiment had left for the front and I was beginning to feel restless. The news about Anzio made me all the more impatient to be off. I felt I was missing fun, especially when I heard that my great friend Nick Mansell had been sent there.

Carthage – Marrakech – Caserta

'I thank God for this fine decision, which engages us once more in wholehearted unity in a great enterprise.' Thus Churchill had cabled Roosevelt from Carthage on 28 December 1943. He added: 'Here the word is "Full steam ahead".'

The decision had been to retain fifty-six landing-craft for tanks in the Mediterranean, which – it was estimated – would enable Operation Shingle to proceed within a month.

'Shingle' was to be what Churchill termed a 'cat-claw' near Rome, a two-divisioned amphibious lift at a spot not yet decided on. It had been suggested before, on a much smaller scale, though abandoned when the Allies' advance began to slow down and then virtually halt before the Germans' Gustav Line, at Italy's 'waist' about half-way between Rome and Naples.

In actual fact further far-reaching decisions had to be made by Roosevelt and his chiefs of staff in Washington before the steam could really be released. Behind those decisions were the divergences in Anglo-American policy about the whole strategy of the war and the overriding priority, agreed at Teheran with Stalin, that the cross-Channel attack, Overlord, and the landings in the South of France, Anvil, should take place in May. As Churchill lay on his bed recovering from pneumonia, he had time to reflect on the Italian campaign. In spite of the Teheran Conference it was a scandal that after so much effort the Allied Fifth and Eighth Armies should 'stagnate and fester'. Shingle would also draw away essential German forces from northern Europe and the Russian fronts; the vital airfields at Naples and Foggia must be protected from counter-attacks.

With the departure of Eisenhower to England to prepare for Overlord, the primacy in Mediterranean operations was in British hands. As it was considered that General Sir Harold Alexander had mastered 'the difficult art of managing Americans', he remained Commander-in-Chief of the land forces in Italy, while the senior administrative and politico-military job of Supreme Allied Commander went to General Sir Henry 'Jumbo' Maitland Wilson. General Mark Clark was in command of the American Fifth Army, on the western side of Italy, and General Sir Oliver Leese in due course took over the Eighth Army on the east. Shingle would thus be a Fifth Army responsibility.

While Churchill convalesced at his 'beloved' Marrakech, the plans proceeded. As Clark said, Churchill was 'hell bent' to get his way, blasting through all objections about supplies and reinforcements and whether German strength had been under-estimated. He even suggested that Overlord might be delayed until early June, so that there would not be so much of a rush to send the landing-craft from Italy to England. 'I do not think,' he said, referring to promises at Teheran, 'U.J. [Uncle Joe, i.e. Stalin] is the kind of man to be unreasonable over forty-eight hours.'

Not until 8 January could Clark safely write in his diary: 'Operation Shingle is on!' On the 11th he wrote to Churchill: 'I am delighted ... I have felt for a long time it was the decisive way to approach Rome.' At last he had sufficient means to do the job. 'I am fully conscious of the necessity for launching the attack at the earliest possible date and have set 22 January as the target date.'

Clark's command post was in the enormous Bourbon palace at Caserta, north of Naples, later to become the seat of Allied Forces Headquarters (AFHQ). His intention was to attack from the Cassino area up the valley of the Liri – the obvious approach – a few days before Shingle. Anzio and Nettuno were chosen because of the suitable beaches nearby and because of Anzio's port. Twelve miles inland lay the Alban Hills, which dominated not only the approaches to Rome but the two main highways to Cassino. The Beachhead forces would consist of VI Corps, under General John P. Lucas, 'the best American corps commander', as Alexander reassured the War Office in London, with experience of amphibious operations. VI Corps would contain initially the 1st British and 3rd US Infantry Divisions, with some Commando and armoured elements, the crack US Ranger force of three battalions and the 504th US Parachute Regiment with a battalion of the 509th. In other words, the strength of the Shingle venture, envisaged once as comprising twenty-four thousand men only, had now risen to over 110,000.

'We have every confidence in you,' Alexander told Lucas. 'That is why you were picked.' But Lucas was full of forebodings. He felt like a 'lamb being led to the slaughter'. Manpower was insufficient, the expedition was 'diminutive' and hopes were set far too high. As for the attitudes of Alexander and Churchill, he was amazed by the 'ignorance of war displayed by leaders of people who have been at war for so many years'. Shingle to him had the 'strong odour' of Gallipoli, and 'apparently the

same amateur is on the coach's bench'. He disliked the 'hermaphroditic' –
i.e. British and American – nature of Shingle, complicating the logistics so
much more, and would have preferred it to have been wholly American.
Finally time was 'pitifully short'. 'Another week might save dozens of
lives. But the order comes from a civilian minister of another nation who
is impatient of such details and brushes them aside ... The real reasons
cannot be military.'

The US official naval historian, Morison, has said that either Shingle
should have been 'a job for a full army, or no job at all'. It was so
inadequate that it was like a boy on a man's errand. Nevertheless, the
whole story of the subsequent battle for Rome was to depend almost as
much on personalities, not only Churchill's but the commanders'. Lucas
was a stolid, methodical Southerner, old before his time but more
sensitive than has often been credited, variously nicknamed Sugardaddy,
Foxy Grandpa or Corncob Charlie because of his pipe. Clark, loving
personal publicity, looked like a Red Indian chief and was described as
'rangy' – Churchill called him the American Eagle. 'Nobody could
control Mark Clark, he controlled himself,' they said, and that was
important when it was a question of being given orders with which he did
not agree by the British. All the same, he got on well with Alexander.
'Alex was a gentleman in every meaning of the word. He was firm, fair
and I liked him very much.' Yet to many Alexander was a remote
character, an enigma: handsome, immaculate, looking as if he were
missing an eye-glass, but difficult to get to know properly and not enough
of a pusher. Then there was old Wilson, whose nickname Jumbo suited
him so well and who could not have been more of a contrast to his
predecessor Eisenhower; he too was reserved and it was as if 'champagne
and oysters [i.e. Eisenhower] had given way to cheese and beer'.

On 12 January a large offensive began on the Gustav Line defences,
with the Fifth Army and the French Corps taking Monte Trocchio, and
the British capturing the town of Minturno, but the advances were slow
and costly. Clark decided on a 'culminating' blow by the 36th US
Infantry Division across the River Rapido at Cassino two days before the
Shingle landings. For by now it was apparent that Cassino was the pivot
of the Gustav Line.

But first there had to be a rehearsal for Shingle. This turned out to be a
muddle and a disaster, putting Lucas into an 'evil frame of mind'. Forty
Ducks or DUKWS, small amphibious transport vehicles, and much else
were lost, due, according to Clark, to the 'appalling mismanagement of
the Navy'. Those lost Ducks were to have been used for the Rapido
crossing, which was a far worse disaster, indeed a shameful catalogue of
confusion and terror, with a loss of 1,681 men, including many who had
gone into action for the first time. The whole show was blamed by the

36th Division's General Fred Walker on Clark's exaggerated personal ambition and his determination to be the first into Rome before the British or French. Clark's own later comment on the Rapido débâcle was that it was better to spill blood 'where we were securely established than at the waterfront', in other words that a major German attack on Anzio and Nettuno, with only the sea behind, would have been far worse. At least he had succeeded in keeping German attention concentrated on the Gustav Line defences.

Clark often complained that the British tried to take the limelight when things went well. Now it was the turn of Churchill, who cabled Wilson on 18 January: 'No one is keener than I in working with the Americans in closest comradeship. I am however anxious that Operation Shingle should be a joint concern and not, as it may be represented, a purely American victory. I notice that in Clark's American Fifth Army, which is at least one-half British, Clark conducts the operation; under him Lucas; the Tactical Air under [General John K.] Cannon [American]; [Air-Marshal Sir Arthur] Coningham, on whose experiences I was specially counting, has been sent home most inopportunely by [Air Chief Marshal Sir Arthur] Tedder – [General Ira C.] Eaker [American] will be commanding strategical Air; and an American Admiral [Admiral Frank J. Lowry] is to command the Naval Squadron. Finally I see that Major-General Crane US Army has been designated as Military Commander of Rome.' He pointed out that Alexander and his staff had been responsible for the 'whole planning and control' of the operation. 'It will lead to bitterness in Great Britain when the claim is stridently put forward, as it surely will be, that "the Americans have taken Rome".' Wilson, of course, was not to make changes in command, but to see that credit was fairly shared.

Shingle would 'astonish the world', Alexander told Lucas. It would make Overlord unnecessary, he even said, no doubt echoing Churchill's hope. This did not help Lucas' gloom. Heavy opposition was expected, and the troops were equipped for this eventuality. Churchill wrote in his memoirs: 'It was with tense, but I trust suppressed, excitement that I awaited the outcome of this considerable strike.' Lucas' brief from Clark and the planners was firstly to 'seize and secure a beachhead in the vicinity of Anzio', and secondly to advance on the Alban Hills – but whether 'on' meant 'to' or simply 'towards' had been left vague, no doubt deliberately. Rome was not mentioned in his orders. On the other hand Wilson, on 20 January, told the British and American Chiefs of Staff that after the beachhead had been established VI Corps had a 'final objective of cutting two main roads about twelve miles south-east of Rome', which clearly showed that the Supreme Allied Commander at least thought Lucas would advance *to* the Alban Hills. Indeed, Alexander's Operation

Instructions had specifically said that the objects of the operation were to 'cut the enemy's main communications' in the Alban Hills and to 'threaten the rear of the German XIV Corps at Cassino'. At the last minute the idea of a further diversionary landing at Civitavecchia was given up. Also the 504th US Parachutes were not to make a parachute drop inland from Anzio but to be used instead as ordinary infantry: a decision it would seem that was concealed from Churchill.

Whatever the British had hoped for from Shingle, Clark and Lucas had determined that the first necessity was to consolidate the port and the beaches, and to leave any offensive operation to a second phase which would have to be decided upon according to the success of the landing.

On the 21st the weather forecast was good: 'Fair to cloudy, wind slight to moderate. Sea slight, no swell. Visibility mainly seven-fifteen miles.' So that at any rate was encouraging. After the armada of 374 ships had set sail from Naples and elsewhere, Alexander cabled 'Colonel Warden', Churchill's code name: 'Just back with Admiral [Sir John] Cunningham from visits to convoys at sea about seventy miles from Naples. All well by 4 p.m. No sign of enemy air. Attacks by II US Corps [at the Rapido] disappointing. Too early to judge. I am leaving Naples at first light tomorrow in a fast motor boat to visit the landings and see General Lucas ... Hope to be back tomorrow evening.'

Soon after H-Hour, 2 a.m., the next morning came the message: 'Personal and Most Secret for Prime Minister. From General Alexander. Zip repeat Zip.' The landings had begun.

Brindisi

The early capture of Rome would, it was hoped, help to solve the political crisis that hung over the Badoglio government in Brindisi, down in the heel of Italy.

'The fact is that the Italians are going through a period of disillusionment and the full tragedy of their plight is only now becoming apparent,' wrote Harold Caccia, a Vice-President of the Control Commission, to Harold Macmillan, who was British High Commissioner on the Advisory Council. The Italians had believed or at least hoped that with Mussolini thrown out the war in Italy would now be regarded as a joint enterprise for the liberation of their country, and that the resources of the Allies would 'turn shortage into plenty'.

The brutal truth was not only that the Italians, as co-belligerents, were still being looked on as a defeated enemy, but that most ordinary people in the liberated South were far worse off materially than before. The remnant of the Army was being treated with distrust, apart from one unit of brigade strength which had been sent to the Gustav Line. Little wonder that the government was lacking in drive and inspiration.

Not that the Allies could altogether be blamed for the miseries that total war left in its train, especially during such a hard winter – though it was the opinion of Robert Murphy, Macmillan's American opposite on the Advisory Council, that the tragedy of the long battle up the length of the country could have been avoided if the Allies had acted at once and decisively after the fall of Mussolini in July 1943, and Operation Shingle might never have been necessary.

Beautiful Palermo was half in ruins, many picturesque and architecturally important smaller towns were devastated. As for Naples, the glorious Parthenope of the Greeks was not only a shambles but morally degraded, an ironic sequel to the gallantry and idealism of the Four Days uprising in September. The Allied bombing of the port had been intensive, and wrecks of some hundred and thirty ships clogged the harbour. The Germans had blown up the sewage and water systems, and left booby traps and delayed-action mines. There was typhus in the overcrowded back streets, and black marketing was rampant. It was reckoned that forty per cent of the women had taken to prostitution. As you drove into the city there were placards warning Allied troops that this was a particularly dangerous area for venereal disease.

What would be the fate of Rome? Intelligence contacts had reported that the bridges, public services and main hotels were already mined. Since the Allies had never recognized Rome as an open city, there were naturally fears, voiced particularly by the Vatican, that this could have sinister implications. However, as long ago as on 29 June 1943, Allied policy had been summed up in a letter from Roosevelt to Archbishop Cicognani, the Apostolic Delegate in Washington, who had sent him a communication from the Pope: 'I trust His Holiness will understand that should the conduct of the war require it, recognized military objectives in and around Rome cannot be ignored. There is no intention to attack or damage non-military objectives or the historic and art treasures of Rome.'

There was a simple reason for the Allies not wanting to recognize Rome as an open city: they hoped soon to capture it and use it themselves as a centre of operations. There was also the possibility that the Germans might turn such a declaration to their own advantage and simply move in their forces. For these reasons the Foreign Office persuaded Washington to maintain a 'sphinx-like attitude' on the subject to the world at large.

As Harold Caccia said, the alarming food shortage in Rome would be eased by the time the Allies reached Rome as more agricultural land would have been freed. He had added that he had heard his American colleagues say roundly that the British had 'better be left to sort out the Italian mess because they will have to live with the aftermath' – implying that the United States would regard the Mediterranean as a British sphere of influence after the war. The fact that there had been a change in the supreme command from American to British, from Eisenhower to Wilson, Caccia said, 'assisted the process'.

The Pope had also long ago, before the Armistice, expressed his concern to Roosevelt over the plight of the Italian people, and the President's reply had been: 'It is my intention, and in that I am joined by the people of the United States, that Italy will be restored to nationhood after the defeat of Fascism and will take her place as a respected member of the European family of nations.' The question was whether Fascism in Italy could now be considered to be defeated. In the opinion of Churchill, Italy had yet to 'work her passage'.

There were those in the State Department in Washington who saw the British support of King Victor Emmanuel and Marshal Badoglio – the

victor of the Abyssinian war — as 'blind and stubborn'; it was also
strengthening the Communist party. Most Italians, they believed, were
outraged by the flight from Rome and considered the king, his son
Umberto and Badoglio to be mere symbols of Fascism. In actual fact on 6
November Churchill had written to Roosevelt: 'Victor Emmanuel is
nothing to us but his combination with Badoglio did in fact deliver the
Italian fleet ... Why should we add to the burdens of British and US
soldiers on their march to Rome by weakening their aids?' To which
Roosevelt had replied that at present he was too far removed from first-
hand conditions in Italy to comment, but that 'the old gentleman [the
king] I am told clicks only before lunch'.

Earlier Churchill had said to Macmillan: 'Our policy is to broaden and
increase the leftward emphasis of the Italian government. I am clear that
any reconstruction of the Italian government had better wait until we are
in Rome. In Rome lie the title-deeds of Italy and the Roman Catholic
church.' When Macmillan had visited Marrakech, he had been treated
with another Churchillian catch-phrase (to be repeated later in Parliament
and not much liked by Italians): 'When I want to lift a pot of hot coffee, I
prefer to keep the handle,' by which Churchill meant that he wanted to
keep the status quo. Military victory had to come before politics.

But Washington's attitude had toughened, as Robert Murphy found
when he was summoned there. He was told that he must hasten the king's
abdication, an important factor being that Roosevelt had before long to
face an election, and the support of Italo-American voters was important
to him — nearly all of them being opposed to the monarchy, or at least
to Victor Emmanuel and Badoglio.

The American candidate to lead a new Italian government was Count
Carlo Sforza, an ex-Foreign Secretary and ambassador to Paris in pre-
Fascist times, and for many years an exile in the United States. Sforza's
opinion of the king was that he was a 'frightened and non-existent'
character and that Churchill had the 'most wrong information' about
him. His plan was that the king should abdicate, not in favour of Umberto
but of his grandson, and that he, Sforza, should become Prime Minister in
place of Badoglio, who could be Regent. Churchill's opinion of Sforza
was scathing: a 'useless, gaga, conceited old man' and a snob. 'I do not
believe,' he told Roosevelt, 'he counts for anything that will make men
kill or die.'

Apart from Sforza and Benedetto Croce, the world-renowned Liberal
historian and philosopher, both in their seventies, there were no political
figures of any weight in southern Italy. Both Macmillan and Murphy
found Sforza garrulous and over-theatrical, a contrast to Badoglio, who
was of peasant stock. When Macmillan visited the 'gnome-like' Croce he
found plenty of reasons to distrust his views. Communism, for instance,

was more of a fashion than a force, he said. Croce was extremely anti-clerical, but supported Sforza's plan to replace the king with his grandson.

In point of fact in Rome Montezemolo's Military Front, which supported Badoglio, was well organized. However, all the national politicians of stature, many of them also in Rome, were ranged against these 'Badogliani' and belonged to the CLN. The Communists in particular were militant and at least as well organized as the Military Front. If, therefore, the Germans were to withdraw from the city, leaving a hiatus before the Allies arrived, there was real danger of civil war, or even a situation like the Paris Commune of 1871.

Whatever detractors of British policy in Italy might feel, in Bari there was the British-run radio station which did its best to broadcast impartially all points of view to German-occupied Italy. A congress of the southern representatives of the CLN was also 'authorized' for the end of January in Bari: a great milestone after twenty years of suppression of free speech. The Allied secret services, the OSS, SOE, and MI6 (British Military Intelligence), had their links in Rome, independent of one another; all received information from CLN sources, and the British had contact with the Military Front – they also had the stronger connection at the time with partisans in northern Italy and the Balkans.

The French representative on the Allied Advisory Council in Italy was René Massigli, and Macmillan had a great regard for him, though the relationship was not always to be easy. It was something of a sensation, as well as a sign of the importance that Moscow attached to the Council when Andrei Vyshinsky was appointed to it by the Russians. Macmillan found Vyshinsky 'the image of every Conservative mayor or constituency chairman; it was difficult to visualize in him the cruel persecutor of the Russian terror.' Needless to say, on arrival, Vyshinsky wanted to know how many Fascists had been tried and how many shot. The best that Caccia could do was to 'murmur something' about nearly fifteen hundred in prison – 'but Vyshinsky obviously thought this a very poor result after three months' work.'

On 14 January, as plans for Shingle were being finalized, Macmillan's office sent a radio message to London: 'Nobody here holds any particular brief for the present Italian administration, but there is no doubt that the decision to carry on with it up to Rome is the right one. This implies that it must be allowed the minimum amount of oxygen necessary to life ... There is no adequate material available in South Italy from which a Government with real authority could be formed with or without the abdication of the king.'

What nobody bargained for was that it was going to be a very long time indeed before the Allies entered Rome.

Anzio

At first there was no moon. There were stars and a slight breeze, which made the waves slap – too loudly? – against the flat bottoms of the landing-craft. It was one of those miraculous, clear, still nights that sometimes occur in an Italian winter by the sea.

0100 hours, 22 January. The Anglo-American invasion force was less than a mile out from Anzio and Nettuno. The first assault would be in an hour's time, the British to the north, the Americans to the south of the towns, while the American Rangers would make a landing on the main beach of Anzio itself – suicide, most people thought. Many of the men had only learnt of their eventual destination after embarking. Some had also taken part in the Salerno landings, four months earlier. Nearly everyone expected the same kind of bloodbath.

The huge convoy, escorted by cruisers, destroyers, minesweepers and submarines, on leaving Naples the previous day, had headed straight out into the Mediterranean. 'As we sailed past Capri, I wondered if it would be my first and last time to see it,' a Sherwood Foresters officer wrote home. The Germans presumably were too preoccupied with the Allied attacks on the Gustav Line near Cassino, for not a single enemy aircraft was seen. Some men were even able to sunbathe on the decks. When dusk came, the convoy had veered back towards Italy. For those who felt like it, there was time for some four hours' sleep.

The British 1st Division's landing area, known as Peter Beach, was to be on a narrow sandy stretch behind which were dunes, umbrella pines and scrub. X-Ray Beach, where the US 3rd Division and 1st Armored Division would land, led to flatter ground – arable and grazing country – that had been the mosquito-ridden Pontine Marshes until reclaimed by Mussolini in the 1930s. Whereas, in the first instance, the British sector would be bounded by a small river, the Moletta, that was fed upstream by deep bramble-filled gullies, the Americans would have as their south-eastern limit the Mussolini Canal, up to sixty yards wide and with banks on either side, a natural barrier against tanks. The men were not told of any special objective, but they knew that the idea was to strike inland towards the Alban Hills rather than straight towards Rome.

Now the ships facing Peter Beach were in their battle positions. The silence was eerie. An armada of thousands of waiting men, jam-packed together, weapons at the ready. Any moment they could be discovered by the Germans, and hell would burst from that hidden shore: a hell of screaming shells, withering rods of tracer and stark, merciless flares that would turn the landing-craft into easy targets. What hope would there be for anyone after a direct hit? Yet there was comfort in the feeling that there were so many others waiting in the darkness outside. When faced with the prospect of hand-to-hand battle and the possibility of heavy casualties, one can only be sustained by the thought, it can't happen to me.

Guardsman Dick Bates of a Scots Guards anti-tank platoon was in the second 'flight', half an hour after H-hour, an even longer period of tension therefore. The American crew of his landing-craft had spent the journey drinking and playing cards; it was clear that they didn't like their job one bit, which was hardly encouraging. There were several six-pounders on board, too. People thought highly of Bates, who had been a corporal but had lost his stripes for nicking oranges in Tunis on his birthday. Now, in full equipment, he waited, longing for a cigarette. A neighbour, unseen in the blackness, tried to ease his limbs, then dropped his rifle, with a terrifying racket.

Captain Nick Mansell of the Signals was probably one of the very few who knew Anzio from peacetime. He remembered the bathing huts and the yachts, with the white casino and pier, the purple mesembryan-themum over the orange rocks, the marvellous fish restaurants. In ancient times the town had been Antium, where Coriolanus had died and where Nero and Caligula had been born. He remembered the ruins of Imperial villas, crags of narrow bricks, and collecting bits of coloured marble polished by the sea. Further up the coast the Emperors had bred elephants. To Mansell the Alban Hills were no menace, or vague rampart that had to be scaled. To him they meant the Pope's summer palace at Castel Gandolfo, where his grandfather had seen Pius IX riding among cypresses on a white mule, followed by cardinals in scarlet, and Lake Nemi, the mirror of Diana, and the famous chestnut woods, haunt of dryads and where there were hoopoes. The trunk road to Cassino below, the so-called Route Seven, was none other than the Appian Way. He thought of friends in Rome. Old Tina Whitaker, who would burst into grand opera. Mario, who produced such delicious *fettuccine* near the Ripetta. Vittoria Sermoneta, snobbish but fun. Vera Cacciatore, who looked after Keats' house by the Spanish Steps. Were any of them alive? He said nothing

about any of this on board. He knew his companions too well. They
wouldn't care a button about dryads, and had probably never read a word
of Keats.

Further back out to sea was a contingent of a hundred and fifty
somewhat apprehensive Carabinieri, whose job was to 'maintain public
order' among the civilians of Anzio and Nettuno after they had been
captured. Sergeant Andrea Villari came from Genzano, near Lake Nemi,
and looked forward to seeing relations again after a year in Naples. He
also had an aunt running a shop in Aprilia, a model village started by
Mussolini on the main road from Anzio to Rome. She always had a good
supply of wine from the Castelli, as the towns in the Alban Hills were
called.

Although in the Brigade of Guards, Major Lord John Hope was due to
land in the American sector, since he was with the British increment to
General Lucas' VI Corps headquarters. Several higher ranking British
officers were worried about Lucas, whose so-called caution appeared to
them to be merely a pathological slowness, and who at fifty-four acted as
if he were 'ten years older than Father Christmas'. Hope thought him a
funny old Southerner, with that corncob pipe, and rather liked him. In
many ways the two could not have been more different, Hope an Old
Etonian and the son of a marquess. 'Lookee, Hope ...' Lucas would
generally begin his sentences.

Lucas was on board the *Biscayne*, Admiral Lowry's flagship, originally
an aircraft tender, on whose deck an armour-plated 'house' had been
built. General Patton had said to him encouragingly: 'John, there is no one
in the army I'd hate to see killed as much as you, but you can't get out of
this alive.' Lucas had tried to joke: 'I'm just a poor working-class girl
trying to get ahead.' Now he wrote in his diary: 'I think we have a good
chance of making a killing. I have many misgivings but am also
optimistic. I struggle to be calm and collected and, fortunately, am
associating intimately with naval officers whom I don't know very well
which takes my mind off things.' He found Lowry 'one of the world's
gallant gentlemen and certainly one of America's most distinguished sea-
dogs'; and since Lowry was not much more than five feet tall he was just
the right size for the *Biscayne*. Major-General Lucian K. Trustcott,
commander of the 3rd Division, slept on a sofa in the same cabin. There
were those like one of the less important on board who thought
that it was crazy to have two such important 'turkey's eggs' in one
basket.

Now there was a slip of a moon. Suddenly the quiet of the night was
shattered by British rocket ships pounding each of the landing beaches.
The noise was fantastic, monstrous, horrifying. Each rocket contained
thirty pounds of TNT, and 780 of them were discharged in two minutes.

The aim was to blast away wire and land-mines. Any defenders who were not killed would be totally stunned. Then at last the barrage ended. Lucas waited, ears singing. One after the other the assault-craft slipped ahead, towards the unknown.

Still no answering fire. According to the timetable the first men would be ashore ... The radio signalled to the *Biscayne* that reconnaissance troops were pushing well inland, beyond the dunes. And so the extraordinary truth became clear to Lucas: far from being another Salerno, Shingle had 'caught the Germans off base' and there was virtually no opposition. 'We achieved what is certainly one of the most complete surprises in history.'

The first British unit to reach Peter Beach had been the 6th Gordons, followed by the 2nd North Staffs. The din of the rocket ship had been unexpected and truly terrifying. A snag was found almost at once. The assault-craft ran on to a sand bar, and on stepping from the ramp men found themselves in water up to their necks – the cold was a shock even in the crisp night air. They struggled ashore, dripping, fully laden. It was discovered that all the mines had by no means been exploded – they were of the wooden variety. A corporal lost a foot; another man was literally blown in half. At last a path was cleared. The sappers quickly laid pontoons from the sand bar, and submarines acted as markers for incoming landing-craft. By the time Bates came on shore, tiny hooded lights were there to guide you through the mines. Again, incredibly, no opposition. Even the concrete pillboxes were not manned.

Prisoners were, however, taken: three drunken German officers returning from a night in Rome. A motorcyclist was flushed out and his pillion passenger shot. Some other Germans were found hiding in a barn. They said that they had only come to Anzio to shoot cattle for food. On being searched one was found to have a packet of nude girlie photographs, evidently from a Roman brothel.

The blurred horizon sharpened into daylight. The dunes were tangerine colour, streaked with grey and sulphur yellow. Then came a kind of esparto grass, beyond which were brambles, myrtles and umbrella pines. Later you could even see the Alban Hills, like arms outstretched, though hardly in welcome. Now loudspeakers guided men ashore. Vehicles of the Assault Brigade were being unloaded over wire net runways, under the supervision of the landing officer, Major Denis Healey, politician to be. The landing-craft looked like enormous open-mouthed whales, as lorries, jeeps, ducks and guns came tumbling out of the holds. Officers began to recognize features from air photographs: an ancient watch-tower built once against the Saracens, silos and farm buildings – though all deserted. It was like landing in a ghost country, where ghosts could turn lethal.

In point of fact the unloading took unexpectedly long, because of the sand bar. This could have meant disaster, even massacre, if there had been opposition. Platoons fanned out into the *pineta*, half expecting ambushes. Suddenly, at last, from up the coast somewhere, a German 88 mm gun woke up and began lobbing over shells, making white fountains among the crowded ships, some of which scattered. A destroyer darted off to deal with it.

The sky now was comfortingly full of Spitfires and Kittyhawks. Some hours passed before Nick Mansell could get ashore. His great fear had been that he would disgrace himself by panicking under fire, but the quiet and the strangeness exhilarated him. He was not even shocked by the sight of the entrails of that North Staffs fellow. Any moment he too might step on a mine. Beyond the *pineta* there was a coastal road. At a crossroads he saw: 'Via Severiana – Roma 52 km.'

The American landing on X-Ray beach near Nettuno was easier – the approach shallower and the dunes less precipitous. Frogmen had gone ahead to clear mines. For those watching during the first tense minutes it was a sight impossible ever to dismiss from memory, as the files of GIs waded into the black with rifles held above their heads. There were some accidents. To his horror Ted Wyman of the US Navy saw the cable part on No. 3 boat. 'Forty men fully equipped were thrown in a struggling mass in the water. The boat hung straight down ... No one knows how we got those men aboard, many of them with broken arms and legs' – one of the men was never found. After a while some shore batteries opened up feebly, but they were soon silenced. Again there were mines, and some unpleasant casualties. By midday the Americans were three miles inland, halfway to the vital town of Cisterna, on the road to Naples. Much of the 3rd Division's artillery and tanks were already ashore.

It was ironic that a tower to the right of X-Ray beach, Torre Astura, built on the site of Cicero's villa, should be full of romantic associations for Germans – for it was here that the fifteen-year-old Conradin of Hohenstaufen fled in 1268 after the battle of Tagliacozzo, later to be publicly executed in Naples. The canal ran inland from the tower, towards a number of modern two-storeyed farmhouses, or *poderi*, which Mussolini had given to indigent peasants, mostly from the North. The Americans found that families living nearest to the beach had been evacuated, and that the farms were empty. The first four bridges over the canal were blown. Near one of them a woman and child, apparently living in a cave, leapt out and ran in terror towards the woods, leaving behind them a large white cow with curved horns. There was some trouble with a pugnacious herd of buffaloes, which had to be countered with tommy-guns. 'Steaks tonight, folks,' yelled Private Jim Weinberg of the 504th Parachutes as his jeep raced eastwards. But the hope was a forlorn one, for the buffaloes' carcasses were to find their way to the kitchens of VI Corps headquarters.

The Rangers' task – to land on Anzio beach and clear the harbour – was the most daring of all. Handpicked volunteers known as Darby's Rangers, after their commander Colonel Bill Darby, they had had a magnificent record in Tunisia and at Salerno, and their endurance and self-confidence were due to Darby's inspired leadership. They were the natural spearheads in any big action. Now their objective was the casino, a white-washed building of the Art Nouveau period with statues along the balustrade. 'When I run out of the landing-craft,' Darby had told the planners at Caserta, 'I don't want to have to look right or left. I'll be moving so fast . . .' Which was what he did; and again there was no opposition. A few German bodies, horribly gashed by shrapnel, lay on the esplanade. By 0645 all three Ranger battalions were ashore. Some dazed, ashy-faced 'Krauts' emerged from rubble and were found to be engineers sent from Rome purposely to destroy the mole – they were to have begun work that morning. Booby traps and mined buildings were also quickly dealt with by the Rangers. The casino was discovered to be built on large cellars hollowed out of the tufo – much appreciated when the time came for German bombardments.

Out to sea a mine-sweeper struck a mine and went down in three minutes. Soon after dawn six Messerschmitts broke through and set fire to some vehicles. Other, more serious raids followed, and some bombs were far too close. The sky was filled with drifting black puffs of smoke. Lieutenant Wyman was to write: 'I still don't like the dirty taste in the air from a near miss.' Then a landing-craft, carrying some of the 504th Infantry, was hit. 'It wasn't long before some small boats began to bring the casualties out to us and we hauled them up over the side. Poor sodden lumps of flesh some of them were, with their faces and hands black from flash burns.'

Alexander and Clark had had one encouraging report from Lucas, at 3 a.m., to the effect that the landings had been made and progress continued, but there had been nothing more by 5 a.m. when they set off for the Beachhead by speed boats from Naples. However, on the journey Lucas' bizarre code message reached them: 'No angels yet Cutie Claudette,' which being interpreted meant that no tanks had been encountered and that American and British troops were advancing.

Before daybreak Truscott's 3rd Division had rounded up some two hundred Germans. Truscott was very different from Lucas: wiry, no nonsense, a soldier through and through, with deep-set grey eyes – 'Old Gravelmouth' to the British. It had been he who had conceived the idea of the Rangers. By 10 a.m. he felt free to return from the front to his command post on the shore. His Chinese orderly, Private Hong, knew that he had had nothing to eat and therefore prepared bacon, eggs and toast 'over an open fire as only Hong could make it'. Somehow he had managed to bring three dozen eggs with him from Naples. As Truscott was eating his first Anzio breakfast, on the hood of his jeep, up came General Clark to congratulate him, along with General 'Wild Bill' Donovan of the OSS, a small OSS contingent having landed with the Rangers. 'Yes, they would love to have some breakfast.' More visitors arrived. At 12.30, as Truscott was preparing to leave, he heard Hong remarking to the sergeant: 'Goddam, General's fresh eggs all gone to hell.'

Lucas had not landed, and indeed did not come permanently ashore until the next day. He had also insisted that General Penney, commanding the British 1st Division, should stay afloat with that part of his forces which were to be a 'floating reserve'. As the British were having difficulty with the sand bar, he took a small boat and visited Penney, who was on board the *Bulolo*. Mines were a problem so he had to go far out to sea, the journey thus taking him an hour. It was frustrating, not to say confusing, for the unfortunate Penney to be told: 'Alert your boys. They will be attacked at four.' Lucas was not sure that the British 'had put forth the maximum effort to overcome their handicaps'. 'The Royal Navy doesn't seem to be as versatile in the substitute of methods as our old sailors are.'

If Penney in Clark's estimation was 'not too formidable a general', Penney had the same feeling towards Lucas. Penney had an attitude that was slightly intimidating to his juniors, although fundamentally he was kind and generous: 'a very good telephone operator', he was described by Clark, a reference to the fact that he had been in Signals. He was also a meticulous man who 'did everything according to the book', and had been somewhat alarmed when Alexander had given him this appointment. He had not even been allowed ashore by the time 'Alex' came to inspect progress.

Guardsman Bates was busy digging a slit trench – somewhat resentfully, since it was not for his benefit but for the Irish Guards – when there was sudden commotion. And there was the mighty Alex, instantly recognizable because of his red headband. Everything was so calm, just like an exercise, and – as the Scots Guards official chronicler was to say later – Alexander, in his fur-lined jacket and riding breeches, for all the world was like a 'chief umpire visiting the forward position and finding it to his satisfaction'. Later Alexander congratulated Lucas. 'You have certainly given the folks at home something to talk about,' he said.

Meanwhile the 1st Recce Troop – under the command of Lieutenant J. S. Baker and therefore known as 'Bakerforce' – had gone up the coast road and encountered some enemy. They blew up the bridge over the Moletta, much to the annoyance of higher command, and an armoured car turned turtle in the mud. The North Staffs pushed up through the

Padiglione woods along a track eventually christened Regent Street. A
forward patrol reached a viaduct bridge in the Campo di Carne, Field of
Flesh. No one realized how grimly appropriate this name was to be. The
bridge came to be known as the Flyover, eventually the most crucial point
in the entire Beachhead struggle.

The Americans had also seen some Germans around Cisterna. But a
rumour raced round the Beachhead that an American jeep had reached
the outskirts of Rome unchallenged. By nightfall Lucas had landed some
36,000 men and about 3,200 vehicles. The Beachhead had about eighteen
miles of coastline and a depth of five to seven miles. Only later was it
learned that the Germans had already amassed 10,000 men on the
perimeter. The Allied airforce had made about twelve hundred sorties.
Penney's boys waited but were not attacked at four or at any other hour
that day.

Most people assumed that by first light on the 23rd the Allied advance
guard would be sweeping on to the Alban Hills, and thence to Rome. As
people were fast realizing, however, Lucas was by no means a 'galloping
Napoleon'. What was more, Clark had said to him in Naples: 'Don't stick
your neck out, Johnny. I did at Salerno and got into trouble.' He had also
said: 'You can forget this goddam Rome business.'

That night officers of the Grenadier Guards played bridge and slept in
pyjamas. And Wynford Vaughan-Thomas, the BBC correspondent,
wrote to his colleague, Denis Johnston, in the South: 'It is just normal
military fuck-up with an American accent. We are commanded by a dear
old pussy-cat who purrs away, that we are all happy on the Beachhead,
and, in a sense, we are.'

A few Italians emerged from cellars, though they were soon driven back
as the German bombardment began to increase. The Germans had
evacuated nearly all the inhabitants of Anzio and Nettuno, only leaving
men to run essential services. Nettuno was the larger, a fortified medieval
area with a castle, while Anzio had more of the air of a tourist resort. Both
towns were dominated by the large Renaissance villa that stood on a hill
covered with pines and evergreen oaks and belonged to the bachelor
Prince Stefano Borghese, who had been put in charge of the local workers
as 'mayor' by the Germans.

Borghese was in point of fact owner of most of the land around Anzio
and Nettuno, and had been allowed to keep his fifteen servants. Naturally
he had heard the uproar of the rocket ships. When dawn came he dared to
walk out on his balcony, and there, beyond the formal garden and the
pines, he saw the harbour packed with landing vessels and Ducks. Almost
at once two American soldiers with walkie-talkies came up the drive. He
went to meet them and just in time managed to prevent them from

shooting his dog. They treated him with little respect, not believing, so he found later – after having seen the palace at Caserta, the second largest in Europe after Versailles – that a prince could live in such a modest building of only a hundred rooms, and made him and his servants line up against a wall. Then he was removed to the Paradiso, Colonel Darby's casino, and kept there for questioning for twenty-four hours.

The 150 Carabinieri brought from Naples were finding that they had very little to do at Anzio.

Some of the ejected families had gone to the towns in the Alban Hills, while others lived in caves in the Padiglione woods, having brought their household treasures with them. The children loved the life, in spite of mud outside and smoke indoors. Old huntsmen and shepherds told them the legends behind the name of various localities: Buonriposo (good repose) ridge, Acqua del Turco (water of the Turk) and Femminamorta (dead woman). At Cavallo Morto you were supposed to hear a dog howling for its friend, a dead horse. The menfolk used to take vegetables to Rome, at first by train, but when the bombings got worse by foot, which usually meant spending some nights away. Once the Germans had come demanding women, but old Zio Peppe had managed to thwart them. 'Not when it is raining,' he had said. Signora Silvestri lived in a cave with some friends and relations. After the Armistice she had been joined by her son Ennio, who had been in the submarines. They had heard the rocket ships and seen flashes. Obviously the Allies had landed. The older men were in Rome, so at daybreak Ennio and the boys climbed trees to try to get some sort of view. It was a terrible anti-climax when at last they met a platoon of soldiers, in camouflage jackets – from the shape of their helmets, familiar from newspapers, evidently British – emerging from the bushes with rifles and bayonets pointed menacingly at them. The officer was suspicious and made them put up their hands. The boys were then forced to lead the way to the caves and then, as roughly as before, ordered to tell their families to come out. The encounter, however, ended happily, with glasses of wine and *pecorino* cheese in exchange for cigarettes and a tin of 'M. and V.' (meat and vegetables). Signora Silvestri thought the officer looked so young. 'When will you be in Rome?' he was asked. '*Presto, molto presto,*' he replied, and the platoon moved on to Campo di Carne.

Not all children were so fortunate. During that afternoon Fusilier Christopher Hayes was digging a trench near the dunes at Peter Beach when he heard sobbing. Then he saw grass move and a girl of about five or six appeared, with black curly hair and in a filthy torn frock. He realized that she was heading straight for a minefield. Grabbing his bren he rushed towards her. She began to scream: '*Mamma, Mamma.*' But he picked her up and carried her to the safety of his unit.

Hayes and his mates could not speak Italian. For some reason they understood the girl was on holiday, and it seemed possible that the parents had been killed or had run away during the bombardment. At last they found some blankets and Italian uniforms in a wrecked vehicle. They managed to get the dress off and wrap her in the clothes, and then Hayes suddenly saw a name on a label. He shouted 'Angelita!', and the girl came running to him. So perhaps she was Spanish, for the name in Italian would have been Angelina – a child of refugees from the Civil War?

Now dark was falling. Tomorrow they would find Italians to look after her.

★   ★   ★   ★

In the whole story of the 'fuck-up' there still remains one question not satisfactorily answered, and this concerns the use of the British decoding machine Ultra, which by then was capable of picking up most German messages about troop movements and displacements. Ultra had made it clear that Shingle would be unopposed, so why was Lucas so surprised? One imagines Clark at the time must have had little faith in Ultra's capacity, or have felt that it was outweighed by other anxieties. Indeed he has said since, in explanation: 'We had broken the German code and could read messages from Hitler to "drive us into the sea and drown us ..." Knowing of the impending onslaught it was necessary to dig in.' But this is confusing the facts, for Hitler's messages came long after the landings had happened, and Ultra recorded that many reinforcements, including armour, had to come from *outside* Italy.

Clark has also said: 'Our big mission in getting to Anzio was to keep reconnaissances out in front ... And the reinforcements came slow because of the turn around by boat and the fact that I didn't have many reinforcements because I was fighting so hard down in the Southern front. There were those who have said: "You could have gotten into your jeep and driven to Rome" '. To do that would have been fatal, 'the end of the war as far as you were concerned'. There was no possibility of going ahead and capturing the Alban Hills 'in the face of the concentrated troops that were ordered to meet us and did meet us'.

This is also a slight confusion of the facts. Eugen Dollmann of the SS in Rome has made a typically cynical comment on those days: 'The Americans put up their tents, said their prayers, had a good meal, and then lost an unique occasion for finishing the war within the year.'

Monte Soratte – Albano

The Germans, said Alexander, were easy to deceive but not so easy to panic. The Allies, said Kesselring and his chief of staff Westphal, showed an amazing lack of imagination; they worked strictly according to plan, security was the all-important factor. They were not daring enough. If, for instance, there had been a secondary landing in Calabria at the time of the Sicilian landings, they would have had an 'annihilating victory'. A landing near Rome in September 1943 instead of at Salerno might have had the same effect. Similarly, a landing at La Spezia instead of at Anzio-Nettuno could have given the war a decisive turn.

As far as Shingle was concerned, these opinions of each other's weaknesses appeared to be justified. Kesselring was taken badly off guard, and the result could have been a disaster. The tension those first days was tremendous, but he certainly did not panic. The news reached him by about 3 a.m. By 5 a.m. German units were already heading towards the Beachhead. By 7.10 a.m. orders had been given for reserves in the North of Italy to march south. Other units were also withdrawn from the Gustav Line, and the High Command or OKW (*Oberkommando der Wehrmacht*), which was under Hitler's direct control, agreed to send divisions from the South of France and the Balkans.

Kesselring's headquarters were at Monte Soratte, a strange mountain outcrop – like a huge wave about to break, Byron had said – to the north-west of Rome near the Sabine Hills. He had moved there after the Allies had bombed Frascati. The devastation of this delightful little town in just one hour, with the resulting civilian casualties and ruin of its famous sixteenth-century villas, had appalled him. Not for nothing had Hitler called him an Italophile. Soratte was a less inhabited spot, though beautiful in itself and admittedly of archaeological importance, associated with Hannibal and Constantine the Great, Pliny and Virgil. Usually Kesselring would fly from Soratte to the front at dawn, returning at dusk, to avoid interference from Allied aircraft.

As he had been commissioned into the Air Force, he wore the Luftwaffe uniform. Because of these Air Force associations Hitler was inclined to be more lenient towards him than he was to some Army leaders, but Goering disliked him. Hitler's support was important, since it was he who was ultimately head of all armed forces. Hitler tried to keep control of strategy on every front, to the extent of pestering local commanders with niggling details. As far as Italy was concerned, the orders were that every yard should be fought for. There were those who considered Kesselring's fondness for the Italians a weakness. All the same he had been shocked by the 'base treachery' of the Italian government at the Armistice.

In appearance Field-Marshal Albert Kesselring had a round, rather jolly face (he was nicknamed Smiling Albert), somewhat in contrast to the autocratic features of General von Vietinghoff-Scheel, who commanded the Tenth Army on the Gustav Line, and General von Mackensen, in command of the Fourteenth Army in North Italy. There were those who thought him over-optimistic, and Vietinghoff considered that he tended to drive men too hard.

Admiral Canaris, chief of military intelligence in Berlin, had visited the Italian front earlier in January. He had been questioned about Allied shipping activity in Naples, but had announced that there was 'not the slightest sign' that a landing would take place in the near future. He had actually left Italy on the 21st. Marshal Graziani, Mussolini's Minister of Defence, had asked Kesselring on that same day where his next line of resistance would be if Rome fell, and Kesselring had answered that he was not even considering the possibility of the enemy reaching Rome. He added that while the Anglo-Americans obviously wanted Rome for political and propaganda reasons, their strategic centre of gravity had now switched to the Atlantic. Italy, he said, was of secondary importance to them.

For all this, when on 12 January the French and British began their attacks on the Gustav Line, there was considerable concern at Soratte. Vietinghoff demanded that the two Panzer Grenadier divisions resting near Rome should be sent to reinforce him at once. Westphal records that a 'bitter tussle' ensued. To agree would mean that Rome would be 'laid bare', with a minimum of troops to guard the coastline from Civitavecchia southwards. Finally on the 18th Kesselring sent Vietinghoff the two divisions, as well as the headquarters of I Parachute Corps which had recently reached Rome.

One of the unknown quantities, in the event of an Allied advance near the denuded Rome area, would of course be the reaction of the Romans themselves. The events of 9–10 September, following the Armistice, had shown that there were possibly dangerous elements, especially if supplied with enough weapons and ammunition. In December Kesselring's headquarters had prepared a comprehensive alarm system, in case of landings in any part of Italy. If there were an Allied landing near Rome, the code-word would be 'Richard' and immediately all the machinery would go into motion.

The Germans' advantage lay in easier communications. It was true that the Allies had air superiority and could attack convoys and railway lines. However their tactics were usually predictable, and it was the opinion of both Kesselring and his chief of staff Westphal that Allied bombing would have been far more effective if they had simply concentrated on certain key areas.

On 18 January Kesselring felt it advisable to form a *Kampfgruppe* or Battle Group out of the 4th Parachute Division, stationed at Perugia. This Battle Group would consist of two battalions, each of about 650 men, and had to be ready for immediate action anywhere. Because of the lack of training time all its members would have to be veterans, fully experienced. The commander was Major Walther Gericke, a fine soldier who had greatly distinguished himself in Crete. The two battalion commanders were also chosen for their outstanding qualities – Captain Hauber and Major Kleye – and the assembly point was Isola Farnese, on the site of the Etruscan city of Veii, near Lake Bracciano, a few miles north of Rome.

Kesselring, worried about manpower shortages, had also ordered an emergency general alert throughout Italy. He had been uneasy about the Allied advances, and there were signs that the Americans might consider an attack nearer Cassino itself. However his staff kept warning him that this continuous stand-to was tiring his troops, and so he decided to countermand it on the very night of 21 January. As he said in his memoirs: 'I had only myself to blame.'

Two days before, Gericke had reported to the Corps Commander General Schlemmer at his headquarters at Grottaferrata in the Alban Hills. He had been told that he could not expect fuel or ammunition sufficient for his requirements until the 22nd.

At 5.30 a.m. on the 22nd the signal reached Gericke from Schlemmer: '*Alarm! Feind beiderseits Nettuno gelandet!*' – 'Alarm! Enemy landed each side of Nettuno!' He was ordered to despatch one battalion immediately in lorries to the Alban Hills.

In point of fact the first alarm had been raised thanks to a corporal of the railway engineers. He had sped off into the night from Anzio on his motorcycle and by chance had encountered a Lieutenant Heuritsch of the 200th Grenadier Regiment, and it had been the latter who had passed on the news to the commandant at Albano, who in turn had alerted HQ.

Not until 10.30 a.m. could Gericke, now with Schlemmer, receive some reinforcements, from an assortment of sources including the platoon that had been guarding Kesselring's headquarters at Soratte and, especially welcome, a company of Tiger tanks. He thereupon established his own command post at Albano. Shortly afterwards he was given his orders: he must secure the railway station at Campoleone on the main Rome–Naples line, and make a reconnaissance towards the newly built agricultural settlement of Aprilia some three miles further along the main road to Anzio.

Kesselring was convinced that the Allies intended to seize the Alban Hills. The whole German strategy would thereby be in danger, and it might not be possible to retain the Gustav Line. There was no reason either why Rome should not be the real Allied target. As Westphal has said, 'The road to Rome was open, and an audacious flying column would certainly have penetrated the city.' In effect, there were three main routes out of the new Beachhead: the central road along which Gericke was now making a reconnaissance, the coast road to Ardea and Ostia, and the road towards Cisterna on Route 7, the Appian Way. Vietinghoff was so dismayed at having to part with some of his troops, especially as the Americans were now on the attack in the South, that he telephoned Kesselring advocating withdrawal from the Gustav Line. He was ordered to stand fast.

It happened that elements of the Hermann Goering Division were resting not far from the Beachhead, so these were ready at once. Mackensen in North Italy was also ordered to make forces available from his Fourteenth Army; they were on the move by evening.

The whole coastline could clearly be seen from Albano. To Gericke the scene was like a peacetime exercise, with ships unloading and aircraft cruising overhead. Battalion Hauber was sent to occupy Campoleone. Because of the shortage of vehicles Battalion Kleye did not arrive until 5.30 p.m. At 7.05 p.m. Gericke received a radio message that the village of Ardea near the coast was still free of enemy, though some weak patrols had been encountered nearby and driven back (presumably 'Bakerforce'). So a company from Battalion Hauber was sent to Ardea, destined to become an important command centre over the next weeks. Battalion Kleye was spread along the difficult country – full of gullies and deep fissures, filled with scrub – between Ardea and Campoleone. The area was so large that Kleye was told that each platoon must prepare for circular defence.

The central road between Campoleone and Anzio seemed the most obvious route for an Allied advance. It was almost straight and ran through undulating countryside scattered with farms, with a single-line railway track alongside it. The Germans called the road *Die Allee*; to the Italians it was Via Anziate.

Lance-Corporal Joachim Liebschner found himself with that part of the Battle Group that was holding the road near Aprilia. Aged eighteen, he came from Silesia, and this was his first time in the front line; when only sixteen he had volunteered for the Waffen SS – the élite of the army – but had been turned down because of his age. Now he was acting as runner-batman to Lieutenant Weiss. His unit was full of confidence, but as the day wore on spirits became dampened because of the heavy loads that had to be carried and because of the muddy countryside, which affected Liebschner particularly since he was supposed to take messages by bicycle.

Enemy shells began to drop, and some men were killed. There was a feeling of frustration now, of not being able to hit back, or to attack. A sergeant, in charge of one of the heavy machine-gun groups and who had given Liebschner hell during training, complained about stomach trouble and fell further and further behind until he sat down under cover of a small bridge saying that he could not go on. He was whimpering and crying like an infant; Liebschner knew that he had been wounded on the Russian front and that his past experiences had probably made him lose his nerve, but fellow-paratroopers were less charitable and muttered about 'court-martial'. They left the sergeant sitting in the mud and never saw him again.

Lieutenant Hermann commanded an anti-tank unit belonging to the Hermann Goering Division. His men were well rested and had been expecting to be thrown into the Cassino battle at any moment. The alarm only reached him at 11 a.m., but within forty-five minutes the guns were hitched up and ready to move. During the march there were constant attacks from 'Jabos', as Allied dive-bombers were known. 'They had acquired the art of hedge-hopping and made life hell for us. Open roads always resulted in a race with life and death for us. Speed and manoeuvrability were our only weapons.' All Hermann's men could do was to fire back with rifles. 'They must have laughed at us, apart from the one who didn't get away. He had been very cheeky and even waved to us.' On one of his return journeys the concentrated fire of the entire unit 'got him straight in the face'. 'He pulled up his aircraft too late; some of the tracer bullets had hit his engine and it caught fire. He dipped his left wing and hit the ground.'

When at last his unit reached the slopes of the Alban Hills, Hermann climbed on to the roof of a villa. The landscape looked so peaceful in the last pastel flickers of the setting sun: to the left Monte Circeo, the fabled abode of the enchantress Circe, and then the neat farmsteads in the drained marshland, and the low shoreline and the wine-dark sea. Peaceful until you turned your eyes towards Anzio and Nettuno, and there saw the flotilla of enemy ships unloading arms and ammunition. Even more chilling than the landing-craft was the sight of a cruiser and its escort of destroyers. Hermann knew well enough how deadly the fire of these ships could be, and the massacre it could cause if directed on land targets. 'When darkness came we had to produce a lot of noise in order to fake large assemblies of German units.'

The anti-tank guns were moved into position along the Appian Way, towards Cisterna, but as yet Hermann had no infantry protection. General Vietinghoff was sending up other units of the Hermann Goering Division from Cassino, and they would probably arrive in the morning. Some contact, mercifully slight, was made with American tanks after nightfall. Hermann wanted to give the impression that his force was much larger than it really was, so all through the night he moved his guns up and down the road, firing them at intervals.

The 65th Division, stationed at Genoa, had also been ordered south. Wilhelm Velten was in a cavalry platoon; the horses were used for reconnaissance and despatch work. In point of fact there were virtually no vehicles in the Division. 'We are the poorest devils in the whole Wehrmacht,' people in his company used to say. When the order to move came, the horses had to be left behind and the men were put into civilian lorries, furniture vans, luxury coaches, anything that could be commandeered in a hurry. There were complaints about food during the long journey south, particularly about the quality of that staple German food, the sausage. 'If a Tommy dared to eat a piece of this sausage,' a corporal said to Velten, 'he will know that he has won the war.'

The final stage of the journey had to be on foot, but by the time the Division was able, belatedly, to reach the Beachhead perimeter the dramas and doubts of that first day were over. Velten's platoon found that it also was to take up positions at Campoleone station.

I Parachute Corps Headquarters, having arrived from the Gustav Line, was now put temporarily in charge of the German defences. By 20.30 a message came that Aprilia was free of the enemy, but civilians reported that the viaduct bridge at Campo di Carne was occupied by British troops. New units kept arriving at Albano, sometimes without warning and usually without ammunition. This involved constant reshuffling and improvisation. All would depend on how quickly the Allies acted the next day.

Rome

Screams in the night. The spatter of machine-guns. People running, the sound of nailed boots. Then a single cry, a shriek of agony, and silence again. Not a shutter was opened; nobody dared to look.

A motor bicycle roared past. Silence again.

A typical Roman night. But it was 24 January, and the Germans still had not left.

This happened in Via Lisbona, in a smart suburb to the north of the city. Two hours later yet more screams awoke Luisa Arpini in Via Paraguay, the adjoining street. She realized that they were coming from the flat next door. She also realized that the Fascists or the Gestapo must be taking away the Jewish family hiding there. She heard a woman's voice: 'No, no, no.' And then a man's name was called: 'Dino, oh Dino, Dino, Dino.' The horror of it would haunt Luisa all her life. She was sure the Jews had been betrayed for money by the *portiere*, a peculiar man. Then the door of a vehicle slammed. The vehicle drove off. Silence.

On the other side of Rome the British Minister to the Holy See, D'Arcy Osborne, had also woken. 'I heard some shots, so went and looked out of the *salone* window over a dead, moonwashed Rome; it was disconcerting but romantic to hear the silver silence shattered by a mysterious machine-gun, very close indeed, spitting death anonymously at nothing but silence and moonshine. Grim and beastly and sinister and evil and symptomatic.'

'Sabotage goes steadily forward,' wrote the American nun Mother Mary St Luke in her diary. The next morning an explosion in old Rome barely missed damaging Palazzo Borghese, which the Germans were using for storage. A lorry had been parked in the courtyard, but someone had just managed in time to remove a suspicious looking parcel on the running board. It would have been tragic if those wonderful loggias and colonnades had been destroyed.

The bomb would have been planted there by the Gapists. Elsewhere their efforts were more effective. On Via Appia and Via Casilina several German vehicles were ambushed and blown up, thereby blocking convoys which were then dive-bombed by the Allies. Telephone wires were cut, road-blocks blown up, sentries sniped or gunned down. A very powerful bomb had been set off in the buffet room at the main railway station; at least thirty German officers and men were killed or wounded. As a punishment for this General Maeltzer, the military commander of Rome, had the curfew put back to 5 p.m. Anyone seen on the streets after that hour would be shot at sight. This meant that people had to start for home at 4 p.m., and shops were shut at 3 p.m.

Everybody seemed to be on edge, as if soon a supreme choice would be expected of you, a choice involving rejection or sacrifice, cowardice or glory: a test of conscience greater than on 9–10 September. Only the signal was needed – but that signal was slow in arriving. By day Allied planes flew high in the clear wintry sky, making white scrolls and streaks; and now distant artillery (or bombs?) could be heard from the direction of the Beachhead. Was Rome's apocalypse, at last, to hand? The end of the city of the Caesars, and of St Peter?

The little market town of Velletri, in the Alban Hills, was said to have been crushed by bombardments. The Whitakers were told that scores of women had been killed while queueing for food, and among them was 'our poor gentle Signora Bartoli, whom we loved so much and who looked after our *podere*'.

Major Sam Derry's escaped prisoners were impatient, wanting to make their contribution – to act, to fight. Some of them were getting too cocky, and Derry had to be severe. He sent a warning to Trooper Basil Thorpe: 'I have received a full report of your atrocious behaviour ... After the liberation you will have to answer the charges, which are already serious.' And to Private Parcheso, who from his name presumably had Italian blood: 'It has come to my notice that you are taking unnecessary risks, which may not only lead to your recapture, but to the recapture of your comrades ... You are to remain in hiding and only go out when absolutely necessary.' One of Derry's charges was a particular problem, namely a British general, Gambier-Parry, who would have been a prize indeed if recaptured by the Germans. Just before the landing Derry had arranged for the general to have a billet in a walled-up room that could only be reached by a plank forty feet above the ground. However, Gambier-Parry had seemed happy enough there, especially since – as he said – he had, at long last, access to a bath.

Derry was as confused as anyone else about the Allies' intentions at Anzio. Now there was the bad news that Centro X of the Military Front had suffered another arrest: Ettore Basevi, partly Jewish, who produced forged identity cards (having with incredible boldness stolen watermarked paper from the Government printing office) and the occasional underground newssheet. Fortunately Basevi was not sent to the Gestapo-SD headquarters at Via Tasso but to the Regina Coeli prison and only briefly.

The arrested Centro X radio operator, whom Derry had used, was Umberto Lusena; he was in Via Tasso, and this inevitably meant that he would be tortured. He too was a brave man, a major from the Parachutes who had made several trips north to contact escaped prisoners working with the partisans. When Princess Nini Pallavicini escaped from her palace, the Centro X transmitter had been in her bedroom. The palazzo contained a rambling but magnificent series of salons and panelled rooms, and it was here that Military Front leaders often met. Since Nini was the widow of a war hero and by birth associated with another hero of Garibaldi's time, it was assumed that her house was unlikely to be molested. She had walled up the best of her famous collection of pictures, including Botticelli's *La Derelitta*, in the cellars which were once part of the tomb of Constantine. She also had harboured a number of Army officers who had to be fed by means of lowering baskets from upper windows.

Two flats, at Via Firenze and Via Chelini, had been made available to the O'Flaherty-Derry organization for hiding escaped prisoners. Now, however, the Nazis knew about them, and it was a question of finding more private individuals who would take the risk of helping. Derry was in some difficulties since two of his 'billeting officers', Lieutenant John Furman and Private Joe Pollak, had been caught – the former was in Regina Coeli, the latter was thought to have been shot. The two main providers of accommodation hitherto had been a half-Danish film producer, Renzo Lucidi, and a jolly, warm-hearted Maltese, Mrs Chevalier, known to her British guests as 'Mummy'. On one occasion Lucidi had taken John Furman (very unItalian-looking) to hear *The Barber of Seville* at the Opera. A high-ranking German officer in the audience admired Lucidi's attractive wife, so Furman had suggested that she should ask him to sign her programme. The German was delighted to do so. When the programme was returned he was found to be none other than that lover of good food and wine, that *rubicondo pagliaccio*, rubicund clown, General Maeltzer – who, to his credit, at Christmas had brought a hundred and fifty British and American prisoners out of camps for a dinner at a luxury Roman hotel, followed by a service at the American Church in Via Nazionale, which he attended.

Derry was worried that 'Mummy' might still be in danger, since the Gestapo had already once visited her flat. Nevertheless, she insisted that it should always be available for escapers, to the delight of her five daughters. As it happened, Renzo Lucidi was eventually to be arrested. Much more serious was the position of another helper, Nebolante, who owned the Via Firenze flat. Not only was he arrested but he was badly beaten up at Regina Coeli.

Unlike its counterpart in London, Wormwood Scrubs, the more euphonious Regina Coeli (Queen of Heaven) prison – sunk as it is between the Janiculum and the river embankment – seems very much within Rome. In times of peace women even go up on the slope behind and shriek out messages and family news to their men inside. It consists primarily of five *bracci* or arms leading out of a communal hall where religious services can be held. Each branch, containing the cells, has two upper storeys, with more cells, in front of which are platforms from which warders can keep a watch on goings-on below. In January 1944 the *terzo braccio*, or third arm, was the most dreaded, for it had been allocated to the Gestapo for political offenders.

Furman's particular worry was about the American Air Force sergeant arrested at the same time. The sergeant had been badly concussed after bailing out and now suffered from hallucinations, sometimes imagining himself to be Goering or Hitler. It was believed that the warders were baiting him.

On 25 January there was a surprise. Furman and the other Allied prisoners, including the sergeant, were told that they were to be transferred to camps in the North. Derry, when he read the news in a note smuggled out by a prison barber, prayed that they were not to be shot. Furman and his friends, however, were happy and 'dreaming of daring escapes'.

It was a different story for those escaped prisoners lucky enough to be in the Vatican's Gendarmerie barracks. Life might be boring, but at least whisky and cigarettes were in relative profusion. The Pope, with his usual 'incomparable charm', as Osborne said, had sent them his 'affectionate benediction', adding that he supposed that even though they were not Catholics they would not object to a blessing. Officially, at any rate, he did not know about another group of prisoners hidden in an old granary attached to the American College, near the Propaganda Fide on the Janiculum. The College was a training centre for missionaries, including some Germans and Japanese. Lieutenant Colin Lesslie of the Irish Guards, a future film producer, was in charge there. He had had a rousing welcome on arrival from O'Flaherty: 'Well, well, me boy, our first Irishman!' Lesslie had been captured in Tunisia and had escaped in September. On reaching Rome he had made his way to the British Embassy, which for some peculiar reason was not then under German surveillance; the Swiss caretaker, Costantini, had whipped the dust-sheets off the ambassador's bed and here Lesslie had spent several comfortable nights until removed by O'Flaherty first to Via Chelini and then to the American College.

Lesslie's charges were an assorted bunch, including several American student doctors of Italian extraction, GIs and British soldiers, a South African padre and several political refugees. Monsignor Montini had sent a corporal from the Pope's bodyguard, Antonio Call, to keep a watch on them. Call's job was also to keep contact with diplomats interned in the Vatican, and every evening he had to report back to Montini. If, for instance, a diplomat wanted to have a haircut, he had to apply to Call for a permit from Montini, and then to the Italian ambassador to the Holy See, and then to the appropriate Ministry. He would be allowed out for two hours and accompanied by Italian police, and later handed back to Call.

Call also did cooking up at the American College. Every now and then a cow would be sent up from the Vatican for slaughtering. Well stewed beef became a familiar diet.

News had reached the CLN that an American secret agent was in Rome. A meeting was therefore arranged for representatives to meet Tompkins on the 24th at his contact Cervo's house. Tompkins was ready with his dramatic proposal that he should arrange with the Fifth Army for a parachute drop in the Borghese Gardens. According to his information there could be no more than fifteen hundred Germans in the city at the utmost. He also had clearly been told by his boss in the South, General Donovan, that on no account did the Allies want an armed clash between the Italian right and left, whether between the Badoglian Military Front and the CLN, or the opposing wings of the CLN itself. As a lone American major he now had the task of persuading the CLN representatives that their main duty was simply to channel their efforts into getting rid of the Germans.

The meeting was headed by Riccardo Bauer, who ran the military junta and was one of the heads of the Party of Action. Bauer, a Milanese aged forty-eight, imprisoned twice during Fascism, modest, with gentle blue eyes, came to be regarded after the war as an almost saintly character. Giorgio Amendola, the Communist leader, was also present at the meeting. Tompkins was a little amused by the precautions. 'Partisans were posted for blocks around Cervo's house with submachine-guns, hand grenades and automatics wrapped in paper to look like parcels.'

It appeared that potentially there were about eight thousand partisans in Rome, and about half that number again outside, as well as escaped Allied prisoners and, of course, Montezemolo's men. Some of the provincial partisans were, however, escaped criminals, often pursuing private vendettas and acting as highwaymen. Tompkins was told about the CLN meeting on 18 January after Badoglio had demanded by radio from Brindisi that the CLN should submit to his command, and how, not surprisingly, it had been rejected. He was more than ever aware of the sinister implications of this rift between the CLN and the Military Front. Amendola, it seems, found Tompkins too peremptory and remembers him saying: 'Now is the time to show the stuff you're made of.' In the middle of the meeting Cervo placed a radio message from the Fifth Army in front of Tompkins: 'It was a warning not to move on any account, that the liberation of Rome was temporarily postponed.'

Tompkins could scarcely conceal his reaction to this news. There could of course be no question now of parachutists being dropped within Rome. The same message contained a top priority demand for information on all German troop movements towards the Beachhead; this was at least something that could be passed on to the Italians. The meeting broke up lamely.

No wonder Amendola was not impressed. As far as he was concerned, the evidence was still clear that the Germans intended to withdraw from Rome. Preparations for the general insurrection would continue.

'Make life impossible for the occupying forces' was in effect the slogan for the whole European Resistance. It was decided that efforts of the three parties of the left in Rome should be intensified, and particular help would be given to the *Gap di Zona*, the Gapist groups in the Alban Hills. The Communists in any case were already organized on military lines. They had divided Rome up into areas, each under separate commands, and allied to them was an organization of students and professors at the University. There were several secret arms deposits, known as Santa Barbaras, after the patron saint of the artillery; one of the most important was in Via Giulia. Some women, such as Captain Marisa Musu, were enrolled in the Gaps as fighters. Others were in charge of vital subdivisions dealing with hospital work, supplies of food and money, contacts with families of those who had been arrested or deported – among the main organizers being a school teacher, Laura Lombardo Radice, also a captain and later to marry a major in an 'Assault Brigade', Pietro Ingrao (many years later Speaker of the Italian House of Commons). The work of sabotage and collecting of arms was in fact under the Saps (Squadrons of Patriotic Action), whereas the Gaps were in charge of the 'elimination of fascist spies, enemy personnel and enemy war material'. The Socialist Party and the Party of Action were too small to be so highly organized: 'all head and no tails', like tadpoles. Anyway at this crucial moment solidarity between left-wing leaders seemed vital.

Meanwhile Tompkins, against his republican instincts, felt constrained to get in touch with the Military Front. He was not impressed by their rose-coloured, tissue-thin Bulletin, produced by the unfortunate Basevi's successors, and realized how inaccurate was some of the radio information on German troop movements that Centro X was relaying back to the South. He did not meet Montezemolo or General Armellini, the new commander of the Military Front, and indeed was not then aware of the qualities of Montezemolo, whose name lives now as one of the great symbols of heroism during the Occupation.

Montezemolo was aged forty-four, an aristocrat, selfless and very religious. He disapproved of Gapist-type activities and asked the Front to avoid such actions within the city, for fear of Nazi reprisals. After the arrest of his friend, General Simoni, he knew his turn could not be far off. Gold-rimmed spectacles and a moustache were hardly enough of a disguise for such a distinctive figure. Indeed he felt the whole Front was doomed unless Rome was liberated soon.

On 23 January a message arrived from Bari: 'From Allied Command stop The hour has come for Rome and all Italians to fight with all means possible and with all their strength stop Refuse to work for enemy on railways or elsewhere stop Sabotage wherever possible . . .' On that very day Frignani, the Carabinieri chief, had been arrested and taken to Via Tasso. And on the 25th Montezemolo was arrested and joined him there.

Tompkins was horrified by the news. What if Montezemolo talked under torture? But Montezemolo's followers and family had more confidence in him.

The treatment Montezemolo received was possibly worse than old Simoni's. It was said that he returned from the torture room with a dislocated jaw, eyes that were black and swollen, a bloody froth on his lips. He was tortured so regularly, and the pain was so intense, that his captors provided him with a deck-chair to sit on in his cell. Stories of what was being done to him spread quickly. Since Simoni was a friend of the Pope, the family had been to ask the Holy Father to intercede with Kappler. 'There is little I can do, alas,' he had said, and it was obvious that he knew precisely what sort of atrocities were being committed at Via Tasso, under the direction of that cool, blue-eyed head of the Gestapo-SD, whose only sign of annoyance would be when the duelling scar flared red on his cheek. The Simonis knew well enough, however, that the Pope himself was in danger, and that there were rumours that he might be deported to Germany. Nevertheless he did manage to arrange permission for special food and clean laundry to be sent, and there were hopes that the family might be allowed to visit Simoni. It was different for the Montezemolos, who would have been arrested if they had shown themselves publicly. The Pope arranged for Monsignor Montini to be in charge of Montezemolo's case.

Like Simoni, Montezemolo never spoke. He had spent the night before his arrest at Palazzo Rospigliosi. Nini Pallavicini, whose turn was to come soon, had begged him not to leave, but he had insisted on going to a meeting with Armellini at the house of Filippo De Grenet, a diplomat. After lunch Armellini had left, accompanied by Montezemolo's secretary, Michele (Chicco) Multedo. As they came out Multedo realized that they were being watched. 'Don't look up, keep walking,' he muttered. As they rounded a corner, Montezemolo and De Grenet emerged; they were arrested at once.

Armellini's wife Aileen now found herself rushed from one hiding place to another. She was nursing a baby, so terrified of losing her milk. First she hid in the Blue Sisters' clinic, then went to the empty and icy flat of the well-known Roman tailor Ciro, with only a few sticks of *pasta* to eat. Finally, to her utmost alarm, she was taken to the TB sanatorium on Monte Mario, where there was a German road-block right at the entrance, and 'this made me tremble every time my husband came to see me.' 'As the crow flies there was nothing between us and the Anzio Beachhead, the windows rattled all day and night from the gunfire, and at night the Very lights and explosions were very clear. The place was full of phony sick like me. I was very depressed and so cried a lot, but this helped really as people took pity and brought milk for my baby ...'

Meanwhile, some of the grand prisoners at San Gregorio were actually released. Not only that, but the remaining six – one an Englishwoman – managed to escape under the wire fence, thanks to a young Sicilian, an ex-Carabiniere officer. The Gestapo regarded Roman high society as being in the special domain of Dollmann, who not unnaturally was furious at the news. 'Enough of this Roman aristocracy!' he cried, adding: 'I have given orders for the Duchess of Sermoneta to be sent north tomorrow.' No doubt the duchess was now the most important blatantly pro-Allied aristocrat who had not yet been taught a lesson – Princess Pallavicini and, earlier, Prince Doria and Princess Isabelle Colonna having escaped the net and gone into hiding. On 28 January, therefore, her butler entered her drawing-room, 'to announce not dinner but the police'. She was put under house arrest. 'You must consider yourself in prison,' she was told, 'as though you were at Regina Coeli.' Vittoria Sermoneta was an accomplished flirt, even with policemen half her age, and she too managed to slip away, down the passages and back staircases of the honeycomb-like Palazzo Orsini. She took refuge at the Spanish Embassy, where she heard that her house was 'forfeit to the nation' and all her furniture was to be sold at auction.

The incredible Monsignor O'Flaherty had actually been warned by the German ambassador, Weizsaecker, that he would be arrested if found outside Vatican property. For Kappler regarded him now as an arch spy.

O'Flaherty did take a few precautions but not very many, and it was miraculous that he did not find himself in Via Tasso.

O'Flaherty had originally been outraged by Fascism when in the summer of 1942 he saw Jews being made to dig sand out of the Tiber. Earlier in the war he had also visited prisoner of war camps in Italy, and had started then to arrange for messages to be sent back secretly to their families on Vatican Radio. Naturally, therefore, after September 1943 many of his prisoner friends came to find him in Rome. He helped them simply 'because they were human beings'. As he said to Derry: 'I've no reason to be fond of the British, you know. Have you never heard of the Irish Troubles? I was there.' At an earlier stage he himself had escaped arrest by disguising himself as a coal-man. In actual fact Derry was careful not to let O'Flaherty become involved with passing of military information to the Allies. O'Flaherty was aware of this, but did on occasions drop the odd sly hint about troop movements. In the organization he was known as 'Golf' because of his addiction to the game – he had even given lessons to Ciano in the palmy days when the Golf Club was a fashionable meeting place. Other Irish priests also had code-names: Father Claffey was 'Eyerish', old Father Lenan 'Uncle Tom', Father Buckley 'Spike', and Father Flanagan 'Fanny'. Then there was Father Owen Snedden, a New Zealander known as 'Horace'; he was on Vatican Radio. The cheerful and energetic little Brother Robert Pace, a Maltese, was 'Whitebows', because he belonged to the De La Salle order and wore white bows on his black cassock.

Father Spike Buckley had a reputation for being 'game for anything' and after a few 'beakers of the warm South' was accustomed to break into 'Mother Macree'. The Irish Minister, Dr Thomas Kiernan, remained stolidly neutral, and preferred to be unaware of his compatriots' activities, let alone those of his daughter Blon or indeed of his wife. Mrs Kiernan, a large and outspoken woman, was a well-known soprano, Delia Murphy, whose most famous – and favourite – song was 'The Old Spinning Wheel'. She was allowed by the Fascist authorities to visit her farm outside Rome without escort, in order to fetch vegetables, and on several occasions took priests with her. On her return the Swiss Guards did not seem to notice that there were Army boots under the cassocks.

For some the Allied landings had been the cue to throw away caution. Neighbours became suddenly aware of Resistance workers living next door. Jews dared to appear on the streets, such as Piero Della Seta, aged twenty-one, who with three friends had taken refuge after the terrible October *retata* in the church of the Oratorians, the so-called Chiesa Nuova or New Church (although built in the sixteenth century) in the Corso Vittorio Emanuele. The monastery attached to the church was already sheltering several ex-Army and Carabiniere officers, but the four young men were walled up in a small room, receiving food and clothing through a trapdoor. Now, after this strange period of blankness, lasting three months, they had surfaced into the open.

Another young Jew had been sleeping inside an altar. He too took courage and emerged – but only temporarily. Unfortunately Celeste Di Porto, the Black Panther, was on the prowl. Many Jews were to regret their foolhardiness, and some were even to pay with their lives. Disaster also lay ahead for the young Communists who looked after the 'Santa Barbara' in Via Giulia. Either they behaved too rashly, or they were betrayed by an informer.

In the Lateran Seminario there was a sudden panic one night. The CLN leader Bonomi heard a German patrol 'squawking' outside the entrance. 'We thought there would be an invasion. For over an hour we were in an underground passage where it was impossible even to sit in the pitch darkness. What a splendid haul if the Germans had gone down there! Practically the whole Committee of Liberation, from me ... to De Gasperi [Christian Democrat] ... to Nenni [Socialist].' Indeed some of the most famous of the post-war politicians, including Prime Ministers, were hiding in the Seminario.

Nenni had told Bonomi that the three parties of the left resented his stern letter calling for solidarity. Bonomi had replied that he did not want to be dragged into 'adventures' or *conflitti* which would be disastrous for the cause. Meanwhile there was the CLN Congress at Bari, due to be held on 28 January. The Roman CLN could only watch impotently and wait for news, but at least this would be the first democratic congress to be held in liberated Europe, and it could only lead to a resolution attacking the king and Badoglio. Another development, somewhat surprising, was that Badoglio – presumably encouraged by Vyshinsky – had invited the Communist leader Togliatti to return to Italy from Moscow.

A few escaped Russian prisoners of war were in hiding in Rome, and these also came under Derry's wing. There were others at large in Italy, and a group of twenty operated in the Alban Hills, under the command of one Vassily. Rough, huge creatures they were, living almost wild and terrifying the peasants who had to cope with their enormous appetites. They took absurd risks, and as the days passed, and the Germans became more established, they were harried from one hilltop to another. They seemed relieved to be able to join up with the Gapist forces, headed by Pino Levi Cavaglione – a man who had spent six years in prison under the Fascists.

At first things had gone well for Levi Cavaglione's men. Near Albano they had even run into German soldiers who had cheerfully told them, '*Domani noi kaputt* – Tomorrow we are finished,' offering thousand *lire* notes for civilian clothes. Levi Cavaglione sent a patrol down to the Beach-head. A British officer acted coolly, but an American major was very

friendly, giving cigarettes and food, with a warning that men from a
Hermann Goering armoured division were on their way north from
Cassino. The Allied bombing was appallingly indiscriminate. Immense
damage was done to the town of Genzano and in the process Levi
Cavaglione lost several arms deposits.

Large nails were laid across the roads. Military telephone wires were
sabotaged, motorcycles ambushed. Then, *porca miseria*, tanks and
armoured cars moved into the area. Germans were mounting heavy
machine-guns. They burst into peasants' houses, shouting '*Via tutti* –
everybody out.' There could be no argument, no time to collect
belongings. On one such occasion Levi Cavaglione, who was caring for a
wounded comrade, found himself confronted by a young German
officer, slim and elegant. 'Why do you hate us?' the German asked, not
knowing Levi Cavaglione was a partisan. 'You hate us and we are
shedding our blood for you.' Three young British prisoners at that
moment passed in a truck, their faces fresh and well shaved. They made
the V sign and peasants gave them fruit, and then they were off again, to
prison, alive.

Soon came nightmare. A huge dust cloud hung over poor, ruined
Albano. Bombs and more bombs. Germans everywhere. Their mighty
war machine was truly getting into gear. Lorries full of parachutists in
camouflage uniform. Tanks groaning, rumbling; Panzer Grenadiers in
grey, the spread eagle on their lapels. Scores of civilians were killed during
an air-raid. There were bodies everywhere, but the tanks went forward,
crushing them. Genzano was evacuated at two hours' notice, and the
people had to take refuge in the woods on the slopes hanging over Lake
Nemi. Many of the inhabitants of Albano had rushed up to Castel
Gandolfo, hoping for sanctuary in the Papal villa.

Levi Cavaglione and a representative of the Party of Action hid in a
cellar at the village of Ariccia, with various families and two smiling,
bronzed South Africans. Artillery rumbled and thudded below. Myriads
of lights, green, red and yellow sprayed into the dark sky. 'Will the Allies
be here tomorrow?' Levi Cavaglione asked the South Africans. 'Yes,
they'll be here tomorrow.'

On the same day, 28 January, old Mrs Whitaker in the Parioli district of
Rome was writing: 'The battle is raging – how can it end? So near, and
yet so far our liberators.' The Allied bombs had cut off the water supply,
and pails and bottles of water had to be filled from a local pump.
Schwester Weisskopf, her German nurse, was distressed by the manhunts.
She had been told that old men, waiters in aprons, workers in overalls
were being rounded up to repair bombed roads, and of course they were
machine-gunned by Allied planes in the process. Mother Mary St Luke

had taken in thirteen peasants from Lanuvio, near Velletri, where they said hundreds of Americans had been captured. They also said that their houses had been destroyed by the heavy guns of battleships off the coast.

In Trastevere there were *graffiti*: 'We do not want Germans or Americans. Let us weep in peace.' Meanwhile there were more arrests, and more grenades were thrown in the streets. And then came the news that the Fascist Secretary in Bologna had been shot by partisans, and that as a result nine men had been executed. General Gariboldi had been arrested in Rome and was expected to be shot because of complicity in the overthrow of Mussolini. 'Life seems to be turning into a series of plots, counter-plots, murders and reprisals,' wrote Mother Mary. The real agony of Rome was about to begin.

Algiers

I had celebrated the Anzio landings with a bathe in a place we knew as the Sea-witch Cauldron. Soon the weather changed dramatically, and snow fell on Algiers.

I wrote in my diary that casualties in Italy were 'frightful'. One friend had been blinded, another had lost a foot. I was anxious about Nick Mansell at Anzio. I was also getting desperate now to leave, not for any heroic reason, and certainly not for fun. I simply thought I was losing face by staying on at La Pérouse.

Anzio

'But now came disaster, and the ruin in its prime purpose of the enterprise.' So Churchill summed up the days following the Shingle landings.

On 24 January he had telegraphed Alexander: 'Am very glad you are pegging in claims rather than digging in beachheads.' On the next day Alexander reported 'fairly good progress' by both British and American Divisions. The build-up of stores was proceeding well, and the capacity of Anzio's port expanding. Meanwhile, in freezing mud and snow, and across minefields and dense wire, the US Corps on the Cassino front was making another attempt to cross the Rapido; at the same time General Juin and his French Expeditionary Corps prepared for a stroke of daring through the mountains that could outflank the Gustav Line. If both efforts succeeded, then the way would be opened up for an advance along the Liri valley – throughout the centuries an invader's gateway to Rome – and a link up with VI Corps at Anzio.

Churchill cabled on the 26th: 'I am thinking of your great battle night and day.'

The severe weather had also reached Anzio. 'Rain, hail, sleet. In other words a hell of a storm,' wrote Lucas. 'No air raids last night . . . but shells still come in towards Anzio. This waiting is terrible. I want an all-out Corps effort but the time hasn't come yet and this weather won't help matters. Bad for tanks.' But more raids were to come: '8.45 p.m. The biggest yet. The Hun's determined to ruin me and knows that if I lose Anzio harbour I am in a hell of a fix. I went to look at the mess. Trucks are burning and the town is in a shambles, but ships are being unloaded. Casualties have been heavy I am afraid. I think I can attack in a few days . . .'

By now he had nearly fifty thousand combat troops in the line. Still he felt he needed a broader base.

He had taken over the villa of the German commander, who had apparently left in a hurry, for a half-glass of brandy and a sausage had been left on the desk in his office. The main Corps HQ was in a wine cellar, full of rows of barrels, unfortunately empty, and in an ossuary, 'damned depressing', with bones laid out on shelves. Clark had chosen Prince Borghese's house as his own headquarters when he visited the Beachhead.

Lucas found the British sometimes difficult to understand. The British for their part were getting restless and resentful about his inertia. Since tempers at Corps HQ were becoming 'frazzled' as result of the shelling, Anglo-American relations were not helped by these complaints. But there were Americans who were also worried. 'Shit, we ought to be getting on,' a Signal Corps captain said to Nick Mansell as yet another glider bomb landed a hundred yards away from a communication cable they were laying.

John Hope watched red-faced old Corncob Charlie puffing away over his maps and air photos. 'Lookee, Hope, I sure am going to attack. But what am I to attack? What would you attack?' 'Sir,' replied Hope, 'why don't you send a patrol up the Albano road and see what's happening?' 'Well, I might as well do that. Hell, I want to attack.'

That had been on the 24th. The Grenadier Guards had at last been allowed to send up a reconnaissance patrol under Lieutenant Hargreaves beyond the Flyover. The road was straight, over apparently flat ground, and was lined with leafless trees, as in a Dutch painting. Italian peasants waved from small neat farmsteads, spaced evenly along the road, and some were even ploughing with oxen. '*Niente tedeschi!* No Germans!' Hargreaves was in high spirits and his men were proud to be the first to move towards Rome. Their objective was the diminutive railway station of Carroceto, beyond which was the cluster of modern brick buildings called Aprilia on the map and which came to be known as the Factory because of three tall towers. And it was from the Factory that the first serious German fire came.

It was therefore decided that the Guards Brigade, led by the Grenadiers, should clean up the Carroceto-Factory area the next day. Far from *niente tedeschi* the enemy was in much greater strength than had been imagined, and soon there was little cause left for high spirits. Indeed, within the next sixteen days the Grenadiers were to lose twenty-nine officers out of their normal establishment of thirty-five, and five hundred and seventy-nine other ranks out of eight hundred. Lieutenant Hargreaves, a 'model officer' his colonel said, was one of the first to die, killed outright by machine-gun fire.

There now developed a hand-to-hand battle, with bayonets and grenades, while the Italian inhabitants of Aprilia hid in the cellars, and their horned white cattle were left to career madly among the shell-bursts. At last the place was cleared, but it had been at great cost, even though more than a hundred prisoners were taken. So far this was the only 'peg' that could fairly be claimed.

Alexander, immaculate as ever, with his fur collar like an apparition from Czarist Russia, seemed pleased enough. 'What a splendid piece of work,' he told Lucas, watching the unloading of Liberty ships at Anzio. 'I am doing my best,' jotted down Lucas, 'but it seems terribly slow. I must keep my feet on the ground and do nothing foolish ... I will not be stampeded.' Clark had also visited the Beachhead, flying in a Cub only a few feet above the sea. 'He should have known better,' said Lucas, who found him gloomy about the Cassino front, 'where the bloodiest fight of the war is going on' – the men there were exhausted. In his own diary Clark wrote that he felt there would be sufficient strength at Anzio to break out within a week. 'I will then strike out and cut the German lines of communication ... Then I will turn my attention to Rome.'

The code-breaking machine Ultra now picked up a chilling message from Hitler to Kesselring: 'The Gustav Line must be held at all costs ... The Fuehrer expects the most bitter struggle.'

General Lucian Truscott, of the US 3rd Division, had not been especially gladdened to find that his sector was being opposed by the Hermann Goering Division, 'old customers'. He had been sending out small patrols in the direction of Cisterna and had come to realize that they had turned every barn or farmhouse into a machine-gun nest. Further south the marshland had been flooded. The digging of foxholes was nearly impossible; after two feet you came across water. He himself had been hit by a shell exploding near his foot. The wound would have been far worse had he not been wearing boots. Still, his leg had to go into a plaster cast. Nick Mansell saw him arrive in a jeep outside Corps HQ and hobble along the street, taking no notice of a dog-fight overhead and the shrapnel pattering down. Did Truscott realize that Horace had written an ode to the goddess of Fortune, who was the patroness of Anzio? Probably not, but the old girl certainly kept an eye on him.

The British destroyer *Janus* and two hospital ships were sunk. There were grisly stories of trying to rescue legless men from the oily water. Mansell also saw a minesweeper go up. 'It was hellish. A great ugly sheet of flame, with seventeen men inside. A noise like an avalanche of cannon balls. The ship disappeared in seconds.'

The shells kept screaming down from the Alban Hills. For the first couple of days, at sundown, you could see the Hills clearly, a wall of soft blue, rising – so it was said – to three thousand feet, with white blocks of houses like dice and what seemed to be a viaduct near Genzano. At that time the huge sky, full of gathering cumulus, had a beauty that was not connected with dive bombers, ack-ack or the railway gun Anzio Annie. But now that was past. The rain and wind meant misery, and the sky was ugly, the Hills were invisible. On the beaches pontoons had been swept away, and supply ships from Naples were being delayed by gales. It was as if Jupiter had woken up and was not pleased. From the heights of Monte Cavo he was flinging the thunderbolts of old, pelting the Beachhead with hailstones that bounced off steel helmets, and sending out jagged lightning that even struck down the barrage balloons. The dryads in the groves around Lake Nemi must have been terrified.

The task for the British was now to press on along the Albano road, Via Anziate, four miles up from Carroceto station to the village of Campoleone, already in the foothills of the Alban Hills and on the main Rome–Naples railway line. Campoleone and Cisterna, opposite the American sector, were the two places that most people considered should have been occupied within twenty-four hours of an unopposed landing. It was becoming evident that the plain on the left of the road was not a plain at all, but fissured with deep valleys, impossible for tanks. So the road was a long thin salient, nicknamed the Cigar, or the French Letter, take your choice. Nobody was particularly surprised to find that Campoleone was strongly held by the enemy: a discovery which, however, cost many dead and wounded.

A group of wooden huts to the north of the Factory was taken in the chill of the early morning by Captain Hohler of the Grenadiers, but after a while he was driven out. Later the hardly lissom Hohler returned and retook the huts, where he found that a guardsman who had previously been blinded by shell-blast had had both his legs blown off as he lay on a stretcher; there were several other wounded men in there, including the company sergeant-major. Hohler then advanced into open ground. His men dropped all round him. It was like a Wild West movie, a watcher said later, only there were no arrows. Hohler's arm was broken by mortar shrapnel, and eventually he was left with one man, also wounded. Feeling faint, he returned to the hut and sat down on some sacks, where he was joined by a guardsman from another platoon whose bren-gun had jammed. He heard shouts: 'Seconds later the turret of a tank appeared a few feet away with its gun trained on the hut. Almost at the same time there was a gurgling noise, and the company commander [Hohler] saw the bren gunner being led away with a schmeisser jammed into his ribs, having been caught unawares with his gun in pieces. Captain Hohler carefully lay down, put his helmet on his face, turned up his toes, and lay as one dead. The wounded guardsman was led off as well, but the ruse worked, and Captain Hohler was not disturbed again.'

Hohler eventually reached safety and found that the colonel had been wounded too. So many had been killed and wounded in the Battalion that it was a relief when some American Rangers moved up on the right flank. Eventually the Grenadiers were relieved by the Sherwood Foresters, who were appalled to see the squalor in which they had been living – brewing up among dead bodies, old tins, excreta and, of course, mud.

Even more squalid was the house further north that the Scots Guards were forced to occupy – it became known as Smelly Farm. No one could understand how human beings could live there; when shells dropped, you were plastered all over with stinking muck. Dick Bates had had a narrow shave on the way up. The Krauts were lobbing over mortar shells one every thirty seconds, and an 88 mm was sweeping the road. It was no joke. Then the carrier in front stopped suddenly, knocking over a box of grenades. The driver reversed right over the box, and the carrier went up with a huge explosion, killing an officer. As Bates and his mate Bert Huggins unloaded their gun, they spotted three German Tiger tanks shooting up the Grenadier company in the huts. They left their slit trench and immediately knocked out one tank. But they had to pay for this. Another Tiger just swivelled round and blasted away at them. Huggins flew for cover, but he was unlucky – his leg was ripped off. Bates fired again, damaging the second tank. Later in the day, during another attack, Bates single-handedly knocked out a third. He was awarded an immediate Distinguished Conduct Medal and promoted to Lance-Corporal.

One of the rottenest experiences for Bates was when he thought he was lost. He got out of his carrier to ask people in a slit trench the way to C Company. Everyone in that trench was not only dead but turned to raspberry mush. Another thing he had noticed was that the German prisoners you took in this area were ragged and filthy, not like the ones in North Africa.

When General Ernie Harmon of the US 1st Armored arrived at Anzio, Lucas got up, laid down his pipe and said: 'Glad to see you. You're needed here.'

He was needed indeed, even if some British commanders were suspicious of his tough-guy pose, with two pearl-handled revolvers in his pockets. There was a meeting of divisional commanders on the 27th. 'Ernie,' said Lucas, 'I reckon you got to go places.' Harmon stood upright and hoisted his breeches. 'Jesus, I'll go places,' and he stalked out of the room. The story goes that he once went straight to where his men were encamped and said: 'Boys, get into line. Advance.' And they advanced – to hell or victory. No wonder people kept on asking: 'Where's Ernie going?'

On that same day Alexander cabled Churchill that he was not satisfied with the speed of progress and had discussed the situation with Clark, who agreed with him and was setting up a small tactical headquarters on the Beachhead where he would be for the next few days. To which Churchill replied: 'It would be unpleasant if your troops were sealed off there and the main army could not advance from the South.'

Clark arrived on the 28th, as usual with a collection of photographers. On the way he had been nearly killed by a trigger-happy minesweeper, which mistook his motor-launch for enemy. One of the shells hit the very stool on which Clark was sitting. He was untouched, though the deck was 'littered with casualties and running with blood'. Clark now decided not to sleep in Prince Borghese's villa, but in a caravan in the grounds.

An attack had at long last been planned, and not surprisingly it was to be a simultaneous assault on Campoleone and Cisterna. A tragedy, however, caused a delay of twenty-four hours. The Guards Brigade was to have led the attack on Campoleone, but the day before jeeps carrying all the Grenadier company commanders, with the plans, took the wrong turn and ran straight into the German lines. The jeeps were destroyed and the officers shot.

'Well, gentlemen, tomorrow has all the makings of a bloody day,' was the hardly encouraging opening at a VI Corps meeting of commanders. And indeed there followed one of the worst calamities in the whole Beachhead campaign.

The 1st and 3rd Battalions of the US Rangers had been given the task of taking Cisterna. It was a daredevil assignment – mad, if one did not know the Rangers, who had already been spending a tough week in the neighbourhood of the Factory. The Battalions, with a total strength of 767 all ranks, were to creep along the six miles of flat reclaimed marshland along the Fossa di Pantano, an offshoot of the Mussolini Canal, silently knifing and bayoneting German sentries on the way. The 4th Ranger Battalion would follow an hour later along the main road, to clear the way for reinforcements.

Darby said that commanding his men was like driving a team of high-spirited horses. They were modelled on the British Commandos and he knew each one by name. As for Darby himself, his second name was Orlando but it could well have been Achilles. He was handsome, muscular, slim-waisted, with clear blue eyes, always smartly turned out even for battle.

He was outraged at first when he was told what the Rangers had to do. For seven days and nights they had been in the line, practically without sleep, and there was now no time for reconnaissance. But he agreed that his men were right for such a tough mission.

Mansell saw the Rangers marching off so jauntily to the start line. Poor buggers, they were singing 'Pistol Packin' Mamma'. And they were off to Cisterna, The Three Taverns of the New Testament, where St Paul met the brethren from Rome ... 'He thanked God, and took courage; Acts, 28:15,' Mansell jotted down.

The night was black, the mud was freezing. Each Ranger had been issued with a woollen scarf and gloves. Lieutenant James Fowler of the 1st Battalion killed three German sentries single-handed, muffling their screams with one hand while he slashed their throats with a Commando knife. In the deep irrigation ditch three Germans joined the Ranger column thinking it was part of their own patrol; they soon met the same fate as the others. Some now think that the Germans actually heard the Rangers and let them crawl on, straight into a trap.

Suddenly there was a screeching inferno of criss-cross tracer, ripping along the lines of men. The Rangers were only lightly equipped, and fought back with grenades and bayonets. When dawn came the situation was desperate. They were surrounded, crouching in shallow ditches in open treeless country. Cisterna was only eight hundred yards away.

The 4th Battalion was making little progress. Darby was in despair. His staff officer and runner were killed in mortar barrages. Machine-gun fire swept the fields. Every building was a strongpoint. As grim reports drifted back over the radio, he began to realize that he would not be able to save his men.

German tanks advanced on the 1st and 3rd. The Rangers hit back with bazookas and sticky grenades, even jumping on top of the tanks, lifting the hatches to spray the interiors with tommy-gun fire. Lieutenant George Nunnelly, the smiling Georgian, had been shot clean through the head. Darby's classmate at West Point, Major Jack Dobson, had been badly wounded twice. Darby made contact with Sergeant-Major Bob Ehalt, a 'tough original' from Brooklyn. He was told that ammo was running out and the Germans had captured several men.

'Keep them together, Sergeant – you must hold out – help is on the way.'

'Colonel, we're doin' the best we can. They're closin' in on us, but they won't get us cheap.'

Then Darby heard a loud explosion, and the radio went dead. Eyes red-rimmed, he telephoned to headquarters: 'We can't let my boys down – we've got to get through – send us more tanks!'

But still the Rangers hung on, although vastly outnumbered. Seventeen German tanks and flak wagons had been knocked out. The fighting was savage on both sides. Dobson has said that he saw American prisoners being machine-gunned and bayoneted. In an attempt to stop a German column Rangers found themselves killing and wounding some of their own men being used as cover. Mark VI tanks would run up to the edge of ditches, lower their guns and just slaughter the men inside. Darby heard from Master Sergeant Scotty Monroe, famed as a 'specialist' in killing Germans, that the Ranger battalions were hopelessly surrounded. 'God bless you, Sergeant. God bless you!' Darby went into a farmhouse and wept.

Only six men returned from the 1st and 3rd, and the 4th lost fifty per cent of its men, having taken several hundred prisoners. To be told by someone that 'Hollywood would have paid five million bucks to have that on film' was not in particularly good taste; nor was it even much of a compensation that 'we knocked off a hell of a lot of Kraut – in the orchard they were piled one on top of each other'. Darby was shattered, but later put in command of the 179th Infantry Regiment. He was to be killed by an 88 mm shell more than a year later – two days indeed before the German Army in Italy surrendered.

In the British sector the Irish and Scots Guards met ferocious opposition as they led the advance towards Campoleone. The Sherwood Foresters at the Factory had already reported hearing many tracked vehicles, so the Irish Guards knew well what to expect, as their boots crunched on the cinders of the railway track. Frogs croaked, a dog barked, telephone wires twanged, a haystack was smouldering. Then in bright moonshine hell erupted ... Mansell heard later of the courage of a boy in the Signals, Lance-Corporal Holwell, who was with two forward companies of the Irish Guards. Whilst under fire Holwell repaired the only remaining radio set and thus received the order for the companies to withdraw. Seconds later he was killed by a machine-gun burst and his set was smashed.

Tank support away from Via Anziate was almost impossible, because of mud and soggy ground. The scrub-filled valleys to the left were known as wadis. Two ridges dominated them, Vallelata and Buonriposo, soon to become names only too familiar to Allied and German troops alike.

Both Guards Battalions were badly cut up. There were many stories of bravery. Major Bull of the Scots Guards, for instance, had a reputation among some of his men for being a hard old devil out of the line but 'you'd follow him anywhere'. He fought off a tank attack from an exposed slope, but soon afterwards his voice came over the wireless to the effect that he was surrounded. It was said that a German officer was about to shoot a guardsman who had run out of ammunition, when Bull shouted: 'Leave that man alone!' The German turned and with his revolver shot Bull dead.

Now came the turn of the 3rd Infantry Brigade – the Duke of Wellington's Regiment, the KSLI (King's Shropshire Light Infantry) and the Sherwood Foresters. The attack began on 30 January, to be met with deadly and ferocious fire from tanks and Moaning Minnies (Nebelwerfers) sited in railway-trucks. The confusion was 'hideous', a survivor remembered. 'Such a lack of information, and no cover in those vines. Shells screaming and whirring like mad, vicious witches. Sprays of fire all over the place. Shrapnel like hail. Bullets whizzing from nowhere. And on top of that the bloody rain. We were so cold. Half the soldiers disappeared – mown down, captured, or just fucked off, everything you can imagine.' When the Sherwood Foresters at last withdrew, no company was left with more than forty men. The colonel was wounded in the leg and face.

The KSLI colonel strayed into a barn which was all laid out as if for a meal. Round a corner he suddenly saw some Germans behind a self-propelled gun. He lay low until dusk, and then started to creep back to his battalion. All at once a voice from a bush said, 'Don't shoot, Tommy,' and out came three Germans with their hands up.

General Harmon's 1st Armored had driven up in support, using a new unmetalled road that came to be known as the Bowling Alley (usually described as a 'disused railway bed' in accounts of the Anzio fighting), in order to avoid the wadis. A tank drew up near a lone corporal of the Dukes, shovelling earth into a trench whilst tracer whipped overhead. The American sergeant called out: 'What's going on, feller?' 'My friend's grave,' the other said, without looking up.

Then Harmon himself went to see 'what the hold up was' at the Foresters. He found dead bodies everywhere. 'I had never seen so many dead men in one place. They lay so close together that I had to step with care. I shouted for the commanding officer. From a foxhole there arose a mud-covered sergeant with a handle-bar moustache. He was the highest ranking officer still alive. He stood stiffly to attention. "How's it going?" I asked. The answer was all around me. "Well, sir," the sergeant said, "there were a hundred and sixteen of us when we first came up, and there are sixteen of us left. We're ordered to hold out till sundown, and I think, with a little good fortune, we can manage to do so." '

Of any British regiment at Anzio the Sherwood Foresters were to suffer the worst casualties, for more were to come. Several recruits from the Black Watch arrived that night. Henry Marking, who had been made Adjutant, had to receive them: 'The officers arrived in the dark, we had to send them on patrol that night, because we had no one else to go out, and they were killed in the night. and none of us saw them in daylight. It was tragic. Can you imagine? Probably they had never had battle experience. It was awful, awful. I heard the spandaus hitting them. Spandaus had such a fast rate of fire, very fierce and harsh — crack, crack, crack.'

* * * *

In Rome Mrs Whitaker wrote: 'Hardly know what to say. Two thousand prisoners, we hear, American and British, marched from the Colosseum along the Corso and up Via Tritone. Schwester Weisskopf saw them. They were making the V sign, and one said in broken Italian, "*Tra due o tre settimane tutti noi a Roma.*" A man was arrested for giving him a cigarette.'

* * * *

Churchill felt very out of touch. 'You have not told me,' he cabled Alexander, 'why the airborne troops were used as infantry. The operation has now changed its character completely from the lightning dash of two or three divisions which we contemplated at Marrakech.' He also added that as the operation had become four-fifths American he quite realized 'the limitations to your personal action'.

A month later he wrote with some bitterness to Field-Marshal Smuts in South Africa how the 'essence of the battle as contemplated by Alexander in all his talks with me was the seizing of the Alban Hills with the utmost rapidity'. It was for this very purpose that he had obtained the US 504th Parachute Regiment, previously under orders to return to England in preparation for Overlord – but their use had been cancelled by Clark. The 'logistic calculations', moreover, had proved to be over-generous. 'If I had been well enough to be at his [Alexander's] side as I had hoped at the critical moment I could have given him the necessary stimulus. Alas for time, distance, illness and advancing years.'

The use or misuse of the 504th Parachute Regiment was one of the many questions brought up in the post-war 'Monday quarterbacking', as Clark termed it, in connection with Operation Shingle. The reasons given for the cancellation of the air-drop were many, including one blamed on General Penney, who thought that as the drop would be near the Flyover, in the British sector, there would be a risk of mistaking American helmets and uniforms for the German equivalent. Other reasons included the possibility of the paratroopers being in danger from long-range naval gunfire, the absence of moonlight on the 22nd and the lack of any rehearsal. Lucas admitted that the presence of these paratroopers half-way to Campoleone might have given him an incentive to join up with them on the first day. Alas, too, for Churchill's dream of 'hard-hitting mobile forces' ...

One turns to Lucas' diary for those crucial days: *30 Jan.* 'Another big raid last night but so far none this morning. One British cruiser sunk, another damaged, and a Liberty ship with 5 days' supply including ammunition destroyed. When she went she certainly shook things up ... The situation, from where I sit, is crowded with doubt and uncertainty. I expect to be counter-attacked in some force, maybe considerable force ... We have taken between six and seven hundred prisoners since we landed. Most of them are down in spirits and obviously glad to be captured but not so the Hermann Goerings. These people are very young, very cocky, very full of fight, and believe they are winning the war ... 4.30 p.m. Clark is up here and I am afraid intends to stay for several days. His gloomy attitude is certainly bad for me. He thinks I should have been more aggressive on D-Day and should have gotten tanks and things out to the front ... There has been no chance, with available shipping, to build

Shingle up to decisive strength and anyone with any knowledge of
logistics could have seen that from the start. I have done what I was
ordered to do, desperate though it was. I can win if I am let alone.

'*31 Jan.* . . . Clark is still here. I don't blame him for being terribly
disappointed. He and those above him thought this landing would shake
the Cassino line loose . . . The disasters to the Rangers he apparently
blames on Lucian [Truscott]. He says they were used foolishly . . . Neither
I nor Truscott knew of the organized defensive position they would run
into. I told Clark the fault was mine as I had seen the plan of the attack and
had OK'd it.'

'Seen the plan.' Hope was longing to say, 'Why don't you go up to the
front and see for yourself?' Lucas hardly moved from his cellar. It was the
Maginot Line mentality all over again. At one VI Corps meeting he
seemed to have forgotten the name of the Alban Hills. He called a meeting
of journalists. After a long pause he said: 'I'll tell you what, gentlemen,
that German's a mighty tough fighter, yes a mighty tough fighter.' No
wonder you could see the morale of some of Lucas' aides deteriorating.

Clark himself had written in his diary: 'I have been harsh with Lucas
today, much to my regret, but in an effort to energize him to greater
effort.'

When Alexander arrived, Clark and Lucas had already decided that the
Beachhead must go on the defensive. Penney was beginning to 'itch at
poor old Johnny Lucas', Clark said. 'Lucas knew he was being sniped at.
He knew the British were going to get him, and they did. They ganged up
on him.' Lucas himself found Alexander 'kind'. 'But I am afraid he is not
pleased. My head will probably fall into the basket, but I have done my
best. There were just too many Germans here for me to lick and they
could build up faster than I could.' Alexander was 'not easy to talk to'; 'he
really knows very little of tactics as Americans understand it.'

But Lucas was not the only one to find Alex inscrutable. The same
applied to some British underlings, and there were those who did not
think he was even intelligent. Others, however, 'worshipped' him. There
was something Olympian about that reserve, that aloofness, that
courtesy. And everyone knew that he had been the last man to leave
Dunkirk.

The twelve-hour trip by sea from Naples was known as the milk run.
By now Anzio also had the reputation of being the hell-hole of the
Mediterranean. The landing-craft would bring back the casualties, up to
350 a ship, and quite a few of them due to shell-shock. For the first time
Ted Wyman, the US naval lieutenant, saw the wonders of blood plasma.
He was often down below helping with the bottles. One man from a
bombed Liberty ship was completely bandaged except for his eyes and
mouth. The only way he could get a smoke was for Wyman to hold the

cigarette and let him take puffs from it. Then there was a doctor whom the crew of the landing-craft particularly admired, he toiled so hard for the wounded. Wyman missed him on one of the trips and asked where he was. A shell had taken off his head on the dock at Anzio.

It was almost impossible for a shell or bomb not to do some damage in the rear areas of the Beachhead. On top of that were the 'hors d'oeuvres', namely anti-personnel bombs, showers of deadly little splinters. Edmund Ball at VI Corps HQ became adept at the Anzio Shuffle, which meant hugging the wall with your head thrust down between the shoulders. He watched the British cruiser *Spartan* blow up, like a tremendous Fourth of July celebration. Most evenings, towards dark, you could see heavy artillery shells floating over, deceptively slowly and red hot from the friction of their passage through the air. Or there might be sneak hit-and-run raids by dive-bombers. And all the while the poor son-of-a-guns at the port would have to be sweating out yet another unloading. Blast was perhaps the main danger.

We come now to Sergeant Jake Walkmeister of the 1st Special Service Force. As the driver of an ambulance known as Walkmeister's Portable Whorehouse, he has been immortalized in a book by Robert Adleman and Colonel George Walton. The sergeant had long, sweeping moustaches which he constantly twisted with two fingers. Somehow he managed to get his ambulance aboard a landing-craft bound for Anzio. In due course, after casting off, the officer who had been in charge of loading went aft to the tiny wardroom. In there was Sergeant Walkmeister, with two quarts of alcohol plainly labelled 'for use of the US Army medical detachments only' and two open cans of pineapple juice. 'A Navy lieutenant was sitting on the edge of a bunk holding the hand of a pretty young lady, and on other bunks lay more pretty young ladies. The officer wasted no time in inquiring how it happened that three or four such peaches were aboard one of the ugliest ships in the US Navy ...' It transpired that the girls spoke no English, only Italian, and had no idea where they were going. They landed at Anzio on 1 February. 'Disembarkation was quick and surprisingly efficient. No colonel appeared to ask awkward questions.'

What these girls thought of their new home is not recorded. However it appears that they were installed in a cottage on an estate that had evidently belonged to a rich Italian, and here Walkmeister arranged that the girls would be ready, for a small fee, 'for parties, festivals or anything needed to take the minds of the Big Brass off their duties for a few hours'. Needless to say he also had secret access to a wine cellar, and lesser Brass had their fun too.

Perhaps the cottage belonged to Prince Borghese. He was not the sort to have been interested in Walkmeister's peaches. However he did occasionally arrange lunch parties for Big Brass. It was impressive to be waited upon by footmen in white gloves, and his cook could do wonders with K rations and garlic.

Meanwhile in the caves of the Padiglione woods the Silvestri family ate its meals round smoky paraffin lamps made out of old cigarette tins. Gep the donkey did not much appreciate the whistling of the shells overhead in this duel of the giants. On the 27th or 28th three young soldiers appeared, obviously British, and after some indecision approached the table where Ennio Silvestri and his mother were sitting. 'Good evening,' said one. '*Buona sera,*' the others replied. 'I am Max, and you?' '*Io Ennio.*' '*Mamma?*' '*Si, Mamma.*' Max and his friends could not speak Italian. They sat down and were offered cheese and wine. Max, who was small and dark-skinned, carefully took some letters out of his jacket, unfolded them and began to read aloud. They were obviously letters from his mother. 'You can see he is an only child,' said Signora Silvestri to her son in Italian. And then: 'He looks like one of us', by which she meant that he looked like a Central Italian. Max seemed happy. He glanced at his watch and got up, shaking hands with Ennio and then – murmuring '*Mamma*' – with Signora Silvestri. He disappeared into the cold night and they never saw him again. For years afterwards Signora Silvestri would say: 'Do you remember that nice young soldier who came one evening and kept speaking about his mother? I wonder where he is now.'

The tower of San Lorenzo stood guard on the coast to the north of the Beachhead, where the road ran over the mouth of the Moletta towards Ostia. Unlike the Astura tower to the south, it was not medieval but built in the sixteenth century and restored by the Roman banking family of Torlonia in 1860. This was the quietest area of the Beachhead at present, though it attracted plenty of shelling and was thus known as Stonk Corner. The tower was extraordinarily well built and able to stand up to innumerable direct hits. It was a natural observation post for artillery spotters.

The No 1 Special Force contingent, whose job it would be to contact Resistance workers in Rome, was also based on the tower of San Lorenzo. It included, among others, Max Salvadori, a young British academic of Italian extraction; Alberto Tarchiani, aged fifty-nine, one of the founders of the Party of Action and once chief editor of the *Corriere della Sera* – both men with distinguished futures; also Michael Gubbins, son of General Gubbins, the head of SOE. The contingent's commander was Malcolm Munthe, Axel Munthe's son, who had been involved in a Prisoner of Zenda type rescue of the philosopher Benedetto Croce from Sorrento just after the Salerno landings. It was a relief to doss down in the tower after sleeping in slit trenches lined with groundsheets. When the weather lifted a little you could see that the Alban Hills were dusted with snow. Each day there were perilous jeep journeys to command posts, and each day the tracks became more pitted by shells, and there were more graves, the crosses often made of bayonets, with helmets laid on the fresh earth. The nights shuddered with explosions – deep, brutal – and there were frequent exchanges of machine-gun fire across the scrubland at the mouth of the Moletta, the sinister ripple of spandaus and crackle-crackle of brens. Towards Campoleone the sky was perpetually aflame. Gaudy Very lights flared up, and up again; they could almost be beautiful, if it were possible to forget the horrors under them.

The Italo-British contingent swapped rations with the American spotter, who said he was half Scottish and half Austrian by origin and came from Pennsylvania. He was very taken by Michael Gubbins. 'That must be the son of a real English gentleman,' he said.

Then alarming news came from the radio contact in Rome. There had been mass arrests of SOE workers. It was decided that Munthe and Gubbins, Salvadori having developed jaundice, must find an Italian to cross the lines by a secret route. As time was to show, this was a disastrous and tragic idea.

A shepherd arrived, thin and prematurely aged. He said he was Princess Torlonia's *fattore* or steward and was full of moans about German looting. The *tedeschi* had used the sacristy of the little church nearby as a latrine. Tarchiani searched out the shepherd's family, who were living in a cave. They were desperate because they were unable to get to some of their cattle, which were starving in sheds in no man's land.

It was to be the job of Sergeant Villari and his Carabinieri to evacuate civilians from the front line. He was worrying about his aunt at Aprilia, which was said to be now totally ruined. A camp was being prepared in the Padiglione woods, and later all civilians would be taken to Naples.

Villari had first to collect a number of hysterical women and children from a barn near Carroceto. It was here that Fusilier Hayes had brought the little girl Angelita, whom he had found on Peter Beach the first day. His unit had had a bad setback after a patrol had been shot up, and there was also danger from British long-range naval guns which too often fired short of their targets. To his astonishment, however, on his return to the barn he found that Villari's truck had gone leaving Angelita behind – the women, too intent on their own woes, had just ignored her.

'We had no option but to get her out of the barn which was now directly under shellfire. She stopped crying as soon as I picked her up and one of my comrades put a greatcoat over her.' So Angelita joined in the advance towards Campoleone. She passed the time playing with empty bren-gun cartridge cases. On 30 January Hayes' company was ordered to pull back a few hundred yards. It was then that a jeep appeared. 'It's the Yanks,' someone shouted. 'Without thinking I picked up Angelita from the bottom of our trench and ran with her to the jeep, pushing her inside on the back between two terrified American nurses. I then ran to help the driver clear a path so he could pass the burning carriers.' There was a whine of a shell – which could have come from the Allied lines – and an explosion. Hayes dived flat. Then he looked up and saw the bodies of the two nurses half out of the jeep. The driver and the steering wheel were blown across the road, but half the driver's body was still in the vehicle. Angelita was quite still. Hayes picked her up and as she rolled over he saw the blood oozing from a large gash in her temple. 'I realized then that Angelita was dead. So were twenty-eight of my comrades who had helped me care for her.'

Villari's aunt was never found. A long while afterwards, when the war was nearly over, a cellar containing some skeletons was discovered at Aprilia; the entrance had been blocked by a shellburst and the flesh of the bodies inside eaten by rats or perhaps dogs which had somehow burrowed through the rubble. Villari thought that certain rags looked as if they were part of a dress he recognized.

On the Cassino front the fighting was as savage as ever. Far from withdrawing, the Germans had sent up reinforcements. On 29 January General Juin was able to tell Clark with great pride that, 'at the cost of unbelievable efforts and great losses', the 3rd Algerian Division had 'accomplished the mission you gave them', which was to capture Mount Belvedere. The French Algerian troops and the Moroccans – the 'Goums', in their distinctive striped clothing – were real mountain warriors; their uninhibited and cruel methods of warfare terrified Germans and Italian civilians alike. After three nights and days of fighting, the US 34th Division had made a small bridgehead across the Rapido and by the 31st had captured the village of Cairo, which was eventually to lead to the almost unbelievable feat of scaling the mountain heights to the north-east of the town, in blizzards and ice, without any possibility of digging foxholes on the rocky slopes.

Nevertheless Clark felt his 34th was near breaking. Alexander decided to give him some troops from Leese's Eighth Army. It had been realized that Kesselring had moved various units from the Adriatic front, and as the Eighth Army was now too weak to make any significant break-through Alexander had decided to leave it as a holding force only. 'Hell, I don't want any troops from the Eighth Army,' Clark said to him. 'No use giving me, an American, British troops. Let the Eighth Army take over in that sector [Cassino town and the Monastery] and let me concentrate on my two fronts, and let me pull loose, and let the 34th Division go up to Anzio.' Alex said no, he was going to give him a Corps. 'What kind of Corps?' It was to be a New Zealand Corps, comprising the 2nd New

Zealand Division and the 4th Indian, just arrived from the Middle East, and 'Tiny' Freyberg would be the commander. 'Well that scared me,' Clark said later, 'because Freyberg was a prima donna, and he had to be handled with kid gloves, very adroitly, very carefully ... He was a great big fellow and had won the Victoria Cross in World War I and had swum the English Channel [not quite true] ...'

It was indeed hard for a would-be prima donna to be put in command of an already established prima donna.

Algiers

A prison compound, which seemed to be mostly for British deserters from the Italian front, had been put up at La Pérouse, and I was shocked by the tough treatment the men got. Most nights I hitchhiked into Algiers and got tight on *mousseux gazéifié*, in spite of just having had jaundice. Assuming that Nick needed cheering up I wrote him a letter full of chatter about his favourite haunts: the Aletti bar, the Bosphore club, the *Echo d'Alger* journalists' bar for late-night anisettes. I told him about a trip through the Little Atlas to Bou-Saada, where I had ridden camels and watched pre-pubescent girls dancing in the nude, thought by the locals to be the height of sexiness.

I doubt though whether he was ever able to read that letter.

FEBRUARY

"Gad, sir, this never happened in the desert!"

"Any complaints, old man?"

Ardea – Albano

Hitler, in particular need of a dramatic success, had sent out an order of the day 'like the call of a revolutionary fanatic', said General Warlimont, Deputy Chief of the OKW General Staff. The Anzio Beachhead was an abscess that must be lanced at once. Every soldier must be aware of the importance of this battle, which was to be fought with 'holy hatred against an enemy who wages a ruthless war of annihilation against the German people and who, without any higher ethical aims, strives for the destruction of German and European culture'. Anzio was of special significance, and must be considered as the start of the invasion of Europe – 'the invasion of the year 1944 is an undertaking which will be crushed in the blood of British soldiers.'

Kesselring had ordered the Fourteenth Army headquarters to move south from Verona. General Eberhard von Mackensen now therefore took the tactical command of the whole Rome area. General Schlemm, recalled from the South, replaced General Schlemmer at I Parachute Corps headquarters, in overall charge of the Beachhead operation.

Mackensen, son of a famous general in the First War and the prototype of most people's idea of a Prussian general – strong-jawed, crop-haired, with a monocle – was also the brother of the last German ambassador to the Quirinal in Rome and had had gruelling experiences on the Russian front. General Heinrich von Vietinghoff-Scheel, commander of the Tenth Army along the Gustav Line, was also Prussian – self-assured, stern, with a small scrub moustache, not particularly popular with the ordinary soldier. By 31 January the key positions around Cassino were still strongly held in spite of a new Allied offensive. Conditions in the mountains were far worse than in the plains and foothills near Anzio, but the Germans had had time to blast into the rocks and build concrete bunkers and gun emplacements. Clark in his diary wrote that he and Vietinghoff were like two boxers in a ring. 'I have committed my last reserve,' he said, 'and I am sure the Boche has done the same.' In fact this was not quite the case; the

German divisions on the Gustav Line had increased – almost miraculously, in view of the chronic weakness both in men and materiel –
from four divisions to the equivalent of six, and more units were to come
from the Adriatic, including the veteran 1st Parachute Division, which
had fought outstandingly in Crete. For the time being it was essential that
the Gustav Line should be contained while the main effort went into
eliminating the Beachhead.

Mackensen's obvious line of attack against the Allied Beachhead forces
was along Via Anziate. This had always been Hitler's plan, although
Kesselring had once thought of an attack along the coast from west to east.
The centralization of strategy under Hitler was an important feature of
most German campaigns, and the Fuehrer's meddling in precise details
could be a drawback. It just was not possible to keep him fully informed
about enemy strengths and conditions of terrain. He did not seem to
realize, for instance, how difficult the country was to the west of Via
Anziate, on account of the gullies. He had given orders for all counter-
attacks to be made during bad weather, when enemy aircraft could not
intervene, but this of course hampered the movements of ground troops.
He also favoured the First War technique of heavy bombardments before
attack, whereas surprise could more often be effective.

Now the British salient towards Campoleone was 'positively demanding' to be attacked. Originally an offensive had been planned for 1
February, but it was delayed partly because of the British attack on 31
January, and partly because of a last-minute false alarm about yet another
imminent Allied landing at Civitavecchia. The front had been divided
into four sectors, which in turn became known as Battle Groups: on the
west from the mouth of the Moletta and Ardea to Vallelata ridge, General
Pfeifer's 65th Division, incorporating the original Gericke Battle Group,
and the 4th Parachute Division; along Via Anziate and incorporating
Campoleone and the men facing Smelly Farm, Graeser's 3rd Panzer
Grenadiers, with headquarters at Albano. These two, roughly speaking,
were opposite the British. Raapke's 71st Infantry Division and Conrath's
Hermann Goering Division were opposite the Americans; the former east
of Via Anziate, including the soon to be notorious Spaccasassi creek and
the hamlet of Carano; the latter division in the Cisterna–Mussolini Canal
area as far as the sea. The components of each of the Battle Groups were
necessarily fluid, a 'witch's brew' of fragments streaming in from all
directions, sometimes containing men who were barely trained or below
the normal age for combat. Actual records are vague, but the hurried
reorganization and regrouping was brilliant staff-work. Often at nights
guns would be moved from one spot to another to give the illusion of
greater strength.

By 1 February the Germans had lost some 5,500 men in the Beachhead fighting, about the same number as the Allies. Battalion Kleye of the Gericke Battle Group had borne the brunt of some of the bloodiest fighting, and it had been Kleye who had shot up the Grenadier Guards officers and captured the maps and plans with the enemy's intentions. Battalion Hauber, which was around Ardea, had had the worst battering from the four Allied destroyers, stationed six miles out to sea. At the end of January Kleye still only had two anti-tank guns, though he had several *Faustpatronen* which could be fired from the hip.

Kleye was now facing the Scots Guards, the Irish Guards and the Duke of Wellington's Regiment. The 65th Division headquarters at Ardea provided him with a 3.7 cm anti-aircraft gun, which was used with nice effect against Sherman tanks advancing along the *Schotterstrasse*, or 'disused railway bed'. In spite of so many losses, Kleye's men had gained from their battle experience, whereas it was considered that the Allies opposite them were low in morale. On 2 February Kleye's battalion numbered six officers, ninety-six non-commissioned officers and three hundred and ninety-six men; by this time it was mostly concentrated on the Vallelata ridge. A great deal of the morale in the battalion depended on Kleye's leadership. As a comrade has since said of him: 'He was a man of decency and faultless character.'

Mackensen was able to launch the first of his 'local attacks', on 1 February, under the direction of Schlemm. This was against the Americans to the south-west of Cisterna; though a 'noisy affair' according to Truscott, it was unsuccessful. An immense Allied air onslaught on Albano had wrecked the 3rd Panzers' artillery communications, and this was another reason for a delay in what was to have been a simultaneous effort to eliminate the tip of the Campoleone salient.

The battle, which began on 3 February, was confused and desperate. The British had been well aware of a build-up; the noise of many tracked vehicles had been heard at night, and a long convoy had also been spotted along the *Schotterstrasse*. But the first phase had been unexpected, namely a flock of about a thousand sheep driven by Battle Group Graeser over a minefield opposite the Gordons at Smelly Farm. Shades, almost, of Cannae. Then came a crazy, brutal nightmare – Nebelwerfers, tracer bren answering spandau, haystacks on fire. At Vallelata ridge, in sleet and rain, Kleye's men went in on the Irish Guards, cheering and shouting; they fell like puppets, as in an old film of World War I. Next it was hand-to-hand, bayonets and grenades, and shell after shell rained down on the Gordons; two of their companies were overrun. It could only be a matter of time before the Germans converged on the Anziate road.

The news that the British were landing part of a new division, the 56th, known as the Black Cats, was in some ways depressing to the Germans, but victory became all the more important and urgent. For a while the

Dukes and the 1st King's Shropshire Light Infantry were completely isolated. Then the British broke through again – thanks to reinforcements from the 56th Division which had been rushed up to the front straight from Anzio port.

On the 4th it was suddenly realized that the British were pulling back down the Anziate road from Campoleone towards Aprilia, the 'Factory'. A radio message to the Dukes' forward company was picked up: 'Every man for himself!' A sergeant of the German 29th Reconnaissance Group had a spandau mounted on a ruined house but could not face mowing down some poor fellows staggering, evidently wounded, through the rain. On these two days the Germans – so it was claimed – had taken nine hundred prisoners. They themselves had lost eight hundred men, three hundred of whom were captured.

It was obvious to Mackensen and Schlemm that the most important objectives now were Aprilia and the neighbouring group of houses and railway station at Carroceto. These two places would be the starting points for the all-out attack on Anzio itself. Graeser would have the job of taking Aprilia, while Pfeifer of the 65th would have to seize Buonriposo ridge and then wheel round north-west to Carroceto.

The British, to draw attention from their retreat on Via Anziate on the 4th, were once more strongly attacking Kleye in the Vallelata direction and around Buonriposo. The *Schafstall*, or Sheepfold, was a German key position, and it was near here that Private Heinz Hackenbeck, aged nineteen, of the 165th Artillery Regiment had his howitzer. The enemy was firing AA shells only a few metres overhead – the noise was terrific. When an American plane was shot down close by and the pilot questioned, it was realized that the enemy threat was more serious than expected. Hackenbeck was ordered to move his gun at once, no joke in that mud, as it had to be manhandled – on other fronts he had been able to use donkeys.

Previously one had not been allowed to fire at night in case flashes gave away the positions. Now headquarters at Ardea gave permission for night firing. On 5 February the guns had to be moved twice. The situation was all confusion, and it was not clear whether the Tommies were about to counter-attack. Two of Hackenbeck's comrades were killed by enemy bombing. Preparations were being made for an artillery concentration on Aprilia. It was a great happiness for him to learn that this major effort was to be made to wipe out the Tommies there.

The attack was to start at 9 p.m. on the 7th. Hackenbeck and his crew rested all day in order to be in good condition that night. When the infantry went in, it was 'Russian fashion', without any preliminary softening up by artillery, in order to take the enemy by surprise.

Unfortunately the night was clear and starry, and the advance was stopped by some hefty fire – mortars being particularly annoying. Red, green and white Very lights soon gave warning of the plight of the infantry. Hackenbeck was now ordered to fire as much as he could. It seemed that casualties were so great that the last reserves were being thrown in. A few Tommy prisoners were herded past. Then at midnight news came that all goals had been reached. Hackenbeck was especially proud to hear that Aprilia was in German hands. He saw a blaze, and realized that the *Schafstall* was alight.

But his joy was brief. The British returned to Aprilia. The next day the enemy attacked with tanks, but were driven back. The sky, at last, was full of German planes, and there were scores of dogfights, until the rain came. More prisoners passed by. So many comrades had been wounded. It was reported that enemy pressure was very strong now, and a counter-attack must be expected.

Hackenbeck's gun was in the middle of a field and very exposed. The ground was so soggy that the gun had to be shored up with bits of wood. By midnight all the batteries were firing. How wonderful it was to partake in a battle without bothering about saving ammunition! And you could see that enemy batteries were being knocked out. Morale was certainly very high. Hackenbeck and his three comrades worked feverishly.

Suddenly two enemy shells exploded very near the gun. Hackenbeck was thrown to the ground, but did not lose consciousness. With a pocket torch he saw that his left leg had been completely torn to pieces below the knee, but thanks to his breeches and riding boot the blood was not coming out very fast, though it was thick. He noticed that his right leg was in good order. He had no other injuries.

Because more enemy fire was expected he was pulled into a trench. This was extremely painful because his left leg was only hanging on by a few sinews. He almost fainted. Then he was put on a stretcher and carried to the Red Cross station three hundred metres behind his gun position. He was given two injections and his boot was cut away. A label was put round his neck: 'Urgent transport'. An ambulance took him off, and he passed out. When he woke up he was at Pomezia on the Ardea–Rome road, and his leg had been amputated, within two hours of his being wounded. At least he still had his knee.

Battalion Kleye was now concentrated in the Vallelata area. 5 and 6 February had been mostly spent in patrolling. An outrageous rumour had been reported of the enemy: the members of one patrol had worn German uniforms and spoke German. The 145th Grenadier Regiment was facing Buonriposo, where the North Staffs were known to be ensconced. The valleys – really the upper reaches of the Moletta – were more troublesome here, filled with scrub and thorn, ideal for infiltration by either side; indeed some German soldiers had lost their lives plunging down ravines in the darkness. The *Dreifingerschlucht*, Three Fingers Ravine, was a particularly unpleasant spot, and one of the most dreaded was *Die Wanze*, the Bug, an oblong knoll near Carroceto south of the *Schotterstrasse*. Beyond Buonriposo ridge were a number of artificial caves, made for excavating what the Italians called *pozzolana*, which was used for cement. The enemy was known to be holding some of these caves.

Movement, as usual, was always by night. You had to be on the alert for small attacks by fighting patrols, straining for any tell-tale movement. Then suddenly, from some unexpected direction, there would be an inferno of grenades and machine-gun fire. Time meant so little. A short encounter seemed like an eternity. You even forgot to be tired.

When the great moment for attack came on 7 February Kleye's objective was Carroceto railway station. Only the Scots Guards stood in the way. The German 145th Grenadiers were ordered to eliminate the North Staffs, and by the next morning it looked as if they had almost succeeded, for the southern end of the ridge was overrun. Battle Group Graeser was now poised to attack the prize: Aprilia.

It was not particularly convenient for Mackensen to be summoned to Hitler on the 6th. Approval was given by the Fuehrer for the final, supreme offensive against the Beachhead on 15 February. Mackensen asked for more troops, but Hitler refused this, the manpower shortage being so acute in Germany. Finally General Jodl, chief of the OKW operation staff, persuaded Hitler to release the Infantry Lehr Regiment, a training unit of some repute – as it happened, one of the worst possible solutions. Mackensen was also promised a few Tiger tanks and four different types of 'secret' weapons, the most significant being one known as Goliath, a miniature tank worked by a remote control that also detonated a charge: guaranteed to demoralize the Tommies.

Rome

Was Luisa Arpini thinking of Nick Mansell on 3 February? On that day, somewhere between the Flyover and Aprilia, he was writing in his diary: 'Last night an extraordinary escape. I was dreaming I was in Rome, and it was very hot, July perhaps. I was sitting with darling Luisa by the Trevi fountain, nearly blinded by the glare from the mad rushing water. Then suddenly it was evening, and we were on a terrace, full of creepers and geraniums, overlooking rooftops and a palm tree. We could see St Peter's and that ugly spire of the English church, and the observatory on Monte Mario. The air was full of the swish of swallows. We were watching the sunset, laughing and drinking Luigi Bigi Orvieto. Luisa said, "Tomorrow we'll have scirocco I think." Then, "This is how I would like to spend my last evening on Earth." And at that moment – literally, I swear – there was a tremendous explosion, and I woke up to find myself buried in mud. A shell had landed not a dozen yards from my dugout.'

Luisa, who of course did not know that Nick was at Anzio, believes now that it was on 3 February that she went to visit a sick friend in Via dell'Anima. Crossing Piazza Navona she noticed a young German soldier with a bandage over one eye. He stopped at the Bernini fountain and seemed fascinated by the figure of the River Ganges with the serpent below. She thought how handsome he was, so fresh and innocent, too young to have been wounded. Some minutes later, looking from her friend's window, she noticed him again. He was going into the German church of Santa Maria dell'Anima. She saw him admiring the theatrical portico of the neighbouring church, Santa Maria della Pace. Then from the house opposite, she caught sight of two youths with a rifle. She realized that they were going to kill the German when he emerged after saying his prayers.

She thought of him in that building full of polished brass and shining woodwork. Probably he was looking at the tomb of Hadrian VI – who had died just before the sack of Rome in 1527, the last non-Italian Pope.

This German must not die! Her friend called her. Later she returned to the window. The youths were still waiting.

Just as the German appeared at the hospice door, a child of about three ran round a corner, and tripped at his feet. He wailed loudly, so the German picked him up and carried him in the direction that the boy had come. The German's life had been saved.

Rome Radio announced on 1 February that ten 'hostages' had been shot the day before at Forte Bravetta, which was to become a familiar place for executions. No reason except sabotage was given.

This coincided with the arrival of Pietro Caruso, a Neapolitan, to take up the post of chief of police. It was rumoured that he had with him a list of nine thousand people to be arrested. As Mother Mary St Luke wrote, he was 'one of the original Fascists, dyed in the wool – burning to show what he could do'. Early in January he had gone to Verona, to be present at the execution of Ciano.

The very day of his arrival in Rome, however, he had had the misfortune to be caught in a mass round-up of men for forced labour. The Gestapo had sealed off the Via Nazionale area and had arrested every adult male, from seventy to eighteen, on the streets or in trams. Some two thousand had been taken, half for road-making and construction work on the Anzio and Cassino fronts, half for Germany. It took Caruso nearly two hours to convince the Germans of his identity. That same afternoon he organized a little man-hunt of his own and managed to bag nearly two hundred more men. Within a week it was reckoned that at least two hundred Italians working on roads round Albano and Grottaferrata had been machine-gunned by Allied planes.

The brutal Via Nazionale round-up was a major psychological mistake, as the German consul-general Moellhausen realized. The shops closed. Rome looked as if it had caught the plague, and from then onwards people would flee if they saw a group in German uniforms. One could feel the hate and the fear. All young men were virtually in hiding. It was a kind of joke that half the city's population was hiding in the houses of the other half. Moellhausen even went to Monte Soratte to ask Kesselring to intercede, and indeed the Field-Marshal did give orders for man-hunts to cease, even though it meant countermanding orders from Berlin. Instead the Germans put up posters, appealing for volunteers to help in saving Europe from the Anglo-Saxon barbarians. But Kesselring's order did not necessarily apply to the Italian authorities. The zealous Caruso sent out circulars to police stations with a target of fifty arrests each per day.

Another fanatic who collaborated with Caruso was Pietro Koch, a dark and dapper, somewhat corvine, thirty-nine-year-old ex-wine merchant from Benevento. He had a squad of men who specialized in tracking down anti-Fascists and then torturing them. It was surprising how many informers could be found, ready to betray fellow-Romans either for money or through personal grudges. At first Koch operated from the Pensione Oltremare in Via Principe Amedeo, but as neighbours were disturbed by screams he moved to another pensione, the Jaccarino, far more conveniently built, with high walls and deep cellars. Scorching showers alternating with cold water, bright lights and pins through the penis were at first his speciality, but his devices soon became more rarefied. There were stories of walls being splashed with blood, never washed off. The Jaccarino was in Via Romagna, not far from Mother Mary's convent. Among Koch's helpers were his two mistresses, Tamara Sangalli and Desy Totolli, a variety artiste; both would laugh and jeer at the victims of torturings. Interrogations were conducted by a lawyer, Avvocato Trinca.

There were other *bande* too, specializing in finding Jews who could be sold to the Nazis for anything up to six thousand *lire* apiece. Needless to say Celeste Di Porto's help was invaluable in this work. She obviously enjoyed women coming to her to implore help and mercy for husbands or sons. The Black Panther would accept presents, a bracelet or a silk scarf, and then say: 'Don't worry. I'll see that he will have a blanket.' Finally her own father decided to go to the German headquarters in the Corso d'Italia to try to reason with her. He was arrested, sent north and never seen again.

Caruso and Koch now planned a major exploit. On the night of 3 February a priest, one of Koch's admirers, battered on the door of the basilica of San Paolo Fuori le Mura, St Paul's Outside the Walls, shrieking for help. The door was opened, and immediately Caruso's men, who had been hiding in the shadows, swarmed into the building and overpowered the guards. The Abbot, a Benedictine, was summoned and insulted. The men said that they had come to arrest the traitors masquerading as pilgrims that he was hiding. As Mother Mary put in her diary, the monks were made to 'wait the pleasure of the gangsters for ten long hours'. Doors were forced, furniture smashed, pictures slashed. 'Outside, in the frosty moonlight, mounted Fascist police sat in their saddles, surrounding the monastery as completely as if it were a beleaguered fortress, while, in silence, sixty-six dark figures of the men who had taken refuge there filed slowly out and entered the waiting lorries, with their guards.' The Abbot had been arrested, along with General Monti, who was said to have been dressed as a monk, various other military men and some Jews. Vehicles, arms, fuel, stores and blankets were also commandeered.

This outrage, a blatant disregard of the sanctity of extra-territorial Papal property, was a matter for Monsignor Montini. Unfortunately, when at last the Vatican could be telephoned, he was at mass. So others had hurriedly to be found, to rush round to the basilica. It was all exceedingly awkward, in view of the fact that nearly every religious house in Rome was sheltering military, political or Jewish 'refugees'. Nevertheless the deed was a contravention of the Lateran Treaty and had been carried out in a manner both loutish and sacrilegious. The Vatican authorities made the maximum protest, and the Germans disclaimed any connection with the incident. The Abbot was released, but not General Monti. But according to the consul-general Moellhausen, Mussolini's message from the North simply was *Benissimo, continuate*. Very good, continue.'

Everyone in the Vatican pretended not to know who was where and what was happening, but everyone did know. Altogether fifty-five monasteries and a hundred convents were hiding Jews. The Franciscans at San Bartolomeo all'Isola had four hundred, the Brothers of the Scuole Cristiane ninety-six, the Stimmatini Fathers a hundred, the Salesian Society of San Giovanni Bosco eighty-three; the Sisters of Our Lady of Sion one hundred and eighty-seven, the Sisters Adoratrici del Preziossimo Sangue one hundred and thirty-six, the Maestre Pie Filippini one hundred and fourteen. In the Vatican itself there were forty Jews (fifteen of whom were baptized). After the first extra-territorial raid, on the Lombardo seminary, there had naturally been much alarm, but 'refugees' soon returned. Many of these religious houses also of course housed *sfollati*, peasants or poor people who had been bombed out by the Allies or evicted from their houses by the German military.

Take the case of Antonio Bartolini. Being half-Jewish only and baptized, he was not affected by Mussolini's racial laws of 1938–39, signed by the king; these laid down that Jews did not belong to the Italian race, and they were thereby debarred from certain careers, but that half-Jews were allowed to be Italian provided that they belonged to a non-Jewish religion. Bartolini naturally was aware that one day things might get worse for people of his sort, and that day seemed to have come after 8 September, 1943. He decided to have an appendix operation; not that he suffered from appendicitis, but some day he might – after all, several of his family had had to have their appendixes out. He had the operation at the hospital of the Fate Bene Fratelli monks' hospital on the island on the Tiber, near the Franciscans of San Bartolomeo. Since the island was close to the Ghetto, the religious houses on it were obvious places of refuge for the Jews, and there were forty-four Jews in the care of the Fate Bene Fratelli.

The operation was not successful, in that Bartolini developed phlebitis and other complications. He had to remain on the island for some months – in a way no hardship, since it is one of the most delightful spots in all Rome (in ancient times it was turned into the shape of a ship). Mostly he was cared for by a Polish monk. By March he was better and thus could not stay in the hospital, so a girl-friend took him by *carrozzella* to the Collegio Teutonicum, where Monsignor O'Flaherty issued him with a fake identity card.

The writer Alberto Moravia was half Jewish and also baptized. In the previous autumn he had been walking through the Piazza di Spagna and had met a foreign journalist, who had warned him that he was on a list for arrest. Moravia had returned home at once, and whilst he and his wife, Elsa Morante, were packing a suitcase the telephone rang. He lifted the receiver and a not exactly friendly voice asked: 'Am I speaking to the traitor Moravia?' Traitor, so now he had become a traitor ... As he was to write later, he suddenly realized the meaning of terror: 'I was a beast in a trap, no longer a person, an individual, a man.' His sense of identity had been replaced by an 'anonymous' instinct of preservation. The Moravias escaped from Rome and spent the whole grim winter in a peasant's cottage at Fondi near the Gustav Line.

There was bitterness among some of the Jews of Rome that their Chief Rabbi, Israel Zolli, was apparently making no efforts to keep in touch with the Community. In point of fact some days before the *retata*, the big October deportation, when Kappler was demanding fifty kilograms of gold in place of two hundred Jews who would otherwise have been deported to Germany, Zolli had not only obtained a promise of a loan from the Vatican but had offered himself as a hostage. Of course he would have been high on the Gestapo's list for liquidation, and other Chief Rabbis in the North of Italy had been deported and put to death. Nevertheless Zolli was to be strongly criticized after the liberation of Rome. Why, for instance, had the Nazis been able to obtain the vital list of addresses of Jewish households when they raided the Synagogue and libraries and had removed sacred and precious books, just two days before the *retata*? Zolli was to retaliate strongly, blaming Ugo Foà, the president of the Community. But the whole question of why that list was never destroyed beforehand has remained unsolved.

Perhaps Zolli's counsels and presence in the Vatican had some influence there. At any rate, after the liberation, to the outrage of many Roman and other Jews, he announced that he had become a Catholic and was changing his name from Israel to Eugenio, the baptismal name of Pius XII.

Among the many priests regarded as heroes of the Resistance was Padre Pietro Pappagallo. He had been born near Bari in 1888, and since 1938 had been at the basilica of Santa Maria Maggiore on the Esquiline hill. His apartment nearby, in Via Urbana, had been a place of asylum not so much for Jews as for Italian soldiers on the run, to whom he supplied fake identity cards. In this work he was helped by a German artist, an ardent anti-Nazi, and after a while he allowed a clandestine radio to be installed in Via Urbana. He was betrayed, apparently, by a woman calling herself Contessa Martini, who had come to him pretending that she desperately needed money, and on 29 January he was arrested by the Gestapo. The Nazis remained in his apartment, waiting for telephone calls and inviting the unsuspecting callers to come round immediately. On 6 February he was taken to Via Tasso, where he underwent 'sacrilegious humiliation'. He was one of the 335 Italians to die in the Ardeatine Caves on 24 March.

Then there was the learned Monsignor Pietro Barbieri, who like O'Flaherty has since also been called a Scarlet Pimpernel, and indeed there was some similarity in appearance between the two priests. Barbieri was at the monastery of the Padri Maristi in Via Cernaia, behind the Finance Ministry. His house was a favourite meeting place for members of the CLN, and many of these would spend the night there. Jews and journalists also took refuge with him, sometimes for a matter of hours, sometimes for days on end. He had eleven beds in his library, and you might well find yourself next to Nenni, De Gasperi, Bonomi or General Cadorna, who after 8 September had fought so gallantly against the Wehrmacht. It was incredible that all this should be happening in such a potentially dangerous area.

In addition, Barbieri did much to help refugees from the Cassino and Valmontone areas. He personally bought large quantities of material for making into clothes. On one occasion he also bought a whole lorry-load of rice and flour from some Germans (who had requisitioned it from an Italian barracks). The bread ration had been reduced to 150 grams a day, if available, and food cards were only issued to those who were registered as living permanently in Rome. There was a soup kitchen near the monastery, and Barbieri would often help the Sisters in the work of distributing up to six thousand portions a day. He would realize that some middle-class families felt ashamed to be there, and would discreetly arrange for them to be fed apart. On occasions refugee peasants brought their pigs and cows with them. The animals too had to be guests of Barbieri for a while.

'We had some dangerous moments,' said one of his Maristi colleagues, 'and we expected to be shot if we were caught. Luckily, though, we didn't hide weapons, only human beings.'

It was said that after the war when Caruso and Koch were sent for trial both men apologized to the Pope for the violation of San Paolo. The uproar that first week in February obviously did have some effect, and there were no other major excursions into extra-territorial property in Rome. Individual priests however were not immune, an outstanding case being that of Don Giuseppe Morosini, whose arrest and execution were the inspiration for the part played by Aldo Fabrizi in that great and authentic film *Rome, Open City*.

The eminent guests in the Lateran Seminario could not but be alarmed by the San Paolo affair, especially as one of them, General Bencivegna, was now in radio contact with the South. Indeed they were warned that it would be better if they moved to private houses. So on 9 February Bonomi and others left, and a restless period of almost daily moves began, from one unheated house to another. The use of marble in Roman rooms never made February particularly agreeable, but this was also an especially cold winter and the feeble gas and electricity supplies were constantly being cut off by Allied bombing.

Several leading Communists had been caught by the Gestapo, and were tortured or put to death. Their 'Santa Barbara', or arms cache, in Via Giulia had been seized on 1 February, and with it some four or five key partisans. The next day Antonello Trombadori, the head of the Roman Gaps, had – in a sense – a near escape. Knowing nothing of what had happened to his friends he made his way to Via Giulia. As usual he whistled in the street outside. There was absolute silence. He became suspicious when a shutter was half opened. This moment of hesitation was fatal and he suddenly found himself arrested. He was taken to Via Tasso, but managed to persuade the Nazis that he had never been involved with politics; so he was treated as a suspect or common criminal and sent to Regina Coeli. Meanwhile his father, Francesco Trombadori, a well-known artist, went to the Vatican and asked if the Pope would intervene to obtain his release. A number of applications were indeed made on Antonello's behalf by the Vatican, though without any success.

Another leading Communist to be arrested was Professor Gioacchino Gesmundo. In his house the Gestapo found a large quantity of four-pointed nails, such as were used by partisans to puncture tyres. He was to die at the Ardeatine Caves; soon after his arrest his sister had been able to visit him and had found him covered with wounds and sores – as they embraced he whispered to her that he had not spoken. The Party of Action suffered many more arrests; they lost some fifty men, forty-five of whom also died at the Ardeatine Caves.

By now everyone knew of the atrocities at the Pensione Oltremare (Koch moved to the Jaccarino in April) and at Via Tasso. Then in Regina Coeli there was the shocking death of another patriot, Leone Ginzburg, a Jew. The Allies appeared to be as far away from Rome as ever. But it did not reduce the ardour of the partisans. They became more determined, more desperate, more daring. This was the new Risorgimento. 'In the Resistance,' said Carla Capponi, the best known of the women Gapists (and like Antonello Trombadori to become a Communist deputy in

Parliament), 'each of us found our mother country. We felt *la mia patria era la patria del Risorgimento* – my country was the country of the Risorgimento; of democracy and liberty.' After twenty years of Fascist repression it was the moment of rebirth and hope and idealism, of faith in Italy and the Italians, not simply a fight to get rid of foreign oppressors. And this inspiration applied to partisans belonging to any party, whether Communists or followers of the Montezemolo 'Badogliani'.

In the months ahead the cities of the North were to suffer even worse retribution than in Rome. But Rome at that moment was a front-line city, a city besieged; and Rome was Rome, *la Città Eterna*. It was perhaps inevitable that the slowness of the Allies should produce a despair, even resentment, when contrasted with the Russians who were already advancing towards Poland (though with what ironic consequences when they got to Warsaw). At Ponte Cavour a blind beggar used to sit with a placard *'Aiutate la barca'*, slang meaning 'help my family'. A joker changed the words to *'Aiutate lo sbarco'*, *sbarco* referring to the Allied landings. And at a cinema when the actor Totò shouted in some film *'Arrivano, arrivano*, they're coming, they're coming,' all the audience stood up and cheered.

Nowadays, in retrospect, the Party of Action, so soon to be dissolved after the war, might seem the most interesting intellectually of the CLN parties, even the most selfless and romantic. The original 'Justice and Liberty' movement had been formed as long ago as in 1929 by exiles in Paris such as Carlo Rosselli and Emilio Lussu. It had sent a contingent to fight against Franco in the Spanish Civil War. By 1944 it contained some of the best liberal–progressive brains in the country, and was the only valid 'laic' left-wing alternative to the Communists; moreover it was strictly republican. The party's clandestine newspaper *L'Italia Libera* was as famous as the Communist *L'Unità* and the Socialist *Avanti!*. The other parties had their heroes and intellectuals, but the Party of Action had an exceptional quota, and only a few names can be singled out, such as Riccardo Bauer, Pilo Albertelli, Carlo Muscetta, Mario Vinciguerra, Ugo La Malfa, and in the South Croce's son-in-law Raimondo Craveri, known among partisans in his native Piedmont as 'Mondo'. Less in the public eye were brave men like 'Furio' Lauri, a Triestino who later worked for No 1 Special Force and would make solo flights to partisan encampments in the North. As Lauri said, 'We had absolutely nothing in those days. It is not easy for a country to express its best, but that was the moment. After 8 September everyone had to make his choice. Of course older people found it more difficult, they had commitments. We were young ...' And likewise another leading Actionist: 'You have no idea what it is like to hate one's country, but that was how I felt when the Fascists were in power, when they invaded France ... In the time of the

Abyssinian war for me Anthony Eden was a god.' But Eden turned out in 1944 to be a 'little man, neurotic, and a Puritan ... For Puritans everything is impure.' Eden, he added, had no idea that the Resistance was the great new impulse in the political history of our modern age. He had no understanding for the poor patriots, those unfortunate idealistic people fighting on the other side of the line.

Carla Capponi, though a Communist, would have agreed with most of these sentiments. She also said: 'It was in the Resistance that each one of us found our patriotism again. And it was in international Communism that I found the joy and pride of being part of the Italian nation, as distinct from the cosmopolitanism that emanated from certain sectors of the anti-Fascist bourgeoisie.'

A feature of the Communist party was the activity behind the scenes of its women, working not only for the partisans but for destitute refugees. In contrast there were the Gap girls, each operating as a team with a boyfriend, such as Marisa Musu and her Valentino. But Marisa was only seventeen and her testing moment was yet to come. The most active pair, and to some the most controversial because of the great number of assassinations and acts of sabotage attributed to them, was Carla Capponi and Rosario Bentivegna. Their story begins almost like the opening of an operetta; Carla, described in an American book as a 'rebel contessa' from Florence, attractive, fair-haired, with some Polish blood in her; Bentivegna, a medical student, an obvious intellectual, dark, bespectacled; Carla in a large house overlooking Trajan's Forum, a place of meeting for plotters; one of their aims, to goad the Germans into retaliation, which in turn would stir up the flaccid Roman public. Carla and Bentivegna took part in the attack on the Barberini cinema, when ten German soldiers were killed and fifteen wounded, and then again at the Regina Coeli – eight Germans killed this time. Just before the Anzio landing a daring attack had been planned on Via Tasso, but it was called off in the belief that the Allies' arrival was imminent. Later Carla and others made an attempt on Pizzirani, Vice-Secretary of the Fascist Republican party, but only succeeded in wounding the driver of his car. On 1 March came her supreme moment, the culminating test of her willpower and idealism, when near the Excelsior Hotel and smart cafés of the Via Veneto she shot a German in the back and seized the briefcase he was carrying. Yet she and Bentivegna still had to plan that major action which would finally outrage the Nazi hydra and goad him into retaliation. It was soon to come, and for the Gapists there would also be betrayals and flight.

Every day the Gapists attacked German vehicles, usually killing a few soldiers. It was now fully realized that the moment for a general insurrection had passed. 'I knew this,' said Amendola, the Communist leader in Rome, 'when I heard German lorries and trucks rumbling all night through the streets of the city towards the South'. In the Alban Hills Gapist partisans were reported arrested by the Allies near Campoleone; later it was discovered that they had been sent to Algiers for sabotage and parachute training, and in due course they were returned, by air. Albano was virtually emptied of inhabitants, many of them taking refuge in the precincts of the Papal villa at Castel Gandolfo. However, on 2 February there was an Allied air-raid on the town of Castel Gandolfo, killing seventeen nuns. There was another major raid on 10 February, with bombs actually falling on Papal grounds. This time there were five hundred civilian casualties. It was said that the Pope received the news on his way to mass in the Sistine Chapel and turned aside to arrange for help.

The Russian partisans – originally escaped prisoners of war – were now reorganizing themselves at Palestrina, further inland from the Alban Hills. In one action they had killed twelve German motorcyclists and had blown up a petrol lorry, which had thereupon attracted Allied dive-bombers – with unpleasant consequences for neighbouring Italians. Many of the Russians had now found Italian girlfriends. Two took part in the murder of the Fascist Secretary at Palestrina. So once more the group was driven up into the mountains, living in shepherds' huts made of straw and mud. They were supplied with food and tobacco by Aldo Finzi, who – such is the wheel of history – had been Mussolini's Under-Secretary for Home Affairs at the time of the infamous political murder of the Socialist deputy Mateotti in 1924. Finzi's house was occupied by the Germans, and as he understood German perfectly and was still living there he was able to pass on valuable information to the partisans. But in due course he was found out, and he was one of those who died at the Ardeatine Caves.

One day Levi Cavaglione went with the Russian leader Vassily and another, Serge, to collect supplies from Finzi's house. On their return they found a peasant woman standing on a threshing floor, weeping. An old man was beside her, his head in his hands. 'What has happened?' 'The Germans,' the woman said, and pointed at the house.

The room was a shambles, crockery broken, the simple furniture smashed, the mirror broken. 'But why did they do this?' 'They asked for wine, and we did not have any.'

There had been four of them. Levi Cavaglione and the Russians set out along a mule-path. It was not long before they found them, under the leafless, dripping chestnut trees. The Germans were singing, with faces flushed and jackets undone. There was a battle. Serge was wounded, but soon the soldiers in grey-green uniforms were writhing on the ground. Three Germans died, but the fourth tried to sit up. Levi Cavaglione stepped forward to finish him off with a pistol shot through the head, but Vassily pushed him aside and walked slowly forward. Then, deliberately,

Vassily gave a terrible kick at the man's face. Levi Cavaglione shrank back, horrified. Many grisly things could have happened in centuries past in this beautiful landscape, perhaps in the time of Hannibal or the Goths, but surely nothing could have been quite like this ... Levi Cavaglione heard the rhythmic crunch of kick after kick, and groans and screams. When there was silence he looked and saw that the face had been turned into a mush of gore. Vassily wiped his forehead. 'I have seen hundreds of my comrades die like that, or whipped to death, in German concentration camps.'

To some extent the Roman CLN had been satisfied, or had to be satisfied, with the results of the Congress of their southern counterparts held at Bari on 28 January. These had been a compromise, simply demanding a new government containing representatives of the six parties of the CLN and, above all, the abdication of King Victor Emmanuel; there would also be a constituent assembly immediately after the end of hostilities. A far more extreme resolution by the Party of Action, in effect nothing more than an attempt at a coup d'état, was never put forward.

There had been no mention of the Crown Prince, Umberto. It was realized that this was because it might be easier to persuade the king to step out of public life if his son were to be Viceroy.

For the time being in Rome Bonomi had other things on his mind, his own safety for instance. But the Socialists were having second thoughts, and Nenni was busy with an 'order of the day'. He wanted an outright declaration that the parties of the CLN would not collaborate in any way with the monarchy, and that it should be swept aside until the constituent assembly could proclaim a republic. This came as a shock to Bonomi. 'It is the first crack in the alliance and a hard blow for the CLN.'

In London a Foreign Office official summed it up: 'All in all, the Italians are not so convinced as we are of the blessings of constitutional monarchy.'

Churchill had sent a secret telegram to Roosevelt following the Bari Congress. It in effect expressed the nub of British policy, against which any number of Party of Action resolutions or Socialist orders of the day were at present powerless:

'I earnestly hope that the existing regime in Italy will be allowed to function at least until the great battles now being fought by the soldiers of our two countries have resulted in our capture of Rome. I am sure now of such authority as remains in the Italian State and the attempt to create a new authority out of political groups [the CLN] with no real backing will add greatly to our difficulties. Moreover these groups when formed into a Goverment, in order to win credit from the Italian people would feel it essential to assert Italian interests in a much stronger form than the King and Badoglio dare to do. I feel it would be a great pity if Badoglio threw in his hand, and our reports show that the Italian Navy might be powerfully affected by action against the king. Much British and American blood is flowing, and I plead that military considerations should carry weight.'

And in the meantime Roosevelt had also had a letter from Badoglio on the old theme: if Italy could be declared an ally, then Roosevelt would have the 'eternal gratitude of the Italians living and in the United States' – shrewdly phrased, with the American elections ahead, of course. The President wrote a note to the Acting Secretary of State Stettinius: 'What do I do about this note from Badoglio? I am stumped.'

To Churchill Roosevelt wired back on 11 February, agreeing. He also added: 'I think, though, that you and I should regard this as a temporary reprieve for the old gentlemen.'

To Badoglio he replied on 21 February, and not quite in the way Churchill would have done. Until, he said, the government of Italy could include groups of anti-Fascist liberal elements within its composition, 'it will not be possible for any Head of Government to organize the conduct of the war on such a broad scale as the status of ally would require'. He then said: 'There is, I understand, a plan for the reconstruction of the Italian Government on a broad political basis as soon as the present critical military situation will permit, and not later than the liberation of Rome. With all these considerations in mind I feel that it would be best to hold in abeyance any major changes in our relationship.' This did at least warn Badoglio that the Americans had in mind the possibility of a broader government before Rome had been entered. And very soon the divergences between the British and American views were to be brought into the open.

By now the American spy Peter Tompkins had donned steel-rimmed glasses and had a new card identifying him as a captain attached to the Fascist headquarters, grandly calling itself the Open City of Rome. He lived in a secret room deep in the warren of the old city. There was a trap-door concealing files marked 'Ammo Dumps', 'Counter-espionage', 'Minefields', etc., and an ammonia bottle was always to hand in case of an SS raid with bloodhounds, now becoming common. It was so cold in that room that he usually had to wear two overcoats.

Tompkins had opted for the Socialists as helpers. Cervo was still in charge of the clandestine Radio Vittoria, sometimes operated from the sacristy of a small church, sometimes from a river boat used in summer by swimmers but a place popular in winter for homosexual assignations – the caretaker, always happy to earn extra *lire*, conveniently closed an eye to whatever went on in the cabins. The radio connections with the Fifth Army base worked quite dramatically well for some weeks. For instance, Tompkins was able to give warning of a German build-up of equipment at Pratica di Mare, behind Ardea, as a result of which the place – originally Lavinium, founded by Aeneas – was blasted by Allied bombers. No doubt this was the reason why Kesselring did not persist with his idea of attacking the Beachhead in a south-westerly direction along the coast and instead adopted Hitler's preference, the Via Anziate. 'Nice going bombing Pratica di Mare,' the justifiably satisfied Tompkins radioed back after the raid.

He also sent recommendations for bombings of troop concentrations in the North, which were promptly carried out, and gave details of German movements through Rome itself, for example on 17 February: 'Traffic through Rome going south on 15th. 230 freight cars loaded with material, 50 loaded with personnel, 100 horse carts, 11 Mark VI tanks, 6 medium tanks . . .' So much for the German pretence of 'open city'. On 19 February he pinpointed Kesselring's exact command post in caves at Soratte, and gave details of units' insignia on trucks and of the names of Fascist agents crossing the lines.

For this work he had a hundred Socialist workers recruited solely for the purpose of watching all the twelve major highways in and out of Rome. His most valuable contact was a young German-speaking Italian lieutenant who was a liaison officer between the Fascist commander of the 'Open City' and the German commander in Rome, General Kurt Maeltzer. This Italian on 13 February was actually asked to accompany Mussolini's chief of staff, Marshal Graziani, to the Alban Hills. Through him Tompkins discovered that the Germans had broken the Allied plane-to-ground radio code at the Beachhead. Another useful, though un-witting, helpmeet was a German NCO at Via Tasso, no less – a stupid man with a taste for brandy, which was supplied to him after a hard day in the cells by another Socialist assistant, 'Franco' (in point of fact Baron Malfatti, later Italian ambassador to France). And in Regina Coeli a warder and a doctor also worked for the organization.

Tompkins was asked to locate the railway gun Anzio Annie, and was delighted to begin a search. Preparing and waiting for a parachute drop of equipment for partisans was one of the most exciting aspects of all the operations in which he was involved. The code words for the exact time and place of these drops would be broadcast by Radio London after the news, strangely thrilling since everyone of course knew that they were messages for partisans: 'The cigarettes have arrived'; 'the sun will rise at dawn'; 'your sister's cow is ready.'

The Voice of America was beamed from Algiers, putting listeners in no doubt that the American public was against the king, but containing too many ingenuous platitudes by Mayor La Guardia of New York. Radio London was by far the most popular and the newscaster became a national figure in Italy, 'Colonello Buonasera', the Anglo-Neapolitan Colonel Stevens, who was always preceded by the famous V sign in Morse code, tara-ta-tum.

Quite how the messages for partisans were worked out was and always will no doubt be a mystery. Those who were concerned at No 1 Special Force say now that they were 'trained to forget', and needless to say no records were ever kept in writing. Many messages must have originated from spy networks in Switzerland, where Allen Dulles was the OSS chief, and then been relayed to London. Colonel Stevens himself never had an inkling of the real meaning of the words.

The British at Anzio also ran a 'black' radio station broadcasting in German. Tompkins used to listen to its late night jazz. By March he had devised a new code based enigmatically on the words 'Screw You'. But the whole of his network was soon to crack with the arrest of Cervo on the Tiber houseboat, after another Vittoria operator had been denounced by the Germans and had revealed his name under torture. Cervo himself was sent to Koch's Pensione Oltremare.

One day a grinning Monsignor O'Flaherty entered the British Legation rooms and brought Sam Derry a letter: 'Back in Rome. Where the hell are you? Only consolation for my sore arse will be when I see your smiling face. John.'

It was John Furman, whom Derry had scarcely expected to see again after he had been shipped north from Regina Coeli. He had jumped from a train, hence the soreness, and had bought a bicycle. At the end of his two-hundred-mile journey he had sent a message to O'Flaherty that a friend was waiting for him in St Peter's Square. Then had come the reunion, and a bellow from the Monsignor, 'In the name of God, John, it's good to see you back.' But Derry and Furman could not meet, Derry being unable to leave the Vatican and Furman forbidden to enter it. By special arrangement with O'Flaherty, Derry would sometimes stand and wave at a window of the Santa Marta hospice, to be watched through field-glasses by Furman from the Collegio Teutonicum.

The number of escaped prisoners in Rome, several from the Anzio front, was swelling, and the cost of keeping them rose in proportion. American bomber crews, six or seven at a time, would arrive largely unaware of the German grip on Rome, and generally expecting to find that the best hotel in the city had been taken over for their reception. Derry tried to persuade most of them to hide in the country, where food was easier to find. Some escaped prisoners never heard of Derry's organization until much later: John Miller, for example, who existed in very simple conditions in the Prati, sharing the meals – often soup made from the husks of beans – with an old woman known as La Nonna. Often prisoners living with peasants outside Rome had the impression that their hosts did not necessarily dislike the Germans. Some No 1 Special Force men were dropped near Tivoli and knocked on a door after dark. 'Don't be afraid,' they said, 'we are not Germans but English parachutists.' The non-committal reply was almost inevitable: 'Well you are all sons of God and welcome to a bed and a meal.'

The British organization in the South in charge of getting escaped prisoners through the line was MI9. Necessarily, most successful attempts were from the Adriatic coast, usually by sea. Harold Tittmann, the American Chargé d'Affaires at the Vatican, was warned by Derry not to encourage American soldiers in the organization to make their way south on foot, partly because of food difficulties, partly because of snow on the mountains – 'Several British ex-prisoners of war, especially Indians, have been seen dead on the mountains, apparently having died of exposure and/or hunger.' Derry added: 'While I realize that it is the duty of all ex-prisoners of war to try to rejoin our forces at the earliest possible moment, I cannot help but feel it is exceedingly unwise to attempt to get through the lines now.'

Nevertheless MI9 (A Force) sent a half-Italian, Peter Tumiati, up to Rome, and in due course Tumiati returned to the South with a microfilm list of names of escaped prisoners and other information baked into a loaf of bread. This was passed to his chief at MI9, Captain Christopher Soames, and as a result successful arrangements were able to be made for getting away 104 prisoners by landing-craft – a group of commandos held a beachhead while they embarked. Tumiati's adventures were often alarming. He would sometimes bring up money for the British Legation from the South, and on one expedition a *contadino* insisted on giving up his bed to him. After about an hour Tumiati found the bugs intolerable, and went to a haystack in a barn. To his horror he heard movements in the hay. Rats? No; only a dozen British escaped prisoners.

By contrast the supply of Scotch whisky in Sir D'Arcy Osborne's rooms – with their stupendous backcloth of St Peter's – appeared undiminished. Maybe Monsignor Montini enjoyed an occasional nip instead of tea on his almost daily visits. Harold Tittmann, who had lost a leg as an airman in the First War, was always welcome. Marchesa Claudia Patrizi, working for Montezemolo's Centro X, was taken to a party in the Santa Marta hospice by Princess Pallavicini and there found not only Osborne, so correct and British, but sundry other diplomats and Jews, not to mention Osborne's peculiar butler John May, a kind of Henry James character, or Mr Know-all, all enjoying their Johnny Walker, except for

O'Flaherty, who was a teetotaller. An American dance tune was put on the gramophone, and an Irish priest gave a good imitation of Fred Astaire.

To some people Osborne seemed overcorrect and formal, the typical Englishman, 'the enemy of untidiness, noise and hilarity', a bit hypochondriac, but as his diaries show he was warm-hearted and loved children, especially the younger Tittmann boy, whom he called Tarzan. His diary of that period was confined to recording BBC news, partly for security reasons, in case the Germans should ever break into the Vatican, and partly for the benefit of the Pope, to whom he would send a typed digest at the end of each day. He found this writing out of news for the Pope a great chore, but had been begged by Montini on the Pope's behalf to continue and at least the work relieved the tedium of that enclosed life. The visits of the Irish Minister's wife Mrs Kiernan were always enlivening and full of jokes. She had got on well with Ciano's wife, Edda Mussolini, early in the war, but had had many anti-Fascist friends as well. Once, after a party in the Kiernans' 'horrid flat' near the railway station, Edda was saying goodbye. As she drew on her gloves she said: 'If I were you, I'd be more careful about whom I'd invite to my parties.'

Much to Derry's embarrassment O'Flaherty had taken pity on their most eminent escaper in Rome, General Gambier-Parry, who was beginning to get bored in his little room with a drawbridge. Now Gambier-Parry was being taken to Irish parties and introduced to high ranking Germans as an Irish 'doctor'. Eventually Derry managed to get the general safely into a clinic run by nuns known as the Blue Sisters; a pleasant and large garden proved adequate for his exercise.

One special party was given in Osborne's rooms for the twenty-first birthday of Paul Freyberg, the son of the eminent New Zealand general at Cassino. Freyberg was a Grenadier Guards lieutenant and had been captured at Anzio. He had escaped and had reached the Papal villa at Castel Gandolfo by climbing over a wall that had been bombed. When D'Arcy Osborne, who was a cousin, had heard about this, he had arranged for Freyberg to be smuggled into the Vatican in a vanload of vegetables. Freyberg was now lodged in the Papal Gendarmerie, familiarly known by Osborne and other 'Santa Martians' as the Ritz.

Rich Romans were able to live moderately well on the black market, sometimes through selling possessions of their own, such as sheets, and one could still get good meals at restaurants at high prices. On occasion British officers were able to get Roman friends to cash cheques which would be honoured, it was hoped, after the liberation. Wing Commander Garrad-Cole was lucky enough to meet a contessa named Cristina with 'blue-grey eyes', and who was so struck by his own eyes that she had him fitted out with suits from the best Roman tailors. A favourite restaurant for 'Garry' and others was the Ostaria dell'Orso, where the barman Felix had once worked at the Savoy. Special allowances were made on the bills. One evening the editor of *Il Messaggero* was dining at the Orso. The next day there was a headline in his paper: 'Rome starves while British escaped prisoners gorge'.

British other ranks had their admirers too. In one case a girl, of Finnish origin, fell in love with her family's lodger, a real Cockney. He taught her English. After the liberation the girl was visited by a woman captain who was assessing compensation for those who had helped escaped POWs. On arriving the captain stumbled on the stairs and nearly fell. 'Jesus Christ,' said the girl, 'I thought you was going to break your fucking neck.'

An alarming situation occurred when a Cameron Highlander, Private Anderson, developed acute appendicitis at Subiaco in the Sabine Hills. Derry appealed to Mrs Kiernan, and in due course a Diplomatic Corps car swept out on the long journey, bearing not an Irish diplomat but the burly Father Spike Buckley. Again thanks to the machinations of O'Flaherty, Private Anderson was operated on in a hospital used for German wounded from Anzio. But he had to be removed immediately afterwards – very dangerous. So Father Spike took the boy to 'Mummy' Chevalier's flat and carried him in his arms up three flights of steps.

This was not the end either. Anderson was very ill, but after a week Mummy was warned of an impending German raid. So once more the Kiernan car had to be requisitioned, and Father Spike took him to the American College on the Janiculum, considered to be the organization's safest billet.

Although O'Flaherty was supposed to be neutral, there were occasions when he might say slyly to Derry (whose code-name was Patrick): 'My boy, there is a lot of funny business going on. The mouth of the Tiber is crammed with wee motorboats. Now, Patrick, what d'ye think they'd be for?' In point of fact they were German E boats, getting ready for a raid on Anzio harbour. Then, when John May told him that there was a German Army boot-repairing shop at the back of the Irish Embassy, O'Flaherty was delighted. During the night many of those boots disappeared over the wall into the garden of the Embassy.

Derry had plenty of contacts for sending back military information to the South, but it was all one way; he never received instructions in return, and this could be frustrating. For instance, he had some ex-prisoners hiding in a valley outside Rome, ready to escape across a viaduct. No Germans were in the area, but Allied bombers (thanks to Peter Tompkins' network?) blew up the viaduct, which attracted the Germans, who in turn believed the work to have been sabotage. So a big *rastrellamento* began; local Italians were rounded up, most of the ex-prisoners too.

The question of funds for the organization was often worrying. Some came from private individuals like Prince Doria or Claudia Patrizi, who sold her tapestries to raise money. Most was supplied by Osborne, a certain amount by Tittmann. Again, secrecy still overhangs the exact methods by which both the British and American Ministries obtained this money in the first instance. Much came on Vatican motor convoys from Switzerland. Other sums were obtained by means of loans from religious foundations or in devious ways from Italian banks. Derry had 2,591 escapers' names on his books in February, 116 being in Rome. The cost per man was reckoned at 131 *lire* a day, and during the month 1,832,590 was spent, including money smuggled into Regina Coeli and assistance to Russians in hiding. Tittmann of course also helped with supplying cash to Delasem, the Jewish organization run by the Capuchin monk Padre Benedetto. In point of fact there was only one American priest connected with the Holy See, Monsignor McGeough, who was of particular help to the score or so of American ex-prisoners.

The Vatican itself necessarily had to avert its eyes from any of the dealings with Delasem. In mid-March the Secretariat was informed that a sum of $16,000 was waiting in London for the Jews of Rome, and it was suggested that this might be credited to a Papal organization known as the Opere di Religione, founded by Pius XII in 1942, and that D'Arcy Osborne should cable instructions to London. Such a proposal, and the implications if ever the Germans got wind of it, obviously horrified Cardinal Maglione, who wrote in a memo: 'I do not intend to give orders or assume responsibility. I do not wish even to make suggestions.'

Some of the money that reached O'Flaherty also appears to have made its way to Centro X, the 'information' centre of the Montezemolo organization. The point of Claudia Patrizi being asked to the party in the Vatican was so that she could carry away two shoe boxes, containing money, each tied up with pink ribbon. She had to take these to the Bar Ronzi and hand them over to the Centro X treasurer, Lily Marx, who as it happened was the girl-friend of Ettore Basevi, the main forger of identity documents. She found Lily, a pretty brown-haired young woman of German-Jewish origin, already seated at a table. 'At last, here I am, Anna,' she said in a loud voice, trying not to tremble. 'These are the children's shoes. Not very good quality but I hope they'll be all right.' 'You're an angel, Giovanna,' replied Lily, loudly too. 'I don't know how to thank you. What can I offer you? A Punt e Mes or a Campari?'

Letters from families of British prisoners in Italy, whether still in camps or escaped and in hiding, would be sent to the Red Cross in Rome. Another Irish friend of O'Flaherty's, Madam Bruccoleri, a widow, worked there. When she came across the name of someone being hidden by the organization, she would slip the letter into her bosom and it would then be given to her nineteen-year-old daughter, Josette, who would take it in a school bag to O'Flaherty in the Vatican. 'I was rather spotty,' Josette modestly says now, 'and probably rather smelly, as there was no soap. I used to go to O'Flaherty's room, half studio and with a bed screened off in an alcove. Very improper for a school girl. I remember him saying to Major Derry, "Don't worry, she's a grand girl."'

In actual fact O'Flaherty had his roguish side. He said to one of his women helpers, a shade older than Josette, 'You know I have a little place in town. How about meeting me there on the quiet?' He added: 'And I won't be in this robe you know.' And she thought he meant it.

Young Josette was very scared sometimes on her visits, in case she was being followed by plain-clothes police. Once in a tram a man dropped a grenade on the floor, and when his coat opened you could see he had a whole belt of grenades. Nobody said a word on that tram. On another occasion there were a lot of monks travelling with her. When the tram lurched the monks clutched the hangers; their sleeves fell back and you could see each one of them had very British tattoos, one being the word Mother on a tombstone.

Once, on entering the Vatican, Josette saw a man in white shoes sitting at a window. 'You're English, aren't you?' she said. He was surprised. '*Perchè?*' He turned out to be Osborne's butler John May. Once reassured, he said, 'I'm waiting for an escaped prisoner but he hasn't turned up.' She also was told that Peter Tumiati, to stop a British prisoner from having to talk, had bandaged his jaw, and that inside the bandage was a map.

Josette was a great friend of Orietta Doria, the daughter of Prince Filippo Doria and his Glaswegian wife. She had been at Palazzo Doria when the Germans came to arrest them. They were in point of fact celebrating Josette's birthday, and she was staying the night because of the curfew. Prince Doria, half English himself, was a man of outstanding integrity, an aristocrat in the great tradition, quiet and unostentatious. Princess Doria, who had the unGlaswegian-sounding Christian name of Gesine, had been his nurse whilst he was in hospital in England (after being injured in a sculling accident whilst up at Cambridge). Both had been adamantly anti-Fascist from the beginning, and had thus put themselves in great peril. Before the war the princess had refused the invitation of the queen of Italy to give up her wedding ring to 'help' in the invasion of Abyssinia, let alone take any notice of those British and American wives who had formed the 'Pro Italia' society at the time of Sanctions. When war was declared Doria was arrested, and had remained in various forms of confinement until Mussolini was overthrown. In the days preceding the Armistice, during the Badoglio period in Rome, he had formed a committee for helping ex-political detainees, and had also assisted another committee for releasing Communists or suspected Communists still in prison. This last committee included the film director Luchino Visconti, the artist Renato Guttuso, and Umberto Morra, a popular post-war director of the Italian Institute in London – Visconti later concerning himself with helping Italian soldiers on the run.

Whilst Josette and the Dorias were at dinner, the door-bell rang. Orietta opened the door and found a down-and-out-looking fellow, who kissed her hand and gave her an urgent letter for her father, saying that they both had been in the same concentration camp in 1940. The prince merely glanced at the letter and put it in his pocket without saying anything. Even though it was a warning that the Germans were coming to arrest him, he treated it as a hoax or a trap. At about 10 p.m., just as they were settling down to listen to the BBC news, Giovanni the butler came to tell them that Germans were in the Vicolo outside. Sure enough, when they peered through the slats in the shutters, they could see that the SS were surrounding the immense palace. Then the telephone from the porter's lodge rang. They must open up at once.

The four of them hid in a lavatory behind a sliding book-case. They could hear the clump clump of the Germans. It was almost the same story as at Palazzo Rospigliosi. The men must have been overcome by the great salons, the gilded furniture, the velvet and the statuary. They would have ventured into that incredible green room hung with Gothic tapestries, and where in normal times there were pictures by Memling, Bronzino and Filippo Lippi – and, above all, Velasquez's formidable masterpiece the portrait of Innocent X, enough to scare away any intruder. Once again, as at Palazzo Rospigliosi, they said they would be 'back tomorrow'.

A palace like the Dorias' is in reality like a hive. There are the prince's own rooms, the state apartments and the picture gallery, and in addition scores of flats of all sizes, some for relatives – 'as big as Selfridges', Orietta has said. It was an easy matter to slip away, having gathered together a few clothes. The prince at first dressed as a priest, while Orietta and her mother dyed their hair black and, it has been said, posed as washerwomen. The princess was small and dumpy, but Orietta was tall, stately and very Anglo-Saxon. In any case the princess was a well-known figure in Rome, black hair or no, and finally she was discreetly advised by a Fascist policeman that she would be wise not to be seen in public. So in due course she and Orietta joined the prince, who – having grown a beard and affecting a limp – was living with the parish priest of Santa Maria in Trastevere and was now a 'professore'.

An Englishwoman, Baroness Diana Corsi, courageously went to Palazzo Doria to rescue some of the family's precious belongings. It was after curfew when she returned on her bicycle with these things in her basket. Luckily she was not stopped by the police. 'My husband was very annoyed with me,' she now says mildly.

Meanwhile Doria was working with O'Flaherty. Strangely enough he also supplied information for both Umberto Lusena, who had been Derry's radio contact until his arrest, and Peter Tompkins' Cervo. When he heard the Villa Doria on the Janiculum was being used as an ammunition dump he was quite prepared to have it blown up.

The princess and Orietta had themselves registered as third-grade employees at the Ministry of Agriculture. They in fact never dared to go out and subsisted only on vegetables. Orietta spent her time doing housework and translating a book on the technique of teaching catechism to children. All around in the ancient streets of Trastevere brave, ordinary people were hiding Allied soldiers and Jews, risking the death penalty.

Stories about the ill-treatment of Colonel Montezemolo at Via Tasso continued to circulate in Rome. A woman cousin had tried to get Dollmann to intercede. Dollmann had been polite but firm. This was a military matter, out of his jurisdiction. Besides, everyone knew about Montezemolo's involvement with sabotage groups and his radio connection with Badoglio. One could hardly expect him to be freed!

Strangely enough this cousin had seen Dollmann at his pensione at Santa Trinità dei Monti; a few hundred yards away Montezemolo's wife and daughters were hiding in the convent attached to that very church. She had managed the interview through Prince Francesco Ruspoli, who was one of Dollmann's particular friends. Ruspoli was interned at the liberation, but had nevertheless been instrumental in arranging with Dollmann for several lesser fry to be released. He was to marry the daughter of Dollmann's landlady.

Montezemolo had a fever for most of the rest of his time in prison. He also suffered from mastoid trouble, probably connected with his broken jaw. Survivors of Via Tasso speak of his extraordinary calm and dignity.

When Signora Simoni and her daughters saw the Pope, he gave them a rosary for the old general. Vera Simoni had gone with her father to the Pope after her brother had been killed in Africa. Simoni had said to the Pope: 'Give me faith. This is a moment in which I need to believe in something.' The Pope had taken them into his private library and had sat behind the desk. As Vera now remembers, 'Father already knew that we were not going to win the war, and he said, "I am not against the New Zealander in the tank who killed my son, but against the system that sent him to war without proper arms. Why send all these people to be killed when anyone can see how useless it is? It is tragedy." Then the Pope had made a gesture for him to be quiet, and he had knelt down and taken out the telephone's connection. He said, "I did that because there are spies everywhere. Now we can speak freely." Then he said something that I shall never forget, he said that it was the *male sceso sulla terra*, the evil descended upon the Earth. And he spoke wonderfully, and gave my father the faith he needed. I could see that the Pope and my father were at one in their ideas.'

On this next visit the Pope did not take out the connection. Through his influence Vera, her mother and sister visited General Simoni at Via Tasso on three occasions. Once Simoni said to his wife: 'Don't worry. Yesterday they took me in front of the firing squad, and at the last minute they said it was a mistake. It was another way of torturing me. But I just thought of you, and all you have done for me, and how grateful I am. As I thought of my life, I felt I could die *in pace con Dio e con gli uomini*, in peace with God and men.' Vera knew that he was trying to give *them* strength. She took him in her arms and hugged him, and he screamed in pain.

When the dirty laundry came back, they would find blood on it. Once they found a little letter: '*Vivo in fiamma d'amore per voi,*' literally, 'I live in flame of love for you all.' Mostly he was in his tiny cell, and allowed twice a day to go to the stinking blue-tiled lavatory. At night the Nazis played the gramophone and had women in. All the windows were bricked up, but once Simoni managed to push out a note through a ventilator hole: 'Simone Simoni – cell 12. Giuseppe Ferrari – cell 2. I am being tortured. I suffer with pride. My thoughts are with my country and my family.' This note was picked up by one of the gaolers, who showed it to Kappler, with the result that General Simoni was given another beating.

An appeal was also sent to Dollmann on behalf of Simoni, but back came the usual courteous reply, in the usual green ink – 'The Person in whom you are interested has been too gravely compromised to be released . . .'

There has been much confusion about the personality of Dollmann, and too often has his role in Rome been muddled with Kappler's, especially in books published just after the war. In his black SS Colonel's uniform he could not help cutting an awesome figure in Rome, accompanied as he usually was by his wolf-hound, Kuno. There was gossip about his relationship with his handsome Italian chauffeur, and with certain effete young Roman nobles – but that was by the way. He was a Nazi, but no bloodthirsty monster, not a Scarpia, and indeed was later to be exonerated of any war crimes. He was frankly a socialite, intelligent and witty, and his often proclaimed love for Rome was genuine. Being called upon to be interpreter on the highest German–Italian levels, he was thus in a position to influence events subtly in favour of the Italians – if he wished.

Dollmann had little respect for General Maeltzer, the 'King of Rome', whom he endearingly called Mr Bum-Bum-Bum. The animosity between him and Kappler, who was in command of the Gestapo SD, was indeed very deep. Kappler, slim, aged thirty-five, grey-eyed, the son of a Stuttgart chauffeur, but of Swedish origin, affected to despise him, and probably was jealous, not only of Dollmann's better education but because he was the favourite of General Karl Wolff, the head of all the SS in Italy. Kappler was intolerant, cold, vengeful, unhappily married and with interests in Etruscan vases, roses and photography. He had adopted a son from the Lebensborn, the Nazi 'baby farm' scheme, where perfect SS specimens of Aryan manhood could mate with perfect Aryan women. He also loved Rome, but not those Romans who had betrayed their former allies and thereby endangered the security of his country and comrades. He believed in the Third Reich, and was ready to carry out orders unquestioningly.

Moellhausen, the German consul, who was acting head of the Embassy in Rome, was half French and nicknamed by his colleagues the 'Byzantine Christ'. Aged thirty, he was not a Nazi and secretly tried to ease the predicament of the Jews, as did his colleague the Councillor at the Embassy to the Holy See, Albrecht von Kessel, known as 'Teddy'. Years later it was revealed that Moellhausen was approached by Kessel to join the plot to assassinate Hitler, but refused.

The position of Weizsaecker, the white-haired ambassador to the Holy See, with his blue 'sailor's eyes', will always remain controversial. His memoirs were to be described as 'teeming with absurdities, distortions and untruths fit to deceive'. According to Kessel, when Hitler considered kidnapping the Pope Weizsaecker found himself 'doing battle on two fronts'. 'He had to persuade the Pope not to say anything too extreme, which might have fatal consequences. At the same time he had to convince Hitler, by ingeniously phrased despatches, that the Pope was not too ill-disposed towards Germany, and that Catholic gestures in favour of the Jews were insignificant and not to be taken seriously.' He went on to say that 'we knew that a violent protest against the persecution of the Jews would have certainly put the Pope in great personal danger, and it would not have saved the life of a single Jew'. Then: 'Hitler, like a trapped beast, would have reacted to any provocation with extreme violence. Kept at bay by the Allies, and their Unconditional Surrender demand, he was like a beast of prey pursued by hunters, capable of any hysterical excess or crime.' Thus, say some, if Weizsaecker distorted the Papal attitude, by emphasizing its innate anti-Bolshevism, he did it in good faith. Others say that this was a manipulation of history, and has been responsible for much of the calumny concerning the 'silences' of Pope Pius XII. All the same, on 29 December Tittmann saw the Pope, who did 'express concern at Soviet successes' which he feared would lead to the spread of Communism in the West. Tittmann had also reported to Washington that the 'consensus among diplomats' was that 'the

Communist danger was the Pope's chief preoccupation at the moment'.

The Pope actually told Weizsaecker that whatever the danger he would not consider leaving Rome, and in the previous October he had even said to Osborne that he would never go unless removed bodily and by force. Early in February there were new rumours that he was to be abducted, even that the Germans were secretly excavating a tunnel under the Vatican. On 9 February, in the Sistine Chapel, the Pope reiterated to the cardinals that he would 'yield only to violence'. He also said: 'We release you from any obligation to follow Our fate. Each one of you is free to do what you think is best.' The cardinals, we are told, 'threw themselves at his feet' and pledged their loyalty.

After the attempted assassination of Hitler in July 1944, Weizsaecker was named as a leader in the plot among Germans in Rome, but in his Memoirs he denied having been an accomplice. At Nuremberg he was sentenced to seven years' imprisonment. He died soon after, a broken man.

The men who acted as the Pope's liaison with the Germans were his own nephew, Prince Carlo Pacelli, and Padre Pancrazio Pfeiffer, of Bavarian peasant stock and head of the Salvatorian Order. Padre Pancrazio had played a crucial part at the time of the October round-up of Jews, and would again in connection with the events that led to the Ardeatine Caves massacre. He also has become a figure of controversy; he had the Pope's complete confidence and developed a very good relationship with the German authorities, particularly Kesselring's chief of staff Westphal, whom he would visit at Monte Soratte, finding him 'helpful, full of decorations, young-looking and *al corrente di tutto*, up to date about everything'. Pfeiffer's testimony about the 'silences' would have been vital, but he died in a traffic accident only a month after the liberation of Rome, without leaving documents behind him. We know now, for instance, that he was in touch with the Capuchin Padre Benedetto, and therefore no doubt with the Jewish organization Delasem.

There was yet another Bavarian who was close to the Pope, and this was a nun, Sister Pasqualina, who was his housekeeper and reputed to have ruled his personal life 'with a rod of iron'.

The Vatican had been officially informed that Kesselring had ordered that the immediate neighbourhood of the Papal domain at Castel Gandolfo should not be used for military purposes. All the same there were more Allied raids. The Pope had given orders for the whole of the palace to be thrown open to the refugees, including the Hall of the Swiss Guards, the Throne Room, the Napoleon Room, even his private apartments. The Barberini villa, part of the estate and built on the ruins of a villa of Domitian, had also been hit; the London Foreign Office was relieved to find that Baedeker had little to say about its merits. The Apostolic Delegate in Washington, Cicognani, protested about the raids. He was promised that there would be investigations, and was referred once more to Roosevelt's letter to the Pope in July 1943. It was perhaps little consolation to be told that this policy would be carried out as far as was 'humanly possible under conditions of modern warfare' and that German forces near extra-territorial properties would only be bombarded if the 'crucial military situation' required it.

Meanwhile bombs also fell on the periphery of Rome. On 13 February Mother Mary wrote: 'Last night British planes flew over the city. German planes rose to meet them, and there was a duel in the air. One big bomb fell in Via Mecenate, not far from the Colosseum, and hit a private nursing home, the Clinica Polidori, wrecking a large part of it and killing the surgeon who directed it.' 'A dreadful time,' wrote Mrs Whitaker. 'Bombardments and sirens constantly. We hear they are still digging out the dead at Castel Gandolfo. Could not sleep after hearing the mysterious aeroplane that flies low over Rome every night. People call it the Black Widow.' D'Arcy Osborne reported to London that thirty people had been killed and six hundred injured in Rome from air-raids on 15 February, and eighty killed and a hundred and fifty injured on 16 February. And Cicognani wrote to Roosevelt: 'With a grieving heart and with a cry that springs from the depths of his paternal soul the Sovereign Pontiff invokes Your Excellency's intervention that Rome may be spared from the horror and destruction of further aerial attacks.'

The fifteenth of February was the traumatic day on which the Monastery of Monte Cassino was destroyed from the air by the Allies. 'One of the major material tragedies of the war,' said Mother Mary. The news stunned the whole Roman Catholic world, and German propaganda made full use of this windfall. Rome and Vienna were spattered with posters showing how the destruction of the abbey was typical of the 'hatred felt by culturally primitive nations towards those with a higher and more ancient civilization'.

It was fortunate that some months earlier the Germans had persuaded the Abbot of Monte Cassino to let them remove the main treasures and books to safety, including material from the Keats-Shelley memorial house in Rome and several cases from Naples museums and the best bronzes from Pompeii. These had all gone to the German headquarters at Spoleto, but after some fuss were taken five months later to the Vatican. There was a grand parade of all the trucks in Piazza Venezia. 'It is difficult to understand the motives,' Mother Mary tersely said, 'after their wanton destruction of the great library at Naples [actually Nola]' – and this library had also contained the archives of the House of Anjou. Later it was discovered that eighteen cases of Pompeian bronzes and jewellery had not reached the Vatican, but had been sent to Germany as a birthday present for Goering.

As danger threatened the Monastery in the early days of February, the Germans had repeatedly claimed that the building was not occupied by their troops. Nevertheless, there was hardly an Allied soldier who was not convinced that it was being used as an observation post.

Paolisi

At last I set sail for Naples, and the sight of it was a sad disappointment. The docks were a shambles, with ships upside down and buildings bombed. The weather was icy, and even Vesuvius was in the clouds. Everywhere you saw beggars, and there were notices about VD dangers and lice causing typhus. It was very different to the *O sole mio* Italy that I had expected.

We were driven off in three-tonners to a village called Paolisi near Benevento. Here too were misery and ugliness: people starving and hating, wretched houses, trucks rumbling endlessly over cobbles, mud. In the chilly mess, where one drank yellow Strega, I heard of more friends who were casualties, both at Anzio and on the Gustav Line. No news of Nick, though. One night we saw more flashes than usual over the bare sugar-loaf hills, and were told that the Monastery at Monte Cassino had been bombed that day. We felt relieved and delighted.

Sometimes when the weather cleared we would climb those hills, where there were wild narcissi. Or else we hitchhiked to Pompeii, to the San Carlo opera house to see *Madam Butterfly*, or to the officers' mess in the Royal Palace where a crazy old peroxided tart sang *Ciri-biri-bim* and *Funiculì Funiculà*. All the same, I was quite glad when I was told that I was to be sent up to the front at Minturno. I was annoyed at not being able to join a battalion of my own regiment, the Rifle Brigade; instead I was to join the Green Howards in the 5th (Yorkshire) Division. Minturno, eighteen miles west of Cassino, had recently been captured and was at the mouth of the River Garigliano, into which the Liri and the continuation of the Rapido flowed. My Baedeker told me that there was a Roman theatre near the town and some interesting Giotto-type frescoes and mosaic work in the churches.

Cassino

The Abruzzi region of central Italy contains some of the wildest scenery in the country – chains of great jagged peaks forming part of the Apennines, some even covered with perpetual snow and intersected with valleys so remote that until recently women there were still wearing traditional dress. The larger valleys are very fertile, producing cereals, rice, vines, olives and almonds, and in the oak woods there are herds of pigs.

One of the main towns of the Abruzzi is L'Aquila, below the Gran Sasso where Mussolini had been imprisoned. The Emperor Frederick II had a dream of making this desolate place into the capital of Italy. Further south is Sulmona, a medieval town with Venetian-looking houses, and near what had been a main camp for Allied prisoners of war. Then comes the Maiella massif and the Adriatic, where by the end of January the Eighth Army had reached a stalemate.

The high mountains continue towards the south-west, but the peaks of Monte Cairo, 5,500 feet, and Monte Baghella, 4,800 feet, are actually in the region of Lazio. The smaller peak of Monte Cassino, at 1,700 feet, stands like the last bastion of the Apennines, crowned by its famous building, mother of all the Christian monasteries, and with a view of incredible majesty. Between the Abruzzi and the sea is the area known as La Ciociaria, with the Liri valley and Via Casilina, Route 6, running through the centre, separated from the Appian Way, Route 7, and towns like Terracina and Gaeta by another smaller but nevertheless formidable range, the Aurunci mountains. The Appian Way here is along the coast, but it weaves inland, through Cisterna and the Pontine Marshes, up to Velletri and Albano in the Alban Hills, and so to Rome.

The first major bombardment of Cassino had been on the morning of 10 September, causing havoc and slaughter among the civilians. People rushed screaming from one ruined street to another, searching for their children. Later that day German tanks and lorries appeared. It became obvious that the town was to be taken over as some sort of military headquarters, and this meant that before long there could be other bombings. The signal was clear, and in a panic the Cassinati fled – their sense of history was too vivid.

For two thousand years the site of Cassino had been a point of vital strategic importance, standing at the head of the Liri valley, only four to six miles wide. As proof there were the remains of a 'Colosseum', built by the ancient Romans for the entertainment of the garrison's soldiers. Mark Antony had chosen to have his villa nearby, to control the roads north and south. Carthaginians, Samnites, Lombards, Saracens, Spaniards and French had fought there. But it was the mountain above that made the place a byword for impregnability.

Originally a temple of Apollo had been built on Monte Cassino. The Monastery had been founded in 529; many times destroyed over the centuries, its walls were as thick as a fortress'. Over a thousand people now rushed up the twisting road known as the Serpentina to take refuge there. Others fled to outlying villages, or to caves in the mountains, joining British soldiers who had escaped from Sulmona and other refugees who had tried to get through the lines and failed. In one village there was an Australian woman who seemed totally unafraid of the Gestapo; her capacity for organization was legendary, and it was said that she had commandeered a number of large saucepans from a nearby ironmonger and had made the locals wear them as tin hats.

A future mayor of Cassino, Tancredi Grossi, took his family – his pregnant wife, two children and his mother, ill with diabetes – to San Michele, once a place famous for bandits. Now they had to face a new kind of brigandage. Farm animals were seized by the Germans, and food became very scarce. Houses and shops were being looted in Cassino itself, and men were being rounded up to work on the Gustav Line defences. Grossi and his brother did not dare show themselves and had a hiding place under the floor-boards for when the Gestapo arrived. Sixty men of all ages were seized and were made to unload trucks at Cassino railway station. Then the Allied bombers came, and after the raid it was found that only six had remained alive.

A German field hospital was established at San Michele, and the Grossis became friendly with the young doctor, an Austrian, a sensitive man, almost ascetic – a contrast to the drunken warrant officers who terrorized the farmers by bursting into houses and demanding wine and women. On the very night that the Germans were preparing to withdraw, Grossi's wife started her birth pangs. It was the doctor who saved her life, though the child died. He was off at dawn, and they never saw him again.

The first Allies to arrive at San Michele were Japanese-Americans – strong, dark-skinned, rather squat. Without even being asked they at once

began doling out biscuits, candy, chocolate and packets of Camels and
Lucky Strikes. Troubles were by no means over however, for the
Germans started to shell the village. The Americans were relieved by
French Algerian troops, who seized whatever animals were left and
behaved as if they were totally crazed by lust. Women and girls were
dragged out of their houses and raped. One widow was raped thirteen
times. Just in time some Americans intervened to protect Grossi's wife
and sister, Grossi himself having been held by Algerians at pistol-point.
One assumes that stories such as these prompted the Pope eventually to
ask the British Minister Osborne if coloured troops could be prevented
from going to Rome at the liberation.

A month after the Allies arrived at San Michele, on 15 February just
before 9.45 a.m., there was a rumbling, a roaring. Scores of heavy
bombers seemed to be converging on Cassino. Grossi could scarcely
believe what he now saw. The Monastery of St Benedict was being
pounded to extinction. It was the end of fourteen hundred years of
tradition, devotion, art and learning.

History will judge, so it has been said, whether the bombing of the
Monastery was justified, but a final verdict seems unlikely. Recrimina-
tions, contradictions and counter-accusations echo from decade to
decade. Was the Monastery destroyed because of those much quoted
words 'military necessity', or could it have been through malice,
Protestant pig-headedness, revenge or even stupidity? Few people now
would deny that, whatever the multiplicity of causes, apparently
conflicting, the result was a tragedy not only historically and spiritually,
but tactically and in terms of human life.

We start with Eisenhower. In November 1943 he reported to the War
Department that 'consistent with military necessity, all precautions to
safeguard works of art and monuments are being taken'. Then Clark.
Church property was to be protected, he said, adding: 'If military
necessity should so dictate, there should be no hesitation in taking
whatever action the situation warrants.' And indeed long before February
Monte Cassino was on the Allied list of buildings especially to be
safeguarded.

There was no hiding the fact that German troops were entrenched
further down the slopes of the mountain. As late as 14 February
Monsignor Montini handed a statement from Weizsaecker to Tittmann
and Osborne affirming that it was absolutely untrue that German defence
works were within the Monastery, and indeed that there were no troop
concentrations of any size 'within its immediate vicinity'. Everything
possible was being done, it was said, to prevent Monte Cassino becoming
a *Durchgangsplatz*, a traffic point. Even if the Chiefs of Staff would have

accepted Weizsaecker's word, the message reached them when it was already too late. Perhaps if the Vatican itself had been able to send an observer to Monte Cassino at an earlier stage, and had given a confirmation that the Germans' many assurances were true, then events would have turned out differently.

The present Abbot and monks of Monte Cassino appear to have by no means forgiven 15 February 1944. They now sell a booklet written by an American of German origin that squarely blames the British. Fred Majdalany's famous book on the battle of Cassino is described as glib, shallow, deplorable, the 'height of effrontery', an 'intricate juggling act', and an 'ecstatic defence of every mistake made by the commanders of the New Zealand Corps'. Freyberg is described as 'patently maladroit in military strategy', with an 'unwonted arrogance'. As for General Francis Tuker of the 4th Indian Division, he was intransigent and quixotic, and promulgated views that were ludicrous and ill-tempered, with an 'air of infallibility and ignorance'.

In 1964 Montini as Pope Paul VI consecrated the rebuilt Monastery. 'We do not wish now,' he said, 'to pass judgement on those who were the cause of this [destruction], but we cannot but deplore that civilized men dared make the tomb of St Benedict the target of pitiless violence.' He also added: 'Because of the duties of Our office under Pope Pius XII We are a well-informed witness to that which the Apostolic See did to spare this fortress, not of arms, but of the spirit, from the grave outrage of its destruction. That voice [of Pope Pius], supplicant and sovereign, unarmed defender of faith and civilization, was not heeded.'

Seven years after the event General Clark wrote in emphatic terms: 'I say the bombing . . . was a mistake, and I say it with full knowledge of the controversy that has ranged round this episode.' He said there was no evidence that the Germans were using the Monastery for military purposes. He had been told that Alexander had decided that the Monastery should be bombed if Freyberg considered it a military necessity. As Freyberg had thereupon said it was a military necessity, Clark as the Army commander had to give the authorization for the bombing. 'I was never able to discover on what he [Freyberg] based his opinion.'

And so, said Majdalany, 'Clark gave the order for the bombing which he afterwards so bitterly repudiated.' Clark was also accused in the British press of trying to 'pass on the blame to anybody else' because he was a Roman Catholic. Cassandra of the *Daily Mirror* remembered seeing German graves that had been tended by the monks just outside the walls. And Churchill said, in any case 'the enemy fortifications were hardly separate from the building itself.'

Lieutenant Peter Royle of the Royal Artillery arrived at Cassino early in February. What he wrote in his diary summed up many people's fears: 'One trained gunnery officer with binoculars could control nearly the whole battlefield by directing shell and mortar fire within a matter of seconds.' On 10 February the Battalion Commander of the 133rd US Infantry Regiment had said that he had seen a telescope at a window on the east face, as well as enemy moving around the base of the building on the north side. This was relayed back to the Chiefs of Staff by General Wilson, who also said that a tank had been noticed dug in to cover the approaches to the Monastery. On 9 February an Italian civilian reported that there were thirty machine-guns and approximately eighty soldiers in the building.

On 13 February General Ira C. Eaker, the US head of the Mediterranean Air Command, who would be in charge of the bombing, had flown with General Devers only two hundred feet above the Monastery. They had reported seeing not only a military radio mast but enemy soldiers moving in and out.

Misapprehensions or not, these facts helped to influence the final decision. Eaker's report must have been known to the other American generals, nearly all of whom were against the bombing, and presumably to Clark. Thirty-five years later there are still those who are convinced that the Germans could not avoid utilizing the Monastery, and they include Harold Macmillan, and many ex-combatants, American and British, of high and low degree.

Kesselring was outraged by the suggestion that the Monastery had to be bombed because his troops were inside it. The thing was a 'baseless invention'. No Germans had been in there since the 'removal of the cultural treasures'. Since Flying Fortresses had been used, he mainly blamed the Americans. 'As the commander-in-chief I therefore declare: United States soldiery, devoid of all culture, have, in powerless rage, senselessly destroyed one of Italy's most treasured edifices and have murdered Italian civilian refugees – men, women and children – with their bombs and artillery fire. Thus it has been proved that Anglo-Saxon and Bolshevik warfare has only one aim: to destroy the venerable proofs of European culture. I feel deep contempt for the cynical mendacity and the hypocritical sentiments by which the Anglo-Saxon command tried to shift the responsibility on to my shoulders and on to my soldiers.' General Frido von Senger und Etterlin, the XIV Panzer Corps commander and therefore Freyberg's opposite number, was aghast too. An outstanding general, despite – according to photographs – his unmilitary headgear, and a cultivated man, he was a Catholic from Bavaria and his later claim to have been anti-Nazi seems to have been justified – indeed he had been a Rhodes scholar at Oxford before the First War. He was always to insist that none of his men had ventured inside, and there is documentary proof that both he and Kesselring gave the appropriate orders for this. Indeed, the Germans often enough proclaimed to the world at large that the Monastery was unoccupied. Yet to some of those who fought against them in 1944 even that is not enough.

Those who lash at the Allies, particularly at the British, for the decision to bomb seem unable to appreciate that not a single pronouncement, whether by Hitler and Goering, or by Kesselring or Senger, could be trusted. And of course vice versa. War propaganda is a dirty business.

Maybe only Protestants would have been ignoble enough to dismiss the 'solemn and firm' declaration made by the eighty-two-year-old Abbot after his escape from the ruins. After all, it was argued in London, the declaration had been drafted by the Germans, and he was in a state of shock and distress. Could it have been possible, ventured a Foreign Office official, that the Abbot would not necessarily have been aware of who was actually in that large and rambling building, especially as in the last weeks he was only left with a handful of monks and brothers, and a deaf and dumb servant?

Clark has written a much quoted description of the fighting at Cassino. He called it the 'most gruelling, the most harassing, and in one aspect the most tragic phase of the war in Italy', the one aspect, of course, being the destruction of the Monastery. 'When I think back,' he continued, 'on the weeks and finally months of slaving struggle, the biting cold, the torrents of rain and snow, the lakes of mud that sucked down machines and men, and most of all the deeply dug fortifications in which the Germans waited for us in the hills, it seems to me that no soldiers in history were ever given a more difficult assignment than the Fifth Army that winter.' The defence works dug by the Germans were truly extraordinary, made of reinforced steel and concrete. 'We found later that during one of our most intense bombing and artillery attacks ... a group of German officers sat in an underground bunker playing cards. They didn't move from the table throughout the attack.' Given that the Germans had decided to build a defensive line a hundred miles south of Rome, Cassino and its mountain inescapably became its hub, and the Monastery was automatically put in danger. How much, it has often been asked, does that absolve them from blame? The Monastery has been likened to a tray of china at a fairground stall for bowling down coconuts. Vietinghoff has said that it was impossible to withdraw from the Monte Cassino feature; not only would it mean loss of important observation posts, but the Anglo-Americans would certainly not bother about any sort of agreement at the decisive moment and would without scruple place themselves in occupation.

D'Arcy Osborne even put up a theory that the Germans could have spread the rumour that the Monastery was being used for military purposes, in order to induce the Allies to bomb the place and give the Germans a fine propaganda weapon.

There had been plenty of advance 'rhubarb', as Clark called it, in the world's press about the possibility of Monte Cassino being destroyed. In early February there had been a debate in the House of Lords on the whole subject of bombing historic monuments, also in connection with the Allied saturation bombing of Germany. In Britain it was taken virtually for granted that the Monastery was occupied, and as the dance of death in Central Italy became ever more terrible, and as the slaughter on both sides mounted, so questions of morality and the preservation of monuments were in danger of being forgotten.

The Archbishop of Canterbury reminded the House of the Italian towns that lay ahead and were also in danger: Assisi, Siena, Florence, Padua, Perugia, Pisa, Ravenna, Venice. 'Think of Rome itself. Rome doesn't belong to Italy; it belongs to the world. It does not belong to any particular time ...' Lord Latham replied: 'I do not wish to see Europe stocked with cultural monuments to be venerated by mankind in chains and on its knees ... The people of this country will not submit to their boys being sacrificed – even one of them sacrificed – unnecessarily to save whatever building it may be.' Lord Samuel spoke of the Germans' reputation as a highly cultured nation. 'But the German army has a malignity which is terrible,' and he cited the deliberate burning of the 866 boxes of archives at Nola and the University of Naples – at the University a sailor had been tied to a gate and burnt to death, the fire engines prevented from reaching the building, and the bookshelves soaked in petrol.

Harold Nicolson announced that he would rather his son should die than let the Monastery be destroyed. 'Works of art are irreplaceable. Human lives are replaceable.' He did, however, add, 'If the war could really be shortened by destroying Perugia, then I might agree to it.' He did not know that his son Nigel was at Cassino at the time.

In spite of Lord Samuel's view of the German Army the world owes a huge debt of gratitude to Colonel Julius Schlegel of the Hermann Goering Panzers. For it was he who in October 1943 had persuaded Abbot Diamare to let the treasures, including the reliquary of St Benedict and the famous library, be removed to safety. If the Allies remembered Nola, the so-called Baedeker raids on Bath and elsewhere, and Coventry Cathedral, Schlegel had been 'tortured' by a 'small inner voice' that reminded him of the basilica of San Lorenzo in Rome and many shattered Sicilian towns and villages. It was he too who, on his own initiative and using trucks that could ill be spared, got the Abbot to allow the majority of the monks and civilian refugees to be evacuated. As far as the latter were concerned, there was another reason. Sanitary arrangements being utterly inadequate, the refugees' habits had already caused a threat of typhoid.

We turn now to those who were actually doing the fighting in the 'torrents of rain and snow'. Who saw the guts of their comrades scattered on that same snow and mud. Who were expecting to die just like that, at any moment. Who remembered their families in Marysville, Ohio, in Lostwithiel, Cornwall, in Waikari, South Island New Zealand, in Birsilpur, Rajputana. And for that matter in Greifenburg, Pomerania. And who wanted to see their families again. An historian or thesis-writer who has not experienced what it is like to be told, under the equivalent of a sentence of death, that you are about to go on a patrol across seemingly impossible country, which could at best result in a bullet through your face or groin, cannot possibly appreciate the feelings of the ordinary soldier, unaware moreover of disagreements, jealousies and strain at top level, trusting that there is sanity in the things he has been asked to do, and trying to believe that what seems like ghastly confusion does really have a purpose behind it. If most of the American top brass agreed with Clark about the Monastery not being occupied, that feeling did not permeate into the lower ranks. Harold Bond, a lieutenant in the Texan Division, the 36th Infantry, has written: 'All of us were convinced that the abbey was a German strongpoint, and that it was being used by them for the excellent observation it gave of all our positions.' And then: 'The tired infantrymen, fighting for their lives near its slopes, were to cry for joy as bomb after bomb crumbled it into dust.'

Sergeant Evans of the 2nd Battalion of the London Irish was in the plain below. 'It just had to be bombed. Oh, it was malignant. It was evil somehow. I don't know how a monastery can be evil, but it was looking at you. It was all-devouring if you like – a sun-bleached colour, grim. It had a terrible hold on us soldiers. I don't think I was convinced that the Germans were *firing* from there, but it was such a wonderful observation post. We thought it had to be destroyed. We just didn't know how the place could be taken otherwise. I am sure what I thought was shared by ninety per cent of the lads in our division.' Sergeant Jenkins of the same regiment earlier on had been in the 1st Battalion's Intelligence on Monte Camino. 'I had a pair of captured German periscope binoculars. You could see the Germans walking around the base of the building, and the road coming down. You could see small trucks. You couldn't see them going into the monastery because you couldn't see any exits or entrances.'

Lieutenant Bruce Foster of the 60th Rifles one morning had been to call on a Guards battalion, camped in a dreary olive grove. 'Since you ask me what I felt about the Monastery, I'll ask *you* something. Can you imagine what is it like to see a person's head explode in a great splash of grey brains and red hair, and have the blood and muck all over you, in your mouth, eyes, ears? And can you imagine what it is like when that head belonged to your sister's fiancé? I *knew* why it happened, I was positive, it was because some bloody fucking Jerry was up there in that fucking bloody Monastery directing the fire that killed Dickie, and I know that still; to hell with all those Pontius Pilates who pretend they were so bloody innocent and had nothing to do with the bombing. Christ, Dickie was the finest, most upright man you or I would ever meet. I am just glad that he died quickly, which is more than a lot of other poor fuckers did up there. It drove me mad to see those chaps at HQ poring over coloured maps and never dreaming of going up to the front line to see what conditions were really like.'

On 5 February, following a bombardment, some forty women rushed to the Monastery from caves and shacks where they had been hiding. They battered on the doors screaming to be let in. Then they were followed by several other terror-stricken civilians. The population of the Monastery now consisted of perhaps eight hundred persons, including the six monks. One man was killed by a stray round, and several people were wounded by shrapnel. Water and food were minimal. The dark, freezing cellars stank of urine, diarrhoea and unwashed clothes. The newcomers' panic never abated. Whenever there was an explosion they shrieked and wailed and rushed frantically from room to room. Typhoid broke out, and some people died, including one of the monks, Dom Eusebio, who had been responsible for caring for the sick. It was a scene for Goya.

On the afternoon of 14 February a pamphlet was dropped signed 'Fifth Army', and addressed to *Amici italiani*, Italian friends. It had been decided, with regret, to attack the Sacred Precincts. '*Il nostro avvertimento è urgente: lasciate il Monastero. Andatevene subito.* Our warning is urgent: leave the Monastery. Abandon it at once.' The effect was a stampede to the Abbot. Eventually a message was sent to a German post, and a lieutenant appeared in the small hours. Here again there has been a divergence in accounts. The monks' booklet simply says that the battle that was raging prevented immediate departure, and that it was agreed that everyone should leave at 5 a.m. on the 16th. The Germans have said that the Abbot had been given 'complete liberty of action' about when to leave and that he chose to delay until the night of 15/16 February, perhaps underestimating the danger and fearing daylight. He had been forbidden by the lieutenant's commander, Major Schmidt, to walk to the Allied lines, as this would mean giving away the German positions, but had been recommended to take a path north to Piedimonte, being less exposed to shelling.

Later Abbot Diamare said publicly that he thought the Allies must have deliberately dropped their leaflets too late in order that there would be no chance of notifying the German command or allowing his people to escape. The warning was indeed dreadfully short, for the bombing came at 9.45 a.m. the next morning. From a military point of view the Allied aim had been to give the Germans as little time as possible to move out their equipment, assumed to be within the Monastery and in the immediate neighbourhood.

Alexander never flinched from taking the ultimate responsibility for the fatal decision. 'Every commander is a lonely figure,' Macmillan said of him, and Alexander said: 'A commander, if faced by the choice between risking a single soldier's life and destroying a work of art, even a religious symbol, can only make one decision.' He used to say to Macmillan, 'I am not a Wellington but a Marlborough,' by which he meant he had to be a diplomat. Under his command were Americans, French, New Zealanders, Canadians, Indians, Poles, Italians and, later, Brazilians. He also had to face the fact that Freyberg was answerable direct to the New Zealand government. There was another aspect in the matter of giving orders. In simple terms it was this: by 1944 the British were pensioners of American lend-lease and rapidly becoming the juniors in the alliance, but in the Mediterranean they had to keep up the pretence of being the masters.

The whole drama of the decision has to be set against the worsening situation at Anzio, where another Dunkirk was a real possibility, and where there was a failure of confidence in General Lucas. Clark had to be at the Beachhead. His deputy at Cassino was General Alfred Gruenther. So discussions with Clark had mainly to be by radio or, on his flying visits to the main front, by telephone. It was ironic that a major attack had now to be made at Cassino to relieve Anzio, when Anzio had been conceived as a means of breaking the deadlock in the South.

On 12 February Freyberg told Gruenther that he wanted the Monastery bombed the next day. 'The division commander who is making the attack feels that it is an essential target and I thoroughly agree with him.'

These are the key words which for some have made General Tuker into a scapegoat.

Gruenther told Alexander's chief of staff, General Sir John Harding – who himself thought the Monastery was occupied – that Clark did not consider that bombing it was a military necessity. 'He believes it will endanger the lives of many civilian refugees in the building, and that a bombing will not destroy its value as a fortification of the enemy. In fact, General Clark feels that the bombing will probably enhance its value.' To which Harding replied: 'General Alexander has made his position quite clear on this point. He regrets very much that the Monastery should be destroyed, but he sees no other choice.' The author of the Monte Cassino booklet, therefore, comes to the 'painful' conclusion that 'those British officers wanted to show their American counterparts how to conduct a war properly'.

Clark says now that he asked Alexander for a written order to bomb the Monastery, and that this was received. However the document has unfortunately been lost.

Two points about General Tuker are often unfairly ignored by writers, including the author of the monks' booklet, and his views therefore deserve to be examined in some detail. The first is that he went into hospital on 4 February and did not return to command his Division. The second is that he did not even want the Monastery to be attacked, and could possibly have prevented it if he had been well. 'I went through hell on earth during the early days urging desperately that no attack on Monte Cassino should be contemplated. I could never understand why the US Fifth Army decided to batter its head again and again against this most powerful position, held by some of the finest troops in the German Army in heavily wired and mined and fixed entrenchments.'

The US 34th and 36th were the Divisions that were doing the battering. They were on the high ground to the north-east of the Monastery. How they even managed to establish themselves there, in such bleak weather and supplied by mules that took seven hours to reach them, is almost impossible to imagine. The icy, windswept ridge known as Snakeshead, fifteen hundred yards from their goal, was the main feature they held, but it was also essential to capture Albaneta Farm and Point 593, which the Germans and Italians aptly called Calvary.

On arrival it became clear to 'Gertie' Tuker that before long the New Zealand Corps, including 4th Indian Division, would have to take over from the Americans. He was an expert on mountain warfare, having fought on the North-West Frontier; and indeed he was to write standard books on military strategy. And for good measure he was an artist and poet. His plan was to 'turn' Monte Cassino by wide flank movements. He went to see General Juin, whom he regarded as probably the finest tactical commander in Italy. 'We were in perfect agreement that the best way to exert the pressure was to follow up his recent success and pass through well to the North.' The next move would be to force a river crossing to the south of Cassino town and 'there establish a strong bridgehead, but necessarily more than that'. He discussed the 'fearsome possibility' of being made to attack Monte Cassino with Juin. 'We had decided to oppose it strongly and point out that if anybody had to attack it directly, then it must be under tremendous air bombardment.'

This did not mean that Juin wanted the Monastery to be destroyed. Clark in his diary records that on 14 February Juin came to see him to try to prevent the bombing. By then the decision was irrevocable. And Tuker himself said: 'No civilized human being would have wanted it to have happened.' When Tuker was struck down by an old ailment and sent to hospital at Caserta, for morale's sake the news was kept from the Division, which had to be put under the command of one of his subordinates, Brigadier Harry Dimoline. Meanwhile, the possibility looked like becoming a reality. As Freyberg said afterwards: 'The whole trouble of Cassino was Tuker being taken ill so suddenly. If he had been there he would have stood up to Mark Clark and argued him out of the direct attack.' Until this was repeated to Tuker he had no idea how heavily Freyberg leaned on him. Tuker considered Freyberg to be 'as brave as a lion' but 'no planner of battles and a niggler in action'. He also thought Alexander was 'indolent' and gave in too easily.

Tuker went on arguing his views by letter. He was amazed to learn that nobody had precise details about the Monastery's construction. Lying in hospital, he sent a subaltern to Naples, and thus obtained a book of 1879 which revealed that the walls were massively thick, at least fifteen feet. To send flesh and blood against that would be plain murder, more than the planners realized. 'If we were to be forced to attack directly, then it would have to be a matter of obliterating the *whole* Monte Cassino feature with bombs day after day and following the bombs with artillery, and then shoving the infantry up at dusk on the heels of the shelling, leaving them the whole night to do the job.' It would be necessary to beat the Germans into complete 'imbecility', and this could only be done by blockbuster bombs. Whether the Monastery was occupied or not, it was certain – he said – that the last remnants of the garrison on the mountain would use it as a keep. This alone made it essential to demolish the building.

The 34th and 36th had lost eighty per cent of their effective strength by the time the 4th Indian relieved them. The last attack they made was on 11 February, when violent rain and snow reduced visibility to a few yards. The Germans had thrown them back from the features Point 593 and Albaneta again and again. So now it was up to the 4th Indian, for Clark did not want any flank movements, but the direct attack.

Tuker wrote: 'I had tried three or four times to get back to my HQ, but each time I collapsed ... On 12 February I managed it and sent for Freyberg ... I stood at my HQ on Monte Trocchio with Freyberg, looking straight at Monte Cassino. I again argued the business ... I reiterated all my reasons. He, as was rather usual with Freyberg when he really did not understand what one was talking about, remained quite silent but did appear to be agreeing. At the end of my talk, which had to be a short one as I was pretty feeble, I pointed at Monte Cassino and said to him plainly and emphatically: "Whatever you do, Freyberg, don't compromise!" ' And Tuker said later: 'I feel sorry for Freyberg, but he should never have been put in command of a corps. He had not the tactical understanding and certainly not the experience in the mountains . . . Most Germans put the blame of the destruction of the Monastery upon the British. The blame is fair and square on the Germans, who knew full well that if they enclosed the Monastery hill within their defences, as they did quite deliberately, then the Monastery was bound to be destroyed if a direct attack was delivered upon the hill. If they did not wish to offer up the Monastery as a sacrifice, then they should never have included it in their defences. They make a fine case out of all this for their own culture and kindness, but I would rather they should have sacrificed the Monastery than that they should have had gas chambers . . .'

'Gas chambers' are an obvious retort in this controversy. Just how much fighting German generals knew about such things, or shut their eyes to them, is an issue on its own. To be fair, the argument is only really relevant as a counterblast to Goebbels' exultant propaganda after the bombing. Senger, in his autobiography, does say: 'Sometimes my friends would discuss the oppression of the Jews. Although we had no precise information, it was common talk that evil things were afoot. We felt ashamed at these developments . . .' He also says that Vietinghoff was 'in harmony' with his views, not only about Jews, but about Hitler and Nazism, and about the need for 'getting rid of the regime'.

The air attack had to be delayed two days, because of the weather and because of difficulties over relieving the 34th and 36th. Below Point 593 fifty of the remaining two hundred Americans were so exhausted and cold that they had to be carried off by stretcher.

It was the first time that heavy bombers had been used in such close support of infantry, and the first time that bomber groups from Great Britain had struck an Italian target. They came over in waves and nearly six hundred tons of explosive were dropped. But it was still by no means the pounding to 'imbecility' that Tuker had recommended, and the great walls on the west were hardly demolished. 'The air attack should have been ten or twenty times as heavy.' Worse, the whole thing had been hustled along so that there had been no time for the 4th Indians to make a proper reconnaissance, and the main infantry attack did not go in immediately but three days later.

So Freyberg, to Tuker, had compromised. Clark said in his book that if it had been an American under his command he would not have allowed the bombing at all – and this presumably in spite of Alexander's order.

On the day of the bombing the 4/16 Punjabis were on a slope near Snakeshead Ridge that looked straight across to the Monastery. 'Almost within touching distance,' said an officer. The 1st Royal Sussex, also part of the 4th Indian Division, was now below Point 593, surmounted by a small fort, built no doubt when the Saracens threatened the shrine of St Benedict; their men lay prone in shallow scrapings behind boulders and scrub – in daylight to raise one's head would have meant instant death by sniper or spandau fire.

At 9.30 on the 15th Brigadier Lovett, on Snakeshead, heard a rumbling in the sky. 'At that moment I was called on the blower and was told that the bombers would be over in fifteen minutes. I started to blow up myself but even as I spoke the roar drowned my voice as the first shower of eggs came down.'

There had been no warning whatsoever. One of the Punjabi companies was just three hundred yards off the target. There were some twenty-five casualties.

What seemed like an atrocious lack of liaison between air and ground forces was, in fact, partly due to intense pressure on Freyberg to attack before the big German counter-offensive at Anzio, which indeed started the next day. Rain was also imminent. The plan of Tuker's deputy, Brigadier Dimoline, had been to capture Point 593 on the night of the 15th, and put in his main attack on the Monastery on the night of the 17th. He insisted that it was physically impossible to advance his timing, which would have been in line with Tuker's recommendation.

The 'hustle' about Anzio was not Freyberg's fault. And Tuker was told later that one reason for Clark refusing his idea about a turning operation to the north was a dearth of essential animal transport. With strongpoints already secured so close to Monte Cassino and at such cost it seemed folly not to make the final, supreme effort.

So Freyberg the lionheart, inspiring leader of men, failed for precisely the opposite reasons to his counterpart at Anzio, Lucas.

A lieutenant in the Royal Sussex had visited the Monastery before the war. 'I remembered the marvellous sense of peace, the sublime view from the Loggia del Paradiso, the kindness of a dear old Benedictine monk in his black robes who showed me round the basilica – such richness, such marble, I'd seen nothing like it, not even at St Peter's. But it was the feeling of holiness, of reverence, that was quite overwhelming.'

The basilica was the first to be destroyed; the frescoes of Luca Giordano, the seventeenth-century choir stalls, the marvellous baroque organ, the high altar were gone. The multi-coloured marbles were pulverized. But miraculously the tombs of St Benedict and his twin sister St Scolastica in the vault below were unharmed. In the afternoon the aged Abbot came into the open. 'The palm trees which had for so long graced the courtyard had been reduced to pitiful stumps. The central courtyard, attributed to Bramante, had been completely shattered, its beautiful pillars and the superb Loggia had collapsed ... On all sides a picture of nothing but ghastly destruction, a picture that proclaimed more eloquently then any words the futility of war.' Moanings, cries of agony could be heard under the rubble. Some people had rushed down the mountainside during the attack, only to be killed by blast and shrapnel. On 17 February a sad little group of survivors left the Monastery, headed by the Abbot carrying a large wooden crucifix. German paratroopers and gunners in their trenches removed their helmets as they watched it pass. A woman who had lost both feet had to be left to die on the way. One lay brother, aged eighty, Carlomanno Pelagalli, went back and returned to end his life in a building that had been his home for fifty years.

Vatican documents released in the summer of 1980 include an account by Monsignor Domenico Tardini – whose rank was the equivalent of Under-Secretary of State – of his meeting on 20 February with Abbot Diamare and his secretary Dom Martino Matronola, to become Abbot of Monte Cassino in 1977. This important account gives some new slants to the controversy. The Abbot told Tardini that the Monastery had already been badly damaged even before mid-January, often by shells falling short; he did not blame either side. He confirmed that there had never been any German soldiers, artillery, machine-gun nests or observation posts within the Monastery. Earlier on some Germans had come in for confession. In January some German officers told the Abbot that it had been agreed with the Vatican that there should be a neutral zone, without any military objectives, for three hundred metres from the walls (no such agreement has been found in the Vatican archives).

It was difficult, said the Abbot, to determine those three hundred metres, given the steepness of the mountain. At any rate they were not respected, and gradually the military objectives were brought closer, until they reached the outskirts of the Monastery. What were those military objectives? The details were mostly given to the Monsignor by Dom Martino. Two tanks – or perhaps they were self-propelled guns – moved round the Monastery at night, firing. Since the Allies were on the heights to the north of the Monastery, and had actually once got within a hundred metres of the walls, it was easy for the Germans to observe them and hit back accurately. Immediately below the Monastery there was an observation post, which at night would flash signals to German batteries pinpointing Allied positions. There was also a cave underneath the Monastery itself, and this was used for storing ammunition. The Abbot protested that these military installations could endanger the Monastery; he received vague promises, but nothing was done.

On 14 February the leaflets were shown to the Abbot. German officers on being told either paid little attention to the threat of bombardment or procrastinated. Eventually, early on the 15th, they said that under a kind of truce (Tardini wrote: 'I think they added, under the auspices of the Holy Father') at 5 a.m. on the 16th everyone in the Monastery could be evacuated. Instead the bombardment came at 9.40 a.m. on the 15th, destroying the Monastery completely and burying many people in a shelter. (A Vatican note says that most of these people were saved, but those who fled in panic were killed.) The usual estimate is that three hundred died.

The Abbot on leaving was given every kindness by the Germans, and was told that the Pope would like to see him in the Vatican. Having been received by the German commander (Senger), he was driven to Rome, but on the outskirts the car was suddenly diverted. The Abbot thought the Pope wanted to see him immediately, but after a long journey found himself at a radio station, and here – exhausted physically and mentally – he was made to speak (the Abbot wept in front of Tardini as he spoke and added that what he had said about there being no German soldiers or military objectives within the Monastery was the truth). Then, when this was over, he was taken to the ambassador Weizsaecker, who offered him a prepared document to sign. The Abbot did not want to sign this before examining it *con calma*. Weizsaecker more or less insisted that he must sign at once. Other *signori* were introduced to the Abbot; they were reporters. Then, said the Abbot, 'I lost patience, I did not want to say anything, and sent everybody *a quel paese* [literally, to hell].' After this the Germans accompanied him to the Benedictine monastery of San Anselmo on the Aventine.

Senger in his memoirs blamed Ribbentrop for this interrogation. He said that the Abbot spent the first night at his headquarters, where he had already been interviewed by a radio reporter. When the Abbot was taken to the radio station he was not even given a meal. Senger protested to Kesselring, who assured him he had nothing to do with such *gaucherie*. Goebbels' propaganda machine nevertheless made full use of such a splendid windfall: 'In the senseless lust of destruction is mirrored the whole fury of the British–US Command, which first announced the capture of Rome by Christmas with great verbosity and then discovered that the road to Rome is just as far as to Tipperary ... Thus it has been decided by Jews and pro-Bolsheviks in Moscow, London and Washington. It is one of the grotesque manifestations of history that

British–US youth risks its life to carry out the Jewish desire to destroy.'

John Miller, the escaped British prisoner hiding in Rome with La Nonna, met a survivor from Monte Cassino. She was so thin that she reminded him of a starving camel. For three weeks, she said, she had eaten nothing but grass. She also swore that she had never seen a single German within the precincts.

The defence of the area to the north-west of Monte Cassino was under the command of the remarkable General Baade of the 90th Panzer Grenadiers – a wealthy Brandenburg landowner, lover of fine brandy, reader of Aristotle and accustomed to wear a kilt over his riding breeches, with a large pistol instead of a sporran. It was from his bunker that General Senger saw the bombing come down. 'Both of us were at a loss to know what this appalling spectacle signified.' To most German soldiers it looked like some vicious act of revenge or disillusionment, as the bombs thudded down, sending up huge angry clouds and spirals of smoke and dust, spurting flames and blackness, like a volcano erupting.

Baade had been of the opinion that the Allies' leaflets were a bluff. He had a reputation for humanity, but according to some Italian survivors they were kept there in the Monastery under pain of being shot, and the gates were barred.

The youths of the crack 1st Parachute Division, heroes of Crete, were said later to have been 'hanging on by their eyebrows' on the mountain-side overlooking Via Casilina. If the Allies had concentrated on blasting them instead of the Monastery, the result – some thought – might have been a break-through. After the Monastery's destruction, of course, the Germans had no need for scruples about moving into the ruins. Having done so, almost immediately they were subjected to yet another major raid by two hundred Allied bombers.

A highly charged German novel by Sven Hassel describes the reaction of a group of paratroopers, as fierce fires now broke out: 'The holy mountain quivered like a dying bull in the ring ... Lance-Corporal Brans got shell shock. He seized his trumpet and started playing jazz. Then he got it into his head that he ought to blow us all up. Tiny managed to wrest the T-mine from him and flung it into the yard ... A paratrooper, who had both legs crushed by falling masonry, lay in a pool of blood. "Shoot me, shoot me! Oh God, let me die!" ... Medical Orderly Glaeser bent over the shrieking man, jabbed the morphine syringe through his uniform and emptied it into his pain-racked body. "That's all I can do for you, chum. If you'd been a horse, we'd have shot you. God is merciful." Glaeser spat viciously at a crucifix.'

The bombing continued by day, and the artillery by night. In forty-eight hours the Royal Sussex lost twelve out of fifteen officers, 162 out of 313 men. Their ordeal on that icy lunar purgatory of a ridge, lit by explosions and with bullets ripping down, can only be guessed at – so few, let alone novelists, are left to tell the story, or wish to remember it. Grenades ran out, because mules carrying them had been blown up by shells on the way. Down below the guns roared in a colossal symphony. 'The night was pricked with belching flames,' wrote the 4th Indian's historian. 'Across the valley stabs of light against the mountainside showed where the shells struck. Sudden glares and steady fires marked exploding dumps and burning houses. The enemy began to loop white flares on to the lower slopes of Monte Cassino. Lines of tracer cut the sky. Then came the distant staccato crackle of small-arms fire as the infantry went in. The Rapido valley filled with smoke, soft as ermine under the moon. On the soar of every flame we strained our eyes, praying that each mounting light would prove to be the success signal and that our men had won home.'

The end for the Sussex came through a coincidence. The Germans sent up three green Very lights, which was the Sussex's signal for withdrawal.

The big attack went in. The 6th Rajputana Rifles were flung against Point 593, to be devastated by crossfire. They lost 193 personnel in casualties. Months later the bodies of a number of their men were found on the summit. The 2nd Gurkhas reached a ridge only three hundred yards from the rear walls of the Monastery, to be faced by German machine-guns fifty yards apart. They plunged into thick briars, tearing them and tripping them, and found them to be riddled with anti-personnel mines. Their colonel fell, shot through the stomach. The little men, although nearly all wounded, fought on and closed with the Germans, slashing at them with kukri knives. Stretcher-bearer Sherbahadur Thapa made sixteen trips through the deadly scrub before he was killed. A wounded signaller crawled back to say that some men had reached the Monastery. None of the Gurkhas who were taken prisoner was heard of again.

At dawn on the 19th it was realized that the position was hopeless, and they too were withdrawn.

Meanwhile, the Maoris of the 2nd New Zealand Division, commanded by General Kippenberger, attacked to the south of Cassino town. Their objective was the railway station, but they came up against minefields, barbed wire and flooding. Nevertheless, they did reach the station, only to find that in daylight they were in full view of tanks and guns stationed at each bend of the Serpentina road above. A massive smoke-screen was put up, but the Kiwi casualties were too great, and they had to retreat back over the Rapido.

Cassino station was another crucial point for the whole Gustav Line.

The New Zealanders did not realize how badly mauled were Baade's Grenadiers facing them. Indeed the Germans had not expected their counter-attack to succeed, as an intercepted telephone conversation between Vietinghoff and Kesselring testifies: *Vietinghoff*: 'We have succeeded after hard fighting in taking Cassino station.' *Kesselring*: 'Heartiest congratulations.' *Vietinghoff*: 'I didn't think we would do it.' *Kesselring*: 'Neither did I.'

Now the winter weather descended once more in earnest and further offensive operations were impossible. French troops, including Moroccans, so greatly feared by the Germans, and an Italian combat team took over some of the difficult country on the Fifth Army's north-eastern boundary. In spite of the hideous conditions, the Italians were glad of this further chance of proving themselves, and their spirit was high.

It was on 24 February that news came that Freyberg's son was missing at Anzio.

On 2 March there was this laconic entry in Kippenberger's diary: 'Corps Conference at 1400 hours. Went with Frank Massey up Monte Trocchio afterwards and, coming down, stepped on a mine and one foot blown off, the other mangled and thumb ripped up. Frank slightly hurt. Picked up by very plucky part of 23rd and amputation done at ADS by Kennedy Elliott. Saw General [Freyberg] and [Brigadier] Jim Burrows before operation.'

Second Lieutenant Niranjin Singh was intelligence officer with the 2nd Punjab Regiment at Ortona. When he heard that his close friend in the 6th Rajputanas had been killed near Monte Cassino, he at once obtained leave to come across. He had his friend cremated on the night of his arrival.

Then he took the long track up to Snakeshead. From there he actually crawled into the Monastery ruins. German rations and equipment were strewn about everywhere. On the way he saw many bayoneted bodies, evidence of hand-to-hand fighting. Then, in the light of explosions, he saw things glistening in the ruins. Gold! It was everywhere. He could not believe his luck and filled his pockets and pouches with as much as he could. Only on his return did he find that the gold was simply gilded plaster – he had been standing in the remains of the basilica, and what he had found were remnants of baroque work from the ceiling.

As daylight approached, Niranjin Singh could see the German gun positions. He was horrified. There were so many of them, blasted into the rock and well camouflaged. He crawled away and was joined by another friend from the 6th Rajputs, who had been attempting to hack out a trench below Point 593. Suddenly they came upon a German trench, and there inside was a German soldier bent over with his head in his hands.

The Rajput took up his pick and gave a great swing. The pick went right through the German's body.

Niranjin Singh had a great admiration for German intelligence. Italian girls were often used as spies, and would cross the lines as 'refugees'. He once saw a girl having tea with his colonel, who said that he had found her crying in the village. The next day she had disappeared. It happened that the Punjabis were able to advance shortly afterwards, and there was the girl once more in a newly captured village. Sometimes these spies were shot – men usually, not the girls.

It was on that occasion that he had to requisition a house. The woman inside, having been primed by German propaganda, was terrified at the sight of this great turbaned man with the curled moustache. '*Mangiare bambini?* Do you eat children?' she quavered in childish Italian. '*No, mangio soltanto uomini.* No, I only eat grown-ups.'

London and Washington were extremely alarmed by the repercussions over the Monte Cassino bombing. On 2 March Victor Cavendish-Bentinck of the Foreign Office scribbled on a memo that 'we had better keep quiet'. The evidence on which the order to bomb was given was 'not satisfactory'. There was no proof, he said, that the Germans were in fact using the Monastery, but they were firing from sites nearby.

Osborne reported that in Rome the staunchest supporters of the Allies were among the clergy, who were willing to believe that there must have been some unknown reason for this apparently useless destruction. A 'raging campaign' had been let loose in the press, however, though the Germans were irritated by the Vatican's 'guarded mildness'.

Extensive investigations by the Vatican did nothing to disprove the Abbot's declaration that neither German soldiers nor German weapons had been inside the Monastery. All the same it was decided in Washington to insist that there had been 'indisputable evidence' that the Monastery formed a part of the German defensive line.

As for Rome, in his Lenten address to parish priests the Pope had said that since Athens and Cairo had been spared he confidently hoped that Rome would be spared also. It would be a 'stain and shame which centuries would not efface' if for military reasons Rome 'fell victim to the devastating fury of this terrible war'.

On 1 March Roosevelt wrote to Cicognani about the air attacks on Rome, confirming that the Allied authorities were committed to a policy of avoiding damage to religious shrines and historical monuments 'to the extent humanly possible in modern warfare'. He then said: 'We are fighting a desperate battle against a hard and unscrupulous foe whose ultimate defeat will accomplish the liberation of Italy and the Italian people ... Our only reason in attacking any part of Rome is because it is occupied and used by the Germans. If His Holiness will be successful in persuading them to respect the sacred and cultural character of Rome by withdrawing from it without a struggle he could thus assure its preservation.'

On that day, 1 March, six bombs fell on the Vatican, very close to where the diplomats lived in the Hospice of Santa Marta. As Air Chief Marshal Tedder once said to Alexander: 'Sorry to say some of the early Popes went airborne this morning.'

Perhaps the last words about the bombing of Monte Cassino can go to Sid Hartnell, who was in temporary command of the 5th NZ Infantry Brigade: 'Too many sacred memories are involved.'

Minturno

My memories of Minturno are all in sepia. We arrived by night, tired, dazed by the sound of guns so near, to find trouble about billeting. Some middle-class woman was having to give up bedrooms to me and my friend Timmy Lloyd, and this made us feel guilty. I was surprised that there were any civilians in Minturno at all, seeing that the front line was only two to three miles away. The guns went on roaring, the house shuddered, the sky was sepia. The woman's face was sepia, the mud outside was sepia.

The next morning I was introduced to my platoon, consisting of Yorkshire miners, who had already had enough of fighting and seemed much older than me. There was no chance to sightsee, and anyway as I learnt later the churches had been virtually destroyed. In the mess at lunchtime we were suddenly told we were going back to Naples, en route for Anzio, that very evening. Obviously some sort of panic was going on up there.

Timmy came up, looking white. 'I think I must have scabies,' he said. 'The MO says I can't go with the battalion to Anzio.' The poor chap knew people would think he was a malingerer, and I certainly was appalled at losing such a good friend; we had been together, often having to share tents, billets and cattle trucks on railway journeys, around Algiers and before that in Philippeville. We had both looked forward to our reunion with Nick.

Anzio – Carroceto

The most famous comment on the Anzio Beachhead – or Bridgehead as he now preferred to call it – is one of Churchill's: 'I had hoped that we were hurling a wild cat on to the shore, but all we got was a stranded whale.'

The whale was not quite moribund, though the Allies had withdrawn from the Campoleone salient and were about to lose Aprilia, the Factory. On 7–8 February the Germans recorded taking 791 British prisoners, mostly from the Guards Brigade and North Staffs. It was 'terrible', said Lucas. 'I wish I had an American division in there. It is probably my fault that I don't understand them [the British] better. I think they suffer excessive losses. They are certainly brave men but ours are better trained, in my opinion, and I am sure that our officers are better educated in a military way.'

Unfortunately he did not conceal these opinions. It was not surprising that General Penney 'seemed rather irritated'. At least no one could compain about the performance of the Allied airforces. In the great battles of the 8th and 9th, 687 tons of bombs were dropped in direct support of the infantry.

Via Anziate remained the very linchpin of the Beachhead. Were the Allies to lose Carroceto they would have to fall back two and a half miles to the viaduct bridge known as the Flyover, which had high banks on either side, an ideal defensive position, in effect the last before the town of Anzio itself. A smaller road ran east and west from the Flyover. The Allies called it the Lateral Road, and the part to the west lay behind not only the two crucial features, the Vallelata and Buonriposo ridges, but the deep thorn-filled wadis of the upper Moletta. If the Germans could reach this road, they would be able to swing round and cut off the Flyover. But these wadis presented a special, intricate kind of obstacle, hell to attack, hell to defend. The most notorious to the British were the Starfish, the North and South Lobster Claws, the Bloody Boot and the Oh God Wadi.

One of the most dreaded areas, especially later, was the junction of three valleys overlooked by some high ground, the Fortress, but called by the Germans *Das Schwalbennest*, the Swallow's Nest. The Germans towards the middle of February had their own *Festung*, or Fortress; this was the area around the *pozzolana* caves still held by the Allies and north of buildings called Pantoni, nicknamed White Cow Farm. Near the *Festung* was another wadi with grim associations for the Germans, *Der Geierschnabel* or Vulture's Beak.

The units of the British division sent in relief, the 56th, were rushed to the front the moment they were landed. They were by no means fresh, but no others had been available. When Lucas had asked Alexander for reinforcements, Alex had merely smiled. As for Mackensen, in addition to receiving the vaunted Infantry Lehr Regiment, as yet untried in battle, he had received large reinforcements from Yugoslavia, the South of France and even Cassino. He had also, 'for political reasons', been given elements of the Italian Fascist Parachute Regiment, Nembo. By 2 February he already had 95,000 men in combat units facing the Allied 76,400. Support from the Luftwaffe had been strengthened, and he had good supplies of ammunition. So he had reason to feel confident.

When Churchill was told that 18,000 vehicles had been landed in 'this small pent-up bridgehead', he was aghast. It looked to him like 'highly organized insanity'. 'We must,' he said sarcastically, 'have a great superiority of chauffeurs.' He was very soon suspicious about Lucas' capabilities, and this was not helped by a cable from Wilson mentioning a 'Salerno complex' and the fact that the Anzio command was 'only geared to work at slow speed'. The reference to Lucas having been 'urged' by Alexander and Clark to take advantage of the original surprise made him write to Alexander himself:

'I have a feeling that you may have hesitated to assert your authority because you were dealing so largely with Americans, and therefore urged repeat urged an advance instead of ordering it. You are, however, quite entitled to give orders, and I have it from the highest American authorities that it is their wish that their troops should receive direct orders. They say that their Army has been formed more on Prussian lines ... and that American commanders expect to receive positive orders. Do not hesitate to give orders just as you would to your own men. The Americans are very good to work with and quite prepared to take the rough with the smooth.'

If Alexander was not satisfied with Lucas, Churchill said, then he must find someone else whom he could trust. Of course the War Cabinet had great sympathy for Alex's heavy tasks, and he was assured of their 'confidence and goodwill' in his further struggles. 'You have I am sure always felt that you have mine.'

The rough with the smooth. Critics of Alexander still feel that the rough was something he too often avoided.

On the 11th Alexander told Churchill that Lucas was 'probably the best' among American Corps commanders, 'but all American higher commanders lack the years of practical battle experience we have had, and this is an undoubted weakness when fighting against veterans'.

Lieutenant Paul Freyberg was among the Grenadiers captured by Battalion Kleye. He had been in the company holding the important group of farm buildings near the spot which the Germans called the Bug, just south-west of Carroceto. Two other Grenadier companies were completely surrounded, many of the men and officers, such as Lieutenant Marmaduke Hussey, having been wounded when trying to avoid capture. The North Staffs on Buonriposo ridge had been wiped out or taken prisoner, and some Irish Guards had been sent there to 'plug the gap'. Between the Bug and the ridge there was a *pozzolana* quarry, known as the Gully, held by No 2 company of the Grenadier Guards and a company of the 504th US Parachute Regiment. Facing them was the No 7 Company of the German 147th Regiment, under Lieutenant Heinrich Wunn, an exceptional soldier who was to receive the Knight's Cross for his bravery on this and subsequent days. Some Italian civilians were unhappily sheltering in caves in the Gully's walls.

Wunn's men were glad to leave the back area, plastered so often by Allied artillery and – even worse – by phosphorus bombs, and where the nights were made eerie by the creaking of a windmill, the knell of death, someone said. The *Schafstall*, Sheepfold, was ablaze that night. It had changed hands often, and had been used as a field hospital; the wounded had lain among starving animals. The first attack was halted, but it was Wunn's determination and courage that drove the men on, and soon they stormed and overran the Grenadiers' anti-tank positions, taking twenty prisoners. They reached a deep ditch, completely choked with brambles – this was the last barrier before the Gully. They rushed up and down trying to find a way through, shouting to one another, hysterically so the Grenadiers thought. In the process there were many casualties from American machine-gun fire, since for once the night was clear and the moon about to rise.

A path had once been cut through the brambles by an Italian farmer. At its entrance stood Major W. P. Sidney, descendant of the great Elizabethan, Sir Philip Sidney, and a relative of Shelley. Behind him was the Grenadier headquarters and behind that Via Anziate. If Wunn broke through at this point, he would cut off the Scots Guards at Carroceto and the London Irish at the Factory. Then the German tanks would have a clear run down to Anzio. The fate of the whole Beachhead was at stake.

Like Horatius, Major Sidney — the future Lord De L'Isle — stood alone, spraying the Germans with tommy-gun fire. The gun jammed, so he began throwing grenades, handed to him by two Guardsmen. 'One of the Guardsmen pulled out the pin too soon and killed himself, and I was wounded in the backside. I bled like a pig.' But he continued to throw the grenades, still blocking the way alone, whilst the enemy threshed in the undergrowth and water. He was hit in the face by a German stick grenade. His opponent Wunn's attack was weakening, and now some American parachutists arrived to take over from the Grenadiers. The moon had risen, and Sidney felt faint. He lay down, while the shooting continued. He remembered a GI saying, 'Gee, captain, I don't feel so well. I think I'll go back to base,' and the captain replying, 'You goddam son of a bitch, you stay where you are.'

Sidney was awarded the Victoria Cross. Of that wild confusing night he said, 'The great thing you had to remember was that the other side was just as puzzled as you were.'

The next morning showed that the ground was strewn with German corpses. But there were only twenty-nine Grenadiers and some forty-five Americans, including wounded, left in the Gully. The rain came down, turning to sleet. Water flooded into the bottom of the Gully, and everyone was exhausted, having barely slept for seventy-two hours. There was no alternative but to withdraw to the Anziate. The Grenadiers were attacked again, and the colonel was killed, shot through the chest.

American Liberator aircraft pounded the German concentrations in front of the Factory. When smoke lifted there would be absolute silence, and then you would see a whole lot of ambulances rushing about. Several German soldiers surrendered, but turned out to be from Luxembourg and only too glad to pass on information.

There was an American tank destroyer, its occupants apparently dozing, near a little farmhouse near the Factory. Sergeant Jenkins of the London Irish was told by his colonel to tell the Yanks to start firing. He went across and was confronted by this huge closed monster. 'Well, I thought to myself, how does one make anyone hear? I began to call out, when suddenly a flap opened and an American officer's head appeared. "Yeah, waddyer want?" I told him, and he said, "Tell your colonel he doesn't command me," and shut the flap again. He was obviously scared. The colonel was not pleased.'

About the time of Sidney's defence of the Gully, the wireless of D Company of the London Irish went silent. This meant that at long last the

Germans had captured the huge pile of rubble that had once been the Factory.

Now all the concentration was on the hamlet of Carroceto, held by two Scots Guards companies and one Irish Guards company. Battalion Kleye, from the west, pushed resolutely onwards, although badly mauled. The Scots Guards hit back with phosphorus grenades, but one by one their machine-gun posts were overwhelmed. Yet the Germans had been so weakened that Kleye doubted whether further advance would be possible. Major Gericke himself now took personal command of the battalion, and Kleye was told that his objective was the miniscule railway station.

Kleye's attack was well prepared. He went forward with two companies, and was able to advance about a hundred yards. Meanwhile, in the east, Battle Group Graeser entered Carroceto from the direction of the Factory.

Then Kleye was killed, by a shell. But one of his lieutenants, Weiss, succeeded in capturing a main Scots Guards strongpoint and took thirty-five prisoners. There were now only sixty men left in the two German companies.

'Rollicking evening in San Lorenzo with cloak and dagger boys,' wrote Mansell in his diary, referring to the No 1 Special Force contingent under Malcolm Munthe. 'Sat round a brazier nearly suffocated by smoke while Mike Gubbins sang "Abdul the Bulbul".' All the while, he added, the Germans were 'pot-shotting' the tower overhead. 'Heard that Munthe has crazy idea of getting some Italian spy through German lines to Rome.'

The 'spy' was with the main part of the Irish Guards in the caves behind Buonriposo ridge, and Munthe and Gubbins had determined to cross open ground to reach them near Via Anziate – in daylight, which was even crazier. Of course they were spotted, and the Moaning Minnies started up. They dashed for a trench, but it had a dead German in it. Five yards further there was another, empty this time, and they leapt in, shoulder to shoulder. To drown the Moaning Minnies Gubbins sang 'Abdul the Bulbul'. As Munthe wrote later: 'The flat field all around was spluttering earth every time a mortar shell landed ... as though invisible mushrooms were popping up.' Then a shell landed on the dead German in the next trench, sending him high into the air. Gubbins sang on.

'He turned in my direction, muttering his song and screwing his face into a wry smile – that was the last time I was to see him alive. A whine was coming down to the left of me. I shut my eyes. A tremendous thud filled our trench. A thud as though someone had hurled a dining-room table against my heart.' Munthe was sure that it was the end. Then he opened his eyes, and to his astonishment he found that he could still see. Gubbins was pressed against him. 'He was on his back, his face looking up, unaltered, but his eyes were open and a fringe of red appeared round the roots of his hair. His helmet was off. The rest of his body was crimson. I saw I was crimson too.'

Mansell heard that when the stretcher-bearers came to fetch Munthe back they had to pull a piece of shrapnel out of his skull. He seemed unwilling to believe that Gubbins was dead and insisted on being taken back to touch his body.

It happened that the 95th Evacuation Hospital was bombed and strafed soon after Munthe reached it. There were twenty-eight deaths, including three nurses, and sixty-four injuries. The news caused an outrage, and it was considered to have been a deliberate piece of barbarism, for the hospital was clearly marked with a red cross. Whatever the truth, it was almost impossible for a bomb or shell to fall in any part of the rear echelons of the Beachhead without causing some damage. There were to be several other incidents. The 95th was simply a large area of dugouts covered with canvas. They called it Hell's Half Acre, and some people actually concealed their wounds so as not to be sent there.

The Irish Guards had reached their caves, in effect long excavated galleries, on 4 February. They had found that here too were some Italian refugees. At first the novelty was welcome. The caves were rain-proof, and fires could be made out of empty shell cartons. During the nights slit trenches outside would be occupied, and when daylight came the men 'like nocturnal animals' crept back into the warmth of their shelter to sleep and wait. One company was sent to reinforce the Scots Guards at Carroceto.

The whole situation changed with the collapse of the North Staffs, followed by the withdrawal of the Grenadiers from the Gully and the loss of the Factory. No 1 Company was sent forward, and nothing more was heard of it until the names of some prisoners were broadcast by Rome Radio.

The caves were visited by Colonel Freeman, a lanky Melancholy Jaques of a Virginian, from the 3rd Battalion of the 504th Parachutes. His comments on arrival were unShakespearean but inspired sympathy: 'Those Krauts, I sure hate their guts.'

The Irish Guards' No 1 Company had encountered Jerries/Krauts/Huns of the 145th Grenadier Regiment. Lt. Ferdinand Schaller of that regiment recalls how the Irish came at him, 'masses of brown overcoats', from all sides. 'There were tanks too. Not a single shot from our own artillery was to be heard. So we used 2.50 and 2.75 cm guns. This did the trick because we

saw those Tommies trying to escape with their brown coats flying open.'
But the Tommies were in a neat trap and many died.

The German artillery had been having difficulties with the mucky
ground. The guns had either to be manhandled or dragged by horses.

The next morning presented a spectacle of devastation. The wadi was
full of dead bodies – German, British and American – and all sorts of
equipment, including a lorry and an anti-tank gun. Schaller passed British
heavy machine-guns still at the ready. The stench of death and cordite was
incredible. But there was so much food about – corned beef, vegetables,
plum pudding – not to mention tarpaulins, gas-capes, socks and blankets.
Schaller made himself tea, using brown ditch water. It was real luxury.

Meanwhile, further inland, thanks again to the efforts of Lieutenant
Wunn, whose company had taken eighty prisoners, the Gully was being
occupied by the 147th Panzer Grenadiers. Among the first to enter it was
Staff Sergeant Bernhard Luy. He at once questioned the Italians about
whether there were any *inglesi* left there. The Italians assured him there
were none, and he said they would be shot if they were lying. '*No, no,
niente inglesi, niente inglesi.*' And indeed they turned out to be right.

This place too appeared to have been used as a supply depot.
Everything was arranged in piles – rifles, ammunition, barbed wire,
spades, uniforms, Red Cross material. There were also motor bikes and
some lorries loaded with food. A lieutenant appeared and said that
nobody must touch anything in case it was booby trapped, but as soon as
he had gone soldiers began prising open the tins with bayonets. The food
that could be eaten cold they ate at once, but anything that had to be
cooked they threw away.

Luy noticed that one of the dead Tommies had a large blue-green ring
on his left hand. He also saw several long-legged pigs running about.
There appeared to have been more civilians in the caves than he had at first
thought. Luy selected a cave rather high up as his command post, so that
he could watch the entrance to the Gully.

When he went down again, to his disgust he saw that the pigs were
eating the Tommy with the ring. He shouted at them but they took no
notice. He was so enraged that he fired at them, and they ran away. A
runner came rushing up to see what was happening. Luy showed him the
half-eaten Tommy. 'Is this what we are fighting for, to be eaten by pigs?'
Together they buried the Tommy. After such horror it was some
compensation later to find a cache of several tins of cigarettes and a lot of
chocolate.

On searching the caves Luy was astonished to find three Tommies
hiding behind a blanket. They had been there for twenty-four hours. He
explored further, and then found a hut with smoke coming out of it. He
thought Italians must be in there, but then discovered that the whole place

was wired in. He shouted 'Open up, open up.' Nothing happened. So he cut the wire and inside were three Americans. Apparently they were cooks and had been left behind in the retreat. So these three 'Amis' joined the three Tommies in the march back to the POW cage. Before leaving, the Amis told Luy that they had killed eighteen sheep, which were hanging at the end of the hut ready for cooking.

In the evening Luy met Lieutenant Wunn, who was very depressed, having lost a whole platoon in an attack on Carroceto. He had run into heavy machine-gun fire, and had heard his men crying in pain and shouting for help well into the next day. Some British stretcher-bearers had picked up a few of them, but after that the Tommies had taken no notice of the German Red Cross flag and had kept on firing.

The defence of Carroceto started reasonably well for the Scots and Irish Guards, with several Germans suddenly surrendering. Evidently the tremendous artillery fire, coupled with the weather, had been too much for the Jerries, and certainly they looked miserable, filthy and soaking wet. It was soon realized that some farmhouses to the north-west were the key positions. Guardsman English and Guardsman Kerr had a great time shooting and bayoneting their way through stables and lofts – 'There's another in that straw. Keep his head down while I fork him out.' But it was Lieutenant Weiss who finally drove out the Guards, taking eighty-one prisoners.

A sudden thrust forward by the Germans took the British by surprise, and Weiss at last reached the railway station – simply a platform along a single track, with a few Fascist-type buildings and a signal box. He was able to take a hundred more prisoners. Now his runner, young Joachim Liebschner, was sent to make contact with Battle Group Graeser advancing from the Factory. To be a runner at the height of a battle was a terrifying job. Liebschner had first begun to feel it when one night he found the body of another runner in a wood; the boy had obviously bled to death with no one to help him.

Two Sherman tanks advanced on to the station platform and raked Weiss' platoon with fire. About thirty British prisoners were able to escape, and Weiss found himself left with twelve men. He retreated into some cellars, only to find that some sixty British prisoners had been herded down there. Luckily a Recce group sent by Major Gericke destroyed one of the Shermans, and the other thereupon withdrew southwards. Weiss was thus able to emerge again, and hand over all his prisoners.

A group of Scots and Irish Guards was still holding a building at the other end of the station. The sound of German tanks rumbling on the road was enough to tell them that 'life was not going to be a bed of roses'. And sure enough a Mark IV Tiger tank soon made its appearance. The Scots Guards adjutant radioed back to Brigade HQ: 'There's a fucking great German tank sitting outside my door demolishing my house brick by brick.' By midnight the whole station was in ruins. The Guards' cellar was full of wounded. Once again it was decided to withdraw. Finally only the remnants of the Irish Guards company and two signallers were left. Little did they know that Weiss' platoon had been reduced to precisely five men – though before long it was to be joined by some of the Battle Group Graeser.

Lance-Sergeant Duffy of the Irish Guards said later: 'The Germans were only a hundred yards away, and we could hear them calling to one another. They started to fire HE . . . Guardsman Murphy – "Old Jock" – had his thigh broken. I went over to Murphy and another 88 mm shell hit me in the back. I was taken to the cellar, which was full of dead and wounded, and lost consciousness. When I came round the cellar was full of Germans.'

So Carroceto was in German hands. On 13 February their Battalion Kleye was withdrawn for a rest. Since 22 January Gericke could claim to have taken prisoner four officers and 541 other ranks, and to have destroyed four tanks. People had been surprised by Lieutenant Weiss' great bravery. He was such a quiet, modest man, originally a lawyer from Silesia, one would not think 'in harmony with war events' – though he had already been wounded five times.

When Carroceto fell Nick Mansell was with the 6th Gordons near the Flyover, 'in a flamingo dawn at a delightful spot they call Horror Farm'. 'So back we go to World War I,' he jotted in his diary. 'Oozing thick mud. Tank hulks. The cold, God, the *cold*. Graves marked by a helmet, gashed with shrapnel. Shreds of barbed wire. Trees like broken fish-bones, or even wish-bones. Rip, rip, rip of machine-guns. Racket of shells screeching, snarling, whirring above like furious witches. Earth shudders. Sadistic. Hot shrapnel tearing through what were bushes. The zip of a sniper's bullet. The repellent smell of stomach wounds – human offal. A haystack is burning. Smoke clouds coiling and reeling above poor old Aprilia. A dead gunner, his head squashed by a tank. Not an attractive sight . . . Voices disembodied: "I'll say this for the Irish, they put up a good scrap"; "Those Jerry buggers were full of vino, they walked straight into our brens, blazing away like merry hell at them they were"; "Maybe I'm a hard old bugger, but I was inured to death long long ago". Scream from a wounded GI – "Medics, medics" . . . Like Agag I lay my cables delicately, for there are *Schuh* mines about. The terrible sight of seeing men go bomb-happy, "yellow". Deliberate self-mutilation. Weeping. The worst moment is dusk, a breathless, anxious hush of waiting. Will we or will we not be attacked? Which of us will die tonight? Something blue near a shell crater. A violet! Yesterday up front a boy with me was badly hurt during a mortar stonk. I tied him up with a bandage off a dead Grenadier. Which reminds me, Guards officers say it is common to turn up your coat collar. I saw a Grenadier subaltern doing just that today. Shame! ... A letter from S today. I think the only thing that keeps me alive is my yearning for her. Woodpigeons in June. New Year's Eve at the Bagatelle; that party with Raleigh. Suppose the old bastard is still wallowing in the fleshpots of Algiers.'

Later that day Mansell wrote: 'A real flurry. Would you believe it? Old Corncob Charlie has actually *been* near here to see Penney and the Guards HQ.'

It had been a strange meeting between the generals. Lucas, red-faced, puffing at his pipe, listened to Penney's exposition of the crisis, the urgency for a counter-attack, the desperate need for reinforcements, and eventually for the British 1st Division to rest and refit. He had finally turned to General Eagles of the 45th: 'OK, Bill, you give 'em the works.' The highly strung Penney noted in his diary: 'No operational appreciation, no orders, no objective, no nothing.' Junior officers, both British and American, were puzzled. The 179th and 157th Infantry went in against the Factory but were driven back with heavy casualties. The force was simply not strong enough, and it was too late and too hasty.

Some prisoners taken by the Americans were insolent and cocky, especially the paratroopers. A major asked where the sea was because the Allies were about to be driven into it. Others talked about the Russians being the real, the common enemy. John McCarthy of Brooklyn took a prisoner whose main worry was whether he was to be sent to Canada or Florida; Florida was his preference. Another prisoner cried because he had lost his comb. Some said that a major attack was to be mounted shortly and were glad to give themselves up before it started.

On the 12th Lucas wrote down: 'Several newspaper men, names unknown to me, got their wind up a couple of days ago and took off wishing to avoid another "Dunkirk". I hear they have been spreading alarmist rumours in Naples and other places safely in the rear ... I will readily admit it is serious. All battle situations are. There is no reason, however, to doubt the ultimate successful outcome of the show. I called in all the correspondents and went over the entire military situation ... They assured me that the weak sisters had departed.'

Churchill was annoyed by the American NBC reports, echoed in the *Evening Standard*, *Daily Mail*, and elsewhere, about 'sweetly flattering hopes' having evaporated, and initiative having passed to the enemy. Roosevelt also admitted publicly that the situation was tense. 'Why all the defeatism?' Churchill asked. The censorship should have been imposed to stop the circulation of these alarmist rumours. He was forced to make a reassuring statement in Parliament. But at Anzio itself there was no disguising that morale was 'rock bottom' in the deep cellars that housed VI Corps HQ, a world of trickling damp, perpetual darkness and centipedes.

Some hopes were raised with the arrival of the commander of the British 56th Division, General Gerald Templer, an electric personality and an energizer, though perpetually looking dog-tired – he lived on his nerves, they said. When Penney was wounded in the head by a shell splinter outside his caravan, Templer took over the command of both the 1st and the 56th Divisions. It was he who had chosen the Black Cat as the 56th's emblem. 'If the tail pointed to the left, you went left. If to the right, you went right. If it was straight, you went straight on, up the arse.' His opinion of Lucas was hard. 'Lucas was absolutely full of inertia, and couldn't make up his mind,' he told Harold Nicolson's son Nigel. 'He had no qualities of any sort as a commander, absolutely no presence; he was the antithesis of everything that a fighting soldier and general ought to be.'

Mackensen's final all-out thrust was planned for the 16th. It was to be called Operation *Fischfang*, or Catch-fish. Hitler took the closest interest in its planning and wanted a creeping barrage 'reminiscent of those used in World War I' along the Anziate. He also insisted that the Infantry Lehr should be to the fore. Both Mackensen and Kesselring were nevertheless uneasy about an attack on such a small front – this would provide too easy and too restricted a target for Allied bombers. It was decided that the main push would be to the east of the Anziate, with a feint attack by the Hermann Goering Division from Cisterna. The Germans were now in the position of having 125,000 men ranged against approximately 100,000. It was just not possible to have a creeping barrage; there was plenty of ammunition but not enough for this. There were also fears that the ground in front of the Flyover would be heavily mined against tanks.

The weather was getting colder. Sergeant Luy found ice on the puddles in the Gully. He had had to cope with some nasty incidents. A guard called Jankowski, a *Beute Deutsche* (i.e. not of German blood), had by mistake fired on a returning recce party, badly injuring some of them. As a result he had a nervous collapse. Then an Italian boy was killed by a rifle grenade. The remaining Italians in the caves, especially the women, set up a tremendous caterwauling. Luy tried to pacify them, saying *piano piano*, making the sign of the cross and kneeling by the body. It was not long afterwards that an Allied *Jak* (fighter) dropped a bomb near the Gully, causing part of the wall to crumble and burying eight soldiers.

After being relieved by the 4th Paras, Luy's company returned to its old position. At HQ Luy was suddenly asked by Captain Richter when he had last had a shit. 'Why yesterday of course.' Richter said he hadn't had one for five days. 'I told him about a place where he could squat in peace, and he went there. When he came back, I realized he had had a bad time and had been crying, for his eyes were red. Then I remembered that for the past five or six days he had been living on Tommy chocolate, which must have caused the trouble. He said to us, "I've done my job, but it was as thick and hard as a shell case." We laughed a lot, but didn't envy him.'

In an earlier stage of the battle, near the Factory, Sergeant Folkerd of the London Irish had been performing his 'ablutions' after breakfast near a well, out of view of the enemy. He noticed an old Italian waiting deferentially for him to finish. There was a quiet insistence, an urgency, in the man's manner, though Folkerd – accustomed only to the Naples dialect – could not understand him. Evidently the help of three or four soldiers was required, and fortunately men were available. They followed him to a barn. 'The old Italian, holding two short lengths of rope, greeted us humbly with undisguised gratitude and pointed to a corner. There we saw a crudely fashioned coffin containing the body of his wife. She had been killed by a shell.' Folkerd and his mates carried the coffin to a grave which the old man himself had dug.

Further east at a Divisional Headquarters battery Philip Norris of Cleveland, Ohio, was in a slightly quieter area, though under constant shellfire. There were some peasants about, 'and when some of the boys started to take logs from a pile in the yard to cover their fox holes we got into trouble'. An old lady started to cry and carry on at a great rate. 'We couldn't figure out why she was so angry, but we left the logs alone, and after that our relations with the peasants were fairly cordial. From time to time we got a bottle of vino from the old man, but his supply finally ran out, so he told us, and we had to go elsewhere.' Only when the peasants had been evacuated did Norris and his friends find out why the old lady had been so agitated. 'Under the pile of logs, beneath the ground, was a barrel of vino ... Certainly it boosted our morale at a critical time.'

Everyone knew that the supreme test, the final clash of arms, was inevitably approaching. There was thus a rush to evacuate all accessible civilians, and these included the nuns who were sheltering in the cellars of the Borghese villa. The assembly point was in the big church a few hundred yards from the landing-craft that would take them to Naples; there were panic dashes in between air-raids and the attentions of Anzio Annie. Families had to be separated, and the sight of waterspouts out to sea was no inducement to go aboard, causing struggles and dreadful screamings. Ennio Silvestri had to leave his donkey, letting it loose in the

Padiglione woods, but managed to bring his pointer Zuga with him. The refugees were finally to end up in a camp at Capua, north of Naples.

Prince Borghese remained at Nettuno with a few essential workers, who were put under his charge. He now wore his father's World War 1 helmet. His greatest anxiety was about his Capodimonte porcelain, which was secretly walled up in an underground passage; Americans from VI Corps HQ were enlarging his cellars and he was terrified lest their excavations would lead to this treasure trove. It was remarkable that throughout the Beachhead fighting only one bomb, an incendiary, should land on his villa, poised as it was on such prominent ground above the port.

General Mark Clark arrived at the Beachhead on the 12th. Lucas found him in good humour. There were widely different reactions about Clark. Some British officers were impressed by his confidence, a relief from Lucas' gloom and 'bumbling'. He was not a martinet. But many Americans on the VI Corps headquarters were irritated by his mania for publicity and the headlines, and there was an institution ironically named 'Mark Clark for President Society'. He had himself photographed with a GI as if sharing a K ration, and then again in the cemetery, with photographers jumping on fresh graves.

On the 14th Lucas wrote: 'General Alexander arrived at 8.30 by destroyer. Always optimistic ... The General has great ideas for breaking this thing. Things like manpower and artillery he waves aside as of little moment. These handicaps must be overcome by an energetic commander. He never sees the logistics of a problem. The picture he sees is such a big one that none of the difficulties appear in it.' Alexander asked to see the war correspondents, so Lucas assembled them 'in my little wineshop after lunch', and there followed a caustic tirade by the Commander-in-Chief about spreading of false rumours. The correspondents were deeply incensed, said Lucas. 'This was the first time it had actually occurred to me that there were some people who really thought we might be in danger of defeat ... A bad case of wind-up.'

On the 15th, the day of the bombing of the Monastery at Cassino, Alexander cabled the War Office: 'I am disappointed with VI Corps Headquarters. They are negative and lacking the necessary drive and enthusiasm to get things done. They appeared to have become depressed by events ... What we require is a thruster like George Patton with a capable staff behind him, or to replace the VI Corps HQ by a British Corps commander and staff. The latter solution is completely drastic, and I should like to know what reaction Eisenhower thinks.' To which the Chief of the Imperial General Staff, General Sir Alan Brooke, cabled back that he and Eisenhower were against a British commander, except as a last resort. Just as an emergency measure Eisenhower would be prepared to spare Patton for a month, but his personal selection for a replacement for Lucas would be 1 Truscott, 2 Eagles, 3 Harmon.

In the long, sleepless nights Lucas found relief in chatting to Captain Mack, the British Public Safety Officer. He spoke about his home and West Point, and about Sherlock Holmes. He thought Sherlock Holmes had been a chief of police.

Alexander's recollection of his talk with Clark about replacing Lucas was typical of his tentative diplomatic approach. 'You know, the position is very serious,' he told him. 'We may be pushed back into the sea. That would be very bad for us – and you would certainly be relieved of your command.' That 'gentle injunction', he was to write, 'impelled action'.

Clark was prepared for the decision that Lucas would have to be axed. 'My own feeling was that Johnny Lucas was ill – tired physically and mentally – from the long responsibilities of command in battle; he died a few years later. I said I would not in any circumstances do anything to hurt a man who had so greatly contributed to our successes since Salerno.' Clark had indeed been putting pressure on Lucas. He had ordered him to put mines along the coast, but on his next visit found that this still had not been done.

It was Templer who had 'got on to the blower' to Alex: 'We'll lose the Beachhead unless Lucas goes.' Of Alex himself Templer said: 'Very few people knew or understood him. He was a very lazy man. To this one could attribute his success in battle. He always had something in reserve.' Some days later, at the very worst moment of the fighting, Alexander called on Templer at 8.30 a.m. 'Could you give me a drink?' He wanted gin. Templer shuddered because he had precisely one double peg left. Then Alex talked about hunting, shooting, Yorkshire, Ireland, 'not a sausage' about the Beachhead. Templer tried to steer the conversation round to the battle, but without success. After nearly an hour Alex said suddenly: 'By God, I must get back to an important conference.' Before departing in a jeep he remarked: 'I have done everything I can to help you, haven't I?'

The Germans tried leaflet propaganda, aiming to spread not only gloom but schism among the Allies: 'Beachhead – Deathshead'; 'The worst is yet to come'; 'British soldiers! General Clark certainly played you a dirty Yankee trick! And who has got to bear the consequences?' And for the Americans there were some anti-Semitic messages about rich Jewish draft-dodgers in New York seducing GIs' sweet innocent girl-friends. These leaflets were especially useful in the front line during outbreaks of diarrhoea.

Then there was the 'Front-line Radio', more popular than the Germans imagined, and for the wrong reasons. The announcer was a woman with a sexy voice and soon to be familiar as Axis Sally, who would intersperse choice grisly tales, lists of prisoners' names in Rome, and news of Russian retreats with boogie-woogie on scratchy records. 'Think it over,' the programme would end. 'Why should you be one of those rotting carcasses? Don't forget to listen in tomorrow. And a big kiss from Sall-y.'

New arrivals at the shattered quay of Anzio were not much encouraged by rows of stretchers with bandaged figures bearing labels like dogs about to travel by train. Innumerable signs – pointing to ration dumps and unit headquarters, or giving traffic instructions – festooned the piles of masonry and twisted concrete. The house with an old Italian sign, *Al Ricovero*, meaning To the Air-raid Shelter, was a favourite joke and known to all as Al's Place. Broken glass was everywhere. As usual the worst danger was from anti-personnel bombs. Above the town would be about thirty barrage balloons.

The British CCS, Casualty Clearing Station, was in the Padiglione woods, but became so overwhelmed with work that another team under Major J. A. Rose was sent up from Naples. On his first night Rose operated on fourteen major cases, including four penetrating abdominal wounds. Later he had some harrowing decisions in the case of gross injuries, when it was realized that men were beyond saving and there was a flood of urgent cases which had to have priority. If possible, 'mercy' operations would be performed – a pretence really. A man one day asked if he could have attention, he had been there twenty-four hours. Rose looked at him and saw he was beyond hope. 'I am afraid you are not quite ready yet.' The man closed his eyes and said: 'I understand.'

On the fatal 16th a succession of men with ghastly wounds continued to be brought to the CCS throughout the day: head wounds, distinguished by loud snoring breathing, protrusions of intestines and brains, shattered muddy stumps tied up with filthy, bloody bandages and yellow pads, fragments of men. Rose heard a plane approaching, but before him lay an unconscious patient with an open wound, the blood welling fast. 'Down boy, down, my knees said, my shoulders hunching, every cell in my body shrinking, crying out to fling myself down.' But he had to carry on.

A bomb dropped. 'God that was near!' The noise of the plane receded. Every one of the theatre staff had kept on working.

Pozzuoli

My Yorkshire miners and I waited a day or so at the port of Pozzuoli outside Naples before sailing to Anzio in landing-craft. The sun had come out for a change. My main memory of that time is sitting in a restaurant where I had been eating chops. Suddenly a ragged old woman dashed in and snatched the bones off my plate and started sucking them.

In Naples I had seen passers-by being haphazardly sprayed with DDT powder by military police. That had seemed horrifying and humiliating, but this was worse.

At Anzio the civilians had been evacuated, so I would not have to look at poverty, or hunger – I hoped.

Anzio – Fischfang

The night of the 15th had been unusually quiet at the front. Templer's 56th Division had now taken over the line from the mouth of the Moletta, along the wadis to Buonriposo ridge, where it linked with the 'Thunderbirds', the US 45th Division. The depleted Guards Brigade with what was left of the North Staffs and other battalions of the British 1st Division were in reserve.

The US 3rd Division was facing Cisterna, and along the Mussolini Canal was the American–Canadian ace commando unit, the 1st Special Service Force or 'Black Devils' under General Frederick – 'an outfit crazier than hell'. It was in these two areas that the Germans were to make their initial attack.

An intercepted radio message betrayed the imminence of a German attack, so at 4.30 a.m. the entire VI Corps artillery opened up. 'The skies split open. Cannon roared and argued; it was like a huge eruption . . . it was the greatest artillery concentration that had yet been fired on the Anzio Beachhead.'

At first light the German guns replied. Nick Mansell put in his diary: 'Deafening, mad, screaming senseless hatred. The whole sky alight. Towards Aprilia flames. Very lights of all colours. Thick brown smoke. Houses, stacks burning. Strange beauty. It made me want to shout and laugh. Ack-ack. Bombs. Smoke biting. Oh Tiber, father Tiber, will I ever see you again? Watching the incredible sight, I heard a man say, "Cor, fuck me," and another reply, "Not bloody likely, Johnson, you bloody crow's nest of shit and sticks."' These were the last words Mansell ever wrote.

The Infantry Lehr, allocated to the 3rd Panzer Grenadiers, made the main attack, as required by Hitler, to the east of Via Anziate. But the attack developed into a massacre. The Regiment broke under shell-fire, and its remnants turned and fled. This was a grave shock to Kesselring, 'disgraceful' he called it. The Hermann Goering Division's attacks from Cisterna were also repulsed. However, to the west Gericke's 4th Paras broke through the British 56th Division, and some platoons infiltrated almost to the Lateral Road. And in the evening the American forward defences astride the Anziate were wiped out. There was now a gap between the 45th's two regiments, the 157th and 179th. Operation *Fischfang* was developing according to plan.

The casualties from Allied bombing were however far worse than the Allies themselves realized. Several German prisoners said that they would rather have been in Russia. Lorries were being piled up with bodies, to be taken for burial at Ardea.

During the night many bombers had made two sorties, and a Wellington would carry up to eighteen 250 lb bombs, or forty-eight 40 lb anti-personnel bombs and six 250 lb bombs. Most came from Foggia, a distance of a hundred and sixty miles, leaving anything up to one and a half hours before each sortie over the Beachhead. Generally speaking, of course, they would have had specifically pinpointed targets, but the order now was to hit 'anything that was lit up'.

When daylight came, for the hard-pressed American and British infantrymen, it was cheering to see squadron after squadron of fighter bombers and even heavies, Liberators and Fortresses, majestically flying over, and to feel the ground shake as the planes unloaded their eggs. On the 16th there were 468 sorties. The Jerries' flak was intense, yet the planes went on in perfect formation. You could see them being picked off in the sky, and just as fast another 'kite' would move into place so as to maintain formation.

Before midnight the Germans resumed their attack, widening the gap further. Gradually during the 17th the Allies were being forced back to the final line of defence, the Flyover and the Lateral Road. German snipers, who had crept through the Allied lines and lain low all night, caused a scare, though for them it was suicide. Eighty Tiger tanks were now thrown into the assault. From time to time, above the noise of battle, you could hear a tank being hit – like a blow on a church bell, followed by an explosion. As one GI of the 179th remembers: 'Those goddam Krauts came on us heiling Hitler and acting as if they were doped up.' A part of the 157th and an artillery company were cut off near Buonriposo and had to withdraw into the caves once occupied by the Irish Guards. On that day, 'the dust and smoke and confusion were such,' wrote General Lucas, 'that little could be seen, and many events occurred which will never be part of recorded history.' And he added: 'A blunt, square salient was eventually driven into the line six kilometres in width.' In spite of this, on the 17th over eight hundred Allied aircraft dropped about one thousand tons of bombs on the German front line positions, a massive quantity and until then the heaviest weight ever dropped in close support on a single day.

On the German side Sergeant Luy's unit had been reinforced with youths aged seventeen to nineteen. They were distributed around the battalion with two or three older soldiers to look after each group. After twenty-four hours' resting the battalion was to go into the attack again, as the second wave behind the paratroopers.

The noise of the artillery on the 16th was so extraordinary that you couldn't distinguish friend from foe. The Allies' warships were also firing again. Later, watching the eager faces of the battalion commander and adjutant, sitting near the wireless operator, Luy knew that things must be going well. Gradually the hammering of machine-guns and explosions of grenades grew fainter. Luy then heard that the German Paras had been halted, and that there had been heavy casualties.

Heavy rain that night made the brooks swell and the going difficult. The battalion was due to attack the caves at Buonriposo, but it was all so carelessly planned. 'Captain Richter was first out of his hole. He shouted orders, but in the inferno of machine-gun fire we couldn't hear much. After a few steps he shouted, "Everybody back!" But we had run into such a heavy barrage that there weren't many of us left … Eventually I made my way to some ruins with two or three fellows, but one man just got up and went forward. I shouted, "Wait, stay here!" He simply raised his left arm and I saw he had no hand. I realized it was Britzius. A grenade went off very close to him. I thought he was finished, but when the smoke cleared he was still stumbling on. I do not know if he survived the war. Then Captain Richter joined us. He too was wounded.'

The Americans defending the caves had used smoke so that the attackers would be silhouetted. From the moans in the ravine that night they knew they had caused a lot of casualties. A German kept crying, 'My name is Mueller, I am wounded,' over and over again. Neither side made any attempt to help him. Shells fell. The voice died down, and then started again, 'My name is Mueller …' A GI could stand it no longer. He pulled the pin out of a grenade, which he hurled over. 'What's your name now, you son of a bitch?'

Further west Gericke's progress against the British (Royal Fusiliers and Oxford and Bucks Light Infantry) was not fully recognized it seemed at Mackensen's headquarters, and was not therefore exploited. Gericke reached the Swallow's Nest and also swung round to attack the wadi known as the North Lobster Claw. The casualties from the shelling were again heart-breaking, added to which the weather was at its most vile. The men were soaked and for two days went without food. They also suffered from lice.

By the 18th the Americans in the caves were virtually isolated.

The German losses had been so great that Mackensen was in some doubt whether he ought to continue the attack. His chief of staff, Hauser, urged him on; they were on the brink of victory, it would be mad to break off now.

The Allies were exhausted, but they did not realize how seriously depleted their opponents had become. During the early morning the 29th Panzer Grenadiers and 26th Panzers virtually eliminated a battalion of the US 179th Infantry. The commander of the 179th was in a state of collapse through sheer lack of sleep, and General Lucas therefore ordered Colonel Bill Darby of the Rangers to take his place. It was the most serious moment of the entire Beachhead battle.

Papers were ready to be burnt in the rear echelons. Cooks, despatch riders, clerks, anybody who could be spared, were rushed to the front. The British 1st Division was brought out of reserve. To make matters worse, the harbour at Anzio had to be closed because of mines dropped from the air. On the 17th the British cruiser HMS *Penelope*, renowned for its earlier service in the Mediterranean, had been sunk by a submarine.

Lucas' state of mind could hardly have been improved by the news that Truscott was to be his deputy jointly with the British General Evelegh, chosen because he got on well with Americans. Lucas knew what was to be in store for him. 'I have done my best,' he wrote, 'I have carried out my orders, and my conscience is clear. I do not feel I should have sacrificed my command.'

Truscott had gone to bed early but soon after midnight had been awakened by his aide Colonel Carleton with the news of his appointment: 'Boss, I hate to do this, but you would give me hell if I held this until morning.' General 'Iron Mike' O'Daniel was to take over from Truscott as commander of the 3rd Division. Truscott at first was upset. He had not been consulted and he was a friend of Lucas'. He also had a feeling that he was being used to pull chestnuts out of the fire. Then he decided that 'this was certainly no time to consider personal preferences.' 'I was a soldier, and I could only carry out the order loyally.'

Truscott's first job was to try to dispel the 'pall of gloom' at Corps HQ. Later Clark told him that he was probably to replace Lucas, but this would not happen until the present phase of the battle was over.

In his unique way Darby put confidence and enthusiasm into the 179th. He singled out malingerers and stragglers and put them on menial duties, such as bringing in dead animals and scooping excrement out of foxholes – all this in front of their comrades. Nevertheless, he was worried about the regiment's low strength and actually suggested that it should be withdrawn into the Padiglione woods. General Eagles absolutely refused to give permission. Every yard of the Beachhead must be held at whatever cost. However, by an amazing piece of luck, the Germans suddenly switched their line of attack further east, against the relatively intact 180th Infantry.

One of the Germans' secret weapons, the radio-controlled midget tank, Goliath, turned out to be a flop, since it easily became bogged down in the mud and was then picked off by anti-tank rifles.

Corporal Frank Cooper of the Gordons was at the Flyover. He spotted one of these strange objects approaching and saw it skid off into a ditch. He at once reported it, and the thing was blown up. Just as well too, for the whole of the Flyover archway was thickly mined, and there could have been 'just one hell of a mess'.

Cooper was a stretcher-bearer. 'You had a strange feeling of nakedness going out into no-man's-land under the Red Cross flag.' About this time he went to pick up a sergeant and two privates who had not returned from patrol. After he and his mate had gone out about a hundred yards a voice called: 'Hey, Jock.' It was a German sniper, all snug, surrounded by grenades and schmeissers. He wanted to swap cigarettes for a tin of bully.

As I myself heard later, Nick Mansell saw them talking, as did some 'monkeys', two-inch mortar spotters. When Cooper returned with the wounded men, the mortars opened up and that was the end of the sniper and the tin of bully.

Because of the crisis, Mansell – although a signals officer – volunteered to man a bren-gun in a platoon commanded by his close friend Jonathan W—. 'Nick was incredible,' Jonathan wrote to me later. 'He was so high-spirited. We were huddled in those miserable slit-trenches, water up to our knees. He told us about summers in Capri, and nights at the opera. I remember trying to enlarge my foxhole and uncovering a corpse, or its leg. I suppose I looked rather wonky because he made me change trenches with him. A spandau was going tat-tat-tat, bullets thudding into the bank. We knew we were in for the high jump. He began to call out silly things to the men like "Mind your hairnet, dearie." The moment he climbed out, a bullet got him, in the neck. He wasn't dead, I could see that, but there was so much blood. I had to go on, it was an attack you see, it was horrible. I loved him, I really did.'

Nick's body was never found.

The American companies of the 157th defending the caves were gradually contracting. Captain Felix Sparks had only eighteen men left in E Company. 'The Germans pressed every advantage. Enemy artillery poured into the Battalion sector without let-up, and German foot-troops appeared on all sides. Battalion medics moved about the area, carrying seriously wounded men to the aid station in the caves, where they were drugged to relieve their pain. Water was needed, but only occasionally could carriers work their way forward to the caves. In a nearby draw trickled a stream in which lay corpses of enemy dead. The water ran blood red, but many of the men filled their canteens, boiled it and drank.'

With more rumours of enemy infiltrations, singly or in pairs, Sergeant Garcia bravely crawled in full daylight to the caves, so that the artillery liaison officer, Captain Hubbert, could radio for Battalion fire. These caves were like tunnels, mostly fifty or sixty feet below the surface, and up to twenty-five feet high, and with six entrances. With wadis on three sides you could only be starved out. Inside were also not only several Italians but some German prisoners. The constant shelling of the entrances reverberated inside, so it was often impossible to speak. Nevertheless there was still a chance for stretcher cases and walking wounded to be evacuated by night to the Anziate, where a truck would await them.

Across the wadi in the German area crouched Sergeant Luy's decimated company. Once more, a man said that what he had experienced had been worse than at Stalingrad; none of his platoon was left. 'A young boy from Saxony who joined us twenty-four hours ago,' wrote Luy, 'came up with a rather tearful child's voice. He said he had no ground sheet. I told him to take one off a dead man lying just outside. I saw him crawl out in the rain, but he only unbuttoned the groundsheet halfway down. Then he came back, yellow in the face, saying that the groundsheet was full of blood. I told him the rain would wash it off. So I went out myself and finished the unbuttoning, and put the groundsheet out in the rain. The dead man was a young lieutenant with curly hair, between twenty to twenty-five. He had caught machine-gun fire in his chest and lower abdomen. I did not recognize him.'

There was another attack. Luy had to take cover behind a dead sheep. It became imperative to call for artillery help, and his lieutenant produced an American intercom radio set. The lieutenant started speaking to Battalion HQ and then handed over to Luy. 'I said, "This is Luy, can you hear me?" "Yes," came the reply, "Loud and clear." It seemed as if I were talking to a huge conference hall with everyone speaking at once. However I directed the fire – more to the left, more to the right, with some success. "Now let them have it." The answer came back, "What do you mean, let them have it? We've only six shots left." Whereupon there was laughter on the line. I couldn't make out what was happening. Then another voice said, "Shame on you, shame on you, have you only six shots? Then we'll send you some." Suddenly I realized we were being listened to by the other side.'

By the end of the 18th the Allies were still just hanging on to their last

defence line, but only just. To the right of the Flyover were the 1st Loyal
Regiment; they held the eastern continuation of the Lateral Road, which
they called Wigan Street, after their home town Preston in North Lancs.
Then came Darby's 179th, then the 180th.

The Flyover, pitted with shell holes like enormous vaccination marks,
iron girders hanging loose like the broken ribs of some decaying
mammoth, had become a symbol of endurance, of survival. If it were lost,
then the Beachhead was lost. At times the Germans had been within a few
yards of the Flyover, and had only been beaten back in hand-to-hand
fighting. Worse, though, the building known as Todhunter Lodge (in
honour of a sergeant) had been lost, and this was actually south of the
crucial Wigan Street. The North Staffs had been sent to help them; even
men from the docks at Anzio were rushed to replace casualties.

Ahead of the Flyover were two roads, Dead End Road and the
Bowling Alley, running eastwards from the Anziate, straight towards the
179th and 180th. This small triangle of churned up mud and crunched up
vehicles had become the pit of hell; and it was near the Bowling Alley that
occurred one of Anzio's legendary acts of bravery.

A company of the US 180th had been reduced to some fifty men,
without any grenades left and only ten rounds per man. There was no
option but to withdraw. The wounded had to be left behind, and one of
them, Private William Johnston, had been shot through the chest and was
thought to be dying. He took it calmly, saying, 'It's okay, fellows. Those
guys paid for it, and they'll pay more. So long.' He crawled back to his
machine-gun, and they made him comfortable and left. He continued
firing until the company had safely gone.

The next morning a lone figure was spotted by an outpost of the 180th
– staggering, falling, getting up, dragging. It was a GI, scarcely able to
talk, Johnston. The Krauts had found him but giving him up for dead had
taken his shoes. He knew he could give information that might save his
comrades, and had been determined to get back.

'My only recourse,' said Lucas, 'was to attack. The only recourse of the
weaker of two opponents is to attack unless he stands still and be cut to
pieces.'

He therefore decided to use his last striking force of any power: the 30th
Infantry, the 6th Armored Infantry and the 1st Armored Division tanks
under General Harmon, for an attack up the Bowling Alley. This would
swing left and join with another force under General Templer at Dead
End Road. Templer would have to use one of his brigades due to land
from Naples that very morning.

Because of the mines dropped in Anzio harbour, the British 169th
Brigade had to be put ashore without its heavy equipment. There were

also dangers from one-man submarines. People said that Templer looked 'flipped', as thin as a rake. So Harmon would have to attack alone; to Lucas it seemed like suicide to send this 'pitiful little force' against the German strength. 'Yet the German attack had to be stopped and I saw no other way to stop it. I decided to let it go.'

The gamble succeeded. Bluff, energetic Ernie Harmon, that 'genius for saying the wrong thing', reached his objective, capturing five hundred prisoners.

Meanwhile the Loyals, having retaken Todhunter Lodge, were being furiously attacked. Their colonel, another who had been unable to sleep, had been forced to hand over the battalion to Major Geoffrey Rimbault, 'as brave as a lion' said Templer. The Loyals had been shelled and dive-bombed at night, and the Germans advanced across Wigan Street absolutely regardless of losses. Suddenly there was a lull. To allow the Germans to be reinforced would be fatal. Templer laid down all the artillery fire he could possibly obtain, and the Loyals and the North Staffs advanced under a smoke-screen.

The incredible happened. The Germans came forward 'in droves' with white flags and hands up. The last bombardment had been too much. Some were trembling, one or two were 'literally gibbering'. Several officers and a battalion commander were among the prisoners. It seemed that they had been told that the Allies were already embarking, but had been shocked and disillusioned to learn that yet more troops were landing.

'Swell work today – keep after them,' signalled Lucas. Thanks to the Loyals and Harmon the Beachhead was temporarily safe. 'German dead were piled in heaps all along our front,' Lucas wrote. 'This was the Hun's last all-out effort. A message from Clark to me read in part: "Congratulate Harmon on his success today. Again I want to tell you that your accomplishments today have been outstanding. Keep it up."'

Kindly words, to smooth the way for the blow yet to come. And whatever the criticisms, Lucas' obsession with supplies and an adequate base had paid off.

In the four days' fighting the Allies had lost about five thousand men, the Germans very slightly more. Since the landings on 22 January Allied and German casualties had each numbered about nineteen thousand, one man in six. The Beachhead had been saved, but the Allies were not strong enough to advance. A stalemate had been reached.

Sergeant Luy was captured late on 21 February. He had just recovered from a brief bout of dysentery. In the darkness of the night the company had split, and he had realized he had wandered into enemy territory. A Very light went up, and he and his men were suddenly surrounded by

Tommies. So now it was a case of 'Come on, come on, hands up.' At once the Tommies began looking for souvenirs, feeling pockets and shouting 'Watch, watch.' Luy pretended he couldn't speak English and said *'Capito niente.'* One little man seized his binoculars. While Luy was kneeling to rescue his spectacles out of his haversack, he was suddenly kicked on the backside. 'I fell on the ground. Someone was shouting, and I heard, "Yes sir, Yes sir." It was clear to me that this was an officer. Suddenly all the soldiers took their rifles off their shoulders and pointed them at us. As soon as the officer went away they put the rifles back on their shoulders and began joking about him.'

Luy and the others had to help with carrying some wounded men on stretchers. More Tommies, artillery men, came up and handed out cigarettes, trying to get into conversation. Luy had some bread which he was cutting with a penknife. Then another officer appeared, snatched the cigarette from Luy's mouth and broke it in half. 'He noticed my penknife and held it up, yelling at the Tommies. Then he closed it and put it in his pocket, and continued his morning walk. One of the Tommies quickly gave me his own knife and indicated that I should finish cutting the bread while he watched for the officer.'

To the west, in the labyrinthine wadis, a special sort of war continued, stealthy and hand-to-hand; here it was said that Germans had a habit of eating a platoon for breakfast. Nobody quite knew where anybody was. There seemed to be no fixed front line. It was almost impossible to evacuate wounded, except along the deep stream-beds, and then there was the danger of grenades being lobbed on you from above.

The undergrowth was gradually being blasted away by grenades and the rifle- and mortar-bombs. Some day Arcadian peace would return to this once lovely part of Italy. But first shepherd's children would have their feet blown off by mines, and people would go hunting for souvenirs, tommy-gun bullets or jagged pieces of shrapnel. Someone would find a German helmet with a hole through it, and he would fill it with apricots and lemons and tie a bow round it, as a present. And wild cyclamen would spring up where the blood of the 7th Battalion of the Oxford and Bucks had soaked into the earth, in unimaginable pain and bewilderment.

Nearer the Flyover and south of the caves was that notorious wadi called the Boot, and here among the craters lurked another dwindling company of the US 157th Regiment. If Templer's task force had been able to move up to the Dead End Road, this company would have been more secure, and their comrades in the caves would have had a lifeline opened up for supplies. As it was, the company was virtually marooned.

The Irish Guards were in their rest area, back with B Echelon. After their earlier experiences, they expected, and hoped, to be despatched quietly to Naples for refitting. Suddenly they were told that they were to relieve the Americans at the Boot. They were not fooled when the Brigadier described it as a tidying-up arrangement, just to get all the British on the left of the Via Anziate and the Americans on the right. 'The sector,' he said reassuringly, 'is very quiet, so you will have no trouble, and your weakness does not matter.'

In due course therefore the Irish Guards reached the Boot, where for four nights they lived under constant attack, a 'savage brutish troglodyte experience'. They also suffered an air attack when anti-personnel butterfly-bombs were sprinkled over them. Icy water swirled at their feet, old and new corpses lay unburied, being impossible to reach because of snipers. 'The bringing up of supplies every night was a recurrent nightmare. Carrying parties got lost, jeeps got bogged and, as the swearing troops heaved at them, down came the shells.' Their colonel, Andrew Scott, always amusing and 'a lot of fun', tried to keep up spirits, but everyone could see he was exhausted, 'You know,' one of his officers said, 'I actually saw him talking in his sleep with his eyes wide open.' A small diversion was provided the first morning by a German walking up in a nonchalant fashion with a bottle in his hand. He said that he had come on his usual errand, to exchange cognac for bully beef or spam. 'Sergeant-Major Pestell explained that the trade agreement had been cancelled "as from now". The German spent an unhappy day deepening Major G. FitzGerald's trench and asking at intervals why Irishmen were in Italy at all.'

Patrols were still being sent out from the caves to neighbouring farms. Some prisoners were brought back, and were initiated to a diet of K rations, not much appreciated. Sergeant Alvin Biggars of Arkansas went out with eight men and was pounced on by twenty Germans who leapt from overhanging trees. He beat them off, killing a few. As he said, 'They ain't so tough when they get into good hard fighting.'.

Private Jim Alcock was a poet. 'It did strike me vaguely that here was my chance to be America's Rupert Brooke. I had nothing to write with anyway. And I was so tired. I tried to think of God; the fact that Jesus died to save us didn't help. I wondered a bit about what the guys with me thought they were fighting for, twenty-year-olds mostly from the Mid-West, never crossed the ocean before – though, come to think of it, a few of them must have been descended from people escaping from per-secutions in Europe. We were just cornered animals, unwashed and ugly. If we killed, we could go on living. Whatever we were fighting for seemed irrelevant. Only suffering was real.'

The 2nd Battalion of the 7th Queen's Royal Regiment had landed on the 18th. It was now selected to take over from the 157th in the caves. On the way there were butterfly-bomb attacks, and the Germans used flame-throwers. Vehicles that were supposed to follow with supplies were pinned down by spandau fire. So by the time the Queen's had struggled through to the caves they were almost in as bad a condition as the people they were to relieve. 'In the caves we found many seriously wounded Americans, while huddled in the back galleries were about thirty Italian refugees – men, women and children – and one large, very bad-tempered pig; to these were now added our own wounded.' Because of supplies being delayed, the Americans reluctantly had to stay on a further twenty-four hours. Before dawn on the 23rd they pulled out, leaving the medical officer with eighteen of their wounded. They had to wriggle along ditches, and about half-way along were spotted and raked by machine-gun fire. The column found itself split in half. Captain Sparks was left without a single man in his company, except for Sergeant Leon Siehr, who worked his way back two days later. Three quarters of the battalion had been lost, and of the survivors ninety were hospital cases, several due to trench foot. Some men had lost their hearing after the constant din of gunfire in the caves.

Ammunition in the caves was so precious that 'every shot had to be a good one'. Now the Germans were mortaring and machine-gunning the entrances 'to the lusty protestations of the pig and the only slightly less discordant wailings of its owners'. Tiger tanks cruised around outside, clanking and grumbling. As food had given out, longing eyes were cast at the pig. Instead emergency rations were eaten – 'an obnoxious mixture tasting like ammunition boots, sawdust and dried mud'. A signal was sent out for 'Uncle 5', the code-word for a Corps artillery concentration, which duly came to pass. But even after this the position was hopeless, and the Queen's were ordered to withdraw on the 24th.

Again the Germans got wind, and very few Queen's men managed to get through, though one party was mistaken for Italian refugees and passed right through the enemy lines without being fired on. Altogether in those two days the Queen's lost 362 officers and men.

On the same day the Irish Guards were thankful to hand over the Boot to the Duke of Wellington's Regiment. The first six Dukes to arrive seemed bewildered by the constant crashing of the shells and the glutinous mud, not to mention the appearance of the 'irrepressible' Captain D. M. Kennedy, red-eyed, grey-faced, with a torn trouser leg and flapping bandage. 'They're new, you see,' said a lieutenant introducing them. 'We only got them this morning.' The Dukes' Colonel Webb-Carter was to write: 'As the tall guardsmen filed out, leaving us the heritage of death and desolation they had borne so long, a peculiar sense of isolation struck us . . .'

At the German 65th Division headquarters their diarist wrote: 'This has cost us a lot of blood. The lion's share of the success must go to the 1st

Battalion of the 9th Panzer Grenadier Regiment under Major Ecker, who has been recommended for the Knight's Cross.'

It was on the 22nd that Lucas had put in his diary: 'Message from Clark. He arrives with eight generals. What the hell.'

Clark sent for Lucas at 8 p.m. He was in his command post in the basement of Prince Borghese's villa. He said that Lucas was to be relieved from his command of VI Corps, and that this decision had been made because he could no longer resist the pressure which came from Alexander and Devers, Wilson's American deputy. That Alexander said Lucas was defeated and Devers said he was tired.

Devers had come to Anzio to see Lucas a week or so previously. 'I was not surprised,' wrote Lucas, 'at General Alexander's attitude. He had been pretty badly frightened, but what I heard about Devers was a great shock. All of us were tired. And I thought I was winning something of a victory. Had been told so by the Army Commander after Harmon's counter-attack.'

Lucas said goodbye to Anzio the following day. 'I left the finest soldiers in the world when I lost the VI Corps, and the honour of having commanded them in their hour of greatest travail cannot be taken from me.'

MARCH

"... forever, Amen. Hit the dirt."

'Go tell th' boys to line up, Joe. We got fruit juice fer breakfast!'

"Tell him to look at th' bright side of things, Willie. His trees is
pruned, his ground is plowed up, an' his house is air-conditioned."

Rome

In her large turreted house, amid silver-framed photographs of the royalty of Europe, old Mrs Tina Whitaker awaited 'the grand apocalypse'. She seemed to her daughters to be the more concerned because her German nurse had been ordered to leave Rome for Berlin, to work in a hospital. 'These Berliners,' Tina Whitaker wrote in her diary, 'are so sentimental, always crying.' The nurse's soldier friend had encouragingly told her: '*Anzio kaputt, Cassino kaputt. Morgen Rom kaputt.*'

It was 3 March. 'The days crawl on sadly,' Tina continued. 'The *contadino* from our Albano property has survived, but most of his family have been killed. Mrs Hodert's lovely villa on Lake Nemi which we occupied in 1940 has been smashed up. Fear of water being cut off. A new man hunt. Our Dr Rocco witnessed a terrible scene. A young woman, pregnant, rushed to embrace her husband, who was being deported. A guard pushed her back violently. She tried once more to reach her husband, upon which the guard drew a revolver and shot her in the face. I counted the sirens ten times this morning. Bombs falling, aeroplanes constantly overhead. Everyone in the house including Schwester Weisskopf [the nurse], but not me and my two girls, in a panic. We had to send them down to the *rifugio*, some early Christian catacombs we opened up recently. From my window at nights I see the red flickering line of Anzio.'

When she was young Mrs Whitaker had had great promise as an opera singer, and in 1881 she had sung before Wagner in Palermo. Now, as the bombs dropped, her daughters heard her break into *Elsa's Dream* from *Lohengrin*.

The incident of the shooting of the pregnant woman, who was also the mother of five children, was the spark that seemed, at last, to ignite the Roman people. She became the necessary martyr; her name was Teresa Gullace and she was thirty-seven, a *popolana*, a woman of the people. Her husband had been one of scores rounded up for forced labour and sent to

the barracks in Viale Giulio Cesare. The Communist women – led by the
indefatigable Laura Lombardo Radice – had helped to stir the fury of
wives, mothers, sisters, daughters, and a great crowd gathered outside.
The boy Peppino Zamboni was taken along by his Trasteverina aunt
Luisa, even though she had no relations there – she could never bear to be
left out of demonstrations. '*Fijo de una mignotta, te venisse un bene, a li
mortacci tua,*' Zia Luisa screeched at the Fascist guards. Some of the
unfortunate *rastrellati* could be seen at the gates, and women battled to
give them packets of food or clothes.

Then Teresa Gullace glimpsed her husband, and rushed towards him.
'She was only five metres away from me,' said Laura Lombardo Radice.
'I cannot swear whether the man who killed her was an SS motorcyclist
or one of those imbecile, arrogant Fascist militia-men. I remember vividly
his pale face, fair hair and black uniform. I saw the woman lying in the
rubbish of the street – she died instantly. The confusion and uproar were
dreadful. An ambulance arrived, and her husband was allowed out to
accompany her body to the hospital. A young man was also killed trying
to escape.' This was the incident that inspired the dramatic scene
portrayed by Anna Magnani in *Rome, Open City*.

Then Laura collected money for flowers, which she laid in the horrid
mess of blood. She had some leaflets printed and circulated that same day.
And in the afternoon there was another demonstration. Here the stories
conflict a little. For whilst it is known that three Fascist 'traitors' were
murdered by Gapists, it is not clear whether it was on this occasion that the
man who was believed to have killed Teresa Gullace was himself shot by
the Communist partisan Blasi. A version is that Blasi just strolled into a
Fascist meeting, singled out his target, shot him dead and then walked
calmly out again. Whatever the truth, the fascination lies in the fact that
this apparently brave partisan – small, virile, nervous, with little blue eyes
– should in the following month turn traitor and betray his own
comrades.

The despair of the Romans now rose like an invisible supplication to
the grey winter's skies. After six weeks the Allies were still at Anzio, any
young man venturing out of doors was in danger of arrest, food was
scarce and prices were soaring; it was very cold, gas and water were often
cut off; there were the grisly stories of tortures at Via Tasso and by the
Banda Koch, and of the executions at Forte Bravetta and Forte Boccea;
and then, above all, there were the bombings with their daily toll of
deaths. At least the Allies did not bomb Rome's historic centre, but many
bombs in the areas of marshalling yards did go clumsily astray. The
bombs dropped on 1 March near the Vatican were, however, believed to
be the work of Fascists, simply to create resentment against the Allies. The
raid on the 3rd in the Testaccio district (some bombs falling on the

Protestant cemetery near Keats' grave, and others destroying part of the Aurelian wall) resulted in many dead. One of the worst was on 19 March, when some hundred people were killed near the Castro Pretorio barracks, which presumably had been the real target; other bombs fell on wings of the Policlinico hospital nearby, causing thirty deaths, and a direct hit on a tram killed sixty people. There were scarcely any precautions taken by the Roman authorities against these raids. Such was the feeling of chaos that quantities of families took to camping out in the Bernini colonnades leading up to St Peter's. A member of the Swiss legation, looking after British and French interests, told Sir D'Arcy Osborne that he had spent one of the most painful days in his life searching for the body of a Frenchwoman among the mangled corpses in the Morgue. The general fear and resentment in the city was palpably beginning to turn into a hatred of the Allies.

Meanwhile the Gapists continued their attacks, blowing up vehicles, eliminating Fascist spies. Outside Rome there was also an attack on Kesselring's headquarters at Monte Soratte. Not surprisingly many arrests followed. Professor Pilo Albertelli, a key man in the Action party, was taken by Koch. So was Tom Carini, likewise betrayed by an informer. Carini was so badly punched and beaten up that he had to go to the infirmary at the Regina Coeli prison. When on his arrest he was confronted by Albertelli in the cell, he could hardly recognize that swollen face. Albertelli's ribs were broken, and each cough was agonizing for him. He had been tossed into the air, and hung up by his heels; needles had been stuck under his finger nails and then heated up. After having been told by his captors that they would fetch his wife and rape her in front of him, he tried twice to commit suicide, once by throwing himself out of a window, once by cutting his wrists with broken watch glass. Eventually he was to die at the Ardeatine Caves.

Another to be executed at the Ardeatine Caves was a simple *contadino*, Angelo Calafati, father of six. He had been hiding escaped prisoners – two Russians, one French and one British, all arrested and sent to concentration camps.

There were said to be 350 prisoners at Via Tasso. Harrowing messages reached the outside world, with rumours of brandings and of disinfectant poured into tubes inserted up the penis. The Jews had to live in the lavatory rooms, and other prisoners had to do their business in front of them. Food would be sent from Regina Coeli. Before it was given to the Jews the guards would sometimes swill dirty water from the lavatory pans over it.

The Gestapo heard of plots to storm Via Tasso, so barbed wire and barricades were set up outside.

*

The two girl Gapists, Carla Capponi and Marisa Musu, had also been at the Viale Giulio Cesare riot. Carla had been arrested, but the women around her had converged on the Fascist police and tried to drag her back. In the turmoil Carla had managed to pass her revolver to Marisa, who in turn slipped a Fascist identity card into her friend's pocket. Thus Carla in due course was able to be released, and was back that evening to help in doing justice to Teresa Gullace's assassins.

Some days later Carla, entirely on her own, set fire to a German petrol lorry near the Colosseum. The fire almost got out of hand, and there was a danger to neighbouring houses. All day long smoke wreathed in and out of the Colosseum's arches, as if the shades of Nero's victims were at last released.

It was after this that Carla cut her hair short and dyed it black.

On 10 March there was an ambitious Gap attack with mortar-bombs and machine-gun fire on a Fascist procession in Via Tomacelli, with plenty of casualties. A reward of half a million *lire* was awarded for information about the perpetrators. When a Communist was arrested shortly afterwards and taken to Via Tasso, other prisoners could hear his screams as he was tortured, alternating with the monotonous voice of the interpreter: 'Tell me who threw the bomb at Via Tomacelli. Tell me who threw the bomb at Via Tomacelli.'

In more fashionable circles in Rome jokes were at least occasionally possible. A rich Florentine, always bedecked with jewels, had rushed during an air-raid to a *rifugio*, there to be joined by other women. They all knelt and prayed before a statue as the bombs thudded outside. When the lights came on the Florentine found that her companions were from the local brothel, and that they were all praying to a naked statue of Bacchus.

It was a common sight in Rome to see ladies in high heels pushing prams with demijohns of water in them. *Coprifuoco*, curfew, parties were the fashion – you had to spend the night at your host's. Mrs Bruccoleri, although Irish, was chased by her porter's wife with a knife 'because of the Allied bombings'. And Baroness Corsi, English, had a bad time with her maid, who was caught stealing. 'Denounce me if you dare,' the maid cried, 'and I shall have you sent to a concentration camp.'

German officers and men on leave or passing through Rome were not necessarily aware of this current of hatred and fear. They made eyes at the girls, and waved from the turrets of their tanks. There were marvellous concerts, and at the Opera one could hear Beniamino Gigli and Maria Caniglia.

Lieutenant Ferdinand Schaller, for instance, was released from the wadi country west of Buonriposo ridge at Anzio, and within hours of being in the front line arrived unwashed and unshaven at the Hotel Regina. He bathed and had a meal from a table with a white cloth. It seemed unbelievable. Then he went to find the rest of his company on the outskirts of the city. A wealthy Italian couple was most hospitable – the man had originally been concerned with importing meat – and offered him a bedroom upstairs. Schaller ate with the family before a log fire, and also played their piano. One evening his men had a *Fest* or party and staged a march-past for him, riding one another as if on horses, to English dance music.

Some German soldiers were stationed below Tivoli at the villa belonging to the Jewish family of Nathan. Obviously they loved being there. 'The uncanny thing,' a Nathan daughter said later, 'was that they kept everything in perfect order, even leaving money, but when they finally left the whole place was mined and could have been blown to smithereens. It was the British who stole our grand piano. But the Germans shot our dogs, which the British would never have done.'

Intelligence reports reaching G2 at Caserta still maintained that the Germans were preparing to defend the city 'to the last', ringing it with road-blocks and anti-aircraft batteries. Famous monuments and public buildings were being used as ammunition dumps. On the other hand there was no indication either that the Allies would recognize Rome's open city status. Suspicions deepened at the Vatican about the Allies' motives when they refused to give a promise not to let aircraft fly over Rome on 12 March, the fifth anniversary of the Pope's coronation, and when a big concourse was planned in St Peter's Square. Osborne was particularly upset about this. He felt at least the promise could have been given as a courtesy. After all, the Vatican had interceded with the Japanese about Allied prisoners, and had been exceedingly generous to him and his staff, not to mention the ten British escaped prisoners who were being housed absolutely free.

Protests about bombings in Rome reached King George VI, Churchill and Roosevelt from all the South American countries. The Foreign Office was impatient. 'We cannot enter into polemical telegraphic and other correspondence with the Roman Catholic hierarchy in Ecuador and Peru.' Finally Roosevelt was driven into making an official pronouncement: 'Everyone knows the Nazi record on religion. Both at home and abroad Hitler and his followers have waged a ruthless war against the churches of all faiths. Now the German army has used the Holy City of Rome as a military centre. No one could have been surprised by this . . . It is a logical step in the Nazi policy of total war.' He also added that the Allies had made freedom of religion one of the principles for which they were fighting.

All this while the 'scrimmage of power politics' continued between the six parties of the southern CLN and the Badoglio government in

Brindisi; and in Rome the CLN was still being rent by argument. Churchill was obviously very bored by Italian politics and repeated in the Commons a version of the 'coffee-pot' half-joke that he had once made to Macmillan: 'It is hard enough to understand the politics of one's own country; it is almost impossible to understand those of foreign countries ... When you have to hold a hot coffee-pot it is better not to break the handle [i.e. Badoglio and the King] off until you are sure you will get another equally convenient and serviceable or, at any rate, until there is a dishcloth handy.' This was not seen as at all funny by the Italians, and indeed caused outrage, with the threat of a ten minutes' token strike in Naples 'to tell Mr Churchill what our country wants'. Then came more anger, about a rumour that a third of the Italian fleet would be handed over to the Russians.

Roosevelt, as always with the Presidential election in view, was getting alarmed by the British attitude. The fact that in Turin and Milan there had been a general strike, the first in occupied Europe, had shown that a new militant spirit was rising in Italy. Then there were continued complaints that Fascist sympathizers were still grouped round Badoglio, and that the king was irretrievably tarnished. On 7 March he cabled Churchill that 'our advices from Italy indicate that the political situation there is rapidly deteriorating to our disadvantage and that an immediate decision in breaking the impasse between the present government and the six parties is essential'. He was afraid that Allied authorities might have to use fire against anti-Fascist groups. The United States government favoured the southern six parties' proposal that the king should abdicate and the powers of his successor (either Prince Umberto or his son) should be delegated to a 'Lieutenant of the Realm', possibly Croce. To which Churchill replied in emphatic terms. He had no confidence in Croce, let alone in his *bête noire* Sforza, or for that matter in any southern politicians, 'ambitious windbags'. 'I understand from Macmillan,' he wrote, 'that Croce is a dwarf professor about seventy-five years old who wrote good books about aesthetics and philosophy ... Vyshinsky tried to read the books and found them even duller than Karl Marx.' In the midst of such a 'heartrending battle', he said, it would be wrong to get rid of Badoglio's 'tame and helpful' government. Churchill was of course anxious for a broad-based government, but this should wait, he repeated, 'until the battle has been gained or, best of all, when Rome is taken'.

If Churchill had been able (let alone had the patience) to listen in to the explosive and utterly inconclusive conference, lasting eight hours, between the leaders of the CLN parties in Rome on 18 March, he would probably have doubted whether an all-party government would ever be possible.

Then everything, suddenly, appeared to have been turned upside down by Russia's announcement that it was ready to establish diplomatic relations with Badoglio's government – evidently preparing the way for its recognition of Italy as a full ally, quite contrary to any agreement hitherto at the Moscow or Teheran conferences. Russia had also asked Badoglio for facilities for its airforce in southern Italy.

The Russian representative on the Advisory Council was now Alexander Bogomolov, in Vyshinsky's place. As Bogomolov, whose behaviour was described to the Foreign Office as that of a 'penitent cobra', was unable to clarify Moscow's motives, it was obvious that this crafty move had been arranged by Vyshinsky before his departure. Badoglio, of course, was delighted, if only because two hundred thousand Italian prisoners were in Russian hands and might now be released. The greatest danger – and indeed it was probably the Russians' aim – was that the wedge between the Americans and British would now be deepened. The whole foundation of the Advisory Council and the Control Commission would also be undermined. As Macmillan said, the Russians were looking forward to more plums out of the Italian cake. 'We cannot disguise a diplomatic defeat if that is the proper description of a process by which we have been deceived by a tortuous and disingenuous policy pursued over a number of weeks by an Ally whom we were treating with complete good faith and frankness.' And the US ambassador in Moscow, Harriman, cabled the Secretary of State: 'We have a long and perhaps difficult road while the Soviets learn how to behave in the civilized world community.'

As it happened, Allied aircraft did keep away from Rome on 12 March. Mother Mary St Luke joined the enormous crowd in St Peter's Square. It was a cold and windy day. There was a strong rumour that the Holy Father would make some important announcement, perhaps about the withdrawal of the Germans from Rome. Mother Mary noticed that there were no Germans in the crowd – no doubt they respected the new temper of the Romans. On the way to St Peter's she noticed a strange thing, namely the sound of footsteps, 'the feet of a multitude converging on one spot', but no voices, let alone laughter.

The Pope appeared on the balcony without any ceremony, his lone white figure standing out against the grey stone of the basilica. His speech, in Mrs Whitaker's words, was a *grande delusione*, just 'platitudes' about the need for prayer, faith, hope and charity. He annoyed some people by his impartiality, and his appeal to the 'vision and wisdom' of both sides in the war to save Rome from ruin. When it was all over a so-called Catholic Communist priest, Don Pecorano, created an uproar by shouting 'Down with the Germans' and 'Long live Peace.' This was followed by others shouting 'We want bread.' Then Communist women, headed again by

Laura Lombardo Radice, distributed leaflets blaming the presence of the
Germans in Rome for the continued bombing by the Allies. As
excitement grew and red flags were waved, mounted police rode into the
crowd, firing shots into the air. People began to flee, and Mother Mary
and other nuns pressed themselves against the walls of Castel Sant'Angelo,
'while frightened men and women ran past like leaves in the wind'.

On the 14th the raids resumed, and in earnest. To Mother Mary that
day was the worst since 19 July 1943 when San Lorenzo was hit and there
were a thousand casualties. 'Bombs fell in streets where queues were lined
up for water from emergency pipe lines, and simply wiped out entire
groups. One woman was beheaded by the blast, the body of another was
thrown on to a telegraph wire.'

This happened whilst Lily Marx was on her way to her boyfriend
Ettore Basevi of the clandestine Centro X information centre. Thanks to
Monsignor O'Flaherty she, a Jew, was officially Chancellor of the
Legation of Haiti and therefore living in extraterritorial property. Apart
from being in charge of finance for Centro X and editing its daily
clandestine bulletin, she was an expert forger of permits and identity
documents in Gothic script, and was now bringing a consignment to
Basevi. When she heard the bombs she was terrified, and then to her
horror on reaching Via Nomentana she found the street blocked off. 'Oh
my God, my God,' she thought, 'Ettore's been hit.' She begged the police
to let her through, saying that she was his wife. But he was safe, by a
miracle. His neighbour Virginio Gayda, the famous foreign editor of the
Giornale d'Italia, and author of so many tirades against the British and
Americans in the early war years, had been killed – ironically whilst
having an English lesson.

In the dells of the Vatican gardens the mimosa was now in bloom. Sir
D'Arcy Osborne, dignified and calm, would be seen exercising his aged
cairn terrier and admiring the camellias in the occasional sunshine.
Sometimes he would be with his friend Tittmann, who would limp along
the paths with his two lively boys, 'Haroldino' and 'Tarzan'. The gardens
had a formality which reminded Osborne, in spite of those great dark
flames of cypresses, of public parks at Ilfracombe or Scarborough; there
were some fairly ostentatious buildings around, but his favourite spot was
a little Renaissance pavilion of the time of Paul IV – away from all the
saluting and bowing from the hips within the Vatican and even St Peter's.
Now the war had brought to the gardens a genteel shabbiness mixed with
typically Italian exuberance, but Osborne never tired of gazing at
Michelangelo's dome, especially in the evenings, when it seemed to swim,
enormous and iridescent, a contrast to the ugly power station and the
radio masts. It was even possible to walk in the gardens at nights, the

disadvantages being frogs, which might be squashed underfoot, or Ethiopian priests, who were almost invisible with their black garments and black faces. The only time the gardens were closed was when the Holy Father took his constitutional.

The French ambassador, Bérard, being pro-Pétain, was not on speaking terms with Osborne and Tittmann, who referred among themselves to his wife as the 'Marquise de Vichy' and to his typist as the 'Marche Funèbre'. Eyes therefore had to be averted when passing in the Vatican gardens, not always easy on account of the Bérards' sheepdog, Judith, which seemed to have an aversion to pets of Anglo-American ownership.

The mysterious lone aircraft known as the Black Widow was heard no more over Rome. Actually it had been found out by AFHQ at Caserta that the bombs dropped on 1 March had been from a British plane. The pilot of a Wellington had mistaken his target during the bad weather, as a night photograph now showed. This discovery could not of course be made public, but AFHQ in making a clean breast to the Air Ministry in London felt impelled to add that the captain had been Pilot Officer McAneny 'who is of Roman Catholic faith', adding that 'unfortunate incidents cannot be prevented without imposing unacceptable restrictions on our air operations'.

Since the bombing of Monte Cassino the Derry–O'Flaherty organization was finding some difficulty in getting billets for new arrivals, mostly from the Anzio Beachhead. Among those who hid 'lodgers' were the film stars Gina Lollobrigida and Flora Volpini; and the Vatican had taken in two American airmen. There were one or two flurries of anxiety, when for instance a British officer stole the pennant off General Maeltzer's car, and another was arrested by German soldiers and fought his way to freedom. Lieutenant Bill Simpson was in a bar when some German officers entered, 'accompanied by a flat-nosed giant', none other than the heavyweight boxing champion Max Schmeling. Simpson could not leave without arousing suspicion, so he decided to offer drinks all around. In due course he found himself having to join in a sing-song round the piano.

A piece of good news for Derry was the sudden appearance of a British soldier of Czech origin, Joe Pollak, a key figure in the escape organization, who had been recaptured by the Germans in January and believed shot. This bouncing little man, with a gift for languages, had been through some wild experiences. He had, among other things, originally been in charge of sending out funds from Derry to Sulmona, where many ex-prisoners were hiding with Italian families. His name however had been betrayed to the Germans by an Australian sergeant-major. This had led to a chase through the streets of Rome, ending at a building near Santa

Maria Maggiore. Stupidly he had spoken to the porter in Italian: 'I am an escaped British soldier. Please help me.' Since he was small and dark, and dressed in civilian clothes, the porter thought he was merely a pickpocket on the run, and therefore replied: '*Ed io sono il Papa*, and I am the Pope.' So Pollak was caught, and after further adventures taken to Sulmona. There again no one would believe he was British, and he expected to be shot as a Jewish spy. After contracting pleurisy in a damp cell, he was put on a train for Germany. He escaped during an RAF bombing attack, and for a while travelled to Rome underneath a lorry carrying German soldiers ...

The Gapists continued their attacks with increasing confidence. On 20 March three German motorcyclists were ambushed on the Appian Way. On 21 March a German truck was attacked near St John Lateran, and an officer was seriously wounded. On 22 March a lorry loaded with troops was attacked in Via dell'Impero; four Germans were killed and some wounded. On the same day there was an encounter with a patrol in Via degli Annibaldi, with one killed and one wounded.

Carla Capponi took lessons in converting mortar-bombs into hand grenades. She and Rosario Bentivegna, both much in love, had taken part in several actions together as a team, and now they and other Gapists were plotting two major operations for 23 March, a day of special significance since it was the twenty-fifth anniversary of the founding of Fascism. The first action was to plant a bomb under the stage at the Adriano theatre, where all the leading Fascists in Rome would be gathered. The second would perhaps be even more devastating: to ambush and blow up a column of some hundred and fifty German police on its daily march through the centre of Rome. If both those actions succeeded, this could be the signal for a general uprising.

The second plan was under the command of Carlo Salinari, whose *nome di battaglia* was Spartaco. For some while those police had marched on an identical route, always at the same time, clumping in their nailed boots and singing in a way particularly irritating to Romans, from Piazza del Popolo through Piazza di Spagna and past the Spanish Steps, then to Via del Tritone and up the narrow Via Rasella. It had been realized by Salinari that Via Rasella was the ideal place to entrap them. The plan was to detonate a huge bomb, which would be concealed in a street-cleaner's cart. But who would be right for this task? Salinari asked Carla her opinion. Not surprisingly she suggested Bentivegna.

For his part Salinari was inclined towards Blasi. Carla, however, was not sure about Blasi, who was a *piccolo artigiano* (literally, a small artisan) and lived off stolen goods. He was a married man and always worried about money. Bentivegna was university educated, very courageous and an optimist, definitely not a worrier. So Salinari suggested Blasi as

Bentivegna's number two. Here again Carla was doubtful. She would have preferred Marisa Musu.

However it was not yet decided whether Marisa Musu or Carla should undertake the Adriano theatre operation. For there had been a change of plan. Instead of the bomb under the stage, a pram with another bomb would be pushed into the meeting by one of the girls. There would only be fourteen seconds between detonation and explosion.

Little did the Gapists know that the Germans had been debating whether they would even allow – in view of the Via Tomacelli incident – such an important gathering of key Fascists in a public place. Finally General Maeltzer took the decision: the meeting would not be at the Adriano theatre, but at the heavily guarded Ministry of Corporations.

So the Gapists were foiled of one supreme act of defiance. The result was that neither Marisa Musu nor Blasi became Bentivegna's number two at Via Rasella; it was to be Carla.

Cassino – Anzio

By 19 February General Freyberg had decided that an all-out assault on the town of Cassino itself was his only solution. This, 'Operation Dickens', would be followed by a massive push up the Liri valley, towards Anzio and, eventually, Rome.

Clark, his mind primarily on Anzio, was 'really shocked' at the proposal that the Monte Cassino feature should be bypassed. He had realized that Freyberg was coming to the conclusion that it was impregnable. The plan was to pulverize the town from the air, followed by an artillery barrage from every gun that could be mustered with tanks and troops in its wake. In other words, Freyberg was at last accepting General Tuker's tactics.

After discussion with Clark, Freyberg agreed on a double attack, on both the town and the ruined Monastery, some of whose walls were still standing to a height of forty feet. The bombardment of both targets would be far heavier than on 15 February – like nothing indeed that had ever been attempted before. In effect, therefore, it would be an experiment, which if successful could be similarly used at the time of Overlord, and as such it appealed to the US Commander of the Mediterranean Allied Tactical Air Force, General John K. Carr, who was ready to 'whip out Cassino like an old tooth', and to the Commander of the US Army Air Forces in Washington, General Hap Arnold. Most Americans in the higher levels of the Fifth Army were, however, full of unease.

Freyberg would have to capture two strongpoints, shown on maps as Points 435 and 192 but known in the Cassino drama as Hangman's Hill and Castle Hill. The former, only three hundred yards from the Monastery and nearly on the same level, was an exposed knoll on which stood the gallows-like shape of a ruined pylon – the 1/9th Gurkhas were to have the fearsome job of scaling it. The latter place, also known as Rocca Janula, in palmier days would have been considered a romantic spot, surmounted as it was by a tower and with wooded slopes where nightingales sang in May; the 6th NZ Infantry Brigade and the 19th NZ Armoured Regiment were to capture this and the main part of the old town clustered below.

It had been insisted by Freyberg that three days without rain was a prerequisite for the attack. He 'brushed aside' complaints that it would be difficult for tanks to get through the debris. General Eaker wrote to General Arnold in Washington: 'I am anxious that you do not set your heart on a great victory as a result of this operation. Personally, I do not feel it will throw the German out of his present position completely and entirely, or compel him to abandon his defensive role.' The streams were swollen, he said, and the land had become a quagmire. Added to which the Germans had their artillery on the high ground, and all the defiles were heavily mined.

The multi-national regrouping of Allied forces showed how important it was to have a diplomat like Alexander in overall command. The New Zealanders relieved the Japanese-Americans. To their left, at the entrance of the Liri valley, was the British 78th Division brought over from the Eighth Army, with the Americans on the Tyrrhenian coast. To the right were the Indians, and beyond them the Algerians.

The Germans had also reorganized. General Baade's 90th Panzer Grenadiers had been relieved by the 1st Parachute Division, described by the historian of the opposing Indian battalion as 'one of the greatest fighting formations ever to take the field'.

The code signal for the Allied attack was appropriately sporting, even if cricket was a closed world to Americans: 'Bradman bats tomorrow'. Unfortunately for Freyberg's plan it rained every day for three weeks, and postponement followed frustrating postponement. Thus the Germans had time to fortify the cellars in Cassino town. Meanwhile the New Zealanders shivered under their gas-capes in ruined farmhouses and sodden foxholes, to the accompaniment of an apparently endless swish and crash of shells, punctuated by cracks of bullets from snipers hidden like marmots in the rocks above. Up on Snakeshead and the bleak ridges near the Monastery the Indians had to contend with blizzards. Every day it was reckoned there would be fifty casualties. Mortars crunched down, and again there were snipers, always snipers. Mines were the great dread.

The scribe of the 4th Indian Division recounts two stories of this period. One is of the 'proud death' of Subedar Subramanyan of the 11th Field Park Company. He went with others to rescue a British officer trapped in a minefield. A shrapnel mine was detonated. 'In the four seconds which elapsed before the mine sprang Subedar Subramanyan threw himself upon it and saved the lives of his comrades by absorbing the burst.' The other story concerns Major Clements of the 11th Field Regiment. 'He had ended a long and exhausting tour in a spandau-swept artillery observation post a few hundred yards from the rear walls of the Monastery. On his return to his battery he found a letter from his mother who besought him, should he ever be in the neighbourhood, not to fail to visit the famous Benedictine hospice.'

A word must now be added on the behalf of mules – in spite of their love–hate relationship with the human species, often tipping the scales towards hate. It was essential to keep clear of the teeth and hooves of these 'four-footed playfellows' and one was not sure whether they responded best to Urdu, French, Italian or broadest Brooklynese. Nevertheless without mules the Gurkhas – at any rate – felt that the battles in Italy would never have been won. Alas, there were too few of the animals available, and casualties among them were high.

General Heidrich was the formidable, and to some arrogant, commander of the German 1st Parachute Division; 'he tolerated no weakness, and had no thought for his own comfort'. But the 'soul' of the defence of Cassino town was Colonel Heilmann of the 3rd Para Regiment. To those two men the parachutists owed the inspiration that gave them such a reputation for esprit de corps and toughness. Heilmann's courage was legendary; he was said to drive a white sports car in places under enemy artillery observation.

Lower in the hierarchy, Lieutenant Heinz Austermann was with the 1st Pioneer Company that had the job of strengthening some of the cellars in the area of the Fishmarket, beneath Castle Hill. All the country nearest the river was under water, which had even penetrated the churches where floated the mouldering corpses of over a hundred Italian civilian victims of former raids – now a feast for rats, too fat even to swim any more. The streets outside were cobbled and narrow. Mattresses and sofas had been dragged into the cellars, so life was almost comfortable. It was somehow reassuring to be told that the castle above had been built when the Hohenstaufens, Germans, had ruled in Naples.

From windows of the less damaged houses you could actually see New Zealanders moving into the outlying streets. During the first days of March hundreds of lorries could be counted in a single day – all out of range of German artillery. Such activity made the paratroopers realize that a new attack could not be far off, and they were ready for this trial of strength.

The attack began on 15 March.

Almost the only good news, said Clark, that he could remember about this time was that, because of his 'preoccupation' with the Italian campaign, 'I had been relieved of all further responsibility for the "Anvil" invasion of Southern France.' General Wilson in particular had been lately pressing for the entire abandonment of the project. Few wartime issues had shown such acute divergence between American and British strategists. The Americans had seen Anvil as part of a great pincer movement in the final invasion of France, with Clark as its commander, but the British, traditionally a sea-power and thus accustomed to using external lines of communication, had always favoured the policy of attrition — smaller actions in various parts of Southern Europe, including the Balkans — resulting in the syphoning off of German troops from the main theatre. Now, because of the failure to capture Rome, and the shortage of landing-craft, the resources for a major landing in Southern France to coincide with Overlord were obviously no longer available. It was agreed by the Combined Chiefs of Staff that the campaign in Italy would have to have overriding priority over all operations in the Mediterranean.

Less controversial, indeed welcome, was Operation Strangle, a bombing offensive against German communication centres, road and rail, to the north of Rome. In this, for the time being, the information from the American OSS agent, Peter Tompkins, played an important part, though it was soon to come to a halt with the arrest of his radio operator.

And it was at this moment of particular stress, Clark later remembered, that he was being niggled by directives from Churchill insisting that in personal memoranda the word 'through' should never be spelled 'thru', and 'theatre' never 'theater'.

At Anzio, between 20 and 28 February, fighting had been confined to local actions, particularly in the wadis. A feature of this hand-to-hand warfare was that neither side was certain where exactly the other was. People lived like savages, faces smeared with mud, clothes never changed, creeping and pouncing in the darkness, lunging with bayonets, firing blindly into bushes at the least rustle. The Germans made various unsuccessful attempts to overcome the Swallow's Nest, alias the Fortress, which was strewn with the unburied bodies of their Sturm Regiment.

And the rain pelted down. Signallers, dog-tired, tried to keep the communications going, stumbling into gullies and shell-holes, equipment soaked, fingers numb. A company of the Sherwood Foresters was attacked by flame-throwers within an hour or so of relieving the Queen's. Everyone in it was killed or captured. A culvert under the Anziate road gave some welcome protection until the rain turned the water into a river, washing away earth over shallow graves and revealing a khaki-covered arm or a boot. Everyone was exhausted, hardly noticing now the shrieks of the sobbing sisters, the multi-barrelled Nebelwerfers. The Foresters' adjutant would give the signal for an all-out 'stonk' by the American artillery, and next morning would forget that he had ever done it. At least one could be sure that a great percentage of German shells were duds.

Brigadier Scott-Elliott of the Oxford and Bucks, in a wadi way out beyond the Lobster Claws, would regularly get a telephone call from his boss Templer. 'Hullo, Jimmy, that you?' 'Yes.' 'Good, still there.' And Gerald Templer would ring off.

Colonel David Wedderburn of the Scots Guards was hit whilst at B Echelon, the rest area, and died of his wound. 'He was a fantastic person,' one of his corporals remembers, 'very tall and good-looking, a good athlete, smashing.' The same shell – not a dud for a change – had hit an umbrella pine, causing an air-burst. It had also killed two Scots Guards majors, two subalterns and the colonel's driver, and had wounded another. Captain Peter Tunnard, unaware of this, arrived at Corps HQ to see a fellow Scots Guards officer (Lord John Hope) and found him absolutely grey, having just heard the news. 'If ever morale was to touch rock bottom, it did so that afternoon.' Since 22 January the Scots Guards had lost fifteen officers and 122 other ranks killed, nine officers and 303 other ranks wounded, four officers – including the Padre and Doctor – and 213 other ranks missing. The Irish Guards and Grenadiers had lost an equivalent number.

Because of the overwhelming Allied artillery the Germans found it virtually hopeless to lay telephone wires at the front. In the wadis, communications with the observation posts had to be by runner. Corporal Liebschner would occasionally have to take messages back to 65th Divisional Headquarters. He would find General Helmuth Pfeifer sitting there in a cave all alone, behind a blanket screen with wooden props. 'Yes, I'm Pfeifer,' the general said the first time. He made you sit down on a trestle bed. There would only be a few radio operators outside the cave.

Pfeifer, always simply dressed, and walking with a stick, would sometimes stay all night with an officer at a particularly dangerous position, talking to him, giving him courage. It was said that he longed to die a soldier's death. He had been wounded five times; he was to be wounded again and on 22 April 1945 he was killed by a dive-bomber, just before the war ended.

On about 23 February Liebschner had to guide his lieutenant to Pfeifer's cave to receive the Knight's Cross. Liebschner slept a good hour or so while Lieutenant Engelhardt chatted with the general, and was awakened to see the cross glittering in the candlelight. Engelhardt was also carrying a bottle of wine, a present from the general.

Once Liebschner was chased and machine-gunned by a two-tailed Lightning aircraft when bicycling along a track. The Allied ships firing up the wadis were the very devil. Liebschner usually shared a trench with a young architect; to take their minds off the shelling and the soaking blankets they used to plan ideal houses together – how many bedrooms, where a nursery would be, even colour schemes.

Sergeant Bernhard Luy after his capture by the British was cross-questioned by an American Jew, who spoke faultless German. His jacket pockets were emptied, a process which was watched with great interest by his Tommy captors. Then Luy and other Germans were put into the hold of a Liberty ship bound for Naples. Luy was uneasy about the ship, which he thought was poorly built. When dark came, the engines were switched off, and the Germans were told that they were lying beside an island; the crew would not travel by night for fear of U boats.

The prisoners were awoken by a hammering sound and the noise of people rushing about. The guard had disappeared and the only door was locked. The hammering increased like a rhythm. Now people above were shouting, and some prisoners began to panic, shouting, '*Aufmachen, aufmachen,* open up, open up.'

'Surely,' Luy wrote, 'they were not going to let us drown like rats. Suddenly a hatch opened. Somebody shone a torch and rolled down a rope ladder calling, "*Rauskommen, schnell, schnell.*" We all climbed up. When we got to the top we saw that the boat was very close to a rock, which obviously had caused the hammering. The boat was tilting, and you could see sailors disembarking. People were sliding down ropes on to that rock, which was getting overcrowded. We realized we were to be the last, and were worried if there would be enough room. However, now we could see Tommies putting down ladders from the cliff tops, and Americans climbing up. Suddenly there was a heavy explosion in the middle of the boat, and quite a panic followed ... some Blacks stretched a net, and the rest of the Americans jumped, followed by the German prisoners. A few of my friends missed the net and were sucked under the boat, others jumped into the open sea on the other side. The rain was heavy, and there was quite a storm. Out of forty-six prisoners ten were lost and some had broken limbs and other injuries because of the rocks ... Later the Tommies marched us through a village, and some Italians appeared with knives, indicating that they wanted to cut our throats. The Tommies seemed to expect this and fired shots, which made the Italians run away. We were taken to a big house near some beached ships, but the Italian woman there refused to make a fire even though we were wet through. A British corporal, however, brought hot tea, biscuits and some wood for the stove.'

The next day, by a subterfuge, Luy found that the name of the island they were on was Ponza, which was where Mussolini had first been interned after his arrest in July 1943. What was more, it transpired that they were in the very house where Mussolini had then lived.

On Hitler's insistence another major attack had to be made on the Beachhead. Once again he intervened in tactics, demanding that the main effort should be against the American sector in the south, between Cisterna and Nettuno. He believed that the country there was easier for tanks, and also felt that the Allies would be forced to remove their reserves from the Via Anziate area, which would then be laid open for one more final thrust to split the Beachhead in two. Mackensen and Kesselring were forced to accede.

Dummy tanks were placed in the Alban Hills and Ardea areas, but here once more Peter Tompkins in Rome was able to tip off the Allies and they were not foiled. He was able to provide locations of some of the newly sited long-range artillery, as well as the railway gun Anzio Annie – but even so the latter could never be silenced, since snakelike it disappeared too quickly into its tunnel.

The attack was planned for 28 February, but delayed twenty-four hours because of torrential rain. In spite of Hitler's directive, Mackensen soon found that he was having most success at Carano nearer the Anziate, against the 509th US Parachute Infantry. A company was overrun, and for a while matters seemed really serious. 'God,' their colonel, Bill Yarborough, remembered, 'we were attacked with everything, including flame-throwing tanks, and still didn't give up.' The Germans, knowing that it was a sensitive area, kept hammering away. 'The word was whatever you have you hold. It was one hell of a fight, and we thought that the German attack was really going to roll over our final protective line. It came within two hundred yards of it, I guess. And then all the Corps artillery we had was churning up the ground in front of us. The Germans came forward in their usual disciplined way and tried to dig in their weapons; but, boy, the stuff that was flying in the air around there. Nothing could live, and so they finally stopped.'

At 6.30 p.m. on 1 March Kesselring ordered the attack to be called off. In two days the Germans had lost nearly three thousand men and at least thirty tanks, without any worthwhile gains.

The next day being clear and brilliant, the Allied planes came out into the attack, and in a very big way, concentrating on assembly points and gun positions, from Cisterna to Campoleone and Velletri. 201 Fortresses and 96 Liberators, escorted by 176 Lightnings and Thunderbolts, dropped 349 tons of fragmentation bombs. 'Christ, General,' Truscott's aide said to him, 'that's hitting a guy when he's down.' But Wynford Vaughan-Thomas, the BBC correspondent, thought that 'the great flight of aircraft looked strangely beautiful, remote, and efficient, as they came in from the south in an endless stream, jettisoned their load of death with a clinical detachment and swung back for more'.

There could have been little enthusiasm by the German task force sent against the Canadian–American Special Service Force, on the lower reaches of the Mussolini Canal – such was the reputation of these 'Black Devils'. And indeed it made no progress whatsoever.

'The Krauts were afraid of us,' said one Devil, Stoney Wines. 'They had been told that we took no prisoners and that most of us were ex-convicts and would show them no mercy.' General Frederick had the idea of printing stickers with the words 'The Worst is Yet to Come' in German, and these would be pasted on the foreheads of Germans killed during patrols. 'Killing is our Business' was also the Devils' motto, and night raiding the speciality. As a Canadian journalist wrote, 'When a tough job comes up, the Black Devils take to it like a duck to water. They revel in danger. With blackened faces and armed to the teeth ... they make desperate silent killings, and come back as dawn streaks the Italian sky, bloody, weary, torn but grimly satisfied.'

General Frederick was an unlikely figure to command this 'mob': slight, pale, neat, with a little moustache. Often he went on patrols himself, 'just to check conduct'. On one occasion a patrol of Forcemen was caught in a minefield, and a heavy German barrage opened up. A stretcher-bearer was hit, and his fellow turned angrily to the nearest soldier: 'For Christ's sake, don't stand there. Grab the other end of this litter!' The soldier obeyed, and only at base was it discovered that he was Frederick.

Morale among the Allies had quickly begun to rise now that Truscott was in command of VI Corps. There was a feeling of positive action, of determination. Truscott moved his headquarters out of the cellars to a wine shop, and on a wall he had a cartoon by Bill Mauldin with the caption, 'The hell this ain't the best hole in the world. I'm in it.' While he held his briefings, shells would be crashing down in the square outside and anti-aircraft guns clattering away almost deafeningly.

He was a quiet man, usually dressed in breeches, leather jacket and a white scarf. People said his head was too small for his helmet. The British liked him and he liked them. He believed in being seen. To some extent, Clark said, he was of the Patton variety. 'But he wasn't as hard-boiled as Georgie was, and he wasn't quite the showman that Georgie was ... he [Truscott] was a dashing cavalryman.'

During the succeeding month the 504th Parachute Infantry and the Rangers were withdrawn from Anzio, to be replaced by the 34th Infantry Division. In the British sector, now the smallest, Templer's 56th Division was being replaced by the 5th Division under Gregson-Ellis from the Garigliano; the three Guards battalions were also withdrawn and their place taken by the 18th Infantry Brigade. Truscott thus had five divisions under his command, two British and three American, plus the irrepressible Black Devils, who carried on their private war in the old Pontine Marshes across the Mussolini Canal.

Since 22 January the total American Beachhead casualties were reckoned at 10,775; the British were 10,168, and the German 10,306 – officially, but probably greater.

Hitler was at Berchtesgaden, whilst his 'Wolf's Lair' in East Prussia was being fortified against Russian air attacks. He was in a poor mood, and his girlfriend, Eva Braun, found him old and sombre. It was, therefore, not the best of times for Kesselring's youthful-looking chief of staff, Westphal, even if he was friendly with Hitler, to tell him that the German strength at Anzio was no longer adequate, and that the sacrifice of troops must be stopped at once.

This did indeed precipitate an outburst of Hitlerian rage, and it was demanded that twenty officers of all ranks should forthwith be sent up from the Beachhead, to account personally for such a shameful business. As Westphal said: 'Hitler would have done still better to visit the front himself and be convinced of our aerial and artillery inferiority on the spot.'

Westphal spent more than three hours with Hitler, and was often interrupted. 'At the end he [Hitler] said, with obvious emotion, that he knew well how great was the war-weariness which afflicted the people and also the Wehrmacht. He would have to see how he could bring about a speedy solution. To do so, however, he needed a victory.'

The group of officers was led by General Walther Fries of the 29th Panzer Grenadiers, and Hitler grilled them for two days. Fries gave as the decisive causes of the failure: 1 The complete air superiority of the Allies; 2 The fire superiority of enemy artillery, including naval guns; 3 The fact that it was impossible for the Germans to commit their heavy armoured forces at the critical time because of the soft swampy ground, travel off the highways and hard surfaced roads not being feasible to any extent. The co-ordination between enemy artillery air observers and their own artillery had been excellent, with disastrous effects also on German artillery sites. Hitler then said: 'In other words, you believe we should have fighters?' The answer could only be in the affirmative.

Fries vigorously objected to the suggestion that his troops' morale had been low. In so many cases reinforcements had been insufficiently trained, and they had immediately been subjected to enormous strains. Even, he said, the most superior infantry force is no longer able to advance if it is being smashed by massed artillery fire and air attacks. Only ten per cent of the German losses had been due to infantry weapons; fifteen per cent had been due to enemy bombing, seventy-five per cent to artillery.

At the end Field-Marshal Keitel said to Westphal: 'You were lucky. If we old fools had said even half as much the Fuehrer would have had us hanged.'

On the subject of Nazism, an artilleryman of the German 65th Division has said: 'There were Nazis in the Army but on the whole we fought for our country and not for Hitler. Everybody knew that after the sorrowful and sad end of the First World War we could not expect anything good should we lose the war. In my opinion the Germans were only better soldiers because there was no other choice. We were so poorly equipped after the end of the so-called *Blitzkriege* that we had either to be brave or give up. The Allies could save lives because you had more and better weapons ... As sons of their mothers our soldiers wanted to come home safe, and as partners of their comrades they did not want to let them down. I think something like this is in every honest army.'

And another, from the same division: 'Did *I* feel that we were defending civilization against the barbarian hordes? Yes, I did, but only in relation to the Russians. The Russians were our enemy number one. The fear of those "sub-humans" entering our country and plundering, burning and raping as they went along (which in fact did happen) forged the German nation into the kind of war-machinery which still fought on when all hope of victory had long gone. As regards the British and the Americans, they were simply pawns in the plot of International Jewry to achieve world domination. There was always a certain respect for the British, even at the height of the bombing, for fairness, but the Americans did not have this reputation – they were considered flamboyant, too rich to be true, rather insensitive. On newsreels one could see over and over again how ignorant were the captured American air-crews. They really had no idea what they were doing and why they were fighting: just paid mercenaries ... The German front-line soldier did *not know* about the concentration camps, nor about any other crimes committed by our side. And that applied to the vast majority of civilians too. The only crimes which we soldiers were aware of were those committed by the Russians and the Allies. I know it is very difficult for the British and Americans to understand, but unless they do they will never be able to explain why sixty million people were able to fight the rest of the world and keep them at bay for over five years – Pfeifer's voluntary death only makes sense in these terms.'

In effect, stalemate had now been reached at Anzio, for the Allies were also incapable of further attacks. Mackensen, however, guessed that if the

Allies succeeded at Cassino an attempt would be made by them to break
out of the Beachhead. In this he was right, for Truscott was planning just
such an operation, codenamed Panther, which it was hoped would start
on 19 March.

For the Germans, however, it was important to keep up aggressive
patrols and raids. The Allies must never be allowed to feel that they had
the whiphand at Anzio.

★   ★   ★   ★

And so I landed at Anzio docks on 2 March with the Green Howards.
Within ten minutes I was nearly killed by a shell from Anzio Annie, the
railway gun. Within three days I was at the Fortress, and there I stayed for
a fortnight – not so very far from the wadi where Nick Mansell had died,
though I did not know it.

'Quiet, yer bloody fool,' were the words that welcomed me at the
fortress on arrival at night. 'Jerry's only seventy yards away.' As I wrote
afterwards to my brother: 'My first shock was the sight of no less than
eight dead Jerries in various stages of decomposition. They were too far
gone to be removed. Anyway perhaps they were a useful deterrent to any
more hostile patrols. But the smell of them – and the smell of human shit
and empty tins – was atrocious. Eventually I got used to these bundles
with wax faces. People had been looting their wallets, and photographs
were scattered around. I picked a photo up but was ashamed to pinch it,
and I couldn't even take a postcard of Romulus and Remus.'

By day it was fairly quiet at the Fortress, but at night shells whirred and
sighed continually overhead, and there were air-bursts. Machine-guns
spattered, Jerry mortars coughed, ack-ack crackled, bombs crumped. The
sky was like a deadly fireworks display. 'One day I saw a helmet moving
across a gap,' I went on in my letter. 'Often we heard voices. Further away
we could see a spandau post on a ridge – too far to snipe at the men
walking so obviously on the skyline, and too near for our mortars, and
anyway we didn't want to attract fire on our positions. It was all so
ridiculous, I even saw a German relieving himself on the hillside in full
view.' I had brought the Everyman edition of *War and Peace*, but only
the *Peace* parts were suitable for front-line reading. Two Germans, who
turned out to be Danes, wandered into the British lines carrying a dixie of
greasy stew, which I tasted and found 'filthy muck'. One night I heard a
German patrol creeping about in the undergrowth, making bird noises.
'Ten yards away from me there was distinct movement. We positively
hared into our trenches, and I belted off with a tommy, and Corporal
Humphrey with a bren. Then Corporal H. chucked a grenade and one
was thrown back at us. This went on for a bit. Next morning Davis said he
had seen a dead Jerry just where I'd fired. My first kill! . . . Everyone is so

amazingly cheerful. You don't actually feel depressed at all – it's a strange feeling, almost thrilling in a way. Like a child's game on a large scale, and what's more you can laugh at these idiotic things.'

My feelings changed somewhat, as I confessed in my diary, as more friends were killed and I became affected by the 'frantic' strain of sleepless nights and of watching for German patrols. Sometimes the odd sniper's bullet ripped the groundsheet over my head, and mortar bombs would fall short. Then there were the 'commando slopes' to be climbed with clanking water-tins. Socks were perpetually soaked and blankets sopping. Then I was sent to a forward observation post for three nights, and here my platoon was only thirty yards from the Germans. You could even creep forward along the wadi and see above, among the branches, the silhouette of a heavy machine-gun against the night sky. 'The men were blue with cold and nerves when I crawled round with the rum ration. You could hear the Jerries plainly laughing and talking, and coughing as they dug. One's name was Gustav.' Then a man called Sutton took fright and threw a grenade, and all night long we could hear a wounded Jerry gurgling and crying. 'I crawled up next morning to fetch the body, but it had gone. I saw the blood though ... It continued to rain and we felt miserable. Next night they mortared us and machine-gunned down the wadi so that we were flat against the sides. It was all I could do to keep the "bomb-happies" in check. Then some grenades were thrown, but, mercifully, no casualties.'

And so back to B Echelon, sleep, and even a little 'convalescent sun'; and at nights the older and hardened Green Howards officers played nap and drank rye whisky.

That German machine-gun I had seen probably belonged to the 2nd Battalion of the 11th Parachute Regiment, and could thus have been a part of the runner Liebschner's company. Orders had come through for the 3rd Battalion to replace the 1st and 2nd, which had been constantly in the line without rest since their arrival. On the night of 15 March, therefore, the very night on which my platoon was withdrawn from the forward position, Joachim Liebschner was taken out of the line too. It was raining hard as usual, he has told me, and all through the next day he slept. For the first time in weeks he felt dry. He was given his back pay, which seemed a lot of money. In the evening he played pontoon and lost everything. A month earlier he would have been very worried, but now he didn't care. He had drunk a lot of wine, and he crawled back into the straw, feeling extraordinarily happy, warm, dry and glad to be alive. The next day he had his first haircut in two months.

Cassino

Early in the morning of 15 March most of the Allied top brass – including Alexander, Clark, Freyberg, Juin, Devers, Eaker and Leese – assembled at the village of Cervaro, three miles south of Cassino. In this 'picnic atmosphere', they were to watch the annihilation of the town and its defenders.

The weather was perfect for bombing. Within a couple of days perhaps the great ordeal of the battle of Cassino, now in its third phase, would be over, and that would lead to the realization of Winston Churchill's dream, the link-up with Anzio. As zero hour approached everyone fell silent. Then there was a distant drone, and soon this grew into a rumble and a throb. Fleets of black specks could be seen, trailing long straight scarves of white vapour. Then these specks turned silver, and the planes were suddenly overhead – Liberators, Fortresses, Marauders, Mitchells – a thousand feet up; and then they dipped and opened their bellies. The war correspondent Christopher Buckley saw 'sprout after sprout of black smoke' leaping from the earth, coiling upwards like 'some dark forest of evil fantasy'. Even from that distance the VIPs found the noise stunning as it reverberated from mountain to mountain. The very relentlessness of the attack was in a shameful way exhilarating. This was revenge for Coventry, Warsaw, Rotterdam, London.

On another hillside Tancredi Grossi also watched, petrified, as the bombs fell on the place of his birth. The tall buildings, the ancient remains, the Cyclopean walls, the elegant villas, the pretty modern houses – all gone. For six months Cassino had endured its horrors, but 'in our hearts there had always been the hope that the town would not be entirely destroyed'. Now Grossi was witnessing its final throes of death.

Some of the men of the German 1st Pioneers in Colonel Heilmann's 3rd Parachute Regiment were stationed in the cellar of the town prison, only a hundred yards from the Allied lines. They had heard the New Zealanders moving around and talking during the night, but by first light

1 In the calm of a perfect winter's morning the British land at Peter Beach, north of Anzio
(Photograph by Denis Healey)

22 JANUARY 1944

2 The Americans land at X-Ray Beach, south-east of Nettuno
(National Archives, Washington)

3 The author, en route for Anzio

(*Raleigh Trevelyan*)

4 Two members of the author's Company during an attack across the Moletta river, Anzio
(*Imperial War Museum*)

5 Americans in a bazooka attack on farmhouses near the Mussolini Canal
(*National Archives, Washington*)

6 Jews digging sand out of the banks of the Tiber, 1942
(*Publifoto, Rome*)

7 Captured American and British soldiers are marched up Via Tritone, Rome, 1 February 1944
(Publifoto, Rome)

8 The rollicking 'king of Rome', General Kurt Maeltzer, with Maria Caniglia, diva of the Rome opera, in her costume for *Tosca*, early May 1944 when she sang with Beniamino Gigli
(Publifoto, Rome)

10 'You have the eyes of a hyena.' Drawing of Captain Kurt Schutz of the Gestapo at Via Tasso by Michele Multedo. Schutz commanded the executions at the Ardeatine Caves

(*Michele Multedo*)

9 Mother Mary St Luke
(*Robert L. Hoguet*)

11 Monsignor Hugh O'Flaherty in his office
(*Col. S. C. Tomlin*)

12 Italian Alpini troops
  encamped at Monte
  Marrone, near Cassino,
  30 March
      (*Imperial War Museum*)

13 Italian women escaping
  from the shell-battered
  village of San Vittore,
  near Cassino, February.
  The American tanks have
  been knocked out by
  mines
(*Keystone Press Agency Limited*)

14 The bombing of Cassino town, 15 March. Castle Hill (Rocca Janula) to the right, the lower slopes of Monastery Hill to the left

(Keystone Press Agency Limited)

15 Germans bringing in their wounded at the Fishmarket, Cassino, 17 March. New Zealanders
are inside the house on the right

(Georg Schmitz)

16 General Helmuth Pfeifer of the 65th Division visits an advance post in the Fosso di Carroceto, typical wadi country

(Wilhelm Velten)

17 American and British prisoners carry stretchers behind the German lines, about a kilometre south-west of Aprilia

(Wilhelm Velten)

18 Near the Lobster Claw wadis. In the foreground graves of men who fell during Operation Fischfang, 16–19 February

(Imperial War Museum)

19 White tapes guide a platoon past a minefield protecting a sand-bagged headquarters on the way to the Fortress, early May

(*Imperial War Museum*)

20 Wounded GIs

(*Anzio Tourist Office*)

21 German propaganda leaflet: on the front a luscious pin-up, on the back a grisly shock

(Wilhelm Velten)

22 At a fair, Sulmona. When the German corporal hit the bullseye, a photograph was automatically taken. He did not realize that he was surrounded by escaped PoWs. Left to right: Joe Pollak (British private), a French naval officer, Gilbert Smith (British officer), 'Duke' (American officer)

(Joe Pollak)

23 A GI shares his rations with
an Italian boy
(Anzio Tourist Offic

24 At the Moletta crossing, 23 May. Private Mornington Sutton, a member of the author's platoon, has stepped on a mine, and is carried by German prisoners. The German on the left has been bandaged by the author

(Imperial War Museum)

25 German guards at St Peter's. The entrance to the Santa Marta hospice is through the archway to the left

(Publifoto, Rome)

26 The Americans enter Rome

(Publifoto, Rome)

27 The Germans retreat from Rome, 3 June. Taken by Harold Tittmann's elder son, from the Santa Marta hospice. In the foreground are carts camouflaged with greenery

(Harold H. Tittmann 3rd)

28 The Pope meets Allied war correspondents, 7 June

(Imperial War Museum)

29 The lynching of Donato Carretta, director of the Regina Coeli prison, in September 1944. After this picture was taken he was beaten with oars until he drowned

(*ANPI, Rome*)

30 Field-Marshal Albert Kesselring arrives for his trial by a British military court, Venice, February 1947

(*Mrs Aubrey Gibbon*)

there was complete quiet and the Kiwis had obviously been withdrawn –
to escape the bombardment, so it turned out. Sergeant Georg Schmitz
had just returned from his nightly digging and was getting ready to eat
when he heard a wave of bombers approaching. He scarcely bothered, for
Allied bombers flew over daily to targets in Northern Italy. Then, when
he felt the earth trembling and heard the explosions, he knew what he and
his comrades were in for.

'The first wave dropped most of its load near the station, but before we
could think straight there was a second wave coming, and this time we
were in the midst of it. The air vibrated, and it was as if a huge giant was
shaking the town. The bombs came nearer and nearer, then the thunder
faded away. Well, we had been lucky. Dust and dirt got into the cellar,
into our eyes, ears and mouths, tasting of bones.' Another wave. The men
clung to one another, 'as if we were one lump of flesh'. Silence again, and
unbelievably they were still alive. They couldn't see. Any sound seemed
to come from a long way off. After a while a dim light appeared at the
cellar entrance. Schmitz went upstairs, and saw that the whole row of
houses opposite had disappeared. Only one house was left standing, and
this was where he knew there was a group of his comrades. He wanted to
run across, but yet another wave of planes could be heard.

After the next load of bombs, it was like night again in the cellar. The
men tried to feel their way through the stifling dust to the entrance, but
there was nothing there except rubble. 'This was terrible. We were buried
alive. Frantically we started to claw in a mad haphazard way at dirt and
stones. And then there was another wave just overhead . . .' During a lull
Schmitz at last managed to scrape a passage into the upper world. The
people in the house opposite were still alive – they had been sheltering
under a stairway. He went to search for another group north of the prison,
and discovered that they had dug themselves a hole underneath a tank
which in turn was sheltered under a massive stone archway – indeed
excellent cover. Schmitz called out a few words of encouragement and
returned to the prison, which was still standing. His men were clutching
the columns that supported the building. Back he went the way he'd just
come. But yet more bombs had completely changed the landscape, and
for a while he lost himself. Then he found that the stone archway and the
tank had been obliterated. His friends would be under that pile of broken
masonry, 'but there was nothing we could do except weep and rage.'

It was clear to Schmitz that he and any survivors must get away at once.
He suddenly remembered a cave below Monte Cassino, so during another
lull they made a dash, just reaching it in time; and there they found the 2nd
Battalion headquarters and eighty paratroopers. They all waited,
weapons in hand, until the bombardment finally would end, so that they
could rush out and take up positions of defence.

At noon it did seem to be over. To the Germans' amazement – since the town was supposed to have been evacuated of all civilians – some eight families, including children, tore out in a panic from other caves, below Castle Hill. They were crying out, tumbling over debris, falling into craters, some of which were the width of a street, clambering out again. Down came the Allied artillery – a 'creeping barrage' that was to last over two hours. It was pitiful to see the Italians being hit and falling. A few survivors struggled towards the Via Casilina.

These were not the only civilians to die that day. At Venafro and other villages on the edge of the Abruzzi mountains one hundred and forty were killed by bombs from heavy aircraft that went astray, as were ninety-six Allied soldiers, many of them Moroccans.

The German Corps Commander, Senger, was on his way to see General Heidrich, who was at the Regimental headquarters, when the bombing started. Later he remembered the blast throwing him backwards and forwards. Afterwards when things died down a little, Senger walked by himself over ground that seemed deserted by human beings. But every now and then men would bob up from hidden batteries and then rush back again to cover. The splintered trees, the smell of cordite mixed with fresh earth, the jarring explosion of shells, the whistling of shrapnel, red-hot, made him feel isolated. 'What I saw and felt took me back twenty-eight years, when I experienced the same loneliness crossing the battlefield of the Somme.'

There was a loneliness, too, when the New Zealanders entered the ruins of Cassino, the bleak loneliness of death. It seemed incredible, therefore, when a machine-gun opened up, somewhere among the peaks of rubble. Then there were rifle shots, and grenades were thrown.

Far from being annihilated, these Germans – emerging from their cave and even some cellars – did not seem even to have been stunned. As it happened, some three-quarters of the 3rd Parachute Regiment had been killed, and one company had been reduced to seven men. Later, one of their battalion commanders, Major Boehmler, remarked how the New Zealanders had looked so confident, advancing 'gaily' and 'for the most part in close formation'. Their tank commanders behaved as if they were on a ceremonial parade, head and shoulders exposed. He added: 'They were the first targets of the German snipers, and over many a tank commander his turret crashed down for the last time in his life.'

And as Freyberg had been warned, the bomb craters also served to impede the tanks. The New Zealanders tried to flatten the craters with bulldozers, but the drivers were even easier targets for the snipers. All the same, as Boehmler said, the Kiwi troops reacted quickly; they were as 'alert as gun-dogs', and their own snipers, who soon got into action, were 'devilish good shots'.

A corporal of the 25th NZ wrote: 'Entering Cassino was a vision of the end of the world, past description. It was like some ghastly warning. Would this then be the fate of Rome, or for that matter Paris, or London, or Berlin, or even Auckland? Marching into those ruins brought out a kind of sadism in us. We were really enraged when the Jerries hit back – they had no right even to be *alive*. They were behaving like machines. Some bugger near me was hit, and he went screaming straight towards the Jerries, not in pain but in sheer fury, like some frantic wild animal scrabbling through the ruins which were covered with a sort of white marble dust – and, God, did that dust dry up your throat. Of course they got him. I can only describe Cassino as looking as if it had been raked over by some monster comb and then pounded all over the place by a giant hammer. There were these vast craters, you see, which when the rain came that night, filled up like lakes, deep enough to drown a wounded man.'

Allied Air Force critics of the next day's battle said that the infantry follow-up was 'puny', and certainly there was an unexplained delay in the area of the station. But the dark night, the flooding, the sheeting rain and the mud all combined to confuse communications. It was an extra-ordinary – though typical – feat of the Gurkhas to scale Hangman's Hill, literally by using a goat track up an almost sheer face and wriggling along it man by man. When daylight came many Gurkhas were revealed to the defenders of the Monastery and promptly decimated. However the remnants of the company dug in on the south slope and were able to be reinforced, in time to beat off a German counter-attack.

Some of the Gurkhas had lost their way on the night march to Hangman's Hill. Now they obediently reappeared. One of them, Rifleman Manbahadur, had taken shelter in a wrecked tank, and from there he had shot a German sergeant in the throat. He had emerged to bind up the man's wound, and when he reached his fellows brought with him an abundant and welcome supply of American cigarettes that he had chanced upon en route.

The fortitude of the Gurkhas during that next week is one of the most moving sagas of the Italian campaign. It seemed impossible that these small brave brown men, from a remote land thousands of miles from Europe, could exist up there, without enough cover from enemy fire, let alone the weather, and without enough to eat or drink. Yet they were the Allies' great hope. If only they could hold on, if only they could be reinforced, an attack could be launched on the Monastery itself, and this long, long, bitter struggle might be brought to an end. The Allied artillery began to drop smoke on Monte Cassino, the object being to prevent artillery observers from bringing down fire on the New Zealanders, who were building a Bailey bridge over the Rapido below. But the smoke drifted on to the Gurkhas, choking and blinding them. Worse, the shell cases and smoke canisters came showering down, causing several casualties.

Two-thirds of the town, including the railway station and Castle Hill, had been captured by the New Zealanders. Dead tired – some of them not having slept for forty hours and without any outside communications – the Germans had formed themselves into 'hedgehogs', notable strong-points being the Continental Hotel, the Hotel des Roses, a *palazzo* known as Baron's Palace, the Roman 'Colosseum' and the 'Hummocks' (presumed, according to guide-books, to be the site of Mark Antony's villa and his 'nameless orgies' – 'Orgies! Lucky sod!' as the corporal of the 25th remarked). In the corner of the Fishmarket stood a house which a handful of German pioneers under Lieutenant Cord (soon to be struck down by a machine-gun) had turned into a fortress. There were New Zealanders in the building next door, but the Germans had the advantage and could lob mortar-bombs into the upper windows. The battle for these points was to last for days, with wounded from both sides crying for help from the rubble.

Colonel Heilmann, because of the severe shortage of manpower, had brought a company of bakers and butchers in to the line. He inspired his men with the feeling that the eyes of the Fatherland were upon them, and they were ready to risk their lives. General Heidrich now laid on a big artillery concentration, and this also slowed up the New Zealand advance.

The Allies once more bombed the Monastery, where the ancient Brother Carlomanno, last survivor of the Benedictine monks, and a few starving sheep and goats roamed in the vomit-sweet stench of death. The Germans took refuge in the underground passages and were unscathed.

British pioneers having refused to face the admittedly very dangerous task of taking supplies to the Gurkhas, this was done by companies of the 4/6 Rajputana Rifles and some gunner volunteers. Only eight casualties were involved; nevertheless, it was decided that from now onwards all supplies would have to be dropped by air, even if a great number of packages would necessarily miss their target. Two or three men had to subsist on a shared one-man K ration per day. Radio batteries were usually smashed, and several men were sniped when trying to recover packages which had rolled down the mountainside. Some blood for transfusions landed on the Monastery ruins and was actually used by German surgeons.

Reinforcements also reached Castle Hill. After a day of confused fighting in the maze of ruins in this phantom town, it became obvious that the battle was reaching stalemate. The New Zealanders were not making the progress hoped for. Clark wrote in his diary: 'Freyberg's enthusiastic plans are not keeping up to his time schedule. I have repeatedly told Freyberg from his inception of this plan that the aerial bombardment alone never has and never will drive a determined enemy from his position ... Due to General Alexander's direct dealings with Freyberg and the fact that this is an all-British show, I am reluctant to give a direct order to Freyberg.'

Officially Freyberg was still part of the Fifth Army. As General Juin was to realize a few days later, Clark – whilst being appalled by the carnage – was worried lest by the world at large he would be regarded as responsible for a defeat. 'I hate to see the Cassino show a flop,' Clark put in his diary.

Freyberg had another ambitious plan for breaking the stalemate on the 19th. All would depend on some delicate co-ordination, though luck as always would have to play its part.

The 28th (Maori) New Zealand Battalion would launch an all-out effort to capture the area of the two hotels in the town, and the Gurkhas, reinforced by the 1/4 Essex Regiment, would make a frontal attack on the Monastery from Hangman's Hill. At the same time Freyberg would put a surprise into effect, something which could well be his great trump card. All during the past weeks his sappers had been carving – unknown to the Germans – a track for tanks, known as Cavendish Road, across the mountains north of the Monastery, a remarkable achievement not only of engineering but of endurance and secrecy. Whilst the Gurkhas and the Essex attacked from the south, tanks would sweep on the troops defending the building from the rear. As Fred Majdalany has said: 'It was hoped that the appearance of tanks from this direction would cause something like the consternation that greeted Hannibal's elephants after their Alpine crossing.'

So much, however, would have to depend on the Essex, who were ensconced on Castle Hill. They were to be relieved by the Rajputana Rifles during the previous night and would then have to climb Hangman's Hill, ready for the attack at 6 a.m.

Unfortunately, luck was not to be on the side of the Essex. For a start, on the evening of the 18th stray tank shells hit the Castle walls, burying a number of their men. Then, later in the night, almost a whole platoon stumbled over a 150-foot precipice. Finally the Rajputs were not able to reach the garrison holding the Castle until well after midnight. This meant that the attack on the Monastery had necessarily to be delayed.

The Essex might have been encouraged if they had known quite how worn out and desperate were the remnants of the German parachute company at the foot of Castle Hill. When reinforcements from a Pioneer battalion reached the parachutists, the newcomers were literally embraced by the lieutenant in command. Spirits however recovered quickly, and there was a sudden eagerness to get going.

As morning approached the Germans attacked. Platoons of the Essex and Rajputs 'disappeared in a smother of enemies', and the Germans swept on with their new-found vigour. A kind of medieval battle developed at the top, with defenders firing through loopholes and attackers trying to scale walls and being beaten back with rifle butts. The Germans almost seemed not to care about casualties, and at last were driven back. But the Essex were left with three officers and sixty men on their feet. There had been a terrific expenditure of ammunition, and mortar barrels, crimson hot, had even curled and bent.

As for the Essex companies that had set out during the night for Hangman's Hill, only seventy men got there, and thirty of them were wounded.

Down in the town the Maoris were not meeting with much success. Although they took a hundred prisoners, they were repeatedly hit by a tank half buried in what had been the lobby of the Continental Hotel. In the Fishmarket the Germans drove the Maoris into bomb craters, some of which were fifteen feet deep. Little did the unfortunate Maoris know that these craters were mined. The Germans threw in grenades, and there would follow great hollow-sounding booms – and then silence, the silence of an immediate extinction.

The corner house in the Fishmarket was still held by the Germans, with the New Zealanders next door. Each side respected the Red Cross, until one incident when the New Zealanders took a German stretcher-bearer prisoner. No doubt there had been an order to the Kiwis to bring in prisoners, but this was too much for the Germans, who were enraged by such a breach in the rules of war. They battered the New Zealand house with everything they had got, including anti-tank rifles. As one of them said: 'We finished off the inhabitants of that house by the evening. None got away.'

A further blow to the Allies was the failure of the attack by the tanks, an Indian-American affair, along Cavendish Road. The appearance of Shermans and Stuarts did indeed cause consternation, but the Germans soon rallied and found it only too easy to knock them out with their *Faustpatronen* and bazookas. When the tanks blew up they blocked the track and the rest could not pass – it was as simple as that. Without sappers to help, without even supporting infantry, the expensive gamble failed. German paratroopers were even able to leap on the turrets and drop T. mines inside. Twenty-two tanks were destroyed or damaged.

That afternoon Freyberg called off the frontal assault on the Monastery by the Gurkhas and Essex.

To Christopher Buckley, Cassino had become the 'ultimate quintessence of war'. Half a mile away from where he sat in his trench, he wrote afterwards, 'men were hurling at one another lumps of jagged metal, everything that could tear and rend the living flesh, crush and shatter the bone . . . A wave of total and overwhelming despair swept over me. It was all going to happen again, so many times more. One had to cling hard to the purpose and meaning of it all. One had to steel oneself to recall the shrill hysterical screeching of Hitler, Goering's brutally triumphant smile at Munich, and all the obscene bestialities done in secret in the black night of a concentration camp.'

The British public was by now thoroughly alarmed by press and BBC reports. Winston Churchill therefore wrote, as gently as he could, to Alexander: 'I wish you would explain to me why this passage by Cassino, Monastery Hill etc., all on a front of two or three miles, is the only place which you must keep butting at. About five or six divisions have been worn out going through these jaws. Of course I do not know the ground or battle conditions, but, looking at it from afar, it is puzzling . . . I have the greatest confidence in you and will back you up through thick and thin, but do try to explain to me why no flanking movements can be made.'

Alex replied patiently, describing the geography and winter weather, the extraordinary tenacity of the German paratroopers and why attempts at outflanking movements had failed. He had, he said, to decide within the next twenty-four hours or so whether to call off the operation and consolidate gains, or whether to continue with yet more efforts to capture the Monastery. For some while he had been planning a future regrouping within the Eighth and Fifth Armies, with 'an attack on a wider front and with greater forces than Freyberg had been able to have'. This other attack would have to wait until 'the snow goes off the mountains, the rivers drop, and the ground hardens'.

A conference was held on 21 March, St Benedict's birthday, at which some generals such as Juin thought that the battle should be called off. Clark, said Juin, was 'anxious and nervous', and in his diary Clark admitted to being discouraged, though later he was won over by Freyberg's subordinates, who were determined to fight on until the objective was gained. So it was agreed to continue for a few days more, though Alexander was to review the situation each day to decide whether or not to call a halt.

The German command was also worried. Heidrich even told his Corps

commander Senger that he doubted whether his vaunted 1st Parachute
Division, the 'Green Devils', could hold Cassino town much longer. The
station was still in the hands of the New Zealanders, and the Royal West
Kents had managed to relieve the defenders in the Castle. The main
supply route to the German lines was down the dangerous and steep gully
known as Death Valley, between the Monastery and Snakeshead Ridge,
the path being marked by the bodies of dead mules.

Corporal Karl-Heinz Meier, just returned from wedding leave in
Germany and a veteran of the siege of Leningrad, found himself one of
those in charge of bringing supplies and ammunition along Death Valley.
On his return journey, which took two hours, he would fetch back the
lightly wounded and the possessions of those who had been killed.
General Heidrich had decreed that the severely wounded had to be
transported in daylight under the Red Cross flag along Via Casilina.

Meier and his friends found that mules would bolt as soon as artillery
started up, and then there would be the dreadful task of catching them and
rescuing the loads. It was thus decided one night to do without animals,
but this turned out disastrously, since his men fell about and hurt
themselves, occasionally badly, and the journey took twice as long. So
back they went to those sometimes stubborn and sometimes panic-
stricken mules. Prisoners were often made to help in carrying wounded.
'We kept cigarettes and chocolates in our pockets for the worst cases,' said
Meier, 'whether friend or foe. We felt really good when we managed to
get them back safely, and they in turn would shake our hands and give us
their *Danke* or Thanks.'

The Germans were proud of their gunners, Colonel Heilmann claiming
that 'we achieved the great feat of gaining, for a while at least, superiority
of fire'. And it was true that the 4th Indian Division suffered some
ferocious bombardments. A New Zealand NCO, watching from below,
wondered how men could survive in such exposed places. In the darkness
he saw how 'shells and mortars crashed among the rocks, burst in spraying
red circles of flame on their flinty surfaces and sent their echoes rolling
down the hillside'. The Allied guns then replied 'with a hurricane of steel'.
'I thought I could see the occasional flash of grenades. As the storm
subsided through the comparative silence came the rip of an occasional
spandau and – by contrast – the slow rattle of a bren in reply. The Indians
were still there!'

By 22 March General Heidrich's depression had passed and he felt that
the battle was turning in his favour. He was right. Freyberg had to
concede that the New Zealand Corps had exhausted its strength. On the
23rd Alexander gave the command for the attack to be halted. In nine
days the Corps had lost three thousand men.

There was now the problem of getting the Gurkhas down from Hangman's Hill. An order by radio to withdraw could not be risked in case it were intercepted by the enemy. Three officer volunteers therefore agreed to take up the instructions by word of mouth, bringing with them three carrier pigeons, by name St George, St Andrew and St David (since one officer was English, one Scots and one Welsh), which would fly back with the acknowledgements. In the end only two officers and one bird — the honorary Englishman — reached their destination intact. Unfortunately, St George did not care to fly in the dark and spent the night adjusting his plumage; but a little after first light he dutifully returned home.

And so, on the night of the 25th, the withdrawal began. In order to divert the Germans' attention, the Monastery was heavily bombed and the Royal West Kents sent out fighting patrols. It was an eerie journey for the Gurkhas down the hill, shielded by that curtain of fire, the noise of the shells mercifully drowning the sound of feet slipping and stumbling on the rocks. Ten officers and 247 men made the journey, and they could hardly believe their fortune when they reached the bottom unmolested. However a number of badly wounded had to be left behind, in the hope that they could be collected by stretcher the next day under the Red Cross flag.

At least that was one story. The Germans maintained that 'excessive use' was made of the Red Cross. Major Boehmler's version was as follows: 'Heavily bandaged and with a prominent display of a Red Cross flag, they made their way in small groups and in broad daylight to Rocca Janula [Castle Hill]. From there they slipped through the two hundred yard gap between the Castle and Cassino. The paratroops let them pass unmolested, and the commander magnanimously refrained from prying too closely into the nature and severity of their wounds. Consideration for a gallant enemy could not have done more!'

It was a surprise to everybody the next morning to see the swastika flying from the top of Hangman's Hill. This object became a favourite for Allied pot-shotters but nevertheless remained in situ for an amazingly long time. The Gurkhas were furious when the German propaganda machine gave out that the Hill had been recaptured after 'hard fighting'.

The end of the third battle of Cassino coincided with a blizzard. The 4/16 Punjabis, when they were relieved from the high ridges, were in as bad a state from the numbing cold as their American predecessors had been before the bombing of the Monastery. Their diarist wrote: 'The shape of the now shattered Monastery loomed out in a mantle of snow as if to hide from us her scars of battle. It was a fitting farewell.'

A German machine-gunner's comment in his diary was less romantic: '25 March. There has been a heavy fall of snow. It is whirling into our post. You would think you were in Russia. Just when you think you are going to have a few hours' rest to get a sleep, the fleas and bugs torment you. Rats and mice are our companions too.'

The weather had contributed much to the great defensive success of the Germans. Nevertheless, the stamina and bravery of the paratroopers had astonished the world and were to develop into a legend. Boehmler was annoyed at the insinuation, once again, that the defenders of Cassino were 'fanatics'. This was nothing but 'an excuse with which to cover up a military blunder'. True, he said, the paratroopers had been brought up in the 'lies and dogmas' of the Hitler Youth Movement, like other young Germans of their age, but the secret of their success, he said, could be summed up in three qualities – comradeship, esprit de corps and efficiency. 'Those were the foundations upon which the German parachute arm was built; and they are the foundation of every corps d'élite.'

It had been another victory for the Germans, though, as Senger knew, it could only be a temporary one. German writers have said that Freyberg failed because he had been too indecisive and had wasted his reserves. This is simplifying matters too much. As Senger has also said, this battle was one of the most perplexing and difficult operations of the war. For the German people it provided, in spite of the casualties, some welcome optimism and new faith in their ultimate invincibility.

And so, for a while, in this vast stricken graveyard, in this Golgotha of bereavement, with mines in its sockets and booby traps in its cavities, both sides were at last able to settle down to what was modestly called the quiet period. At Anzio they had their wadis filled with mud and brambles; here the wadis were of broken bricks, bits of marble flooring, and jutting beams, with gables of crazy masonry where snipers hid, watching and waiting for any careless flicker of movement during the hours of daylight. As at Anzio it was hard to know at first just where one's enemy was exactly. 'The first time I heard "Lili Marlene",' said a Lancashire Fusiliers officer, 'was soon after we had taken over from a Kiwi platoon, and I heard a Kraut whistling it in the very next house. Cripes, did it nearly give me a heart attack – I thought the house was unoccupied.' Another said: 'The rats were revolting. They were so fat. We know they were gorged on the hundreds of bodies nobody could reach. We used to catch them and put them in empty sandbags and chuck them into a place where we were sure a German observation post was stationed after dark. People speak of the sense of space at Cassino and of the clear nights, and of the black shape of the Monastery glowering, as it were, above us. There *were* clear nights later on, but there was often a hell of a noise too. A mine would explode and you would know some poor bloke on patrol had copped it. Sometimes there would be a scream, you've no idea how chilling; I once heard some chap calling desperately, a woman's name, always fainter, as if saying goodbye for eternity before he died this agonizing death. But I remember too the reflections of stars in the pools of the craters, like eyes, and as the weather got better the fantastic uproar of the croaking and quacking of bull-frogs from the river. Christ, there must have been billions of them. I also remember at dawn one day seeing the German part of the town covered with little Nazi flags. Hitler's birthday! Those Krauts could be cheeky. One chipped into a wireless conversation with "Hey, Tommy, got any socks? We've run out."'

'And I remember,' a private in the German pioneers has said, 'being sent to collect in dead bodies for burial. They had been piled in a big crater by both sides over the weeks. It was probably the most terrible sight I have ever seen. Green faces, swollen; and all those eyes – staring, loathing. And the rats. The stench was colossal. Even gas-masks were no use. We had to put first-aid packs soaked in cologne over our mouths and nostrils.'

Denis Johnston of the BBC remembered visiting the town prison, held by the British. To reach the unit latrine one had to sprint across what was known as Spandau Alley – no fun. Among the graffiti was written: 'Boy, do we long to be constipated.'

In the open country to the west of Cassino there was a tenseness of a different kind, for here it seemed as if the Germans in the hills above had absolute dominance. Lieutenant Peter Royle of the Royal Artillery remembered taking up a position on 29 March: 'I could see the flashes of exploding shell fire about one mile ahead every twenty seconds or so. Being shelled is always frightening, but on this particular night I had a lot of time to think about it as the columns advanced slowly northwards at 8–10 m.p.h., and by the time we had gone a few hundred yards I was feeling quite terrified. There was nothing I could do except to go straight into the area of exploding shells and pray that we weren't hit. My armoured carrier was my only protection against flying splinters, a near miss or direct hit would be the end . . .' On the next day Royle admitted that he felt on the edge of a nervous breakdown. 'The Americans would have classified it as battle fatigue – it was a mild form of shell shock but it affected my speech and I found it increasingly difficult to speak without a fairly serious stammer . . . I had two main worries – the all important one a real fear and my inability to control my actions, and secondly the knowledge that I would disgrace myself in front of my men . . .' Strangely, it was the mere fact of confiding in another officer about this business of losing his nerve that made him recover a little.

*

Alexander now planned his next offensive for mid-May. The code-name was hopeful: Diadem.

As if not to be outdone, old Vesuvius woke up and erupted for the first time in thirty-eight years. Man-made destruction could not vie with those spasms of flame and red-hot rock flung a thousand feet into the sky. Earth tremors shook the countryside around, and lava poured through villages. As the dust descended thickly, Army hospital staff beneath the mountain prepared to evacuate. The port of Naples was illuminated by night, an advantage – so it was said – to the Germans, on their nightly bombing raids. For Allied aircraft the volcano was certainly a perfect visual homing beacon.

Then, on 29 March, Vesuvius too subsided.

Rome

The first swallows were arriving in Rome as the Duchess of Sermoneta paced the terrace of her hiding place in Palazzo Caetani. For two months she had been 'boxed up like a hunted animal', unable even to look out of a window for fear of being recognized. Suddenly she heard an explosion echo over the roof-tops, then three lesser ones. By now one was used to bombs going off in Rome, but the first seemed especially alarming. It maddened her not to be able to go out and see what had happened.

Luisa Arpini was walking up Via Nazionale, on her way back from some hospital work. The explosions sounded really close and frightened her – the *Messaggero* newspaper offices blown up perhaps? In any case it was something serious, she knew, and she took off her high heels and ran for all she was worth. She found a dirty boy panting and crying in a doorway, and had to stop; he had fallen and cut his knee rather badly. He told her that he had come from the Quattro Fontane and that partisans had bombed a lot of Germans in Via Rasella. Luisa helped him into the house of some friends – who seemed annoyed at being disturbed at their game of bridge.

The boy was Peppino Zamboni. He had been on an errand for his aunt. It was a springlike day but still cold, and he had not liked going barefoot all that way from Trastevere. The terrific blast from Via Rasella had thrown him backwards, and a van had literally been flung against the railings of Palazzo Barberini. The screams and cries were awful. People came running and staggering towards him, he didn't know whether they were hurt or if they were the partisans themselves. He saw some German soldiers rushing away in a panic. Then there was some machine-gun fire and Peppino too began to run – he had been blind with fear and had charged straight into someone, a German. He had struggled and twisted, and soon got away; being barefoot was a help and anyway the German was more interested in catching someone older.

A cloud of dust and smoke now spread over the entire quarter, as Vittoria Sermoneta could see from her terrace. Along the Tiber's embankment frightened people jumped on *circolari* trams and stayed there for an hour, going round and round Rome. There were shots all over the centre of the city. You saw German soldiers in twos and threes, brandishing revolvers and machine-guns at upper windows. Shopkeepers drew down their blinds. Was this to be the start of the great insurrection at last?

The Communist leader who had partly planned this action, Giorgio Amendola, was at that moment in an extraterritorial house off Piazza di Spagna, where he was meeting De Gasperi of the Christian Democrats in order to discuss the crisis of the CLN. De Gasperi asked him what had happened, and Amendola replied that the explosion was probably 'one of ours'. De Gasperi smiled a little: '*Deve essere così* – It must be so.' Then he repeated an old saying: '*Voi una ne pensate e mille ne fate* – You think of one thing, and you do a thousand.' And without more ado, they got down to business, namely the implications of Bonomi having told De Gasperi that morning that he was going to resign from being president of the CLN, which would inevitably mean a drastic split between left and right. When at last Amendola emerged again into Piazza di Spagna, he found an 'inferno' with Germans everywhere. 'Here was concrete proof that we had not envisaged such a furious German response.' This time the affront had been too much, the audacity and success of the partisans had been too obvious. People were running here and there and shouting that the Germans were rounding up all pedestrians ... There was again that cry of terror, only too familiar in recent weeks: '*Stanno chiudendo la zona* – They are closing the area.'

Exactly as had been plotted, the forty-pound bomb had been placed in a rubbish cart, with Rosario Bentivegna disguised as a street-cleaner. Carla Capponi's job was to give him the warning of the Germans' approach. Other partisans were ready with mortar-bombs converted into grenades, which would be thrown at the rear of the German column after the main explosion. More partisans would be ready to block the Germans' escape.

The victims of this assault were from the 11th Company of the 3rd Battalion of the newly formed Bozen (Bolzano) Police Regiment. They were all over-age, too old for fighting and – ironically – could have been considered Italians, since they came from the South Tyrol, annexed by Italy after the First War but in October 1943 incorporated into the Greater German Reich. Because of the increasing partisan activity and the fact that so many Romans were defying the call-up for labour service in Germany, these men of the Bozen Regiment had been sent to Rome to enforce stricter law and order. The Germans could not afford civilian upheavals whilst the critical fighting continued at Anzio and Cassino.

It happened, however, that the normally punctual police company was very late on its accustomed march towards Via Rasella. Indeed, if it had delayed ten minutes more, the whole operation would have been called off by the partisans. Then at last the clump of the Germans' nailed boots and the raucous, confident sing-song, which so irritated the Romans, could be heard. Three abreast, the column of 156 men could be seen beginning the ascent. Carla Capponi took cover from the expected blast. Bentivegna put his lighted pipe to the fuse in the rubbish cart; the fuse ignited at once, and he then placed his cap on top of the cart to signify that all was well. He had fifty seconds in which to saunter to safety.

The noise was far greater than even the partisans expected. The column of Germans seemed to crumple, as if blown down by a great wind, and shrapnel, splintered glass and bits of brick sprayed out far beyond Via Rasella. Twenty-six men were killed at once, and about seventy wounded, some very badly. At the top of the street, in the great baroque Barberini palace, built in part from the stones of the Colosseum, and where both Bernini and Borromini had worked, the teenage Prince Augusto Barberini rushed to the window. Three hundred years before at that very window people had watched one of the most fantastic and extravagant pageants ever staged in Rome, in honour of Queen Christina of Sweden. Now he saw bodies writhing, pools of blood, scattered helmets, smoke. A water main had burst. A few Germans were on their feet, firing pistols in a crazy fashion. If he also saw a young woman throw a raincoat over a young man and dash with him towards the Quattro Fontane, they were Carla and Rosario.

Some of the wounded were carried into the sombre courtyard of what had been the Scots College but was now inhabited by nuns, who ran an orphanage and a soup kitchen. The *portiere* was called Lorenzo. 'Oh yes, I saw them, those men in their grey uniforms, being carried in. They were old, old, from Bolzano, fathers of families. I felt sorry for them, their feet were bleeding, and I took off their boots. Then I heard a lot of shouting down the street. *Disastro!* I got up and ran. If they arrive here, I was thinking, they'll kill me. To hell with those old bleeding men. *Kaputt*, oh yes I knew that word. No *Kaputt* for Lorenzo. I wasn't going to wait for another bomb, or a German bullet, not Lorenzo.'

A child and six other civilians had been killed, and others were to die from wounds. The Germans blamed the Italians for this, the Italians blamed the Germans. Now General Maeltzer arrived, puffing and fuming, his face aflame with too much wine after a long lunch at the Excelsior Hotel. Next Colonel Dollmann of the SS appeared, and Consul Moellhausen, both of whom had been roused by the explosions whilst listening to flowery and boring Italian speeches at the meeting extolling

Fascism's twenty-fifth birthday. Moellhausen was accompanied by
Buffarini-Guidi, Mussolini's Interior Minister. Caruso, Italian chief of
police, was there, and both German and Italian police and members of the
Sturm Division had also by now arrived. The dead bodies had been laid
out in a row. Dollmann was aghast and 'very excited', but Maeltzer was
raving, shouting for revenge, weeping, gesticulating and threatening to
blow up all the houses in the street. The inhabitants of Via Rasella –
including a dentist and his patients, and the octogenarian widow of a
Senator – were now forced out, prodded and beaten with rifle butts, and
made to stand facing the Barberini railings with their hands behind their
heads. Maeltzer was seen to clout a sick old man who did not move
quickly enough. Later, Prince Augusto Barberini saw all the people taken
away in lorries.

The *portiere* Lorenzo had hidden under some stairs. 'Yes, the Germans
were shooting with machine-guns at windows. I saw big holes in the
walls of the *cortile*. It was like an earthquake in there. *Pazienza*,
Lorenzo, I said, you must save yourself. Down I went to the cellar, where
there were nuns, full of fear, and children. Suddenly I became very brave.
"Why are you crying?" I said to the nuns. "Have courage. Think of Our
Lord." You know, I am not a fanatical Catholic, but I believe in God.
There were four other porters down there, it was very dark. Then we
heard Germans coming: *"Schnell, schnell!"* I said to the porters, "Let's
kneel among the boys, and we'll look smaller." The Germans came in
with a torch. "No, no," the nuns cried. "We swear there are only children
in here." So the Germans left. *Dio!* I was lucky, I had an Italian gun with
me and fifty bullets!'

Moellhausen was trying to calm Maeltzer and prevent him from
blowing up the houses. Maeltzer rounded on him: 'There you are, this is
the result of your politics! Now everything will change! I don't care. All
these houses will go up in the air, even if the diplomats fire me tomorrow!'
He threatened to telephone Kesselring and tell him that the Consul was
being obstructive. Dollmann was also insulted. Finally the pale, cool
Colonel Herbert Kappler arrived and took over. This was a matter for his
SD.

When Rosario Bentivegna reached the Capponis' house he fainted. That
night Rome Radio made no mention at all of the explosion.

Moellhausen telephoned Kesselring's headquarters from the German
Embassy to find that the Field-Marshal was at the front. He relayed the
details, which were then passed to the OKW, Hitler's Army headquarters.
Hitler was not well – it had been noticed by Eva Braun that his knees
shook when he stood. Moreover, only a week before he had lost his

temper with Admiral Horthy, the Regent of Hungary, accusing him of an 'Italian-style' betrayal; and on 19 March German troops had occupied Hungary. The Allied planes were ravaging Bavaria, and from Berchtesgaden at night Hitler could see the red glow of fire-bombs on Munich. And the Russians were advancing in the Ukraine.

Kesselring's headquarters was told by the OKW that Hitler was 'roaring'. Not only was the whole area around Via Rasella to be burnt down, but all the inhabitants were to be shot. For every German soldier who had died (now thirty-two), thirty or fifty Italian hostages would have to be killed as a reprisal – and within twenty-four hours.

Dollmann, meanwhile, had telephoned his chief, General Wolff, who said that he would fly down next day. Dollmann had a plan, which was to bring the relatives of the dead soldiers to Rome for the funeral, with maximum publicity, and make the city of Rome pay them reparations. In his memoirs Dollmann was to say that he was totally ignorant of the gruesome retribution that was in fact being plotted. Yet later on he admitted to having been uneasy. 'There was only one power in Rome,' he said, 'who could have done something, and this was His Holiness. Because, you know, Hitler was very cautious with the Pope and did not want an open war. So at six in the afternoon I went with my chauffeur to the monastery of the Salvatorians at St Peter's and asked for an audience with Padre Pancrazio Pfeiffer, who was the head of the Salvatorians. I said: "Padre, I am certain that something serious is about to happen, what I do not know, but you must go immediately to the Vatican and tell His Holiness to intervene at once, at once, at once, either through me or Kesselring, and defer any decisions, defer them, and gain time." And he did this, but what happened in the Vatican I do not know.'

And again, many years later, it was said by Albrecht von Kessel, councillor to the ambassador Weizsaecker, that the Vatican did telephone asking about possible executions. The Via Rasella incident had occurred precisely when the delicate negotiations between the Vatican and Weizsaecker (and Kesselring) were reaching a final stage about the Germans' acknowledgement of Rome's open city status – which in theory would mean the withdrawal of their troops. Kessel has said that he was instructed to relay an evasive reply to the effect that the Germans linked the killing of the police with the fate of the open city and might have to re-examine their attitude.

Kappler went to Maeltzer's office, and both spoke to General Mackensen, who, as commander of the Fourteenth Army facing Anzio, was Maeltzer's superior for the Rome area. 'I remember well my conversation with General von Mackensen,' Maeltzer was to say. 'After I had reported on the incident, von Mackensen asked me what I thought had to be done in the way of punishment, and I answered that for the moment I had no suggestions to make. Von Mackensen, however, insisted that I state what kind of punishment had to be adopted, and I therefore referred to the examples of Paris, Brussels and Nantes, which were in the way of reprisals. I would like, however, to make it clear that during the conversation nothing was laid down, and von Mackensen told me that I would get a definite ruling later. Shortly afterwards von Mackensen phoned me again and asked me what people I had available for a reprisal to be taken. I stated that I had none and that I did not intend to arrest anybody as hostage, but mentioned that the SD might have people available who had acted against the security of the German Army.' Later Maeltzer was told by Kappler that he had about two hundred such people available and that more could possibly be obtained from Caruso. 'I reported the results of this conversation to von Mackensen, who said that he would give me a definite ruling as soon as possible.'

Later again that evening the message reached Kappler from Maeltzer's office that it had been confirmed that ten Italians for every German killed were to be executed within twenty-four hours. Kesselring had returned from the front about 7 p.m., to receive the news of the attack at Via Rasella. To him partisan war was a 'complete violation of international law and contradicted every principle of clean soldierly fighting'. He had already warned the Roman population of serious consequences if attacks continued 'under the cloak of patriotism'. By and large he had attempted to be fairly lenient with partisan activity anywhere behind the lines, even meeting it with 'welfare measures', radio propaganda, etc., and only in March had he issued a directive to German troops on the penalties of looting and the question of behaviour towards Italian civilians. But this was much the most serious incident so far, and a strong reaction was necessary. In due course, after the war, an Italian court of law was to pronounce the bombing a legitimate act of war, but Kesselring would have agreed with Maeltzer who said: 'I am personally of the opinion that this outrage against German policemen does not represent a patriotic deed but common murder.'

Even today it is unclear whether Kappler himself originally recommended reprisals at the ratio of ten to one. Certainly Mackensen thought this ratio fair, provided there were enough men available in Rome who were already condemned to death, and he would appear to have passed on this recommendation to Kesselring, who in turn was responsible for calming Hitler and getting him to scale down his original demand of thirty or fifty and accept the lower figure. And although Kappler was to be evasive about another crucial matter, whether or not he did speak to Kesselring on the telephone, Kesselring later declared on oath that he had been telephoned by Kappler, who was 'elated and happy' because he found he could provide the required number of people already con-demned to death. Kesselring said that he thereupon thanked him 'from the bottom of my heart because it relieved my soul'. He was not surprised, he also said, at Kappler having so many people available, since this was Kappler's 'habit'. 'Kappler was also in close contact with the Italian police who would have been in a position to furnish the rest, if more people would have been required, from the great reservoir of sentenced criminals.'

Kesselring then felt free to go to bed, and early next morning was off to the front again. Yet Kappler was to maintain that he never used the words 'condemned to death' to anyone, he had referred to persons who were 'worthy of death' in accordance with German military law – *Todeskandidaten*, death candidates.

Mackensen wanted swift, decisive measures because 'I, as commander-in-chief of the Fourteenth Army fighting at the Anzio front, could only fulfil my task of holding that front sector if there were peace and order in that city of millions situated immediately behind the fighting lines.' He had made a further stipulation to Kappler, which would have to be kept secret from Hitler, that should the SD not be able to produce a sufficient amount of persons condemned to death, then it should be publicly *announced* that the whole number of the ratio of ten to one had been executed.

Like Kesselring, Mackensen did not ask how the executions would be carried out. It did not occur to him to distrust Kappler, whom he had not met before, but who seemed level-headed and loyal. Later he was to find him 'shifty'. Both Mackensen and Kesselring were to insist afterwards that they had been misled about *Todeskandidaten*. 'Kappler,' said Mackensen, 'was an SD man and as such opposed to the Field-Marshal's and my principle of trying to win over the Italians. He was living in the ideas of Hitler and especially the SS chief Himmler, who thought they could guarantee law and order by terror.' Kappler, he added, had long before made up his mind to 'clean up' the gaols and Jews in Rome to 'assure himself of Hitler's and Himmler's benevolence', and here was his great chance. And Kappler's arch-rival Dollmann was to say: 'The order [for the executions] was an order from God, and this God unfortunately was called Hitler. For me Hitler was a great personality, he was a great man; however he was not my God, and that was the difference. Kappler was the classic policeman of all times, and so he carried out an order which perhaps he could have deferred.'

Kappler himself was to say that when he saw the body of a child in Via Rasella one of his first thoughts was for all the poor children who had died in the Hamburg raids. When interviewed about the executions on Italian television thirty years later, he wept. 'Yes, I was there, but I did not start it,

I did not create those conditions. I carried out orders, and it was very hard. I do not want to speak of it, please.'

The German Embassy at Villa Wolkonsky – in Dollmann's words 'an oasis of peacocks, roses and chirping crickets' – was only ten minutes' walk from Via Tasso. So Moellhausen called on Kappler that evening and found him caressing a sick dog while he drew up his list. 'What you are doing, Kappler,' he said, horrified, 'goes beyond patriotism and war. Remember that you will be answerable not only before men but before God.' To which Kappler replied that for every name he would think three times. There would be no 'injustices'.

Kappler worked all night. By the early morning he had 223 names, only four of whom had in fact been condemned to death. Four others had been taken out of the houses at Via Rasella and seventeen had been sentenced to long terms of hard labour. The rest had committed acts which he himself considered called for the death penalty. 'So I decided to add fifty-seven Jews.'

But even so he was still far below his target. He therefore turned to Caruso and his protégé Koch for fifty more names. Koch could certainly be relied upon for a good supply at his torture-house in the Pensione Oltremare.

Caruso felt he must get the authorization of Buffarini-Guidi, as Mussolini's Minister of the Interior. He drove round to the Excelsior at 8 a.m. to find the Minister still in bed. 'What can I do?' said Buffarini-Guidi. 'You'll have to give him what he wants, otherwise who knows what will happen. Yes, yes, give them to him.' Having received this authorization, Caruso felt happier.

But when Caruso had to tell Kappler that, even with Koch's names, he could not possibly make up the required total from his prisons, Kappler simply said: 'Then find some more Jews.' So Celeste Di Porto, the Jewish tart-informer, alias the Black Panther, was put into action, to scour Rome for friends and relatives in hiding whom she could betray for a fee of fifty thousand *lire* a scalp. Meanwhile Caruso and Koch went to the police station to wrestle with the same problem that had kept Kappler up all night. The only name on Koch's list which was familiar to Caruso was that of one of his own officers, Lieutenant Maurizio Giglio. This Giglio was none other than 'Cervo', radio operator for the OSS spy Peter Tompkins; he had been arrested a week previously.

With the arrest of Giglio/Cervo messages from Tompkins' Radio Vittoria to the Fifth Army had necessarily been halted. Giglio, who after the war was to be awarded posthumously the *Medaglia d'Oro*, the highest Italian award for bravery, had been betrayed by a colleague among

Tompkins' helpers. Brought up as a Fascist, he had volunteered for the war in Greece, but had fought against the Germans by the Pyramid of Cestius on 9 September. He had fled to Naples, where he took part in the 'Four Days', and had then returned to Rome to work for the OSS, having joined the metropolitan police. Scottu, his orderly, had had only a vague idea of the lieutenant's *alter ego*, but had also been arrested.

Scottu has left a day-by-day account of the horrible tortures both he and Giglio endured. Sometimes they would be watched by Koch's new mistress, Marcella Stoppani, who wrote gloating poems about the ordeals of victims. The man who tortured Giglio, known as Walter – 'olive-skinned, ascetic, always wearing a raincoat' – had actually once been a friend of his. On the fifth day of interrogation Walter had suddenly brought a cigarette and chocolates for Giglio, and had attempted to flatter him. 'Quietly,' said Scottu, 'the lieutenant replied: "Walter, you are like Judas!"' On the sixth day, the night of the Via Rasella affair, Giglio was interrogated for twenty minutes and emerged with his face completely disfigured. 'Walter punched him in the mouth. Blood flowed from his cracked lips. As he sat on the bed wiping the blood with his handkerchief he weakly called out for his mother. At that moment Walter, like a beast, raised his foot and brought it down with all the weight of his body, kicking him in the pubic region. The lieutenant, at the end of his strength, uttered a weak cry: "Mamma, Mamma, they've killed me!" As he tried feebly to turn on to his side, Walter let go another kick, as hard as the first, striking him in the kidneys. It was all that was needed. The lieutenant turned as white as a corpse...'

On the next day Walter told the cell's inmates that they were to be turned over to the German SS and they had better write last notes to their families. 'Everyone was crying.'

Tompkins had a brave but hopeless plan to rescue Giglio, who if he had broken down under torture could also have betrayed the entire OSS network. But when the day came for this coup, it was already too late, and Giglio was dead. Eleven other OSS helpers were also shot. Perhaps not surprisingly on the walls of a Via Tasso cell these words were written (and still remain): 'At the OSS headquarters there is a traitor connected with the enemy. E.'

The main clandestine operator for the British, Umberto Lusena, who had also recently been caught, along with four colleagues, was totally unconnected with Giglio; he was a natural *Todeskandidat*. There had been consternation at the British Legation when the little Maltese priest Brother Robert Pace was picked up, as he was also important in the Derry-O'Flaherty organization. However he was released, but the two who had been with him, Andrea Casadei and Vittorio Fantini, were less fortunate, and were due to die.

General Simoni and two other generals were on Kappler's list; so were the fifty-three-year-old priest Padre Pappagallo, Colonel Frignani and several other ex-Carabinieri, Professors Pilo Albertelli and Gioacchino Gesmundo, and of course Montezemolo and the crippled diplomat Filippo De Grenet, who had been arrested with him. Among the Jews were a butcher, Di Consiglio, and his three sons, one aged seventeen.

Montezemolo's cousin, Marchesa Ripa di Meana, had had an audience with the Pope on 19 March. She found him seated behind his desk, emaciated and lined, dressed in white and with a splendid crucifix of diamonds and sapphires on his chest. She told him about Montezemolo's plight and how he could be invaluable in keeping order in Rome when the Germans left, and begged the Pope to intercede with the SD and take Montezemolo into the Vatican. After a while the Pope seemed to shudder. 'He is in Kappler's hands then?' he asked. 'Yes, Your Holiness, and we all know what that means. Montezemolo's tortures have been atrocious.' She saw acute pain flicker across the Pope's face. Eventually he said: 'I promise you we shall do all we can, absolutely all we can.' He took down details, and the Marchesa heard afterwards that he had summoned Monsignor Montini and had given precise instructions – though whatever they were, they were to be of no avail.

The Black Panther had to work quickly, but she was in luck. Her hunting ground was in medieval Rome, round the Campo dei Fiori in particular. Two easy catches were her first cousin, Armando Di Segni, and his brother-in-law, Ugo Di Nola. Then she spotted the boxer Bucefalo. The Fascist police had a job arresting him, and he laid out three of them before being overpowered. He was dragged to Celeste Di Porto's flat to be beaten up and then flung into Regina Coeli. On the wall of his cell Bucefalo, father of two children, wrote: 'I am Lazzaro Anticoli, known as Bucefalo, boxer. If I do not see my family again it is because of having been betrayed by Celeste Di Porto. Revenge me!' And there were others in the day's haul. Altogether at least twenty-six Jews were to die through the good offices of this 'belva umana', the ages ranging between fifteen and seventy-four. Other Jews, in the weeks ahead, were to be deported to the ovens of Auschwitz, with her assistance.

Kappler called on General Maeltzer at midday on the 24th with his list of names, less Caruso's. Afterwards he could not remember whether Maeltzer had asked to go through the list, or whether he had even wanted to know if it included Jews. Maeltzer, who had always tried to dissociate himself from what all Rome knew must happen at Via Tasso, and who tried instead to attract popularity by adopting a sort of Falstaffian bonhomie, had said to Kappler: 'You yourself must take responsibility for the list.' Kappler did remember that Maeltzer had been surprised that only four local inhabitants of Via Rasella had been included.

Major Dobbrich, the commander of the 3rd Bozen Battalion, now arrived and was told that his surviving men would have to carry out the executions. He refused. 'My men are old. They are partly very religious, partly full of superstition, and they come from remote provinces in the Alps.' Above all, there were now too few of them to carry out such a large job, in so short a time. A call was therefore put through to Fourteenth Army headquarters. Mackensen was not available, and it was his chief of staff, Hauser, who answered. No, he could not spare men for the executions. Quite clearly, too, the teleprint from OKW to Kesselring's headquarters had stated: 'Execution by SD.' So Maeltzer, relieved, was able to say: 'Well, then, it is up to you, Kappler.'

In the trials of Kesselring, Mackensen, Maeltzer and Kappler after the war much time was expended on the responsibility for this final order. Although in effect it had been passed from Kesselring to Mackensen to Maeltzer to Kappler, and although Mackensen was to sign the statement saying that the executions had been carried out, it was maintained by the three generals that all this was formality, and that they were really just transmitting Hitler's and Himmler's decision. The SD and the whole SS were totally separate from the Army and they had no jurisdiction over it. This was due to Hitler's extraordinary insistence on centralization.

Kappler, therefore, returned to his office at Via Tasso and informed his men of their duty. It was agreed to shoot the Italians in batches of five, and that the officers would shoot first, a 'symbolic necessity'. Speed was essential, and no time could be wasted. Any religious assistance was out of the question therefore. A single shot per person would quicken things too; death should be instantaneous if the shot entered the cerebellum at close range.

One problem was how to dispose of the bodies. Digging a mass grave would take too long. Kappler then had a brainwave: why not find some large cave or grotto, or a catacomb even? He then heard that a thirty-third policeman had died in hospital. On his own initiative he increased the total number of hostages to be killed to 330.

An ideal spot for the executions was quickly found: some *pozzolana* caves off the old road to Ardea just outside Rome, near the catacombs of Domitilla and the Church of Quo Vadis, where St Peter had met Jesus as he fled from persecution. The place became known as the *Fosse Ardeatine*, the Ardeatine Caves.

Caruso at this late stage was still having difficulty in making up his fifty names.

★

SS General Karl Wolff's plane from the North did not reach Viterbo until 3 p.m., by which time the executions had already started. He was met by Dollmann and together they drove to Kesselring's headquarters at Monte Soratte. Wolff's ill-humour was by no means improved by partisans sniping at their car. Whatever Kappler had in hand was not going to be nearly sweeping enough for him and Himmler. He was bringing instructions for all Communists and other suspects to be 'eliminated radically'; what was more, in the most dangerous areas of the city every male between the ages of eighteen and forty-five must now be rounded up immediately, and shipped to Germany for labour duties.

Prisoners at Via Tasso were aware of sudden commotion in the corridors, some minutes before 2 p.m. Doors were flung open, and German voices barked out: *'Los, los!' 'Raus, raus!'* Sometimes names were called. Then three warrant officers appeared at the entrance to the crowded cell where old General Peppe Gariboldi, nearly seventy, had mostly lived since before Christmas. Another series of barks: 'You, you, you and you.' This time no names were given, and the selection seemed at random. The general was not chosen; none of those who were taken from his cell had ever had a trial.

Several prisoners had difficulty in walking – Montezemolo, for instance, had had the nails pulled out of his toes, and he was also unaccustomed to strong light. Others were full of hope, believing that they were to be transferred to Regina Coeli. When outside, however, their hands were tied with cords behind their backs, and they were crammed into vans, used once for transporting meat. Those left behind, such as General Gariboldi, were ordered to make up parcels of the men's belongings and place them in piles in the corridors. This seemed to them a sure sign that the owners were destined to be killed.

Captain Schutz had been put in charge of the executions. Before leaving Via Tasso he told his squad that anyone who baulked at the job – even if he were an officer – would be shot also. The vans drove past St John Lateran, where so many of the CLN were hidden, past the little church of the martyrs Nereus and Achilleus alone among umbrella pines and cypresses, past the red hulks of the Baths of Caracalla, past the tomb of the Scipios, through the Aurelian Walls at the Porta San Sebastiano with its twin turrets; then they turned right off the old Appian Way into the beginnings of the sad and beautiful Roman Campagna; past the Catacombs of St Calixtus, past the little *trattorie* with their wooden benches under vines, almost unchanged since the days of Keats, Byron, Goethe and Buffalo Bill. At the entrance of the quarry Kappler was waiting. He had investigated the tunnels in the reddish earth; they were like a maze, some a hundred yards long and fifteen feet high, ideal. As the

first load of prisoners descended, he gave the assembled Germans a brief
talk on their duties and reminded them that the order had come direct
from the Fuehrer himself. He felt moved, almost tearful.

SD guards had been posted all round to keep civilians away. They did
not realize that Nicola D'Annibale, a peasant who minded pigs, was
looking all the while from a spot near the Catacombs of St Domitilla.
D'Annibale was petrified, but what he saw was later to be evidence of first
importance. He saw prisoners being divided into groups of five, all bound
to one another. They went into a tunnel, and later he heard shots, but no
cries. Some of the waiting prisoners shouted 'Italia!' One was a priest and
he was asked for blessings; this was Padre Pappagallo. When Pappagallo
lifted his hand, the man tied to him was suddenly freed. This was Josef
Raider, an Austrian deserter from the German army. He attempted to
escape but was caught, then recognized as a deserter. His life was thus, at
the last minute, spared. An SD man was to remember: 'They died quietly.
Most of them prayed. An elderly man whom I knew to be General
Simoni comforted everybody.'

Once deep inside the tunnel, the prisoners had been made to kneel, and
machine pistols had been held a few inches from the napes of their necks.
In the insufficient light of torches Captain Schutz had given the order to
fire, and in due course a medical orderly had checked to see that the men
were dead.

Kappler now selected a prisoner that he himself would kill. 'Four other
officers did the same. We led the victims to the same place and, in the same
way, a little behind the first five, they were shot.' Outside D'Annibale saw
the empty vans turn round and leave. Within a short while they would be
back with more prisoners.

At Anzio the *pozzolana* caves had been a refuge. Here they were a place
of doom and of not always instantaneous death.

The vans had gone to Regina Coeli. On reaching the prison, twelve SD
men got out with several lengths of rope, and made for the *terzo braccio*,
the wing kept for the Nazis' political prisoners.

At that time there were about four hundred male prisoners in the wing,
fifty females and several children belonging to Jewish inmates. Eleonora
Lavagnino, a lawyer who had been arrested for helping escaped British
POWs, was in the lavatory washing mess-tins, a privilege granted only to
female prisoners. On the way back to her cell she saw about twenty male
prisoners grouped in front of the offices on the ground floor. 'This was an
unusual sight. I then saw three or four pairs of German SD, in uniform,
with papers in their hands, going from cell to cell opening the doors and
shouting out names.'

Guglielmo Morandi was in a cell with Lusena, the man who had been a radio operator for the British. Lusena had only recently arrived from Via Tasso and had been allowed a shave. Through the bars of their cell they saw people being hauled out roughly, and noticed that they were usually not even allowed to take belongings. 'A guard stopped in front of our cell and threw open the door. We all stood up. The Nazi's eyes searched the list of names, crossed out some that he had already called, then looked up and shouted: "Umberto Lusena".' 'The name,' said Morandi, 'lay heavily in the still air of the cell – hard, inexorable, not permitting any doubt.' They all turned to look at Lusena. 'Only the pallor of his face, a result of the ordeals he had already suffered, was a little accentuated. He looked like a child who had been caught doing something wrong.' As Lusena bent to pick up a small bag, he said: 'They are going to shoot me.' But Morandi, thinking he was merely to be sent to a concentration camp, gave him a piece of his bread for the journey.

Eleonora Lavagnino reached the women's floor. In one of the cells she saw a Dr Pierantoni giving an injection to a female prisoner. A member of the Party of Action, he had been arrested about forty days ago. Miss Lavagnino then met two agents of the *Feld Polizei* who were looking for the doctor. They called out his name. 'When the doctor answered, the agents entered the cell and took him away without even allowing him to finish his work. I tried to speak to Pierantoni but was unsuccessful. I was then pushed towards my cell by the Germans with their usual words: "*Komm komm, los, los.*"'

Peering through the grilled window she watched the ever-growing group of prisoners in the courtyard below being sorted into Jews and Aryans. The doctor was very noticeable in his white coat.

Morandi saw a young Carabiniere officer, Fontana, with them. Fontana's wife had been arrested at the same time as her husband and now she was permitted to wave goodbye from a balcony. The prisoners in the courtyard had their wrists tied behind their backs. 'First, however, they were stripped of all their belongings. Some even had to give up their shoes. The Italian *Guardie di Servizio* then threw themselves on these things like jackals.' He heard Fontana shout: '*Ciao, Nina, coraggio.*'

The prison had become a desert. The departure of the trucks rattled the window frames. That night Morandi was to miss hearing Fontana and his wife calling to one another from their different floors.

Kappler was back at Via Tasso, worrying because Caruso had still not completed his list of fifty men. Then he was told about indiscipline at the Caves. Some prisoners were being finished off with rifle butts, and an officer called Wetjen was refusing to shoot, in spite of Schutz's warning. So Kappler rushed round, to find that his men were indeed becoming 'spiritually depressed'. 'I spoke to Wetjen as a friend, as a comrade.'

Kappler then put an arm round him and drew him into a tunnel where five men were waiting to be shot. 'Whilst he was firing I was myself firing at his side.'

Next Kappler ordered a rest period, during which some of the corpses were stacked on one another. He had brought cognac from Via Tasso and now advised his men to drink. When firing resumed, it was often found easier and less wasteful of space to make prisoners climb on the piles before kneeling to be executed. Kappler returned again to Via Tasso.

Thanks presumably to the cognac, the soldiers became careless. It took several shots sometimes to kill a man, and there were cases of heads being blown off. Lieutenant Guenther Amonn arrived rather late, when about two hundred prisoners had been killed. Captain Schutz ordered him to take his turn at the shootings, but Amonn was nauseated by the sight. 'I raised my gun,' he said, 'but I was too afraid to fire. The four other Germans fired one shot each into the backs of the necks of the other prisoners, who fell forward. Upon seeing the state in which I was another German pushed me out of the way and shot the prisoner I had been detailed to shoot.' After that Amonn fainted.

Meanwhile some local people, particularly monks who were guides at the Catacombs of Saint Calixtus, had heard repeated muffled shots and were becoming suspicious. Their evidence was again to be of importance.

By 4.30 p.m. Caruso's list was still not ready. In a fury one of Kappler's lieutenants stormed into Regina Coeli and ordered eleven men to be seized at random. Within the hour the victims were dead.

Antonello Trombadori, the Gapist leader arrested early in February, thought the men were being taken away for labour duties. He asked to join them, since he thought he then would have a chance of escaping, but his request was refused. As it happened, several days later he was taken to work at the Anzio front and did manage to escape during a bombardment.

The Germans had never suspected Trombadori of being a Communist, so he had been spared torture. The Actionist Tom Carini, however, had been less fortunate; he had been so badly beaten up that he was in the Regina Coeli with a suspected fracture at the base of his cranium. Nevertheless he featured on Caruso's final list.

When Carini's name was called, he believed he was going to be released. He tottered down the stairs where he met the chief male nurse, who had heard rumours about hostages in the city and had hastened to Regina Coeli. 'Where are you going?' 'I have an order for release. I'm leaving.' 'Back you go to bed, quickly.' And escorting Carini upstairs, the nurse explained the dangers. Soon Carini was in bed again with an ice pack on his head. But once more his name was called. His state of health was no obstacle to the Fascists, and this time he knew he was to die.

He found himself facing Carretta, the director of the prison. Three Germans were just leaving the office as he arrived; they seemed in a hurry, as if they had just concluded some business. Carretta had, generally speaking, done what he could to ease the prisoners' conditions, and indeed some weeks back had secretly arranged for the Socialist leader Saragat to escape. He now said to Carini: 'They have eleven men too many, so I am allowed to delete eleven from our list – ten Jews and you. So back you go to the infirmary, and don't you move from there.'

The executions were finally over at 8 p.m. Engineers now sealed off the tunnels with explosives. In point of fact 335 people had been killed, including seventy-five Jews and ten men who had been rounded up near Via Rasella. Kappler was to blame the Italian police for the extra five names, and his own men were either too tired or had had too much cognac to be bothered about such a small matter. He claimed that he left the Caves an hour before, but one of his men said he was there to the end. That evening he addressed all under his command in the Gestapo mess: 'The reprisal has been carried out. I know it has been very hard for some of you but in cases like this the laws of war must be applied. The best thing for you all to do is to get drunk.' Most were drunk already.

At Monte Soratte General Wolff – intensely irritated and red in the face – confronted Kesselring with Himmler's demand, which in effect would mean evacuating one million Romans. Kesselring was calm, pointing out that such an operation would mean withdrawing three divisions from the front line. Moreover, taking into account enemy air strength, such a vast movement of personnel on the main highways outside Rome would result in huge casualties. In the end it was decided that Wolff would meet Kappler, the consul Moellhausen and others at midnight at the Excelsior Hotel.

According to Dollmann, when he and Wolff entered the Excelsior, they found Kappler looking like a 'true executioner', his pupils 'flaming from deep livid eyes' after nearly two days without sleep, the duelling scar on his cheek looking like a raw snake. 'General,' said Kappler, in a parade-ground voice, 'the order for the reprisals has been carried out.' Dollmann said Kappler then gave the figure as 335, but in later years Kappler maintained that he did not know about the additional five until the next morning, and other Germans said that he also at that time concealed the fact that he had gone beyond the authorized 320.

A subtle communiqué was hammered out for publication the next day; in this the phrase 'Badoglian Communists', as perpetrators of the 'vile crime' at Via Rasella, was used for the first time. Inevitably the right would deny any such association, and there was a chance that the whole

Roman Resistance might be split in two. The communiqué continued: 'Investigations are being made as to the crime being caused by Anglo–American influence. The German High Command is determined to crush the activities of these villainous bandits. No one will be allowed to sabotage the renewed Italo–German co-operation. The Command has ordered that for every German who was murdered ten Badoglian Communists should be shot. This order has already been executed.'

Himmler was telephoned at 2 a.m. The small hours were not the best time to suggest that his plan for the evacuation of most of Rome's male population should be abandoned. As Dollmann said, his threats were positively Neronian. Then everyone went to bed, to be ready for the funeral of the Bolzano policemen when Wolff would make a speech.

The Papal representative who called regularly at Regina Coeli was Cardinal Nasalli Rocca. He had been told by a prisoner that several people had been taken away to the firing squad. Greatly alarmed, the Cardinal had hurried straight to the Pope. 'When I told him what I had learnt in the prison, the Pope covered his face with his hands and murmured: "It is not possible, I cannot believe it."' Nasalli Rocca was asked to return to Regina Coeli for more news. 'The guards there confirmed that many prisoners had been sent to be shot.'

Earlier on the 24th the *Osservatore Romano* had, in its usual ambiguous and careful language, appealed to all Romans to refrain from acts of violence, the implication being that reprisals might result. Detractors of Pius XII have since claimed that this proves that he must have known what was in store. In point of fact there is only one document in the Vatican archives referring to Via Rasella and possible reprisals on that day. It is a note made at the Secretariat and the time shown is 10.15 a.m. A certain Ingeniere Ferrero, never identified, from the civil headquarters of Rome had given details about German and Italian casualties, adding that 'up till now the countermeasures are unknown, but it is foreseen that for every German killed ten Italians will be shot'. Vatican historians have re-emphasized the fact that Via Rasella was a serious blow to the Pope's strategy for saving Rome from destruction, and added that it would seem likely that someone such as Padre Pancrazio or Prince Carlo Pacelli would have gone to the German authorities to ask for moderation, in the same way as they had often done in individual and less important cases. There is nothing about any warning from Dollmann. The whole of Rome expected some sort of German reaction, possibly violent, but nobody knew it would be so swift. As for contacting the German Embassy, there is only documentary evidence after the massacre, when details of victims of the reprisal were requested by the Secretariat on 22 April – the embassy denying any connection with the affair; earlier, on 29 March, an official at the embassy, when asked about political detainees, had said that all enquiries should be sent to No. 155 Via Tasso.

As Dollmann has said: 'This is a page of history destined to remain a mystery.'

The curfew was now at 1700 hours again. Then the bread ration was reduced, from 150 to 100 grams a day. 'Another turn of the screw,' wrote Mother Mary St Luke, the American nun, in her diary. When she read the communiqué about the reprisal, she felt 'a shiver of horror', as did most other inhabitants of Rome.

Carla Capponi was stunned; she felt 'a terrible desperation, anguish'. Bentivegna was overcome by 'wrath, pain and outrage at so cowardly a reprisal'. His impulse, he said, was to take revenge, to kill. 'For the first time I understood the ferociousness of the enemy we faced.' Amendola could not shake off a feeling of individual responsibility. He and the other Gapists who took part in the Via Rasella affair were to be criticized for not giving themselves up before the executions. Yet they were never asked to do so. The executions were announced by the Germans as a *fait accompli*. 'But,' Amendola said, 'quite apart from the circumstances of those times, we partisans had a duty not to give ourselves up, even if our sacrifice could have prevented the death of so many innocent people. We were a unit in a fighting army, we were also part of the headquarters of that army, and we could not abandon the struggle and go over to the enemy with all our knowledge of the organization's network. We had one duty: to continue the fight.'

And so on the 26th the Gapists issued their own communiqué, with that very message: the partisan war would not cease until the total evacuation of the city by the Germans.

It was still assumed that only 320 Italians had been killed. The *Osservatore Romano* now printed another announcement, careful as always not to take sides, on the one hand expressing grief for the thirty-two victims at Via Rasella, on the other 'for the three hundred and twenty persons sacrificed for the guilty parties who escaped arrest'. The Communists saw this as a double barb, but the Germans were not pleased either. Kesselring – who after long arguments with Wolff had finally stalled Himmler's plan – did not like the word 'sacrificed'. He therefore told his chief of staff to ask Kappler for clarification about the Vatican's further claim, by word of mouth, that innocent people had died. Once more, Kesselring was later to maintain, he had been assured that 'all those who had been shot had been condemned to death'. Nothing had been said to him either about the fifty-seven Jews who had been included.

'You cannot imagine,' Luisa Arpini has said, 'the grimness, the dread of those days. Nearly all of us had a friend, a brother, a father, a husband who *might* have been assassinated by that horrific Gestapo. Near me there lived the family of a dear little housepainter called Gigi, who had been caught in a man-hunt some weeks back. Perhaps the Nazis felt he was a partisan, because he went straight to Via Tasso. The wife was desperate for news. There were fantastic rumours – seven hundred, eight hundred had died. Of course it leaked out quickly that the executions had been at the Ardeatine Caves. We heard that a priest from St Calixtus had actually managed to get into one of them and had seen bodies – true, as we now know. Then Gigi's wife had a typed note from Via Tasso saying her husband was dead, not how or why. Even after the liberation of Rome she still tried to make herself believe that he had really been deported to Frankfurt or somewhere. All the same, she decided to go to the Ardeatine Caves, and asked me to go with her. We brought flowers – gladioli. But the smell ... The memory still makes me feel sick. You noticed it hundreds of yards away. The Nazis had dumped rubbish at the Caves' entrance to camouflage it. I am afraid I said I could not go on, but she insisted ... Eventually the Nazis put more explosives there and the place was really sealed up, and they kept guards outside.'

On 26 March there was a further German communiqué, published in the *Messaggero*. Part whitewashing, part threatening, it in effect affirmed Rome's open city status. To many Romans it seemed mere bluff. To the Vatican, after all the weeks of negotiation, it must have read somewhat sourly. At least the Germans had not carried out their threat to re-examine their attitude.

The communiqué claimed that it had done everything possible to 'deprive the Anglo-American adversaries of every pretext for the senseless bombardment of the city of Rome', yet the 'terroristic attacks' continued. Now all military movements across Rome would be prohibited, and there would be no German troops whatsoever in the city, apart from police and hospital personnel. Soldiers would not be allowed leave in Rome, even to visit St Peter's. If, however, Badoglian Communist elements took advantage of those measures in order to 'carry out cowardly ambushes', the German High Command would find itself obliged to take what military measures it deemed necessary. 'Thus, the fate of Rome and its civilian populations rests exclusively in the hands of the Roman population itself.'

The arrests continued. The black market continued. The miserable bread ration continued, and the bread mostly consisted of ground chickpeas, maize flour, elm pith and mulberry leaves. People were hacking trees and benches in the parks for firewood. Every day in Piazza Navona the church of Sant'Agnese tolled for the dead. Water was short;

the shabby women clustered with their buckets round the fountains. The Allied POWs were moved from new billet to new billet, but by the end of the month twenty-one had been recaptured. The walls all over Rome were scrawled with provocative *graffiti*, often sarcastic about the Allied slowness. Three women had their heads shaved by neighbours for sleeping with Germans. Not all those who received notes from Via Tasso about their relatives' deaths still had hope. The parents of Maurizio Giglio put in the paper that 'torn with grief they requested their friends neither to call nor send messages of condolence'.

Families were allowed to collect belongings of those reported dead. In the seam of a shirt this note was found: 'I dream of the hills around Siena, and of my love whom I shall never see again. I shall become one gaping wound – like the winds, nothing.'

On the 30th Mother Mary wrote in her diary: 'There is a sort of vague, dissatisfied, ominous feeling in the air. Some German cars and lorries have gone, and a good many soldiers with them, but barriers are still up around the German offices, and they are guarded by sentinels with machine-guns as before. Those who have gone outside the city have not gone far, and can pounce in on us whenever they wish to do so.' The Allied bombardments had died down, but not in the suburbs, and there was a good deal of shooting in the streets at night.

The Communist underground newspaper *L'Unità* published an article 'Avenge our Martyrs', and called for 'war to the death'. The Action Party paper *L'Italia Libera* had a headline: 'We shall not bow to Nazi terror'. Meanwhile Kappler and Kesselring's headquarters were secretly considering how the plan of the still insistent Wolff could be effected in case of any new *Schweinerei*. That moment was soon to come.

APRIL–JUNE

Anzio

By the end of March the Beachhead had become, to use a military euphemism, static. The failure at Cassino naturally meant that Truscott could not proceed with his Operation Panther, designed to coincide with a breakout in the South. Mackensen also abandoned his own plan for a new offensive. Both sides were worn out. There was a need for rest and refitting, in readiness for the big Allied offensive that must surely come in the late spring with the good weather.

In mid-April the Allied Combined Chiefs of Staff decided that Operation Anvil could not now possibly be launched simultaneously with Overlord, scheduled for early June. According to Clark's reckoning three weeks might be needed for the Fifth Army troops in the South to link up with VI Corps at Anzio. By now he had some 130,000 men on the Beachhead, over 90,000 of them being Americans, a fair proportion of whom had been there since the earliest days.

The drive by XII Air Support Command to disrupt German rail, road and communications north of Rome, Operation Strangle, continued inexorably. Between 15 March and 10 May there were 4,807 sorties. General Eaker divided Italian towns containing historic and religious monuments into three categories. Those which were in no circumstances to be bombed without his authority were Rome, Fiesole, Florence, Venice and Torcello. In category two were Ravenna, Assisi, San Gimignano, Pavia, Urbino, Montepulciano, Parma, Aosta, Tivoli, Udine, Gubbio, Volterra, Spoleto, Ascoli Piceno, Como, Pesaro and others listed enigmatically as Borgo, San Spolone and Aquia, presumably Borgo San Sepolcro and L'Aquila. 'The bombing of these towns,' Eaker directed, 'which have at present no spectacular military importance should be avoided if possible. If, however, you consider it essential for operational reasons that objectives in any of them should be bombed, you should not hesitate to do so, and I accept full responsibility for the results.' In the third chapter of this Apocalypse were such towns as Siena, Orvieto and Perugia — 'There are important military objectives in or near those towns which are to be bombed and any consequent damage is accepted.'

The expenditure of high explosive rained on Italian marshalling yards, railway lines and bridges was vast, but the Germans merely increased their round-ups of Italian male civilians and, with the help of the Todt labour organization, repairs were quickly made. Strangle proved in the end only to be a nuisance, and the Germans — masters always of improvisation — managed to keep their traffic going.

It was still expected by the Germans that there might be further Allied landings, possibly at Civitavecchia or Tarquinia, or even at Ostia. Although troops were regularly withdrawn from the front specifically to help in building defensive positions around Velletri and before Rome, they had to be kept on the alert at night. By and large units would stay three weeks in the line and were then withdrawn for ten days' construction work. This compared with the Allied habit of keeping men in the line for ten days, then bringing them back for two days in reserve followed by six days' complete rest. Further south, between Cassino and Anzio, a new defensive area, known as the Hitler Line, was also being built; in some places it was even stronger than the Gustav Line.

The Beachhead perimeter now measured sixteen miles along the coast by five to seven miles deep, 'no larger than a medium-sized Western ranch'. The British still guarded the Flyover on Via Anziate; this area was held by the 1st Division, with General Penney back in command. To the west, taking in most of the wadi country and as far as the swampy pools and dunes at the mouth of the Moletta, was the 5th Division under General Gregson-Ellis, whose gaunt figure in khaki shorts, very British, amused Truscott so much. The American 45th Division, commanded by General Eagles and with men from Oklahoma, Colorado, New Mexico and Arizona, was to the east of the Flyover, at the beginning of the great flat stretch of farmland known to some as the Billiard Table. Facing Cisterna three other American divisions alternated during the next months: the 3rd (General O'Daniel), the 1st Armored or Old Ironsides (General Harmon), and the 34th Iowa Infantry Division (General Ryder). Then along the Mussolini Canal as far as the sea were the Black Devils, the 1st Special Service Force, under the remarkable General Frederick.

Stories about the Black Devils buzzed round the Beachhead and the less outrageous appeared in home newspapers. There was 'Gusville', for example, a group of ruined farms from which patrols would go out but where animals still maintained a kind of life. Its mayor, Lieutenant Gus Heilman, boasted that it had no strikes, unemployment or black market, and was able to run a well-stocked bar through bringing back booze from raids far in the enemy hinterland. His colleague George ('The

Mustache') Krasevac once guided a whole herd of cattle back through the minefields. The Force surgeon managed to deliver five Italian babies for a fee of two eggs apiece, later increased when he heard that the chaplain had been given a chicken for a christening.

The Force also kept a prophylactic station for men who were lucky enough to chance upon farmhouses behind the German lines where there were young wives or older daughters. Such escapades were fewer when the 'Heinies' began sowing more anti-personnel mines. On one occasion tanks had to be sent to rescue a number of severely wounded men. Sergeant Knox remembered a tank trundling up to the surgeon, Evashwick. 'A boy was sitting on the tank with one leg up ... the other having been blow off. The Forceman called to Evashwick: "Hey doc, got an extra foot around this place?"'

As the weather improved, and honeysuckle came into flower, and narcissi and cyclamen appeared in this 'arsehole of Italy', so the trenches dried out and were reinforced by beams, doors and girders taken from Nettuno and Anzio. By day there was relative quiet, but the horror returned each night, with the stealthy combat patrols, grenade duels and mortaring. It was the War of Little Battles. Observation posts would have to be manned, and maybe a trip-flare would be set off, illuminating the landscape in stark aluminium-coloured detail, and spandaus would rake the frozen figures. Mines were the greatest dread, particularly 'Bouncing Betties'.

The thousands of propaganda leaflets caused a diversion. Some were frankly obscene, some useful as pin-ups. There were also surrender passes. Most leaflets were purposely grisly – 'The road to Rome is paved with skulls', etc., with appropriate illustrations – and there were others with subtler messages: 'Ask your pals in the 5th and 56th English Divisions whether they are shedding blood as you are. The Limeys have good reason to keep mum, for – as history proves – other peoples have always been the cat's paw of England.'

'Jerry's Front Line Radio', starring Axis Sally of the low-keyed sexy voice, alias the Berlin Bitch, and her helper George, continued to be popular. Her programmes usually began with the words 'Hullo suckers', and her signature tune was 'Between the Devil and the Deep Blue Sea'. After the routine boogie-woogie there would be some choice tale: 'Heard about Private Jones? He had all his guts blown away by a *Schuh* mine last week, but went on living twelve hours. Nasty things *Schuh* mines.' Then would follow messages from POWs enjoying the good food and comforts of captivity. Sally also seemed well informed about happenings on the Beachhead: 'Well, boys, how did *you* like the blasting you got last night?'

As Truscott said: 'Life was tense as it always is when men are close to death. But we learnt how to survive.'

At the other end of the Beachhead, in the British zone, I also listened to Sally, avidly, enjoying the banality and always hoping that in her catalogue of prisoners my batman-runner Vickers, recently captured, might be included. I counted myself lucky to be living for three weeks – as against the usual ten days in the line – in a deep and therefore shell-proof hole under a cowshed, once excavated by Americans and with a good store of K rations, tinned pineapple, sweetcorn and chewing gum left behind, a relief from bully beef and 'conner', Maconachie's stew. Unfortunately, there was also a legacy of crab lice. Water was very short, only enough for two mugs of tea per person a day. Illumination in the dugout came from a smoky paraffin lamp made out of a cigarette tin. 'If,' I wrote to a girlfriend in London, 'we do venture to poke our dirty unshaven faces over the top by day, the light is so dazzling we have to blink. What one has to go through to save civilization. There's no water for washing. Yet we are a merry enough dugout – all walks of life. The Honourable Society of Moles and Earthworms.' And later again: 'Excuse paper – hands are filthy and it's loot from a farmhouse anyway. I don't mind dancing with you all night, but when it comes to being platoon commander, wireless operator, guide, stretcher-bearer and general liaison stooge all night long it's a bit of a strain. As you would say: my dear, the noise and the shrapnel!'

In my diary I was less flippant. 'Dusk, and these awful nights. A Jerry patrol slipped in behind one of my forward sections and nabbed a corporal. We are very uneasy. I'm determined we shall be offensive from now on, and I'm laying ambushes, snipers everywhere, booby-trapping the wire. My knees are so sore from crawling.' And later: 'The men seem dispirited. They've been on the go since the invasion of Sicily and are worn out. It's terrible to see what war can do to a man's will. I'm always coming across those people – mostly old soldiers and excellent fellows – who are entirely shaken and a bag of nerves, a captain among them. Bomb-happiness is a dreadful thing. Jerry knows it too. His propaganda is very subtle, though often stupidly crude ... Today I'm organizing a burial squad to deal with dead cattle and sheep. We have a dead horse near here. It stinks. Mosquitoes are now hatching out.' And later: 'We are beginning to bore one another in this hole, and I'm sick of the smell of feet. Then these grouses. Why don't we advance? What are we fighting for? Why don't they send out the strikers to take our place?'

On Easter Sunday we had powdered eggs for breakfast. In the Padiglione woods the Old Ironsides organized a multi-denominational service at sunrise in their 'Church-in-the-Wildwood', erected from trees felled by enemy shells, and invited some of us across. We declined, perhaps luckily, as a bugle call besides summoning the worshippers also attracted the German artillery . . .

An underground cinema was constructed nearer the town of Anzio itself, seating thirty-five 'and no queueing'; this was for when we came out of the line to rest, and for people who existed permanently in rear areas – though nowhere in the Beachhead was safe from bombs or shells. There were also concert shows, with costumes looted from the town, and sometimes starring professional entertainers – but the Americans, we heard, found the humour of a British pair, Ramsbottom and Enoch, 'unrewarding'. The pipers of the Scottish Horse, complete with kilts and sporrans, did however provide a sensation for the Yanks. Nevertheless, first priorities when we emerged from the front were (a) sleep and (b) 'disinfestation' at the mobile showers.

I once went with another subaltern in the Green Howards, Charles Newton – half French, as lively a character as Nick Mansell – to a show called *The Waggoners*. 'I hadn't laughed so much for a long time.' I wrote in my diary: 'The "leading lady" was most voluptuous, heavily rouged and with a low-cut dress. We all whistled and cheered, he might have been Betty Grable. Later we heard he had been ordered to tone it down. Such is the all-male atmosphere in the Beachhead. The whole place is fraught with what Charles calls sulphur.'

Beetle-racing became a mania for some; a Green Howards favourite was called Mae West, carrying a lot of money as well as weight. An ex-New York bartender, Corporal Joe Boyle, rounded up some mules, donkeys and horses, 'as nifty a bunch of steeds as ever turned a quarter of a mile in thirty-five seconds flat'. He formed a Beachhead Racing Association, the high spot being the Anzio Derby, with a can of C rations for the winner, and another of spaghetti and meat balls for second place. The Derby was won by Quartermaster Stable on Six-by-Six, who surged ahead of Suzie and others such as Slow Motion and George, 'a white jackass well anchored under 240 pounds of Pat Burns of Brooklyn'. All this to the strains of the 3rd Division band playing its famous hymn, 'The Dogface Soldier March'.

On my return from my three weeks' sojourn under the cowshed, I found that the 'lads' at our rest area, B Echelon, in a *pineta* by the sea, had excavated roomy sleeping-holes, each containing real beds filched from Anzio with camouflage nets as mattresses. Most of these holes had been thoughtfully provided with notices, such as 'Seaview Hotel', 'Good Eats Café', 'The Nook', 'Hawkers and Shells Not Welcome', or 'Sunny Side Up'.

Front-liners were never allowed to venture into Anzio town, strictly the domain of VI Corps HQ, port authorities and suchlike. Anyone arriving at the port from Naples during the day would find himself plunged in an unpleasant greasy smoke-screen, through which could be discerned numerous barrage balloons which kept off the dive-bombers. Some signs might also be visible: 'You are Here', 'Beachhead Hotel – Special Rates for New Arrivals'. Further inland they became more menacing: 'No traffic in daylight beyond this point', 'Danger – Shelling. Make No Dust'. The unloading at the port continued with marked unconcern (at times) for Anzio Annie, whose shells were like an express train running full tilt overhead, and for the plumes of spray constantly spurting up from random shells. Indeed, between March and May 1944, Anzio had the reputation of being the seventh busiest port in the world. On 29 March no less than 7,828 tons were brought ashore.

There were days, or more usually nights, of great disasters down at the port. On 3 April, for instance, 150,000 gallons of petrol went up and several men were scorched to death. Every day, too, there were casualties from 'Popcorn Pete', the anti-personnel bomb. Hospitals continued to receive direct hits. Altogether nearly a hundred medical personnel were killed by shellfire, including six nurses. German 'human torpedoes' or E-boats looked like being a menace until it was realized that their pilots became hopelessly sea-sick. Occasionally some intrepid saboteurs, dressed in Allied uniforms, would land on beaches in small boats and then be blown up on the mines. One group actually claimed to have a mission to assassinate General Clark.

The Beachhead during this period of 'lull' was a great place for sightseers, known to the Americans as Gadabouts and to the British as Swanners – senators, members of Parliament, self-important journalists, Russian observers. To Anzio hands there was always some sadistic pleasure in noting the anxiety of these people to return home as quickly as possible. Often the visitors would express a wish to 'fire a gun' and would then be directed to a twenty-five pounder reserved for that purpose. A Colonel Robert Spears, an Ordnance officer, made a special trip from Palermo just to be able to snipe a German, so that he 'could hold his own with his son', who was a pilot in the Pacific. He was in luck. 'The Colonel nuzzled his cheek against the stock of his 103, squinted down the sights at the grey-green tunic ... Now he was ready for retirement. The old Colonel had killed his German.' And somebody else, in Germany, had lost a son.

A surprising scourge among new recruits or those who had been on short leave to Naples was VD. I was really upset when my sergeant, who acted as a kind of father to us all in the platoon, announced that he had got it and must go into hospital. I could not believe that he had 'stooped' to what Neapolitan pimps called ficky-fick, he a married man. In my innocence I was also a bit afraid lest he had caught it from American blankets, like the crab lice, or Timmy Lloyd's scabies, and that the rest of us might also be contaminated.

Italian civilians were not finally evacuated from the Beachhead until April, though a few hundred were kept back for jobs such as mess waiters and cooks at Corps HQ or as hospital orderlies. Captain Mack, British Public Safety Officer, used to visit a farmer who had insisted on staying on in a danger area. The man lived in his cellar, and one day Mack was amazed to find a girl cooking something there – she was his daughter. Mack warned him not to let her outside, in case she was spotted by a nearby American unit. He called again and found an American sitting in the cellar; but the man was a deserter. The GI couldn't keep his eyes off the girl. So Mack quickly disarmed him and called the military police – but in so doing the secret was out and the farm came under siege. The girl had to be despatched, as the Italians succinctly say *precipitevolissimevolmente*, to Naples.

There were said to be three hundred deserters, both British and American, at large on the Beachhead. At first nobody made out where they could hide themselves in such a small area. John Hope, the British Guards officer at VI Corps, used sometimes to take time off bird-watching in deserted gardens to the east of Nettuno, making his way along a very deeply dug ditch. 'Once I saw some washing hanging out, which I thought was odd. Then I saw something shining beneath a lot of old sticks. I kicked at it and found a large cache of new tins. I thought: "My God, those deserter bastards must be in the wood here." I turned a corner and was confronted by two unshaven GIs, one with a red beard, with rifles. I knew it was touch and go. "What are you doing here?" one of them asked. I showed him my British badges, and when I said I was bird-watching they burst out laughing. They pretended they were just back from the front.' As soon as he got back, Hope reported the affair to the American Provost. After some difficulty, it was agreed to send a jeep. Hope, to his alarm, was asked to sit on the bonnet. 'As we approached the ditch, Red Beard and his companion jumped up and ran like hell into a tobacco field; the men in the jeep belted off into the crops. God knows whether any were killed. No expedition was organized to go into the bushes to find out who was there. Men just couldn't be spared.'

Hope was delighted one day to see a pair of bee-eaters, which appeared to be nesting in the German lines. He also saw several golden orioles.

In the front line you might hear a cuckoo at dawn. Nightingales sang day and night, and people complained they were becoming bird-happy. The more the nightingales were frightened by two-inch mortars or volleys of grenades, the more they sang – and the more this so-called music of the moon seemed callous to those who crouched in shallow fox-holes and who saw their comrades die.

If we British felt that the 'soya link' was no substitute for the sausage, so the German soldier complained about the composition of his *Wurst*, that almost sacred item of the national diet. Sergeant Fritz Wolff, who belonged to a butcher company in 65th Division, was eventually given money to scour the countryside for pigs. Amazingly, he was in the end generally able to find one pig per day. Animals for slaughter were in very short supply around Rome, especially beef, and Field-Marshal Kesselring had forbidden the killing of milking cows, as he said that milk for Roman children was more important.

The *ersatz* coffee, supposed to be made from roasted wheat, was nicknamed *Muckefuck*, and cigarettes were rationed at three a day. By and large, food at the front was better than in rear echelons. In spite of Axis Sally's eulogies, any Allied POW who managed to escape from a camp pronounced prison food to be vile, mostly potatoes and cabbage.

Lieutenant Schaller, returning from his comfortable leave in his Italian friends' house, was relieved to find himself attached for a while to the 145th Regiment HQ, under Colonel Claus Kuehl, a man of some charm, aged forty-five, with a passion for dance music. After visiting front line positions they would return to peppermint liqueur and Schnapps, though the colonel would only allow a Spartan meal of sandwiches in the evening. Early in April Schaller had to return to his original unit, which was at the hated *Dreifingerschlucht*, Three Fingers Ravine – no-man's-land there being just as far as you could chuck a grenade. His batman was almost at once killed from a splinter in the groin. If, like me in my cowshed, Schaller suffered from lack of washing water and from lice, he fared better on Easter Day, receiving from base tobacco, Schnapps, cake and one fresh egg, hard-boiled.

A derelict Sherman tank was used as an observation post, and Schaller sat inside it throughout daylight hours. His radio set broke down, which meant that he could not direct artillery fire. This was a nuisance, as you could actually see Americans of the 45th Division shaking out their blankets in the morning. They seemed to have diarrhoea, because they were always dashing out to ammunition boxes which they used as lavatories.

At last his radio was mended, and the artillery opened up on Schaller's targets. Did those Americans rush into the bushes! They retaliated with a grenade-thrower, but of course Schaller directed the artillery on to that too. When night came, he made a reconnaissance and found several bodies, including German ones from earlier actions which nobody had bothered to bury. Colonel Kuehl visited the unit and was so upset by these dead Germans that burial parties were at once arranged.

When Schaller was not in his observation post he spent his time looking for lice – fifty to sixty a day were not rare. Whenever he returned to HQ he was always astounded by the greenness of the meadows and the trees, just coming to life, in contrast to the blasted ground, like cocoa powder, at the front line.

Lieutenant Richard Oehler was in a Signals Company. By the end of April, he noted, the average German soldier in his foxhole felt an 'uncanny disquiet', a kind of dread of the unknown, though at the same time this gave him a heightened readiness for battle. At least, with the drier weather, the ground would be nicely hard for the Tiger and Panther tanks, always superior to the Allies' 'hardware'. But the German Air Force, by contrast, had been so weakened that it mostly kept out of the skies by day, even when the Allied observation plane, known as the *Lahme Ente*, Lame Duck, came trundling overhead. At night it was different, and one heard bomber formations speeding for Anzio. The enemy anti-aircraft defences were massive, but the planes obviously found some good targets, judging by the pulsing red glows in the sky. 'I am sure,' wrote Oehler, 'that few of my comrades will forget the firework displays on those nights.'

His company was moved back to Ninfa, west of the Alban Hills, and positioned in tents and straw huts on the mountainside opposite the village of Norma. Ah Ninfa! A place of magic beauty, a village deserted for at least a hundred years, its towers and ruins reflected in pools and streams. The American wife of Prince Bassiano had begun to turn the whole place into a garden, with water-lilies and climbing roses, but now the Bassianos had fled to Rome and the undergrowth was taking over again. And high above, past the olive groves, was Norma, perched incredibly like a kestrel's nest on the barren cliffs; and opposite it Sermoneta, with its romantic castle and the Borgia dungeons.

Oehler's company had the job of blowing up no less than twenty-eight bridges when the Allies would launch their attack.

On 18 April I was back at the Fortress. As before I tried to be breezy in my letters to my London girlfriend: 'My dear, fancy beating off patrols all last night, with mortar barrages, flares, tracer everywhere! Such a strain on the old nerves. We have to climb a thirty-foot vertical slope to get to this place!'

To my brother I wrote more frankly: 'Here we are stuck in the shittiest position on the edge of a hillside and completely under observation from the enemy. We can't so much as stir above the top or snipers are at us at once. We just crouch at the bottom of our trenches and hope for the best, listening to the distant report of a grenade-thrower, waiting for the whistle of the falling grenade, and then hearing the explosion, maybe twenty yards away. The German adjusts his aim and there is another report. This time the thing explodes only fifteen yards away. And so on ... The dry ground is now like iron and it's difficult to dig deeper. Only Charles Newton cheers us up. Last night the Germans were talking and shouting across the valley, and he shouted back, '*Ruhe da, wir koennen nicht schlafen*, Shut up, we can't sleep.'

And in my diary: 'GOD THIS IS A BLOODY WAR. First of all the position I occupied six weeks ago is now the target of vicious Jerry attacks, just across the valley from here. I just cannot forget having to listen to a wounded corporal sobbing and crying ... Then last night two of my men were wounded, one a stretcher case, I swear the worst thing I have ever seen ... Charles at least could be funny, even hilarious, about Jerries rolling egg grenades down a slope, trying to get them into his platoon's weapon slits. He says Brian Ryrie, who fought so bravely, had a bottle of whisky in his trench and that was the only thing that kept him going during a rifle grenade attack. One of Brian's men became so hysterical that he had to sit on him ... There is a feeling that our defences are being gradually nibbled away. Dusk is the worst time. Will there or will there not be that big attack we now expect? Who among us will survive the night? ... I had a real trouncing from our second-in-command about What We Are Fighting For. In a nutshell. He said that all this talk about crusades made him retch. The Four Freedoms, *Herrenvolk* and German "inhumanity" were incidental as issues. Wars are like mass migrations of insects – a matter of impulse. Rarely had they anything to do with sentiment; their roots were nearly always buried in much more intricate matters, mainly economic, over which the emotions of the little man, be he British or American or German, had absolutely no control. And so on.'

The Fortress had been a far more restricted place than in March. Major Gericke's war diary shows how the 4th Paras had been gradually encroaching on it. His policy had been to 'give the enemy no peace' and to boost his men's morale by a succession of small successes. On 11 March he recorded taking eleven prisoners, on 19 March forty-five, then forty-seven. He claimed that most of the '*Schwalbennest*' was in German hands by 23 April (I left on 25 April).

There followed for me a spell at B Echelon: 'This could be glorious country,' I now wrote. 'Charles and I did a little tour in a jeep – brilliant moon and dark trees shrugging their shoulders; even an illicit bathe by moonlight.' Then I found myself in the North Lobster Claw wadi, among the graves of men who had died two months before, mostly belonging to the Queens and the Oxford and Bucks, in a 'wasteland of churned up earth and craters'. From my trench the Alban Hills and Velletri were easily visible in the freshness of morning light.

This time, for a change, I found my platoon had the advantage over the Jerries, and I would sometimes crawl out in the now sweltering sun to ruined houses to do a spot of sniping. But it was not long before remorse overtook me: 'Yesterday I did a terrible thing. There was an attack scare and we had a hundred per cent stand-to. I went forward to an old trench on the ridge above us to have a "dekko". Like a fool I only had a grenade with me, and to my surprise I saw a Jerry get up and walk, about two hundred yards away. I went back and fetched a rifle, and then saw a head looking over the top which I fired at. It fell backwards straight away. I knew I had scored a bullseye. I was thrilled. Shortly afterwards I crawled up to the Jerry wire to get my field-glasses, which I thought I'd left there. As I wriggled into a big shell-hole, about fifty yards from me I happened to notice a very blond Aryan, as Charles would say, looking the other way, combing his hair. I tried to fire three rounds with my Winchester and of course – as always in such cases – it was jammed. Back I went to fetch a rifle, and then, watched closely by my platoon, I fired at this wretched chap. He threw up his hands with a gasp, which I clearly heard, and collapsed. Then the meaning of what I was doing hit me. Oh God, oh God, let me out of here before I do any more such things . . . At Company HQ they joked and called me "Killer" or "Crippen", which makes me all the more miserable.'

This happened on 10 May. Alexander's great offensive, Diadem, opened at Cassino on 11 May.

At the end of April the American 3rd Division had carried out two small but bloody actions, known as Operations Mr Black and Mr Green, in the region of Spaccasassi (Break Stones) Creek, which their predecessors, the 45th, had thankfully handed over to them. The hero of the former action was Pfc John C. Squires, who – in spite of his eighteen years and never having been in action before – coolly took over command of his platoon when the NCOs were knocked out. Single-handed, he captured twenty-one prisoners, one by one, from the 29th Panzer Grenadier Division. Squires was later killed and posthumously awarded the Congressional Medal of Honor.

Operation Mr Green was notable for its use of the 'psychological attack'. Loud-speakers warned Germans that more and heavier artillery fire was about to come, and they had better surrender before it was too late. German NCOs could be seen rushing from hole to hole to pacify their men.

The 3rd Division's successes with these two operations helped to raise morale, for up to now the enemy had been gradually pushing forward.

Since, in that flat and bare country, and unlike some of the British sector, any vehicle stirring during the hours of daylight could be watched from the Alban Hills, movement was naturally sparse. It was not surprising, maybe, that one track to the front was called variously Via Dolorosa and the Burma Road. Now, at last, there was a slight feeling of offence rather than defence.

It was also noticeable that the Germans had virtually given up raids on shipping. Instead, their chief targets were supply dumps, landing strips and troop concentrations.

Captured German documents gave these casualty figures: 4–8 April, 82 killed, 403 wounded, 14 missing – Allied prisoners 11; 14–18 April, 97 killed, 342 wounded, 82 missing – Allied prisoners 12; 19–23 April, 107 killed, 340 wounded, 48 missing – Allied prisoners 9; 24–28 April, 116 killed, 447 wounded, 56 missing – Allied prisoners 43; 29 April –3rd May, 132 killed, 531 wounded, 11 missing – Allied prisoners 23. The German deserters were usually *Beute Deutsche*, i.e. from occupied countries. Of the German prisoners, few under twenty-one proclaimed themselves as anti-Nazi though not many were politically conscious. All those in the 65th Division praised General Pfeifer. General Greiner of the 362nd Division, opposite the US 3rd Division, however, was generally disliked. '*Die Division Greiner/Wird immer kleiner/Zum Schluss bleibt einer/ Und das ist Greiner*, The Greiner division/Gets smaller and smaller/At the end there will only be one man left/And that will be Greiner.' He was felt to be conceited and tremendously ambitious, and had actually said that he would never leave the Beachhead until his division could be loaded on a single truck.

There was also scorn for Captain Aschmann commanding the 7th Battalion zbV, who was considered *feige*, chicken-hearted. The zbV, or Special Service, was composed of court-martialled men and physically fit criminals on probation, some being veterans. The morale of these men was not very high either, and cannot have been improved by the fact that they often had to encounter the Canadian–American wild boys, the Black Devils.

During April Alexander and Clark did not visit the Beachhead. Clark had been summoned briefly to Washington. In the meantime Truscott was preparing alternative schemes for the great breakout, after the Gustav and Hitler Lines had been breached. On 5 May Alexander visited VI Corps headquarters and at once selected the scheme known as Operation Buffalo as the most feasible; it called for a thrust to a gap south of the Alban Hills towards Valmontone on Route 6, the aim of which would be to cut off the retreat of the right wing of the German Tenth Army.

Alexander also told Truscott that he reserved for himself the time for launching this attack.

Truscott decided to alert Clark about this at once, and the next day Clark arrived, obviously annoyed by what he considered to be an attempt by the British to run his Army. What was more, he was determined that his men should have the glory of being the first to enter Rome. And in any case, he was not at all convinced that a drive for Valmontone would cut off the Germans; it would certainly leave them holding the high ground in the Alban Hills.

'I asked Alex,' said Clark, 'please to issue orders through me, instead of dealing directly with my subordinates.' Alexander climbed down at once, and as for who should go to Rome first, he said: 'You see where I've drawn the boundaries, Wayne. Rome is in your area. Rome is yours. You take it.' Clark then remembered him saying: 'If you can't take it, I'll send the Eighth Army over to take it.' To which Clark hastily replied: 'Don't worry, Alex, if it can be taken, we'll take it.' All concluded therefore in a nice gentlemanly way – for the time being.

Rome

Disgusted and disillusioned by the quarrels in the Rome CLN, its president Ivanoe Bonomi wrote in his diary on 23 March: 'Today, in the silence of my little room [in the Lateran], simple and austere as is right for young seminarists devoted to divine service, I have written my letter of resignation.'

So now there was a vacuum among the six parties. Some further manoeuvring had also toppled General Armellini, who had been in command of the pro-Badoglio Military Front, and his place had been taken by General Bencivegna, considered to be more acceptable to all parties of the CLN. Unfortunately, Bencivegna had broken his leg and was laid up, helpless, in another Lateran cell. This state of disorganization, with all its future dangers of clashes between rival factions, was just what the Allies dreaded, and was not helped by a vigorous and successful drive by the *Nazifascisti* to arrest yet more leading Resistance figures.

But these squabbling Roman politicians were unaware of an imminent wind – gale – of change among their counterparts in the South. This was due to the arrival of the Communist leader, Palmiro Togliatti, code-named Ercole (Hercules) and surnamed Ercoli, who had been in exile in Moscow since 1924 and had been Secretary of the Comintern, no less. 'A weedy little man, with no obvious fire-ball characteristics,' reported a member of Macmillan's staff; but this was wishful thinking. Togliatti's impact was like the arrival of a paladin on a charger. Within a few days he had made his pronouncement: everything must be subordinated to the defeat of Germany, and the Communists would therefore collaborate with Badoglio and the king.

A clarion-call for national unity? A brilliant piece of statesmanship? A cynical move on Moscow's orders? A deftly aimed shot at the Anglo-Americans? The announcement brought consternation to the parties of the left, both in Rome and the North. What price now the Bari Congress of last January, with all those fiery resolutions against the Badoglio regime?

Churchill's first reaction was one of relief. 'It looks,' he told Eden, 'as though we may get pretty well all you asked. As long as we keep that old trickster Sforza out or in a minor position, all may be well.' Others saw it as Russia's way of getting a chance to run Italy's affairs after the war. There was no doubt that Communism was on the increase in Italy, even among the *bourgeoisie* and upper class, and for several reasons, which could loosely be summed up as impatience: frustration over Allied policies and the misery of living conditions in the South, the at present lukewarm help for partisans in north and central Italy, the bombing of towns and the civilian casualties, and the failure to break through the German defences as compared with Russia's successes. As a Foreign Office man wrote: 'We do not inspire burning faith or hold out prospects for a better future.'

Togliatti's decision might have been affected by the efforts of an eminent Neapolitan lawyer, Senator De Nicola, who, with the backing of Croce, in mid-March had persuaded the old king to retire from public life after the liberation of Rome and to appoint his son, Prince Umberto, Lieutenant-General of the Realm, or Regent. So this had been another dramatic step forward, and at long last. It also helped Roosevelt, with the American Presidential election in view. However, as Russia's star was now gleaming so brightly, the Anglo-Americans realized that they must take some positive step to refurbish their own. Could the king be persuaded to retire at once?

The king and queen were living in a great villa at Ravello perched over the Amalfi coast, a kind of Mediterranean Tintagel, someone said. A deputation set out, consisting of Robert Murphy for the USA, Harold Macmillan, Sir Noel Charles (destined to succeed Macmillan on the Allied Advisory Council), and General Mason-MacFarlane. The wily little king played his game well and refused to bring forward his retirement, but he wept when he agreed not to go to Rome at the liberation and to make an immediate public announcement about his decision to hand over to his son on the day of Rome's liberation. General Mason-MacFarlane is said to have been tearful too, as was Badoglio when he went to see the king a little later.

And, so, on 21 April, the government of the South, after much haggling, announced that Badoglio had reconstituted his Cabinet on an all-party basis. Togliatti, Croce and Sforza were to be among the ministers without portfolio. Togliatti told Mason-MacFarlane that he considered Badoglio to have a 'perfectly clean record'.

This U-turn, this *'svolta del Sud'*, was welcomed in Rome by De Gasperi on behalf of the Christian Democrats, and by Bonomi and other rightist leaders. The unease of the Communists, who had little option but to accept their leader's dictum, was watched with some amusement by their opponents, though Amendola records that as early as 3 April he wrote to his northern colleagues saying that they must approve Togliatti's initiative 'with enthusiasm' and recognize that in the past they had been mistaken. The Socialists, rather than be left in the lurch, seemed prepared to give in too. The Actionists, however, were appalled. Much clarification would be needed before the parties of the Rome CLN could be reunited, against a background of increasing civilian distress.

By the first week in April the food situation in Rome was becoming ugly. Ninety per cent of the supplies were black market, centred round Tor di Nona, the site of a medieval prison. Prices had increased tenfold since November: the official ration of bread was a hundred grams, the equivalent of about two slices a day. There were more riots. Bakeries and German food-carrying lorries were assaulted. Worse, Vatican convoys bringing supplies from the North were constantly being mistaken by Allied aircraft for German transport and therefore machine-gunned.

It was assumed that the Germans were systematically trying to cow the Romans through starvation. The Communist women leaders distributed leaflets: '*Donne romane, lavoratori*, leave your work, leave your houses, out into the street and demand your right to live!' Argentina and Spain made approaches to the Vatican about sending flour. The Swiss suggested dropping supplies by parachute. D'Arcy Osborne transmitted a Vatican plan to the Foreign Office — accepted, apparently, in principle by the Germans — whereby Rome could be sent food by ships flying the Papal colours from ports such as Genoa. For the poorest people it was now only possible to subsist thanks to the Vatican's soup kitchens.

There still had been no official Allied reaction to the 'open city' issue. The Roman press gave the total of victims from bombing to date as five thousand killed and eleven thousand injured, which some thought was too low. The Communist women also organized an appeal to neutral countries to intervene with the Anglo-Americans. The continued German presence in the city, in spite of some gestures towards 'de-militarization', was underlined when seven of their parked vehicles were set on fire by partisans in the Circus Maximus.

Water-sellers appeared on the streets, and a bottle of drinking water could be a valued present. Since telephones were tapped, wealthier people spoke in code when they acquired black market food which they wanted to share: 'Moo moo' perhaps for a piece of beef, or 'Buttons' for potatoes. Cooking salt was nearly non-existent. With many public services practically defunct, Rome had become like a besieged city. There were so many rumours. However wild they were snatched at eagerly, so long as they were optimistic. Farm animals were kept in the Villa Borghese. People, desperate for money, stood at street corners selling gramophone records, furs, prams, books, shoes and empty bottles. It was joked that most of Rome listened to the radio under the bedclothes, meaning that everybody was listening to the forbidden BBC news.

Although the American chiefs of staff wavered, the British were firmly against declaring Rome an open city. As usual, it was a matter of the 'known unreliability' of the Germans. In an emergency, the Germans would not hesitate to make the fullest use of communications through Rome, and as things were they were perfectly able to maintain supplies to the southern fronts without using the marshalling yards. Another argument was that recognition of the open city would affect the Allies' prestige; it could be regarded as an admission of guilt. Above all, though, the Allies themselves wanted to use Rome after its occupation. Since they had overwhelming air superiority there would be little question of subsequent attacks on the city by German planes.

Although the disruption of German communications and the 'destruction of economic targets used by or working for the Germans' were of first importance, strict rules had been laid down about precision bombing close to Rome. There were mistakes of course, not to mention some dreadful acts of carelessness. A squadron leader flying a Wellington remembers: 'Far from being given specific targets in Rome we were categorically banned from any attacks on the city and were left in no doubt that any "accidental" bombing would bring trouble to the crew responsible. We carried cameras which were linked with bomb release gear and automatically took photos of areas under attack, so we couldn't have "got away with it" unless we were over 10/10 cloud.'

Bombs did however continue to drop and cause damage in the vicinity of the Papal villa at Castel Gandolfo, where four thousand five hundred refugees were now living. A special plea was sent by the Vatican to spare the sheds housing Caligula's famous barges on Lake Nemi, since three thousand more civilians were there. As day by day agonizing reports came in about the destruction of ancient and beautiful buildings in the North, there were renewed appeals to spare places such as Assisi. Surely *Assisi* could at least be regarded as a 'hospital city'? And what about Orvieto, Chieti ... But again the Allies kept their sphinx-like silence.

'I am against it,' wrote Churchill tersely, about supplying Rome with food by ship. General Wilson considered that the military reasons for not granting such facilities 'far outweighed any possible humanitarian or propaganda value'. As for the road convoys, it was almost impossible to identify them as Vatican vehicles. The Allied Air Forces must have freedom to attack all road transport so long as the enemy was more dependent on roads than on railways (because of Operation Strangle) for their supplies. On 20 April Roosevelt sent a note to Eamon De Valera, Prime Minister of Ireland, reiterating that if German forces were not entrenched in Rome no question would arise concerning the city's preservation; 'the fate of Rome rests in that [the Germans'] quarter.'

But on 25 April Osborne was writing to London: 'I cannot too strongly emphasize that unless we can within the immediate future either ourselves provide for essential supply of flour to Rome or enable the Vatican to do so we shall be inviting a catastrophe by which the sole beneficiaries will be the Germans who, by their demilitarization of Rome, can claim to have divested themselves of the responsibility.'

The late spring burgeoned. The Tiber swirled high in brown waves, as water poured down from the melted snows; along its banks the plane trees were in leaf. In the Vatican gardens diplomats played tennis on the Ethiopian College courts, or bicycled down avenues of ilex, umbrella pines and cypresses. Soon the pomegranates would be in flower.

Lilac was on sale in the narrow streets by the Pantheon – streets stinking of urine. Lilac was on the desk in the interrogation room at Via Tasso – a room stinking of congealed blood. After curfew the sound of cheap dance music, women's squeals and German voices could be heard from upstairs rooms above bars in Largo Argentina and off Via Veneto.

Mrs Whitaker's younger daughter climbed the tower of their villa to watch a night raid over Ciampino airfield. It was like a red spangled net, she said, with 'myriads of sparks dancing in the sky'. On Easter Day there were sirens in the morning, but planes did not fly over Rome. The guns were booming towards Anzio, quite loud, and at the same time the bells of St Peter's were ringing out. 'I looked over the cupolas and terraces shining in the sun and tried to remember that this city is supposed to be eternal.'

Still the executions continued at Forte Bravetta, and a prize catch for the Gestapo was the Socialist Giuliano Vassalli. The Fascist police were having a new drive to round up the rich and the aristocracy. 'Everyone is full of friends arrested,' said Mrs Whitaker. Badoglio's son Mario had been caught. Princess Gangi was apparently locked up in San Gregorio. 'That nice Chicco Multedo', the portrait painter who had been secretary to Montezemolo and Armellini, was in Via Tasso. Vincenzo Florio of the fabulously wealthy Sicilian family and his wife were arrested on a stupid charge of trying to sell the royal family's jewels and also put in Via Tasso, though briefly. The Duchess of Cesarò came home to find that her two daughters Mita and Simonetta (later a famous dress designer), their fiancés and all the servants had been arrested. The film director Luchino Visconti spent three days in Koch's Pensione Jaccarino, without being tortured, and then went to San Gregorio. Joey Nathan, the Jewish banker, was also put in Via Tasso, but moved later to Regina Coeli, again unhurt; the assumption by his family was that he was for some reason being kept as a hostage. It was commonly believed that the Fascist police had prepared lists of all Romans who might be of some service to the Allies when they reached Rome, with a view to deporting them to the North. Most university professors, lawyers, doctors and government functionaries were supposed to have been included on the lists.

The Cesarò household had been arrested for helping Allied prisoners. They spent Easter week in a police station, usually being questioned in the small hours. In due course Mita's fiancé was taken to Via Tasso, where his nails were ripped out. She was made to watch him and a *contadino* being beaten. After a while she fainted. Her mother was able to obtain Simonetta's freedom by promising a Flemish picture in exchange, and she also tried to get her friend Harold Tittmann at the Vatican to arrange an exchange of prisoners for the others through the Fifth Army – hopeless of course. Eventually Mita was smuggled into the Vatican dressed as a Palatine Guard.

When Multedo was arrested, he was found to have a note with the words '*Letizia è bella*' in his pocket. The SD men at Via Tasso were suspicious (and justifiably, for it was connected with a parachute drop of arms), but Multedo pretended to break down under the nine hours' interrogation under strong lights and raved incoherently about religion, philosophy, Carducci's poetry, etc. A doctor was called, luckily an Italian, who pronounced that he had a weak heart, so he was spared torture.

In quieter moments Multedo did drawings of his gaolers. One named Mueller had been a boxer, and Multedo knew that he had tortured a boy from his cell. 'As I expected to be shot, I could say what I liked – those Nazis seemed to respect people who were proud. I said: "You have tortured people," and he replied: "Yes, but I didn't use instruments. I only used my hands." In the distance we could hear Chopin's Prelude No. 15 in D Flat Major being played on a piano. I explained to this great burly Nazi that it had been inspired by raindrops in Majorca and had been played to George Sand, and that she had loved Chopin. You know tears came into his eyes.' There was another SD official, quite handsome, called Schutz (the one who gave the command to fire at the Ardeatine Caves). 'I said: "You have eyes of a hyena." Schutz was pleased at this and told me: "In Germany if you are in the Gestapo and are told that you have human eyes it means that you have eyes of glass."'

Multedo was in a cell usually with five others. There were no mattresses and most slept on the floor. Every twenty-four hours they had soup like dirty water. Sometimes you could hear the screams of Jews being kicked on the stairs. Once there was a cry: 'No, no, not the scissors.' On two occasions Multedo was permitted to be visited by his mother and sister. The second time his mother thought she had come to say goodbye for ever. She was dressed up as for a visit, full of dignity, a true Genoese, and did not weep. She said to him: 'Remember what Madame de Staël said. "Death does not separate us, it only makes us invisible."'

The execution of a young priest, Don Giuseppe Morosini, shocked Rome. He had helped soldiers in hiding after 8 September, and had been arrested because some weapons had been found in his library. The Pope had tried twice to have him reprieved, and the matter had been referred to the Fuehrer himself. Suddenly on 2 April Morosini was told that he would die the next day. His reaction was: '*Ci vuole più coraggio per vivere che morire*, one needs more courage to live than to die.'

Mother Mary St Luke knew Morosini and gave this description of his end: 'He died like a saint and a hero. Having asked as a favour to be allowed to celebrate mass on the morning of his execution, permission was granted to him, and Monsignore Traglia, Vicegerent of Rome, was present at it. The latter protested against the priest being handcuffed on entering the motor van that was to take them to the place of execution . . . Before being blindfolded he [Morosini] kissed his crucifix, blessed the platoon of [Italian] soldiers who were to shoot him, and publicly forgave the man who had betrayed him. Possibly because the executioners were overcome by his quiet heroism, he was not killed by their volley, and fell to the ground, wounded but conscious. He begged for the Sacrament of Extreme Unction, which was administered at once by Monsignore Traglia, after which the commanding officer shot him at the base of the skull with a revolver.'

A Dutch priest, Father Anselmo Musters, was also arrested – dragged from the sacristy of Santa Maria Maggiore. In the Derry-O'Flaherty escape organization he was known as 'Dutchpa'. The SD believed he was a British colonel in disguise, so at Via Tasso he was stripped and beaten up, then kept in a dark cell for a fortnight. Afterwards he was put on a train for Germany, but managed to jump out of his carriage and return to Rome.

There were many such stories. Koch was reputed to have said that if he ever caught O'Flaherty he would have his nails off his fingers before he shot him. Everyone in Rome knew of the kind of horrors that went on at Pensione Jaccarino, thanks to the Allied radio from Bari which also gave lists of names of double agents and traitors. All the same, denunciations were common, and an American escaper, Lieutenant Dukate, was betrayed to Koch by a jealous girlfriend.

It was a sorry time for the escape organization. A little submarine officer, Lieutenant 'Goldilocks' Elliott, an invaluable helper for Derry and living in the Vatican gendarmerie barracks, had walked in his sleep apparently during a nightmare and fallen from a window. Five of Derry's Italian associates had been executed at the Ardeatine Caves and twenty more were arrested soon afterwards. Outside Rome eight recaptured

British prisoners were shot. A letter dated 15 April had reached Derry for forwarding after the liberation of Rome.

'Dear Mother and Father and Family,
This is the last letter I will be able to write as I get shot tomorrow. Dear family, I have laid down my life for my country and everything that was dear to me. I hope this war will soon be over, so that you will all have peace for ever.
                    Your ever loving soldier-son and brother, Willie'

To this was attached a further note:

'Just a few words to tell you that your son Willie was shot because he was caught and arrested in civilian clothes. I assure you that he received the comfort of our religion, and died in peace.
        The Reverend Father Il Cappellano, P. Antonio Intreccialagli'

The number of ex-prisoners picked up in Rome because of denunciations was becoming ever more alarming. Other men, bored with being cooped up in flats, broke out and went into bars and got drunk, and were thus too easily caught. As a result, and because of the high cost of feeding them on the black market, Derry decided that no more escapers could be allowed into Rome. Then there were other escape organizations with which he was indirectly involved – Yugoslav, French, Arab, Greek (known as 'Liberty or Death') and Russian. Recently two Americans had also been admitted to the Vatican gendarmerie barracks.

There were about four hundred Russian ex-prisoners in and around Rome. Tardini, the Cardinal Secretary of State, took a special interest in them. D'Arcy Osborne's butler, John May, was in charge of the Arab escapers. It was a splendid piece of luck for Derry when May suddenly produced a friend who was a spy at the Questura, or police headquarters. This spy, known as Giuseppe, produced all sorts of useful tip-offs about impending raids. Then came a really choice item: Pizzirani, the Fascist bigwig whom Carla Capponi and other Gapists had tried so often to assassinate, was willing to annul all denouncements of escapers for a fee of fifty thousand *lire*. A middle man, however, was involved, and he would want another ten thousand *lire* ... Derry decided that bribes like these were a legitimate expenditure of British funds.

The OSS man, Peter Tompkins, consoled as he was by sundry pretty girls and a fortunate supply of gin and cognac, was also in danger, since both German and Italian police had his description. In addition he found himself plunged in denigrating rivalries with the agent 'Coniglio', who operated in the North and considered himself Tompkins' superior. For a while Tompkins passed information to British MI6 agents (taking a whole month to be relayed back to the OSS base). Finally, with so many helpers having been shot in the Ardeatine Caves, Tompkins decided that he must now get back to the South, either by land through the Apennines or by sea. Once more he disguised himself as a Fascist policeman and reached L'Aquila. The way overland turned out to be impossible, so off this high-spirited American went to Ancona in the hope of buying a boat or secretly contacting some Allied craft which might spirit him away into the far Adriatic and so home. He was still in Ancona when news came of the Allied offensive in May.

If, in Rome, clandestine radio communication with the Allies was now only intermittent, some half dozen well established OSS stations were operating in the North, thanks in part – it must be admitted – to Tompkins' hated Coniglio. Details of help to northern partisans, at this particular period, and of Allied sabotage teams and missions behind the lines tend to be misty and vague, mostly unrecorded, though early in 1944 the British No 1 Special Force had six missions working in enemy territory. The partisan bands on the whole were local, without overall leadership. Nevertheless, rubber dinghies would appear at fixed appointments on beaches in the dark nights, and an agent would be parachuted by some prearranged plan in a remote forest clearing. With the fine weather it was possible to live rough; patriotism was alive, glowing, heroic – and at times relentless. By May it was reckoned that partisans in the North had trebled since February. In the Florence area there was a particularly courageous woman, 'Vera', who organized sixty-five OSS supply operations by parachute.

Yet from the German armed forces' point of view partisan warfare only developed into a real menace in the second half of 1944. Down at Monopoli battle schools and courses in subversion and sabotage were being run by No 1 Special Force under Commander Gerry Holdsworth, 'half hero and half filibuster'. For the time being Corsica was the chief launching place for raids and landings by sea. In late March, for instance, there had been an amphibious OSS raid near Spezia in connection with Operation Strangle; it was successful but the whole team was caught and shot.

Operations were becoming more difficult with the establishment of German radar installations on the coast, and with fast patrols by corvettes and E boats. However on 27 April an OSS agent and two radio operators were successfully landed on the Adriatic coast by the British. The agent had a forged pass 'signed' by a high officer of the German Todt Organization. This he presented to the German commander at Ascoli, who at once gave him and the radio operators a staff car to drive to Rome.

In April and May the bands in the vicinity of Rome were still mostly run by the Gaps. The war had driven them back somewhat from the

Alban Hills, but they were intensely active near Lake Bracciano and
Monte Soratte and in the Sabine Hills, one of the best organized being the
Banda Stalin. A young Italian-born nephew of Mrs Whitaker, who was
in Viterbo gaol on a charge of spying, escaped during an Allied
bombardment and – though far from being left-wing – joined the Banda
Antonio Gramsci in southern Umbria. But these partisan bands also
attracted criminals and were an excuse for banditry and personal
vendettas. Then there was the shocking incident of the 'massacre of
Leonessa' near Rieti on Good Friday, when a woman called Rosa
Cesaretti, mistress of a German lieutenant, led a German patrol which
rounded up some fifty people including her relatives, who were all shot.

As usual the parachute drops were linked to the mysterious code
messages read out after news bulletins on Radio London (such as
Multedo's *Letizia è bella*). Bonfires would be lit to guide the planes. Radio
London announcers, who knew nothing of the meaning of these
messages, admitted to being in cold sweats in case they got a word wrong,
which might result in lives being lost.

Some Germans were also deserting to the partisans. Operation
Sauerkraut was an OSS 'black' propaganda scheme. Carefully screened
German POWs were infiltrated in uniform behind the lines; their job was
to circulate a forged announcement by Kesselring to the effect that he was
resigning his command knowing that the 'war is lost to Germany' and
that only senseless slaughter could ensue. Operation Cornflakes consisted
of dropping fake German mailbags filled with subversive letters to real
addresses with copies of an apparently underground newspaper *Das Neue
Deutschland*. Both had a fair success.

Radio Bari was operated by the Allied organization known as PWB,
Psychological Warfare Bureau. It concentrated on giving impartial news
and opinions on Italian subjects and was greatly respected for its honesty.
For instance it had recorded the speeches of the various parties at the Bari
Congress. It also had a programme especially for partisans, *Italia Combatte*.
And for a short while the Germans had their answer to *Italia Combatte*
with their Radio Baita, purporting to be run by a partisan called Barba di
Ferro, Beard of Iron, in the North.

There were plenty of stories circulating in Rome about atrocities
committed by German soldiers near the front line, such as massacres of
whole families and the exposure of mutilated dead bodies. Some of these
were hard to substantiate, a product of what Kesselring called 'the
exaggerations and fancies so characteristic of the Italian people', but sharp
directives had been issued by him about looting. 'I am not prepared to
tolerate such indiscipline,' he had said on 13 March, 'which brings the
good name of German forces into disrepute.' The penalty would be
court-martial. And somewhat later he announced: 'German soldiers have

behaved like bandits with Italian peasants, demanding goods with pistols. These men have lost the right to call themselves German soldiers. I demand strongest action. Every man must know this.' Much later he even decreed that looters could be shot on the spot, but this was counter-manded by Goering and Keitel at the OKW.

On 8 April it was acknowledged that Italian 'terrorist activities' were on the increase, and Kesselring had to lay down rules to safeguard troops. When marching through large towns, for instance, men should be in open formation, with weapons at the ready. 'If an attack takes place, weapons must be used without consideration of passers by. Fire must be opened at once ... Quick action is the first necessity.'

To Kesselring guerrilla warfare was 'horrible and treacherous', in disregard of Article 1 of the Hague Convention. 'The previous com-radeship in arms [with Italy] had turned to brutal warfare,' he was to say. By June 'brigades' had been formed by partisans in the more sophisticated areas, and it became, as he said, a matter of 'unrestricted guerrilla warfare'. There were also some villages, and indeed zones, where the entire population – men, women and children – would be somehow implicated. Partisans, therefore, had to be judged by the German authorities from military standards and 'not on an emotional basis'. What was more, partisan warfare gave individuality the chance to run wild, and 'the southern temperament did the rest'. The 'scale of crimes' against German soldiers included 'shooting from ambush, hanging, drowning, freezing to death, crucifying and all kinds of tortures'. The Germans were thus forced to suspect any civilian of either sex of being a fanatical assassin and could expect to be shot at from every house.

And in this way, said Kesselring, 'one could predict with almost mathematical precision the gradual brutalization of the conduct of war which, steadily increasing, inevitably had to lead to the most dreadful crimes on either side ... One has to admit that illegal and detestable deeds were also committed by the Germans.' Soldiers were liable to see red. It was a vicious circle. Kesselring was to be tried after the war and condemned not only because of the Ardeatine Caves but because perhaps over a thousand Italian civilians, including women and children, were killed as a result of his two orders dated 17 June and 1 July. The second order, read out at the trial, included these words: 'Where there are considerable numbers of partisan groups, a proportion of the male population of the area will be arrested and in the event of acts of violence being committed, these men will be shot. The population must be informed of this. Should troops, etc., be fired at from any village, the village will be burnt down. Perpetrators or ringleaders will be hanged in public ...' The defence at the trial, however, put great reliance on the context of the times and on words in the same order: 'All countermeasures must be hard but just. The dignity of the German soldier demands it.'

Alexander was also quoted at the trial of Kesselring as saying that as far as he was concerned he thought the warfare in Italy had been carried out fairly and cleanly, though of course it was pointed out that he was only referring to the German conduct towards regular Allied forces.

The reprisals that followed the Via Rasella incident did not deter the Gapists from further *azioni*. One independent band, non-political, was led by a figure worthy of Pasolini's books, Giuseppe Albani, alias Il Gobbo, The Hunchback, aged seventeen. He was immensely brave and ferocious (and much later to die in an encounter with Carabinieri), but did not scruple to rob houses on Monte Mario or to sell stolen bread on the black market. On 10 April the Gobbo's men killed three German soldiers at Cinecittà. This was the signal to put into effect a modified form of Himmler's and Wolff's original plan for whole-scale deportation. The working-class area of Quadraro had long been regarded by the *Nazifascisti* as a 'nest of wasps', so much so that the curfew there was at 4 p.m. Now it was surrounded by police and parachutists, and the houses were systematically searched. At least eight hundred men were caught and sent up for 'productive work' in Germany. It was the largest *rastrellamento* experienced in Rome.

On 16 April a mass was held at Santa Maria Maggiore in memory of three professors presumed executed at the Ardeatine Caves: Pilo Albertelli, Salvatore Canalis and Gioacchino Gesmundo. The interior of Santa Maria Maggiore, like the colonnades at St Peter's, was packed with refugees (and in a highly insanitary condition). After the mass, students distributed leaflets, and the people became excited, shouting '*Viva l'Italia libera!*' and '*Fuori i tedeschi*'. A Fascist corporal tried to arrest two students and gave chase; in a narrow street they turned and shot him dead.

The Nazis posted more warnings. Nevertheless, once more there was an attempt, though again unsuccessful, on the Gapists' favourite target, the Fascist Pizzirani. Two of the partisans involved in this were Franco Calamandrei, who had given the signal for the bomb to be set off at Via Rasella, and Fernando Vitagliano. It was Vitagliano who, in a group of four including Marisa Musu, set out to kill Mussolini's son, Vittorio.

The reason for killing the fairly innocuous Vittorio Mussolini was, ultimately, so that the head of police, Caruso, could be 'eliminated'. For a long time the Gapists had been studying ways of assassinating Caruso, but he was too carefully protected. Now, if Vittorio Mussolini were to die, then Caruso would have to attend the funeral, and that would be an ideal chance to shoot him down, probably from a flower stall.

Young Mussolini habitually left his house at 7 a.m. to fetch his car from the garage. That would be the moment to get him. After the first shot had been fired by the hit man, Vitagliano and Marisa Musu would rush up to finish him off if necessary, while the fourth partisan would be ready with covering fire. However it happened that on the day before there had been a burglary in the house next door to Mussolini's, and unknown to the Gapists some plain-clothes police were in the vicinity.

So the four went straight into a trap. Only Vitagliano escaped, and Marisa was caught after a roof-top battle. The police were convinced that she and the others were common criminals, and battered them with questions such as 'Where is the Gobbo?' and 'What have you done with Colombo's money?', referring to some robbery. In actual fact this was the first time any Gapists had been captured. Marisa was sent to the Mantellate, the women's prison.

Vitagliano had two special friends in his Gap, Raoul Falcioni and Guglielmo Blasi, the author of so many brilliant *azioni*. He was invited by Blasi to join in a raid on a wine shop, but when he realized that it was simply to steal wine from an old man he was horrified and knew that Blasi was little better than the Gobbo. A little while later Blasi was picked up by the police on another thieving exploit.

The arrest of Blasi was of major significance to the Gaps, for at the police station his nerve suddenly broke and he asked to see Caruso. He then confessed to Caruso that he had been involved in the Via Rasella affair and could supply names and descriptions of everyone else who had taken part in it. As proof he said that he would lead the police on the next day to a house near the Colosseum where he was to meet three of them: Salinari, Calamandrei and Falcioni.

Blasi had joined the Gaps in the euphoric period following the Anzio landings. His credentials had not been properly checked, therefore, and it had not been known that he had a criminal background. Since then he had done so many brave things, including the shooting of the murderer of the pregnant *popolana* Teresa Gullace in March, and he had behaved like a great patriot.

Salinari, Calamandrei and Falcioni were arrested and removed to Koch's Pensione Jaccarino. For the time being Falcioni had no idea that he had been betrayed by his friend.

The Pensione Jaccarino, recently taken over by Koch, still retained some of its comfortable furnishings, and Koch and his colleagues were able to enjoy its good supply of wine and – best of all – that rarity coffee. They retained the kitchen staff but had to get new cleaners, since the old ones didn't like the mess in the torture rooms. Koch slept in the Pensione's honeymoon suite. The chief punishment rooms were variously known as the *Buco* or hole (a tiny room with no window where prisoners would collapse from lack of air), the *Carbonaia* or coal-room, and the *Soffitta* or attic, which was also without light and stinking of excrement. When Luchino Visconti had looked into the main torture room, No 15, he had seen two men tied together and hanging by their arms from the ceiling.

Calamandrei managed to escape from the Pensione almost at once. He had had a spell in the *Buco* and, feeling ill, had asked to go to the WC. Since he was exceptionally tall and thin, he was able to climb through the small window and thus warn some other Gapists of the danger. But he was not able to contact everyone, and there were some more arrests, for which Blasi received money from the police. Marisa Musu of course had 'disappeared'; nevertheless Blasi went to her parents and asked for money so as not to give away her name.

When, for the second time, Blasi saw Falcioni coming out of Room 15, bleeding and bruised, he was ashamed, for he knew Falcioni's family well and realized the trouble his wife and children would now be in. So he made a surprising offer: Falcioni could become a chauffeur for the Pensione. Falcioni was able to discuss this with Salinari, who had been badly tortured, and they decided he should accept, as in this way he would be able to play a double game and tip off those Gapists still in danger of being traced.

Here there are slightly conflicting versions to the story. According to Vitagliano, he ran into Falcioni, who told him of this new job. Together they concocted a plan to kill all the Banda Koch, including Koch and Blasi. Each night Falcioni had to drive up to the Pensione in his van and give a special toot on his horn, when Koch and the rest would come out one by one and get into the back. Thus the idea was to shoot each member of the gang as he climbed in, using a revolver fitted with a silencer. All details were exactly planned, even to the extent of having towels to mop up the blood.

On the night before the *coup* Vitagliano slept in Falcioni's basement flat, to have a good rest. He was uneasy when Falcioni came in and casually said that he had confided in another member of the Koch gang. 'I went to sleep, but woke when two taxis arrived, giving that special toot. Falcioni went out, telling me to escape if he didn't come back. But how could I do that? The windows were barred and there was no back entrance. I waited, then two men pushed open the door. The *signora* screamed and switched on the light. My room was still in darkness, but one man had a torch, which blinded me. He fired an automatic, wounding me in the neck and arm. I only had five rounds in my gun, but I fired four of them. I realized that I had hit somebody as I heard him crying out in the bathroom. Then the other man went into the bathroom and threw a grenade. The *signora* went on screaming. Somehow I managed to get to the door, expecting to be shot down – but a third man had gone upstairs, to telephone for help apparently, and one of the taxis had taken Falcioni away. I must have run a kilometre and a half. I was bleeding and only wearing my underpants. I tried to get into a flat, but the owners stopped me because they were hiding a Jew. Then an old woman let me into hers. She embraced me but could only give me a pair of trousers. I hid in the roof all night, and the next day went to a church where the sacristan let me ring up my brother Ugo, who brought me shoes and a coat.'

Marisa Musu, being in a non-political prison, used to receive presents of food from her family. One day there was an alarming, though somewhat damp and barely readable, message in a Thermos flask, to the effect that her real identity was about to be betrayed. The only way to get out of the Matellate was the usual one of faking an illness. So Marisa ate a large quantity of hard-boiled eggs and made herself badly constipated. This at least was a start. On reaching a hospital, she found a friendly doctor who at once pretended she was a rare case which would eventually need an operation. He used to stand at her bed and lecture about her to students.

By this time the police wanted her for interrogation, but the doctor insisted that she was not fit to be moved. A policeman kept guard by her bed. After a while Marisa made friends with the policeman and persuaded him that they should both escape together. After all, the Americans would soon be in Rome, and he would surely be promoted to sergeant for his good deed ...

In the Santo Spirito hospital lay the Actionist Tom Carini, ill for more genuine reasons and still suffering from being tortured by Koch. Two armed guards took turns by his bedside, and it had been made clear that if he so much as got a foot outside that would be his end. Meanwhile his mother had been working on the sympathies of the nuns who ran the hospital, instilling them with maternal feelings for this poor handsome boy. The Mother Superior decided to plan his escape. It was realized that around 2 a.m. a guard was liable to nod off. One night at that time therefore Tom was awoken by someone tickling his feet. It was the Mother Superior, and he saw that the guard was asleep. 'Fila, fila via, off you go, quick.' Still in his bare feet he followed her down the corridor to the nuns' dormitory, and for the rest of the night he was kept there behind a screen, the nuns bringing him chocolate, milk and cognac. In the morning he was dressed as a *monsignore* and during all the hue and cry he sat with the Mother Superior telling his rosary. It was the indefatigable O'Flaherty who got him into the Vatican, and when Tom was safely there O'Flaherty took pleasure in ringing up the Gestapo and telling them this dangerous partisan was now safely in hiding – without apparently compromising the nuns.

Favourite spots for women partisans to hide were maternity hospitals. It was easy to leap into beds, in case of danger, and stuff pillows under the sheets. Dr Giuseppe Pitigliani was a Jewish obstetrician of high repute.

Even after the round-up of Jews in October he continued his rounds, visiting (genuine) maternity cases and not even carrying false identity documents. The Italian police turned a blind eye – and Pitigliani was only too easily recognizable, since he always wore a blue overcoat that had once belonged to an Air Force officer. Occasionally there were police visits to his hospital at Testaccio, and then it was considered prudent for him to slip out of a back window. But throughout the whole period of the German occupation of Rome he was never betrayed.

Sometimes fake illnesses would be arranged by the French Capuchin monk, Padre Benedetto, who ran the Rome branch of Delasem, the organization for helping foreign Jews. It took a surprisingly long time for *Nazifascisti* to become aware of his activities, even though he operated only a few hundred yards from Pensione Jaccarino. He had once even travelled to Milan by car to investigate the possibilities of smuggling Jews into Switzerland. The expenses of supplying food, medicines, false identity and ration cards and clothing grew enormously. The Padre was able to obtain some funds through loans against money deposited in New York and London, usually through Tittmann and his contact Monsignor Hérissé. Or else funds were obtained from Osborne, the Red Cross and occasionally Spanish and other legations at the Vatican. By May two non-Jewish French spies were discovered to be making denunciations about Delasem to the Gestapo, and there were arrests. It was also learnt that a warrant for Padre Benedetto's arrest lay on Kappler's desk. One night the Gestapo entered the house where he was hiding and he escaped over a wall. He took refuge in a convent, shaved off his beard and disguised himself as a nun.

With the arrest of two important Gapists, Silvio Serra and Franco Ferri, the remainder went into hiding for a while. Blasi's efforts had blown the organization to bits. The choice now lay between remaining in hiding in Rome or going out into the country to fight with partisans near the front lines.

Carla Capponi and Rosario Bentivegna decided to make for Palestrina, which had become a main centre for those partisans who had operated in the Alban Hills. In recent centuries the inhabitants of Palestrina – the Praeneste of Virgil and Horace, famous too in the struggles between Guelphs and Ghibellines – had had a reputation for violence and cruelty, and the Germans were finding that their descendants were only too willing to offer help to the partisans. Carla and Rosario arrived after a ten hours' walk, having pushed a single bicycle loaded with revolvers and grenades. Dead tired, they had immediately to attend a meeting with local partisans in a pigstye, full of flies and lit by one candle. It was a hallucinatory experience, with all those half-seen faces around. Some

Russians were there too, unable to speak Italian and communicating only by gesture.

The Germans had ordered the *Comune* to make a list of all males over sixteen. It was decided there and then to enter the *Comune* building and burn all the papers. Some typewriters were also removed.

The town of Palestrina was almost deserted because of carpet bombing, so the next day Carla, Rosario and some partisans went down to the main Cassino–Rome road near Valmontone. Here among the olive groves and vineyards the Russians had been very active and had killed several Germans. Now Carla could see some of those Russians' features – they were mostly terribly ugly, but *simpatici*, and each one had an Italian girlfriend. The partisans – usually just armed peasants and farmers – were indeed an undisciplined lot; altogether there were some hundred and forty in the band.

Because of the Allied air attacks Germans coming on leave from Cassino were too scared to go by lorry and preferred to make the journey on foot, which made them much easier to capture. As they stole food from farmhouses on the way, they were by no means popular with local people. In no time the partisans had bagged forty-seven of them, plus rifles, machine-guns and grenades. All the Germans were put in a cave, conveniently near the partisans' headquarters, which was a straw hut inside a sheepfold. Next the partisans managed to capture a German Red Cross unit, complete with doctor, nurses and medicaments – a great help because one of the Russians was wounded and had gangrene.

The Russian partisans couldn't understand why Carla wanted to ration the medical material. All at once they lost their tempers and began firing in the air. The partisans thereupon all ran away, and the Russians left too, leaving only Carla and Rosario.

After the third day there was no food left for the Germans, nor could they be let out of the cave to relieve themselves. The sun was very hot and Rosario suddenly collapsed. Carla was, therefore, on her own, and she could see the Germans crowding up to the entrance of the cave. Snatching up her machine-gun she sprayed the ground in front and told them not to move. Then she ordered the doctor out and made him revive Rosario.

What to do now though? Night was approaching. Carla and Rosario certainly didn't want to kill all these people. They thought of just slipping quietly away and taking the weapons, when suddenly the Russians arrived, all forgiveness and smiles, bringing food and water and wanting to shake hands. Then the partisans reappeared, so Carla and Rosario were able to go back to Palestrina and leave the Germans to their friends' ministrations.

On another occasion Carla and Rosario were asked to help in driving out some German soldiers from a peasant's house, where the men had killed the only pig and were helping themselves to his wine. Carla shot one of the Germans point-blank and was nearly shot herself. This led to a big dawn raid by the Gestapo the next day, and the Nazis raided other houses nearby where they discovered arms. In one house Carla was appalled to come across the bodies of three brothers and two sisters, summarily shot in front of their mother who had been tied up and was now raving mad.

In the city itself the CLN, still shaken by the *svolta del Sud* and by the consequences of Blasi's betrayal of leading Communists, nevertheless managed to distribute leaflets calling for a general strike on 1 May in protest against the bread crisis and the deportations. There had been strikes in northern and central Italy in March, and those had actually resulted in an increase in the bread ration. For the Romans everything seemed to depend on Allied recognition of the open city status. If this came to pass, then the Germans might really pull out.

As usual the walls were scrawled with slogans and exhortations to strike. The Fascist police cleverly put an abrupt end to this by making porters of houses responsible for subversive writings on their walls, on pain of arrest. And indeed the strike had to be postponed until 3 May. Even then it was mostly a fiasco. The tram-drivers were bribed to stay at work with a fifty per cent pay increase. However, a hundred workers did not turn up at the *Messaggero* newspaper offices that morning, and this did cause a sensation since the *Messaggero* was considered the official organ of the republican government at Salò. As a result eighteen printers were arrested.

On 3 May there was also another big *assalto al forno*, attack on a bakery, and a mother of six children, Caterina Martinelli, was shot dead by a '*Paino*', a policeman of the PAI, *Polizia Africana Italiana*.

Then on 5 May the CLN at last made up its mind to recognize Badoglio's government, which was now situated in Salerno. The parties of the left reaffirmed their republicanism, and the Socialists pledged their readiness to take part in the national insurrection. The Party of Action gave only muted support; 'without assuming political responsibility', it would give every contribution to the war effort and the rapid expulsion of Nazism and Fascism from Italian soil. As a result Bonomi once more agreed to take over the presidency of the CLN in Rome, after forty days in the cold. It was realized by all parties that it was of vital importance that the Allies on entering Rome should find a CLN that was in capable working order.

At Salerno Badoglio was aiming for another major step forward: full Allied status. A sly dig had been passed on to Washington. Were the United States preparing to abandon Italy after the war to Britain and the

Soviet Union? But when Noel Charles told Badoglio that the British and
Americans had received a shock when he had made a separate agreement
with Russia, arousing the suspicion that he was playing one government
against the other, he protested his sincerity in wishing to co-operate with
both Britain and the United States and said that he believed that Italy's
future lay with the Western countries and not with Russia. Churchill, on
hearing this, was kind: 'Was it not natural, when so many people were
trying to boot out Badoglio, and many more were ready to let him go,
that he should have "clutched a helping hand"? One may be vexed at the
Russians for their lack of etiquette, as I often am in many connections; but
to beat up the wretched Badoglio for grasping at the only chance which
would have enabled him to remain in his difficult position much to our
advantage, is, I think, rather hard ... The best medicine for this tangled
situation is a decided victory on the Italian front and I am quite content to
wait until one is gained.'

But there was no question of either the United States or Britain
agreeing to Allied status, and Cordell Hull at once made this clear. For one
thing there would be huge objections from the Greeks, Yugoslavs and
Free French. For another it would entail having to hand over the liberated
territory to Italian administration, and this would be impossible since it
was being used either for military bases or as an operational theatre. Most
important, Allied status would mean that Italy would automatically
become a signatory to the final peace treaty.

The Foreign Office also informed Osborne that the Allied govern-
ments had finally decided against declaring Rome an open city, 'on
military grounds'. If the Germans wished to declare Rome an open city
and keep to their word, then the Romans had nothing to fear from Allied
bombers. But Osborne had to point out that the Vatican food convoys
were still being attacked; on 29 April a convoy of fifty-two vehicles had
been machine-gunned, with a lot of damage. Quoting the Cardinal
Secretary of State he telegraphed back: 'Famine, with all its terrible
unknown consequences, is now hanging over the city of Rome.' The
population, swollen by refugees, was now 'destitute of all resources'. The
only way to supply Rome was by lorry. 'It cannot be believed that the
Allies wish to deprive the population of this ultimate means of sub-
sistence.' Osborne also feared that mobs might be induced to attack the
diplomatic corps in the Vatican and even the Pope.

A detailed plan for supplying Rome by ship was transmitted by
Osborne: two ships were waiting at Marseilles, two at Genoa. The Allied
Chiefs of Staff were still against this proposal, considering that it would
impose unduly severe restrictions on military operations. In any case, it
was pointed out, the Germans had the real responsibility for feeding the
civilian population. Any concession by the Allies would relieve the

Germans of the strain on their communications. 'We are in effect,' Eden said to Churchill, 'blockading Rome.'

'Rome,' Eden added, 'is not merely an enemy city; apart from being the Catholic capital of the world, it is the capital of a co-belligerent state which we hope to occupy ourselves in the near future. Again, is it really in our own interest to risk reducing the population of Rome to starvation with all resulting political and social consequences from which we shall be the chief sufferers when we occupy the city?'

To which Churchill replied: '*Foreign Secretary*. It is with pain that I write these words. Rome must starve till freed.'

For Operation Diadem was near. On 11 May Churchill sent this cable to Alexander: 'All our thoughts and hopes are with you in what I trust and believe will be a decisive battle, fought to the finish, and having as its object the destruction and ruin of the armed force of the enemy south of Rome.'

Cassino – Anzio

Alexander to Prime Minister, 12 May: 'Offensive launched according to plan and up to time. Weather good but heavy ground mist caused some confusion and loss of direction to XIII Corps ... German artillery and mortar fire have worried Poles but I do not think they have had the heavy losses they had first reported. They are continuing their attacks by moonlight with strong artillery support ... On the whole the battle has gone fairly well considering the stubbornness of the opposition. This is the Poles' first battle ... There is no doubt that the Germans intend to fight for every yard and that the next few days will see some extremely bitter and severe fighting.'

Alexander to Prime Minister, 13 May: 'Poles lost all previous gains and now back where they started. They were very depressed but are in better spirits today and are reorganizing for further effort. They have a thousand wounded back through casualty clearing stations ... Our losses have not been unreasonably heavy. At rough estimate, a thousand prisoners taken but may be more.'

Operation Diadem was in many ways a classic battle. If it was Alexander's greatest triumph, it was also a triumph for individual generals under his command, including Sir John Harding, his chief of staff. It was a masterpiece of deception and surprise, a victory for Allied intelligence.

On another level, as the drive northwards developed, Diadem was an example of how conflicting temperaments in high places can change the course of battle just as much as blood, guts and high explosive. The breaking of the Gustav Line and subsequently the next line of German defence, the Hitler Line, symbolized then and symbolizes now for many nations the ultimate in courage and endurance. Perhaps above all it will be remembered in history as a tragedy: a victory through tragedy – the tragedy of the Polish Corps.

The Germans had once again, as at Anzio on 22 January, been caught totally off balance. They had assumed that the Allied assault could not take place before 24 May, and were also expecting landings at Civitavecchia or Leghorn, which had meant having to retain valuable forces in the North. On the very afternoon of 11 May Vietinghoff had left for Germany to receive a decoration from Hitler. Senger, Westphal, Baade and other important officers were on leave. 'I look back on those days in horror,' Kesselring was to say later.

The move from the Adriatic sector of the greater part of the Eighth Army under General Leese had been achieved over the past two months with elaborate secrecy, as had the reorganization of the various divisions. The Germans had little idea of the strength of the French Expeditionary Corps. The extent to which Kesselring and his staff had been fooled was clear to the Allies thanks to the code-breaking system 'Ultra'. The Allies also knew that the German units were in many cases not yet up to strength, with a shortage of junior officers and non-commissioned officers especially, due to the growing manpower shortage in Germany. It was also clear that German forces were being held back in the North to deal with partisans.

It was essential to Allied strategy that the battle around Cassino should be won before the landings in Normandy took place, scheduled now for 6 June. In simple terms the first phase of Operation Diadem would be a four-speared attack: along the coast by the American II Corps; into the Aurunci mountains south of the Liri valley by the French Expeditionary Corps; across the River Rapido by the British XIII Corps (which included the 8th Indian Division and an Italian Motorized Group); and against the Monastery from the north by the Polish Corps. The second phase would be a follow-up in the British Sector by I Canadian Corps and the 78th British ('Battle-Axe') Division. The Americans would drive on to the important coastal towns of Formia, Gaeta and Terracina, on the way to the Anzio Beachhead, whose forces would break out at the appropriate moment. As far as Alexander was concerned, the major role in these first stages was assigned to the Eighth Army (British, Indians, Poles, Canadians, Italians and South Africans), whilst the duties of the Fifth Army (Americans and French) were only sketched out in vague terms to give it flexibility. Clark and Juin however had always been sceptical about yet another frontal attack against the main Gustav Line defences, let alone the Monastery death-trap. They saw the Aurunci mountains, with their three-thousand-foot peak, Monte Maio, as the way to catch the Germans at their weakest. The British however could not visualize that it would be possible to cross such rugged and trackless country within the time limit, and for this reason Alexander insisted that the main air support should be in the Eighth Army sector.

In Alexander's orders there was still nothing specific about that burning question: who would be the first into Rome? It was difficult, however, not to imagine that this was going to be the Americans' trophy, and certainly Clark understood that Alexander intended it. Nevertheless, the true objective of Diadem had been stated in clear terms: the destruction of the enemy south of Rome. Alexander had furthermore, also quite clearly, ordered that Truscott's VI Corps in the Beachhead would when the time came 'launch an attack on the general axis Cori–Valmontone to cut Route 6 [Via Casilina] in the Valmontone area, and thereby prevent the supply and withdrawal of the German Tenth Army'. Subsequently the Fifth Army was expected to 'pursue the enemy north of Rome and capture the Viterbo airfields ... and thereafter advance on Leghorn'. The Eighth Army was to pursue the enemy in the direction of Terni and Perugia, and advance on Ancona and Florence.

The French Expeditionary Corps now consisted of four divisions, two Moroccan, one Algerian and one French. The North Africans looked forward to the attack as a further test and proof of their fighting ability, already famous. For Frenchmen it was a first step towards the liberation of *la Patrie*. General Juin's uplifting order of the day spoke of a struggle which must be implacable and relentless. '*La France martyre vous attend et vous regarde. En avant!*'

The Polish Corps had two infantry divisions and one armoured brigade; for these Poles their role had an even greater significance. As Harold Macmillan has said: 'Recruited largely from eastern Poland, they had been imprisoned in Russian internment camps in 1939 after the Molotov–Ribbentrop Pact and the defeat of Poland by Germany. When Germany attacked Russia they were at last set free and after incredible adventures they marched (like the Greeks in Xenophon's *Anabasis*) until they finally reached Palestine. Now they had re-entered Europe in Italy.' Many of those Poles had lost their entire families. Some were Jews. If the Germans now had eighteen-year-olds in the line, there were Poles in the infantry platoons who were over fifty. Their General Anders himself had been in Lubianka prison. 'Soldiers!' his order of the day ran. 'The time for battle has arrived. We have long awaited this moment for revenge and retribution ... The task assigned to us will cover with glory the name of the Polish soldier all over the world ... Trusting in the Justice of Divine Providence we go forward with the sacred slogan in our hearts: God, Honour, Country.'

The Poles had moved into their assembly areas about three weeks before, having taken over from the Irish Brigade. The language problem was no help as they loaded up at San Michele, especially as the muleteers were Italian and the mules themselves had been accustomed to working with Indians. 'Cor,' a London Irish sergeant, sent to meet the advance party, remembers, 'you might have thought they were taking up bloody elephants instead of mules. The Poles had even brought tents. I couldn't get them to understand that there weren't even slit trenches up there, only sangars — parapets of stone, you know.'

At last the mule train moved off along the Mad Mile. 'There was a fucking great notice up, "Shell Trap — No Halting". Those Polaks understood the meaning of that all right. It was murder along there.'

The journey was seven miles, the track being marked by phosphorescent arrows. The scent from the red clover fields was almost like an anaesthetic, it was so strong, but soon this was replaced by another smell, fusty, persistent and nauseous, the reek of the unburied corpses of mules. Then came the climb, ever steeper, and the slithering and stumbling among boulders. A six-barrelled Nebelwerfer would panic the mules, which would snort and rear. The men staggered on, sweat streaming, lungs almost bursting, as all around mortar shells hissed and whistled. A few scraggy pines. Dwarf bushes. A schmeisser like a dog yapping. The red glow of flares. Then at last they came upon the Irish: coated figures, fully laden, delighted to leave. There were some quick whispered instructions, which only helped to confuse, about the direction of the enemy and the sangars, and they were off. The Poles found these sangars to be mostly three feet high, with a blanket or groundsheet for cover. As a chronicler of the 3rd Carpathian Division wrote: 'We felt heavy at heart. There were two soldiers to every sangar, which scarcely had room for one and smelled of dankness and rot. Rats were scurrying about in search of food.' That first night was spent on the alert, staring into the darkness at the unknown, listening to the spandaus, and to the confusion of howlings, thumps and buzzings. In the morning they heard a cuckoo.

The 3rd Carpathians were eventually to have the task of capturing the Monastery ruins, but first they would have to take Point 593 (Calvary Hill) of such evil repute, and Albaneta Farm, another graveyard of the past. The 5th Kresowas had been allocated the outer sector, and would have to assault Phantom Ridge and Sant'Angelo. All these features having been secured, then the attack on the Monastery could be launched. For Anders favoured the tactics of encirclement, as promoted by Tuker and Juin two months before and discarded.

It was known that the 1st German Parachute Division still held the Monastery, and that it was their particular pride to be there. Great pains had been taken to conceal from them that Poles were now their opponents, including elaborate camouflage and strict wireless silence.

11 May had been a day of heat. Just before moonrise, at 2300, six hundred and fifty guns opened up on the British XIII Corps sector below the Monastery. Three-quarters of an hour later the 1st Royal Fusiliers and the Pathans of the 1/12 Frontier Force, with shells whipping overhead,

launched their first assault across the Rapido. All around was the debris of the disastrous crossing made by the Texans in January. They were hampered by a mist which with the smoke and dust soon turned into fog, reducing visibility to two feet. There were trip wires and mines, and hand-to-hand fighting developed. By daylight they at least had a toehold across the river.

On the left flank the 2nd Moroccan Mountain Division had some hours before been creeping up to the assault position. The shells crashed down on the mountain slopes ahead. Juin had hoped to reach Monte Maio within five hours – but this, alas, in spite of advances, was not to be the case.

Clark in his book has a vivid description of the barrage in the American sector: 'The ridges in front of the Fifth Army seemed to stand out monstrously in a great blaze of light, sink into darkness, then tremble under the next salvo.' Enemy batteries were 'smashed into dust'. But the 88th Division, otherwise known as the Oklahoma Wildcats or Blue Devils – consisting of many men as yet untried in battle – made little headway that first day.

So it was up to the 'fire-eaters', the Poles. Within twenty minutes the 3rd Carpathians were on Point 593, and the 5th Kresowas managed to gain the Phantom Ridge crag. But they paid grimly, because of mines and enemy cross-fire from concrete-reinforced positions. It was a familiar story. The Germans, stunned at first by the bombardment and suffering terrible casualties, soon recovered. Four times the Carpathians were beaten back, and Major Veth of the 1st Battalion of the 3rd Paras counted a hundred and thirty Polish dead before Point 593. The smoke was so thick that the Germans had to wear gasmasks. With the fifth attack the Poles were back on the hill again. It was a night of confusion and butchery for both sides, a 'collection of small epics,' Anders said, 'many of which can never be told, for their heroes took to their graves the secrets of their exploits.' By 2.30 a.m. the Kresowas had lost twenty per cent of their men.

Dr Majewski was at the Casualty Clearing Station. 'I was working on my knees. I was smeared all over with blood. Amid the unearthly cries of the wounded and the dying I went through the mechanical motions of uncovering the wounds and bandaging them. As a guess I'd say that over a hundred wounded, perhaps more, passed through my hands before 2 a.m. Some crawled to us on their own, others were helped by friends, others were slung over shoulders like sacks. The helpers, the wounded and the dying were all in a state of excitement. At times I thought I was dreaming. There was no fear to be seen in them, only a kind of fury and rage ... A corporal came and stood among the wounded, panting and breathless. I was bandaging a stomach wound. I turned my eyes from the monstrous gash and glanced at the corporal . . . His eyes were wild, his jaws shaking. In the dim lantern light his face was like a vulture's. He knelt before me without a word and showed me his back. Through his torn tunic I saw a wound the size of two hands, the shoulder-bone bared . . . He wouldn't let me give him an injection. I said: "I can't evacuate you without an injection." The corporal stood up and said: "I'm not being evacuated, I must go back. I'll be killed, but I shan't let you evacuate me until I've thrown all my grenades."'

At 1400 on the 13th Anders was forced to give the order to return to the start-line. It was a bitter decision.

The crucial day of 12 May ground on. The British in the valley were fully exposed to the German batteries on Monte Cassino. Sepoy Kamal Ram, aged nineteen, of the 3/8 Punjab, single-handed had attacked and bayoneted two German machine-gun posts, which he captured; for this he was later awarded the Victoria Cross. The 1st Argyll and Sutherland Highlanders had suffered many casualties in crossing the Rapido, and boats were swept downstream, but a small force managed to hold on to the far bank. During the day Canadians and Indians succeeded in imbedding two Sherman tanks in the river and on these a Bailey bridge was built. Then three other bridges were completed in the same way; and over them clanked and rumbled troops of Canadian tanks, camouflaged with greenery as if bound for Dunsinane.

The incredible Goums suddenly made a spectacular dash into their mountainous sector, which the Germans had thought virtually impassable. It was said that Juin was always to be seen with the most advanced units. These burnoosed men preferred to use their knives rather than rifles, and quickly dealt with their opponents of the 94th Division, many of whom had been badly upset by the acoustic effects of the bombardment in the mountains. As General Montgomery had once said of them in his typically staccato manner: 'Dark men, dark night. Very hard to see coming.'

Ausonia, at the centre of the defile leading into the Liri valley, was captured by the Algerians. Monte Maio was taken on 13 May. The Goums now pushed on through the ravines and scrub towards the north of Spigno, one of the objectives of the US II Corps, and Esperia, on an encampment overlooking the Liri.

The successes of the French Corps greatly encouraged General Keyes, commanding II Corps. Once more Allied warships came into good use, battering the German positions behind the Gustav Line. The little village with the beautiful name of Santa Maria Infante was rubble after so many air attacks. As the US 338th Battalion advanced towards it, the Germans counter-attacked hard, and there were disasters. If many Germans were killed and captured, many Americans died too. The 338th Battalion S.3 reported to the regimental commander over the telephone: 'Two years of training [have] gone up in smoke ... my men ... about half of them – almost all my leaders.' In the confusion an officer thought some fire was coming from American guns. He advanced alone towards it, waving and shouting: 'We're Americans, stop your fire!' He was wrong about the guns, and a burst of fire silenced him for ever. Sixty Italian peasants also helped as couriers in the battle for Santa Maria Infante; twenty-three of them were killed and several wounded. At last, on the 14th the village, or the site of it, was captured. Spigno did not fall until the 15th.

In his diary General Mark Clark makes it clear that he was disappointed by the progress of the Eighth Army, even taking into account that it had a 'tough assignment' against prepared positions. He felt it was 'not pushing as hard as it might', and that the Fifth Army was really carrying the load.

It seems, at any rate, that he excluded the Poles. Major-General 'Pasha' Russell, who now commanded the 4th Indian Division, might have had a word on that subject, as might individual members of the Black Watch and Royal West Kents, whose Captain Wakeford was eventually to be awarded the VC. Another VC also went to Fusilier Jefferson.

On the 15th Leese ordered the Canadian tanks into the attack. Until just before then Kesselring had not realized that the Canadian Corps had been in the Allied reserve. He was furious: 'It is intolerable not to know whom one is fighting for two whole days.' Then on the 16th the Indians captured the mound that had once been the village of Pignataro. In four days the Eighth Army had advanced four miles at the cost of 4,056 casualties. Suddenly there were signs that the Germans were breaking, on both the British XIII Corps and French fronts. At 5.25 p.m. this telephone conversation occurred between Kesselring and Vietinghoff:

K: 'I consider withdrawal to the Senger position [Hitler Line] imperative.' V: 'Then it will be necessary to begin the withdrawal north of the Liri; tanks have broken through there.' K: 'How far?' V: 'To 39 [two miles north-west of Pignataro].' K: 'And how is the situation further north?' V: 'There were about one hundred tanks in Schulz's area [a 1st Para Battle Group].' K: 'Then we shall have to give up Cassino.' V: 'Yes.'

That evening the Poles began their new assault. The Germans, meanwhile, having discovered their opponent's identity, had blared out propaganda about the Russian advance into Poland and the Katyn massacre. The Polish Corps had been regrouped and, as a result of patrolling and capturing prisoners, now felt more confident about the terrain ahead. Their objectives were exactly the same as before. The Carpathians would neutralize Albaneta and Point 593, thus diverting the enemy from the Kresowas attacking Phantom Ridge and Sant'Angelo. In this way the Germans' escape route from the Monastery would be blocked, and the Kresowas would link up with the British 78th Division already making headway along Route 6.

A chronicler of a Carpathian company described the approach: 'It's so quiet; oh Lord — how time crawls ... Though our boots are wrapped in rags every step is a strain on the nerves. Then ... crash ... a man has carelessly knocked against a stone ... everyone lies flat on the ground, listening tensely ... They haven't heard ... we can go on. Slowly ... very slowly ... stooping, the soldiers make slower and slower progress. They look like ghosts ... But ... suddenly one, two, then a third spandau starts spitting out their lethal bullets ... The boom of grenades ... Staszek Wejman is severely wounded by shell splinters in the head ...'

Then the attack went in. Corporal Feliks Redlarski of the 1st Company: '... Gunner Bobon burns with enthusiasm, like a torch. He is the last of a group of fourteen. His arm, leg and forehead are wounded by stone chips ... Lieutenant Baran gathers up the remains of the 1st and 2nd Platoons and renews the assault. He goes right close to the bunkers, he is wounded in the neck, but does not care. The soldiers surge up, hurling grenades at the Germans. Then with one last cry, "Jesus! Mary," Baran collapses on the rocks like a felled tree-trunk.'

The Polish tanks — each with a name, like 'Pirate', 'Claw' and 'Pigmy' — advanced on Albaneta, gurking fire at the burnt-out hulks of Allied tanks, remnants of the attack in March and now being used as machine-gun posts by the enemy. They were halted by mines, big black dishes not even camouflaged. Sappers, therefore, had to crawl underneath the tanks, for protection from snipers, and the tanks then moved forward inch by inch as the mines were defused by the men. In spite of the hellish din, cries and moans could be heard in the bushes; one didn't know whether they were German or Polish. A German mortar barrage wounded all the sappers, who had to be evacuated. 'We were in utter despair,' said a tank commander, 'being unable to reach our comrades dying in front of Albaneta. With real fury we blasted away at the ruins, and at every suspicious bush or pile of stones.' After a couple of hours the ammo ran out, and they had to retreat backwards, 'like proboscidean beetles'. It had to be acknowledged that the Germans were 'absolutely first-rate soldiers, well-drilled and disciplined'. Luckily there had been no enemy air activity whatsoever.

During the night of the 17th the Poles had gained all their main objectives, including Point 593, but not Albaneta.

As the British and Canadians moved forward in the valley, the overwhelming material wealth of the Allies became obvious to the Germans in the mountains above. All the same Kesselring had to give orders personally for pulling out of the Monastery and the town of Cassino, as otherwise his parachutists would have stayed on — 'the drawback,' he was to say, 'of having such strong personalities as subordinate commanders'. Even then some parachutists chose to remain in their forward positions, to fight to the death.

The first Poles to enter the Monastery, early on 18 May, were Lieutenant Casimir Gurbiel and a platoon of thirteen uhlans of the Podolski Lancers. Through the trailing smoke, and across the ravaged landscape, strewn with tree stumps and blackened corpses from battles of long ago, the silhouettes of these men could be seen moving among the ruins. Then the red and white flag of Poland appeared. 'Mouths dropped with emotion,' wrote Sergeant Choma, 'and the sound of the Krakow *Hejnal* floating across against a background of shellfire now distant brought a lump to everyone's throat ... Then these soldiers, hardened by so many grim battles, by the sight of so many deaths, started sobbing like children ...'

The Germans who had remained in the Monastery were mostly the badly wounded. It was said that they looked like wild animals, on the verge of madness. Only their Captain Beyer seemed composed, but he had lost his leg. Asked why his men had held out so fanatically, he said that they had been told that the Poles did not take prisoners. It was found that corpses had been disposed of by pushing them into large drawers for vestments in the cellars. The great vaulted cellars had easily withstood the thousands of tons of bombs, and contained enough tins of food to feed a whole regiment. Books were still on the shelves. Some fine liturgical robes were rescued to be given to the chaplain.

Nearly a thousand Poles had died in the two attacks, and within the next week three thousand had been wounded, and about three hundred and fifty were missing. Years later a majestic cemetery, with two great eagles at the entrance, was to be created in tiers facing the rebuilt Monastery. There is an inscription: 'We Polish soldiers for our freedom and yours have given our souls to God, our bodies to the soil of Italy, and our hearts to Poland.'

Not far away, on a hill in a small valley, 20,047 Germans lie in their cemetery: a stark black place, with a beauty nevertheless, where hypericum grows vigorously around tiers of graves, usually one for six men — 'just as they had to fight for one another, so are they laid to rest'. At the top there is an iron cross like two girders; at the entrance there are statues of a man and woman grieving for their son. Few places convey so forcefully the anguish and waste of war.

The British Commonwealth cemetery for the Cassino dead by contrast gives an impression of greenness, and has a formal garden and a goldfish pool; it is more personal, graves often bearing messages from families. Here 4,266 men are buried. There are other British cemeteries at Minturno and Caserta.

A French cemetery is at Venafro and contains 3,414 graves. An Italian war cemetery, with 975 soldiers' graves, is at Monte Lungo. 7,812 American dead from Cassino, the Beachhead and all Southern Italy are at Nettuno, in a huge cemetery of seventy-seven acres like a park with avenues, oleanders, viburnums, and a chapel. Statues of two youths, shirtless, in bronze, convey themes of comradeship and the essential vulnerability of flesh. 14,500 other bodies were returned to the United States, and on the chapel walls are 3,094 names of those who were never found.

There are two British cemeteries at Anzio, with 3,369 graves, and a German one, with 27,436 graves, nearer Rome at Pomezia.

On 17 May Churchill had cabled Alexander congratulating him on the Armies' advance. He added: 'There is some opinion here that it would have been better for the Anzio punch to have been let off first. But CIGS [Brooke] and I agree with you that it is better to keep the threat of the compressed spring working on the enemy in the present phase ... My own feeling is that seven or eight thousand killed or wounded would cover your losses on the whole front. All blessings upon you and your men.'

To which Alexander replied that the German reserves in the Anzio area were too strong, and that the enemy had expected that the major thrust would be there. He added: 'I have ordered the 36th US Division [in reserve] to start moving into the Bridgehead tonight. I am trying to dribble them in unseen. When the right moment comes the Americans will punch out to get astride the enemy's communications to Rome. If successful, this may well prove decisive.'

This secret move of the 36th Texas Division – the same which had suffered disaster at the Rapido in January – had, of course, been decided upon with Clark. At that meeting Clark again brought up the question of the direction of Truscott's breakout from Anzio. 'Alexander remained adamant that the attack should be towards Cori and Valmontone [eastwards], regardless of the enemy situation at the time.' Clark pointed out the problems – having to cross mountains, the enemy still holding the Alban Hills and being in a dominant position. He argued that they should keep themselves ready to 'evaluate the situation when the time comes' and that it might well prove that the Cori-Valmontone idea was mistaken. 'We left it thus, with Alexander still feeling it would be best to cut Route No 6 at Valmontone in an effort to trap the Germans opposing the Eighth Army.'

Senger returned from leave to his XIV Corps on 17 May, to find the situation worse than he had expected, particularly in the area facing the Americans. General Vietinghoff had been bombed out of Tenth Army headquarters. The French were sweeping forward at an alarming rate further north, and the British 4th and 78th Divisions had not only cut Route 6 but joined up with the Polish Kresowas. 'I had to report to Kesselring, as usual right in the front line, that for the first time in nine months my Corps' front had been broken through.'

He recommended a withdrawal to the Hitler Line, but even after the loss of Cassino Kesselring refused to consider such a suggestion. The American 338th Infantry having by now captured the coastal town of Formia, Kesselring decided to order the 29th Panzer Grenadiers from the Fourteenth Army reserve opposite Anzio to block the Americans in the area of Terracina and Fondi, further up the coast and both strongpoints of the Hitler Line. Mackensen, needless to say, objected vehemently to this proposal and was responsible for a delay in the departure of the Panzer Grenadiers — one of his actions which was ultimately to lead to his dismissal by Kesselring.

It was typical of Senger that at the height of this fatal battle he should have time to ponder on the fact that in almost identical positions, along what was now the Gustav Line, the Spaniards and French had fought one another in 1504. He also regretted the plight of the small town of Aquino, another key point in the Hitler Line, facing the Canadians; for here St Thomas Aquinas had been born in 1226. Fondi was Horace's Fundi; Cicero had had a villa at Formia and had been murdered on escaping from it, and his head had been taken to be exposed in Rome. In more recent history Terracina had been the gateway to the Kingdom of the Two Sicilies, and at Gaeta — named after Aeneas' nurse — the ancient castle had been defended for four months by Queen Maria Sophia in 1860–1.

The GIs of the 338th, part of the 85th or Custer's Division, might not have known much about this ancient land of the Ciociaria or, given the circumstances, cared. But they would have all been aware that here was beauty of the grandest sort — the steep grey-greenish mountains, still untamed, on the right, the shimmering lapis lazuli Mediterranean on the left, and far away like a pale mirage the hump of Monte Circeo. A lieutenant who 'liberated' the fishing village of Sperlonga was taken aback to find a grotto with Roman carvings inside — in point of fact Tiberius had given a supper there. 'Somehow I believe I shall want to come back to Sperlonga,' he wrote to his father.

It was incredible that in such heat the French should be advancing almost at running pace through the mountains. There was a rumour that the Goums buggered their prisoners, then went in with the bayonet. A report about the Goums reached the Badoglio government a week later. It appeared that the people of Spigno and Esperia had escaped to the scrub woods during the fighting. As the Goums approached and the Germans withdrew, they came out 'convinced that they were meeting liberators, convinced that their days of tragedy were over at last'.

'We suffered more during the twenty-four hours of contact with the Moroccans than in the eight months under the Germans. The Germans took away our goats, sheep and food, but they respected our women and our meagre savings. The Moroccans flung themselves upon us like unchained demons. They violated, threatening with machine-guns, children, women, young men, following each other like beasts in rotation; they took our money from us, they followed us into the village and carried off every bundle, our linen, our shoes. Even those of their officers who tried to intervene in our defence came under their threats.'

After the capture of Esperia, the French made a mistake. They failed to clear Monte d'Oro near the town, and while trying to push through wrecked vehicles were fired on by German mortars above. A light tank was in the lead and as the correspondent Will Lang recorded: 'Screams pierced through clouds of smoke as the Germans poured their fire into the exposed men and machines. The tank exploded with a roar and belched a mass of flame and smoke as the ammunition side caught fire. Other vehicles were catching fire as their frantic, crazed occupants scrambled out, running up the road towards the shelter of thick-walled old buildings in the village.' Lang saw a chaplain, Father Baudoin, his silver crucifix hanging from his neck, dragging bleeding men under vehicles for safety.

The Poles were now preparing for yet another drive, this time against Villa Santa Lucia and Piedimonte. On 19 May Corporal Szymon Jankielewicz was on the table-land behind the Monastery, watching men in gloves gathering up the dead, putting aside wallets and personal objects. Flowers were growing everywhere – poppies, chamomile, irises. He saw the body of a Pole with a tommy-gun facing a German's with a schmeisser. 'Together they fired, together they died.' Without the documents he would never have recognized Lieutenant Betkowski, that brave and helpful man, vital and vigorous. It was 'a scene straight out of Dante: people burned by flame-throwers, naked, their clothes like cobwebs ... not even corpses, but ashy remains that crumble at a touch'.

Villa Santa Lucia was soon occupied. Lieutenant Durlik had the job of capturing a convent, perhaps the very one where the abbess had invited General Senger to meals, the nuns remaining behind grilles in silence. 'I fired my tommy-gun down a long corridor ... Two Germans lay in a pool of blood, two others ran away ... A German shouted, *"Mein Gott!"* and vanished behind the wall. We had surprised the whole bunker team ... We entered the cloisters, shouting *"Haende hoch!"*, but they fired spandaus at us and pelted us with grenades ... There were only three of us left now. We backed into a crypt, and stacked some forty skeletons in front of us ... We could hear Germans talking in loud voices in the next room ... We thought they would try to smoke us out ... One of our own shells hit the upper edge of the entrance. Stones and corpses fell down on us. I took a look: the whole convent was covered with dust and smoke. Here was our chance. I shouted "Run for it" ...'

The Poles had to make four attacks on Piedimonte, capturing it on 25 May.

Clark was not at all pleased to hear from General Lemnitzer, Alexander's American deputy chief of staff, that Alexander had ordered that the attack from Anzio should be launched on 21 May towards Cori and Valmontone. By this time the 36th Division had safely arrived at the Beachhead (Bridgehead to Churchill).

From Clark's memoirs it appears that he saw this as a ruse to let the Eighth Army into Rome first. He wrote passionately about the ordeals of the Fifth Army during its winter campaign: 'We not only wanted the honour of capturing Rome, but we felt that we more than deserved it ... Not only did we intend to become the first army in fifteen centuries to seize Rome from the south, but we intended to see that the people at home knew that it was the Fifth Army that did the job, and knew the price that had been paid for it.' In any event the attack could not possibly take place before 22 May. Alexander came to see him and must have used all his famous diplomatic charm. It was agreed that the Anzio attack would be in the small hours of 23 May, with the main thrust towards Cisterna, and 'flexibility of movement thereafter'. On the same day the Canadians would make a frontal attack on the Hitler Line at Aquino.

*   *   *   *

On the afternoon of 22 May I had to write what I thought could be my last letter to my mother.

The Green Howards had been chosen to lead the diversionary attack out of the Beachhead, a few hours before the main attack against Cisterna, and my platoon was to be in front. We were to attack northwards along the coast and across the mouth of the Moletta, our objective being a group of bathing huts called L'Americano. I was, above all, terrified of the minefields.

I wanted my letter to sound cheerful, but it turned out rather flat: 'I can't write properly, as my mind is so occupied by things that are happening in the near future. I have so many letters still to answer, but somehow I don't feel like it. I only want to write to you. Everyone here is in complete confidence and tremendously excited by it all. By the time this reaches you, you will know what I mean. As soon as I can I shall write again. I wish I could talk to you and not write letters.'

Earlier that day I did let myself go in a letter to my brother, but never posted it. On the night of the 21st I had been on a reconnaissance patrol to see the starting-off point of the attack, which was in the bed of the Moletta itself, the water being only knee deep. 'On the way back,' I wrote, 'I volunteered to be the guide, as a shell had blasted away the white tapes marking the path through our mines. Suddenly there was an explosion, a hot flame seared my neck and I was dazzled by vivid streaks and sparks. The colonel, who was behind me on the same patrol, seemed to be lifted up and thrown into a bush. I was knocked over and lay stunned for a little. I must have stepped right over the mine. I got up and saw a figure behind me all quiet and dark, and another just behind groaning slightly. The first was a sapper officer, quite dead, with his face blown away. I lifted up the other who had stopped groaning. It was Lance-Corporal Atkinson with both legs off. His breath came out with a great gurgling sob and he died. Oh the smell of the hot thick blood on my hands and of the fumes of cordite. They haunt me still . . . I felt responsible . . . I dread this attack . . . I am so afraid of disgracing myself.'

Some time on the day after the attack I wrote again to my brother: 'I am actually writing this from hospital where I am for a short while with five very slight wounds from a couple of grenades . . . Of course our barrage was quite fantastic. We had to go slap through a minefield and the two men next to me were blown up. When I led a section round some bushes, a spandau opened only ten yards away, killing the section leader behind me and badly wounding four others. I chucked a grenade and tore off, only to discover another Jerry trench just below me. The Jerry threw an egg grenade, which hit me on the nose and it bounced back into the trench on to him and exploded. The next few hours were a haze of grenade throwing and tommy-gunning, sand and bits of scrub flying everywhere. My platoon took fifteen prisoners and we must have killed half a dozen.'

I went on to describe how on reaching the furthest point I had nine men left, and how I got wounded. I did not tell how on the way to the start line my wireless operator panicked and deliberately shot himself through the foot. 'Worst thing of all was that one of my very best friends, Charles Newton, was killed. Typical of him, he went into the attack laughing and singing, but an anti-tank bullet got him in the face – I'm sorry to tell you this, but I *have* to tell somebody. He didn't die at once. I pegged out at about 1 p.m., when I was beginning to feel sick and my wounds were stiffening. The brigadier came here and said it was all highly satisfactory and we had achieved our object. Also the main American attack seems to be going extremely well.'

'Stalingrad' – Valmontone

The Allied press was urgently speculating once more whether the Germans intended to defend Rome street by street. Would the city's claim to be eternal at last be ended? Would there instead be a 'smoking mass of rubble', as at Stalingrad – or Cassino?

Kesselring feared a repetition of Stalingrad in a different sense. At Stalingrad an entire German army had been cut off in a vast pincer movement by the Russians, and 130,000 men had gone into prison cages. He thought he could see precisely what Alexander had in mind, and of course he was right: Alex's intention was still that Truscott's VI Corps, on breaking out of the Beachhead, should make for the gap south of the Alban Hills towards Valmontone on Route 6, Via Casilina, thus cutting off the German Tenth Army's line of retreat. Here Mackensen's thinking, as usual, differed from his superior's. Mackensen was sure that the main Allied attack must come up Via Anziate, as in February, and then swing west of the Alban Hills towards Rome along Route 7, the Appian Way.

It had long been realized by the Germans that when the attack came they would have to face far superior fire-power. For this reason they had created their 'C-Line', which the Allies were to call the Caesar Line, a series of fortifications from Ardea on the coast to Campoleone, to the south of Velletri and up to Valmontone, and across Italy to Pescara on the Adriatic. The fortifications were mostly built by the Todt Organization and forced labour from the streets and prisons of Rome, and as at the Gustav and Hitler Lines contained emplacements so deeply and strongly dug that it was hoped they would be immune to bombardment. Then there was another line of defences, not so formidable, in the Alban Hills themselves near Lake Nemi; this the Germans called the Campagna or Rome Line.

From early in May the Germans had noticed that enemy reconnaissance patrols on the Anzio front had been increasingly active. During April the Allies had fired on an average eighteen hundred shells a day. On 11 May, when the Cassino battle reopened, the number had risen to about five thousand, some concentrations lasting an hour on end and not apparently aimed at any particular target. German soldiers used to say: 'Once they start taking aim we shall be in trouble.' But such random firing by the Allies was deliberately designed to confuse, and in this it was successful.

As Kesselring had now removed the 26th Panzers as well as the 29th Panzer Grenadiers from the Anzio to the Cassino front, Mackensen was left without any reserves whatsoever, although the 334th Infantry on the Adriatic and the Hermann Goering Division, refitting near Leghorn, had been promised to him. He had just over five divisions in the line, ranged against five American divisions, two British divisions and the 1st Special Service Force. Mackensen had further anxieties in that he still thought that the Allies were plotting a seaborne landing further up the coast.

Mark Clark had moved to the Beachhead on 22 May. At a press conference in the wine cellars of Nettuno it was made clear that the forthcoming attack would be under his 'personal command'. Reporters felt in no doubt either that after the capture of Cisterna and the next town Cori the objective would be the Valmontone gap. Clark however still had in mind the need for flexibility – a word that was to prove ominous.

On the next morning it was noted that Clark had risen at 4.30 a.m., almost an hour before the big bombardment. The guns had become silent, and there was a strange overlying feel of tension throughout the Beachhead, as before a big race. Over a hundred and thirty thousand men were waiting to take their part in this supreme gladiatorial combat.

The minutes ticked towards zero hour. Watchers saw the Army Commander get into his jeep and drive towards a command post nearer the front.

The US 1st Armored and the 3rd Infantry, under that doughty pair of generals, Ernie Harmon and Iron Mike O'Daniel, would lead the offensive, with Eagles' 45th on the left aiming at special German strongpoints and Frederick's 1st SSF striking across the Mussolini Canal on the right. The British role was to be minor; after the diversionary attack it would be a matter of keeping the enemy on its toes, guessing.

Pfc Gerold Guensberg had recently joined the 3rd, and in the previous afternoon had been in a final parade past Iron Mike, to the accompaniment of the Division Band, interminably playing 'The Dogface Soldier March'. In some ways it was relief to him that the weeks of hard training and the 'chicken shit' of spit and polish were over. He was aged eighteen, and had actually been born in Germany. In the small hours of 23 May he found himself, at last, in a long narrow drain or ditch, ready for the attack. It was so crowded in there that it was difficult to lie down. Nobody spoke. Having listened so much to older soldiers talking about sex – how English women liked it best standing up, or Italian women from the back – his great fear was that he would die before he had 'become a man'.

Guensberg like his companions had of course heard about the Rangers' disastrous attack on Cisterna in January. This was something that everybody now preferred to ignore.

The barrage came at daybreak. 'Just one continuous thunder,' said Guensberg afterwards. 'And overhead squadron upon squadron of aircraft coming in to strafe and dive-bomb the German lines.' At about 6.30 the fire lifted and the doughboys went in. 'While we were waiting to advance down the ditch the first wounded began filing past in the opposite direction. Those with light wounds seemed to have a silly smirk on their faces, as if they had won their tickets back to the US.'

In another ditch further back the war correspondent Eric Sevareid listened to the battle. Any moment he would see violated bodies carried back on stretchers. Out of the racket a man said to him: 'They can hear this in Rome maybe.' And another: 'Are you noivous in the soivice?'

In the morning light a huge column of dirty smoke could be seen above the site of Cisterna. Then later in the hot sun the stretchers arrived on jeeps. People peered at faces to see if they belonged to friends.

Guensberg's column slowed down after a hundred yards, 'as we had to make our way gingerly between remains of corpses, dismembered limbs, scraps of bodies'. A shell must have dropped short. 'We were too numbed to give this any thought ... We climbed out of a ditch and crossed a field. A few German soldiers began running towards us waving their hands high in the air and calling out "Kamerad". They were terrified.' The Krauts were simply told to keep on running in the direction of the Allied lines. Every hundred yards or so you would stop, hug the ground for a while, and then move on again. 'The tactics were simple: you walked when the guy ahead of you walked, and stopped when he stopped. This way we went on for much of the early morning. There was continuous shellfire: especially and unforgettably the German 88s. There was small arms fire but this largely went unnoticed. Here and there in the field or in a dip in the ground there was a GI, dead, wounded or dying. Then we came across German emplacements: some fairly elaborately constructed with steps leading down into a large dugout covered with timber.'

Mines, as always, were almost the greatest concern. Various elaborate ruses had been evolved to deal with them – 'Snakes' for instance, cylindrical rollers pushed in front of tanks and equipped with flailing chains. These were quite successful, and the huge explosions seemed to stun the enemy, so that the sectors where they were used were easily overrun. Iron Mike had another invention, 'Battle Sleds', which towed men behind tanks; but they were a fiasco and were hardly able to advance any distance because of the irrigation channels, fortunately perhaps for the so-called volunteers inside the sleds, who had never expected to survive anyway.

Isola Bella. Femminamorta Creek. Names like these, dreaded so much in the January and February fighting, were now recurring in the battle bulletins. The 1st Armored made better progress than the 3rd Infantry. When Colonel Omohundro in a forward company reported to General Iron Mike that he had been pinned down, the reply came back: 'We have no such words in our vocabulary now.' Resistance by the Germans however became ever tougher. In the confusion of combat and in the white-hot frenzy of elation mixed with tiredness, men emerged as unexpected death-or-glory heroes. Pfc John Dutko, maddened by an 88, leapt up 'like a ruptured duck' and ran towards it, oblivious of machine-gun bullets spattering the ground around him. He was followed by Private Charles Kelly, who saw him kill the two-man crew with a grenade, and then wipe out five others firing his BAR automatic from the hip. Then Dutko charged another post. 'With a single burst he killed the gunner and, staggering forward, fell across the dead German machine-gunner. When I reached him he was dead.' This won Dutko a post-humous Congressional Medal of Honor. Two other men survived that day to win the same awards, Pfc Patrick Kessler and Pfc Henry Schauer, whose nerve they said was 'like ice'.

The 3rd lost no less than 1,626 men on that one day, and Guensberg was among the 642 wounded. As a shell exploded near him and he leapt into a trench, that same old thought raced into his mind: 'Must I be knocked off before I have had a woman?' He was hit by a small fragment that seemed to ricochet off the shoulder of the man in front (much more badly wounded) – small enough, as it happened, to enable him to recover quickly in hospital in Naples, where it was easy to address himself to the problem of his manhood.

The 3rd failed to reach Cisterna, but the 1st Armored cut the railway to the north, and the 1st SSF – though beaten back half a mile by a counterattack from Tiger tanks – actually was astride Route 7. The 45th had had a lot of casualties but had overrun a battalion of the 29th Panzer Grenadiers and captured its commander. Poor weather conditions had reduced the amount of air support. Nevertheless, 712 sorties were flown on that day. It was learnt that the German 362nd Division, opposite the US 1st Armored and part of the 3rd Infantry, had lost half of its fighting strength, whilst the 715th, partly defending Cisterna and partly facing the 1st SSF, had lost forty per cent. The Americans claimed to have taken fifteen hundred prisoners. The Germans said they had destroyed a hundred tanks.

So another day of slaughter, for both sides, lay ahead.

Kesselring was disappointed by Mackensen's failure to hold the Americans. Ultra picked up his signal to Vietinghoff: 'Contrary to all expectations things do not look so good on Mackensen's front.' He refused permission for the Corps commander General Herr to withdraw the 715th to higher ground, since it might create a gap north of Terracina, which indeed was about to fall to the advancing Americans of II Corps – Terracina being the last obstacle to the link-up between the two halves of the Fifth Army. Still Mackensen was worrying about an attack in the British sector, i.e. along Via Anziate, and this made him delay moving units from divisions in that area (the now veteran 4th Para Division and the 65th) to reinforce Herr. Clark and Truscott would have felt more at ease if they had been aware of the growing rift between Mackensen and Kesselring.

ROME

The fate of Rome had been discussed two weeks earlier at a secret meeting in the Vatican, of which the very idea would have outraged some people: a meeting between Pope Pius XII and the head of the SS in Italy, General Wolff. It had been arranged by Dollmann, who has since said that he used as an intermediary Donna Virginia Agnelli of the Fiat family. Weizsaecker, the German ambassador, was not informed until afterwards.

Wolff had to wear civilian clothes. An ironic aspect of the meeting was that it had been he who had been abortively deputed by Hitler before Christmas to abduct the Pope and the Curia. Padre Pancrazio Pfeiffer was present, and the three spoke in German for about an hour. Wolff told Dollmann later that the conversation had been 'very cordial', and that he had found the Pope amazingly conversant with all sorts of details even of a minor nature.

They had talked about the atrocities at Via Tasso. Pius XII had especially asked for the release of the Socialist Giuliano Vassalli (who had been working for the OSS and Peter Tompkins, though the Pope could hardly know this), now in Via Tasso and whose father was an old college friend. On finding Wolff so amenable, he is supposed to have said: 'How many crimes, how many injustices, how many offences against the human spirit would have been avoided if we had met earlier!' And: 'Whatever happens I shall never leave Rome voluntarily. My place is here, and I shall fight until the end for the Christian commandments and for peace.'

During the meeting Wolff had promised to do whatever he could to help bring the war to an end, should the opportunity occur. As he left, forgetting that he was in civilian clothes, he gave the Nazi salute. He was true to his word in asking Kappler to release Vassalli, and he spoke to him about conditions in Via Tasso, though Kappler gave him his 'word of honour' that he had never tortured anybody. Later, the Allied drive from Cassino having begun, Wolff saw the Pope again, and the subject this time was a possible armistice in Italy. Afterwards he flew to Berlin to see Himmler, and then to Hitler's headquarters in East Prussia. Early in 1945 he did indeed initiate secret discussions about an armistice, and after the war he was the only leading SS figure pronounced 'clean' by the Allies. However he was sentenced by a West German court in 1946 for 'high altitude experiments on human beings', whatever that meant, and again imprisoned in 1964.

Wolff, of the pure Aryan type, with his ginger hair and grey eyes, was considered to be a connoisseur of female beauty. One Roman *innamorata*, like a matron in the days of the Emperors, slit her veins for love of him on the day the Allies entered Rome. Around the time of his visit to the Pope, he caught sight of a particularly appetizing woman, partially American, in a restaurant, and, raising his glass, sent across an officer with his card and a message saying that he would grant her three wishes. This Hans Andersen-type gesture was not spurned. The lady immediately asked for milk for her child, a permit to go to the country to get food, and the release of the painter Chicco Multedo, who was her great friend. Wolff granted her the first two, but said he had to refuse the last. All the same Multedo's family was able to procure his release by paying a bribe of two million *lire* to guards at Via Tasso.

As the food crisis developed ever more alarmingly, some barges loaded with bread by the Germans appeared on the Tiber. General Maeltzer, the 'king of Rome', had himself photographed distributing loaves and hugging children. Late in May D'Arcy Osborne reported to the Foreign Office that the Vatican was supplying 100,000 meals a day at one *lira* per person. Finally, General Wilson agreed to allow one food convoy to Rome each week. There would be no more than thirty lorries, which would have to follow a certain route at a set time every Thursday, and there must be no German vehicles accompanying them. But how, Osborne fairly asked, could thirty lorries feed two million people? In Rome, he said, some of the worst hardship was among small employees and the white collar class; he estimated that only about four days' supply of flour was in hand. When Tivoli was bombed, he continued, the water supply was mostly cut off and electricity disappeared. Rome was now a besieged city.

AFHQ's comment on all this was that arrangements for the feeding of Rome on its liberation were well in hand.

If the Allies were still being evasive about the matter of the open city, so the Germans remained evasive about their own intentions if they were to be driven back to the city's outskirts. Now German vehicles were again passing through Rome without restriction. It was rumoured that all the bridges and main public buildings had been mined. Pillboxes had been built outside the walls. On 27 May the Papal Under-Secretary of State, Tardini, summoned Weizsaecker to protest against the mounting arrests and the food shortage, which he felt might result in riots. He also said that he feared that Kesselring would be prepared to abandon the city when the time came, presumably as a result of another visit by Padre Pfeiffer, the Pope's special envoy, to the German headquarters at Monte Soratte. At this the ambassador shook his head and said, 'No, I do not have that impression.' He added that he thought Kesselring was determined to hold the Campagna, the plain around Rome. 'But,' protested Tardini, 'if he does that Rome will be attacked and it will be its ruin.' The ambassador smiled and gave a sibylline reply: 'An attack on Rome will depend on Roosevelt's forthcoming elections.'

Earlier Tardini had also seen Osborne to discuss his anxieties about the possibility of uprisings at the time of the Germans withdrawing from Rome. He stressed the importance for the Allies to send a small force at the earliest moment to show itself in the centre of Italy. 'Such ocular demonstrations of impending Allied control and administration,' Osborne reported to the Foreign Office, 'would, he believed, serve to avert disorders and I think he is probably right.'

Tardini must have realized only too well that the *Insurrezione* was the dream of the partisans, the great moment when the people of Rome would at last rise up and prove their valour, patriotism and ability for sacrifice.

Now there were round-ups every day. Men and boys were plucked off trams or trapped in bars and cafés. More partisans were arrested and executed at Forte Bravetta. The leading trades unionist Bruno Buozzi was sent to Via Tasso. Agents of the Fascist interrogation squad, the Banda Koch, shot down Eugenio Colorni, Professor of Mathematics at the University and editor of the clandestine Socialist paper *Avanti!*. A deadline of 26 May was given for reporting for military service. Headlines in the Fascist newspaper read: 'After midnight punishment will be relentless'. There would be house-to-house searches.

All this to the sinister crescendo of the approaching battle, of shellfire, anti-aircraft fire and dive-bombing. It was said that a thousand civilians had been killed in a raid of a few hours in Tivoli, and many hundreds wounded. Refugees poured into Rome. There were now forty-one in Mother Mary St Luke's small convent.

$$\star \qquad \star \qquad \star \qquad \star$$

On the Cassino front, a new advance by the French on 22 May, at Pico above the upper Liri valley, had made Kesselring 'almost cry with rage'. On the next morning, in sopping mist, the Canadians began their attack, concentrated on a three-thousand-yard front.

It was to be another bloody day, with nearly nine hundred Canadians lost, but by night the Hitler Line had been pierced. The worst casualties were suffered by the Seaforths and the Princess Pats, all of whose platoon commanders died or were wounded.

The attack had been preceded by a creeping barrage, shells dropping at over eight hundred a minute, and was supported by tanks of the North Irish Horse and the 1st Royal Tank Regiment. German artillery airbursts over the thickly wooded country caused terrible gashes from splintered wood; they also decimated their own snipers, who were seen hanging from trees.

A 'killing zone' had been cleared by the Germans, laced with minefields and overlooked by anti-tank guns, Nebelwerfers and dug-in Panther turrets. Some of the Canadian infantrymen were lacerated by British tanks dragging barbed wire caught in their tracks. There were unexpected wadis, and a Churchill turned a somersault into one. Then rain came down, but nothing could quench the flames of the many burning tanks, Allied and German.

One commander of a Sherman troop, who had left his tank to winkle out a machine-gun pit, had the unusual experience of being offered money by its defenders for their safe conduct. In a dugout a stock of new Iron Crosses was found.

On the next day the Canadians entered what was left of the ancient Volscian town of Pontecorvo, and the French took Pico.

As the press communiqués poured out news of the successes of 'General Mark Clark's Fifth Army', Churchill asked Alexander if a little more could be said about British achievements. 'I know of course what the facts are, but the public may be upset.' On 24 May Alexander was able to tell him that five hundred square miles of Italy had been freed in a fortnight and over ten thousand prisoners taken.

The situation for Mackensen was worsening fast. Cisterna, still holding out, was, nevertheless, surrounded. The US 1st Armored was approaching the Valmontone gap. The 36th Division was driving southwards down the coast towards the sad, crushed but now liberated Terracina, to the *Aeneid*'s fabled shore; on its left were the Pontine marshes, flooded again, and on its right umbrella pines and the gold-glittering sea.

On 24 May O'Daniel tried a frontal attack on Cisterna which failed.

But the 1st Special Service Force had broken into the centre of that part of the German 715th holding the area below Cisterna. Kesselring saw that the battle had reached a decisive stage and again forbade any withdrawal from any key position without his express order. However Mackensen, who regarded Kesselring as dangerously over-optimistic, took it upon himself to withdraw the division, though by night to escape Allied dive-bombers. When an attempt was made to get through to the Cisterna garrison, he was told: '*Cisterna antwortete nicht mehr*, Cisterna did not answer any more.' The only hope now of preventing the Americans from sweeping up to Valmontone was the arrival of the Hermann Goering Division, still on its hundred-and-fifty-mile journey from Leghorn and much harassed by Allied aircraft.

On the evening of the 24th Truscott saw Clark, who had asked: 'Have you considered changing the direction of your attack towards Rome?' By this he meant not pressing on towards Valmontone but veering away and taking the geographically shortest route. Truscott was puzzled, since he thought his attack was doing well, and was later to realize the significance of the question. He agreed to keep the option open.

Ultra caught a message from Hitler to Kesselring agreeing to the general principle of the Fourteenth Army withdrawing to the Caesar Line.

War correspondents such as Wynford Vaughan-Thomas of the BBC and Eric Sevareid awaited the big moment which must surely come soon, the link-up with the South and the ending of the Beachhead. Italian labourers were digging graves outside Nettuno in readiness for the dead Americans. Sometimes they were unable to keep up with the amount of bodies; sometimes there would be a score or so of waiting holes, like mouths. German prisoners had the job of unloading the corpses. They were not given rubber gloves.

The days were hot. The nights, the Mediterranean nights, could have been beautiful under that moon. A few ruined villas had bougainvillea and jasmine around their porches, and correspondents could relax there. At least the field hospitals were now not so vulnerable to air attacks. So many boys had lost legs from mines. So many had been blinded by shrapnel. So many would be crippled for life. 'I realized,' said Sevareid, 'I was becoming a little obsessed by the tragedy of these youngsters.'

On the 25th, 655 German vehicles were knocked out.

The fall of Cisterna was announced. Vaughan-Thomas drove up in his jeep and found two soldiers with mine-detectors. 'Go right up into the town, bud,' they said. Bullets were still singing in that litter of broken stones and brick-dust, and Vaughan-Thomas could hear an occasional rattle from a spandau. Some tired GIs crouched in a mess of filthy German clothes and abandoned rifles. Then there was another *sput* of a bullet and they scuttled like frightened crabs into an archway. A small group of prisoners, dumbly obeying, was hustled along by a sergeant with a tommy-gun; their clothing was torn, showing skin, and none were wearing helmets. A tommy-gun sprayed the wall above Vaughan-Thomas' head. A shout: 'Come on, out of it.' More Germans crawled into the sunshine. A battle-weary lieutenant said: 'Well, I guess that about cleans up the town.'

Then at last the link-up, so unexpectedly quick that by the time Clark reached the scene it had to be re-enacted for photographers. The first men actually to meet at this place, nicknamed Borgocrappa, were said to be Lieutenant Francis Buckley of Philadelphia, arriving from the South, and Captain Ben Souza of Honolulu, coming from the Beachhead in the North. A British reconnaissance unit was also present. Cigarettes were exchanged, there were jokes and yarning. It was heart-warming, reported Vaughan-Thomas. In the background someone dared to quote T. S. Eliot: '*Where is there an end to the drifting wreckage, the prayer of the bone on the beach* ...'

A lark sang, even. A white flag was flying from the broken red roof of a farmhouse. Dead Germans lay in the green wheat. Looters had scattered photographs, now limp, around these bodies, and there were letters with writing like birds' footmarks, all smeared. If you could read German, you might have been embarrassed by the endearments of grandmothers, aunts, girlfriends.

The remnants of the German 715th were now completely cut off from the rest of Mackensen's Fourteenth Army, and mostly without radio contact. They had lost the greater part of their heavy weapons. The night of the 25th had been very dark. Lieutenant Richard Oehler had been almost blinded by the exploding shells, and flaming ammo trucks had only served to attract more enemy fire. *Viele Hunde sind des Hasens Tod*, many dogs are the death of the hare. All next day the bombers went on attacking. Oehler drove his vehicle criss-cross over the countryside, but it was no use. He had to abandon it, blowing up the engine with two hand grenades. Exhausted and out of breath, with a motley group from all sorts of units, he eventually climbed to the crest of the Lepini mountains. 'The sun hung blood red over the Tyrrhenian Sea. We threw a sad glance at the valley below, where so many of our comrades had given their last. We had fought as long as we could against the overwhelming power of men and material.'

An American task force from the 1st Armored, under Colonel Hamilton Howze, consisting of three battalions and three companies, was ten miles from Valmontone. But the British Eighth Army was still forty miles away. Only a few reconnaissance units from the Hermann Goering Division had arrived from Leghorn. Truscott was confident that by the 26th Howze would be astride Route 6.

As the Allied planes pounded Valmontone, few people on that day had time to worry about the fate of its baroque Palazzo Pamphili.

Howze has described how on the 25th there were only about eight German tanks falling back in front of him. There was no resistance at all in that lush valley, lined with chestnut woods and oaks. Soon he realized that he was about twelve miles deeper than any other force in VI Corps. He drove back in his jeep all night to Ernie Harmon. 'My message was, "I am in a soft spot, for Pete's sake let the whole 1st Armored come this way!" I didn't want to do it all myself, I didn't have enough strength. I was over-extended and vulnerable . . . Harmon agreed instantly and told Truscott.'

When Truscott returned to his command post, 'feeling rather jubilant', he was met by General Brann, Clark's G3. 'The Boss wants you to mount the assault you discussed with him to the north-west as soon as you can,' he was told. Only the 3rd Infantry, depleted now and battle-weary, and the 1st SSF were to continue towards Valmontone. The main drive would thus be along Route 7.

Clark's decision – subject of what he again terms 'Monday morning quarterbacking by the British' – is one of the most controversial actions in the whole Italian campaign, as controversial almost as the bombing of Monte Cassino. Truscott however has admitted that he was dumb-founded, and Howze not surprisingly has described it as 'one of the worst decisions I ever knew'. When Truscott demanded to see Clark he was told it was impossible, as Clark had left the Beachhead (to be ready for the link-up, no doubt) and could not be reached by radio. It was an order and there could be no argument.

So Truscott had to feign enthusiasm when reporting back to his VI Corps divisional commanders. Generals Harmon and O'Daniel were particularly bitter, but Truscott reassured them by saying that along this new axis 'the Boche is badly disorganized, has a hodge-podge of units'. The focus of attack would now be the towns of Velletri, Lanuvio and the once much fought-over Campoleone. Places like Aprilia and Buonriposo ridge would also have to be regained.

There now ensued extensive and complicated shifts of troop dispo-sitions, which held up any positive action for nearly a day. Howze's task force was allocated to the 3rd Infantry, only just emerged from the Cisterna battle, and the 3rd Infantry and the 1st SSF became part of General Keyes' II Corps. It would be some time, however, before Howze could have backing before Valmontone.

Only on the next day, twenty-four hours later, when it was too late to object, did Alexander receive news of the change from General Gruenther. Alex seems to have behaved with his usual inscrutability, saying that he was for any line of action Clark believed would offer a chance to continue the present success. Then he asked Gruenther: 'I am sure that the Army Commander will continue to push towards

Valmontone, won't he?' Gruenther reported back to Clark: 'I assured him
that you had the situation thoroughly in mind, and that he could depend
upon you to execute a vigorous plan with all the push in the world.' In
actual fact the push towards Valmontone had now become only a token
one.

Alexander concealed any disappointment in his despatches. Only years
later, in his memoirs, did he let himself go. If Clark 'had succeeded in
carrying out my plan', he said, 'the disaster to the enemy would have been
very much greater . . . I can only assume that the immediate lure of Rome
for its publicity persuaded Mark Clark to switch the direction of his
advance.'

He was reticent when Churchill, alarmed, signalled him on 28 May
about using some of his armour in a 'scythe-like' movement cutting off
the enemy's retreat. 'I would feel myself wanting in comradeship,'
Churchill said, 'if I did not let you know that the glory of this battle,
already great, will be measured not by the capture of Rome or juncture
with the Bridgehead but by the number of German divisions cut off.'

Harold Macmillan saw Alexander soon after his interview with
Gruenther. He realized there was trouble because Alex's eye was
twitching, as it would do before a big battle. He asked what was wrong.
'What is right?' Alex snapped back, and told him. Macmillan asked him
why he had not put his foot down. 'Why do you talk nonsense?' Alex
replied. 'How can I give orders?' This was the only time Macmillan had
ever seen him lose his temper.

Clark, for his part, has always made it clear that he was determined that
the Fifth Army was going to capture Rome. 'I was probably over-
sensitive to indications that practically everybody else was trying to get
into the act.' The Eighth Army was lagging behind in the Liri valley. 'The
British had a tough nut to crack, but I don't think it was any tougher than
what we did in the mountains [presumably referring mostly to exploits of
the French, part of the Fifth Army].' If he had attacked the way Alexander
wanted, it would have been like throwing the British a rope. He always
had to be careful about 'making it possible for the British Eighth Army to
get an easy victory by Fifth Army efforts and swinging along on the
successful offensive of the American Fifth Army'.

That was a main factor. And as for the 'chance of trapping a lot of
Germans', it was 'absolute rubbish'. There were other escape routes they
could have used. And in any case, the Hermann Goering Division was
moving up, and Truscott's lines of communication in the Valmontone
gap would not only have been over-extended but overlooked by the
Alban Hills.

The question of trusting or not trusting the perfidious British is one
matter, and whether the Fifth Army deserved to be the first into Rome to

the exclusion of the rest is something else. But the remaining points raised by Clark have some validity, except that as the American historian Martin Blumenson has pointed out (and as earlier invaders knew), capturing Valmontone provided the quickest way to Rome. Clark underestimated the strength of the Caesar Line and of the 'hodge-podge' manning it. Perhaps he still did not pay enough attention to Ultra, it being exclusively operated by British Intelligence. At any rate, again in Howze's words, he consequently 'ran into a stone wall, had very heavy fighting and took many losses'; in other words he ran himself into a stalemate.

Another important matter governing Clark's thinking was that Marshall had told him that it was essential that Rome should be captured before the Normandy landings, and D-Day for the landings was less than a fortnight off.

The units from the German 65th Division and the 4th Para Division, facing the British on the northern sector of the Beachhead, had had to be rushed to the Valmontone gap. An historian of the 65th has written under the heading *The Crisis: 26 May*: 'During the night very few provisions came through to the front line. Some companies were completely without food. In the area of the 65th and 4th Paras all attacks were repelled. East of Velletri, however, the Americans had pushed through to Artena only six kilometres from Route 6 at Valmontone, which carried the supplies for our Cassino troops. A miracle had to happen to prevent the Allies from closing the sack in which most of our divisions in Italy could be thrown. General Clark provided that miracle ... Then the "Stalingrad" south of Rome, which had been the Allies' goal since January, did not materialize. The way back for the Tenth Army remained open.'

Without much air or artillery support, the British on the Beachhead had made little progress. According to the US correspondent Sidney T. Mathews, 'when asked about the reasons for the failure of the British under Fifth Army command, General Clark stated emphatically [in 1948] that their lack of aggressiveness and their failure to accomplish more was due to poor leadership rather than to difference in transport or tactical concepts from Americans'.

The fate of the king of Italy at this precise moment, with D-Day in Normandy also so near, must have seemed small beer to Churchill. On the whole it was left to Harold Macmillan to make decisions.

The question was when or if the king should enter Rome on its liberation, and even if he should be allowed as far as Naples. It was decided that for the time being he would have to stay in Ravello, and that Prince

Umberto and representatives of the six parties would go to Rome as soon as feasible.

The king was also apparently having second thoughts about handing over his powers. Macmillan was incensed by this 'wriggling out' and gave orders that if there were to be 'any nonsense' the king was to be put on a plane and sent to Kenya.

Churchill was more concerned by Badoglio's demands for a 'partial peace treaty'. 'None of these matters,' he told Eden, 'should come up until we are safely ensconced in Rome and chasing the enemy up the Italian peninsula ... Badoglio is very lucky if he gets away to retirement and untroubled demise.' In his draft note, Churchill crossed out all the following: 'Why is it you want to settle things? It is a tremendous mistake for the Foreign Office to settle things ... In Foreign Affairs, if one question is settled, it only gives way to another usually more disagreeable. Please take these words of wisdom from an aged friend. Let me send a nice telegram to Badoglio on the theme of "*dis*quieta non movere", translation "Pig it".'

Churchill was annoyed when he received a long telegram from his High Commissioner Noel Charles about a meeting with the Communist leader Togliatti, who had asked for facilities to meet Italian leaders in Rome when the Allies arrived in the city. Togliatti had told Charles that he wanted to solve the position of the monarchy and Badoglio, and felt that Umberto's position was 'none too good'. He also complained of 'bad discipline' in the Roman Party of Action, though he hoped he could control the situation, provided he was able to get to Rome 'as soon as is practically possible after the arrival of the Allied troops'.

Churchill's draft reply was preserved but never sent, though the sense was transmitted to Charles: 'I do not like Togliatti's attitude. Having boosted the king and Badoglio into a certain position, he now wants to ruin them and no doubt the Communist gang will sing their part. They will certainly pulverize any form of government that can be set up ... You should not hesitate to use language suitable to the rights and dignity of Britain, which has done four-fifths of the fighting against Italy from the day she entered the war. Do not take it all lying down. A good row with the Russians is sometimes a very healthy episode.'

Togliatti as much as the Allied leaders was anxious to avoid an *Insurrezione* in the city. It was a different matter in the Castelli, the towns in and around the Alban Hills. There at the right moment the partisans could be of immense value. The code word for them to strike would be '*Anna Maria è promossa*, Anna Maria is promoted'. And that message came over Radio London on 27 May.

Sorrento

I went to the 186th General Hospital in Naples, a 'head and tails' hospital dealing with head wounds and VD cases. There I had a piece of grenade removed from my cheek. I also fell ridiculously, violently and briefly in love, and it was all to the good when I was sent to convalesce in the Hotel Tramontano at Sorrento.

The Tramontano was an enormous Edwardian-type building, on the site of Tasso's house, with a garden full of camellias, bougainvillea and palm trees, and built on a sheer cliff over the Bay. On the evening of my arrival I looked out at the smooth milky-blue waters. I could just see Naples outlined in the distance and the double hump of old Vesuvius, which was no longer smoking. I thought I had never seen anything so perfect. This, at last, was the real Italy I had been longing for.

A fishing boat had been pushed out. They were going to catch *calamari*. Just in front of the hotel, near the herringbone bricks of a Roman villa, the boat stopped and a man began to sing, a typical Neapolitan tenor. He was singing 'Lili Marlene'.

'Stalingrad' – Rome

Under a radiant sky the juggernaut of war pushed slowly up the narrow Liri valley, obliterating whatever was left of farmhouses and villages, ruining crops and ancient olives. But, incredibly, wild flowers sprang up in the shell holes, it seemed overnight, and after dark the thunder of the guns had its counterpoint in the quacking of a myriad frightened frogs.

The Canadians advanced, their numbers diminishing. Tanks were being held up by an unexpected quantity of blown bridges and by the wadis, and were only too easily picked off by guns sited in the defiles above. Indian and Italian forces, like the Moroccans and Algerians to the west of the valley, were having some success in the mountains, and on 26 May the 8th Indians had captured Roccasecca.

Kesselring called for a 'fanatical defence' of the Liri valley: 'It is the Fuehrer's explicit order and my belief that we must bleed the enemy to exhaustion.' But once again, in spite of the tremendous Canadian casualties, he was being too optimistic, as is clear from a conversation between General Feuerstein of the German Mountain Troops Valentin and the Tenth Army commander:

Feuerstein: I report as a matter of duty that we shall not bring back many men if we have to hold out at all costs.
Vietinghoff: We must accept that risk. Army HQ has given explicit orders to hold the line for several days.
Feuerstein: I regret to report to the Colonel-General that the enemy has already crossed the River Melfa [a tributary of the Liri] in two places.

(On the day of this conversation the Canadian Westminsters' Major Mahony, wounded in the head and leg, won his VC.)

The Germans were also being bled to exhaustion. Even Kesselring was coming to realize that there might have to be a phased withdrawal to the crucial town of Valmontone.

A thick cloud of dust, like a smokescreen, covered the Allied rear echelons. As the agonizing 'text book' advance moved ahead, mile by mile, yard by yard, so each army left behind it the usual detritus of burnt vehicles, smashed gun carriages, broken rifles and valuable precision instruments. If these things had belonged to the other side, you saw them with satisfaction, a good job done; if not, too bad. As for the corpses, if they too were the other side's, and if they stank, the best way to be rid of them was with a can of petrol and a lighted match. There was no time for regrets; after all you were trained to kill, to destroy.

Some vignettes then, recorded by a Guards officer, through a trance of sleeplessness:

'German prisoners made to clear their own minefields; half a dozen blown to blazes. A whole convoy held up because a London Irish subaltern, once a cabaret-singer, was doing his number one act from a scout car, flinging his arms about; the next time I saw him one arm had been blown off. The long black locks of an Italian woman otherwise invisible beneath rubble; muffled screaming. An old man, a carpenter, decapitated – people fighting for his wallet, watch, shirt. A statue of St Anthony, also decapitated. Flames of Jerry guns almost beautiful at dusk; spitting crimson, amber and opal. Fireflies, mistaken at first for the dimmed sidelights of trucks. The greenish waters of the Liri, like Kipling's Limpopo. In the remains of a stinking cellar, by the light of a hurricane lamp, anxious faces around a field telephone, hearing that a company commander is dead. Someone fussing, at the hottest moment of the day, about seventy-four lost overcoats. The whistle of a mortar shell, and diving into a ditch full of blood-red poppies.

'Then trying to snatch a half hour's kip and being kept awake by the earth trembling from the concussion of bombs. And the sour smell of captured Jerry trenches, the same as in Tunisia and the Desert. Was it something to do with their tobacco, or the food they ate?'

If Clark chafed at the Eighth Army's slowness, his 34th and 45th had been truly blocked on the Caesar Line. Like the Canadians along the Liri, they were having to attack on a congested front, only three miles wide, and there was confusion about boundaries. Towards Anzio, in the British sector, the line bulged inwards across the Anziate, taking in the wadi country, and Aprilia, alias the Factory. However the role of the British was still meant to be diversionary, with plenty of vigorous patrolling. In any case their stamina had been much reduced by weeks in the trenches – the 2nd Sherwood Foresters, for instance, had lost the equivalent of a hundred per cent of its original battalion strength, and no less than two hundred per cent of its original officer strength.

On the night of the 27th the Germans pulled back two to three kilometres in order to shorten their own line, and on the 28th they also withdrew from the Factory, which was thereupon reoccupied by the Gordons. Wynford Vaughan-Thomas drove past the Flyover with its now unnecessary sign, 'No traffic past here in daylight', and up to the site of Carroceto station, past the Lobster Claws, the Boot, Puntoni and the gully where Major Sidney had won his VC. Here had been Spandau Pete, there the farm known as the King's Arms. It all seemed on such a small scale now. He reached the Factory. The famous tower had crumbled long ago, and the brick walls of the church were barely standing. But in front of the church the bronze statue of the Archangel Michael, one foot on a dragon, was still there, although slashed by shrapnel.

The Foresters were able to recover bodies of men killed three months before and still unburied. The Loyals took over the beginning of the rough road which the Germans called the *Schotterstrasse*; heavy traffic had churned it up so that now any movement sent up clouds of choking dust. Above, the ground was unpleasantly open and overlooked by familiar features of the past such as the *Schafstall*, the Sheepfold. Mortar shells were constantly being lobbed into the *Schotterstrasse*, and there were bad burns when shrapnel detonated phosphorus grenades carried by the Loyals – so the carrying of these had to be given up. In due course the Factory area was handed over to the 45th Division, the 'Thunderbirds', in preparation for the major American attacks on Campoleone and Lanuvio.

The German 65th Division had successfully resisted the Thunderbirds on 27 May and in consequence had been sent a special message of congratulations from Kesselring, who made a daily habit of visiting advance command posts along all fronts. Then on the 28th the American 1st Armored put in its attack on Campoleone with five hundred tanks. Two companies of the German 147th Grenadier Regiment were lost entirely. The only reserve now left was the 7th Company of the 147th, and this was under Lieutenant Heinrich Wunn, who had faced Major Sidney in February.

Wunn occupied Campoleone church and its surrounding buildings, the tower giving him perfect observation for kilometres around. This extraordinary man typified the doggedness and discipline of the German soldier. He was in his element; 'We cannot lose the war if everyone does his duty' was his favourite dictum. If a comrade was killed he would always see that he was given a burial with military honours, three shots being fired over the grave. Wunn now quickly gathered in any stragglers – runners, artillery observers and anti-tank men who had lost their guns. The American tanks had broken through, but he was able to beat back their infantry. Concentrated artillery fire then proceeded to decimate the majority of the tanks. *Stuetzpunkt* Wunn – Strongpoint Wunn – had become a key outpost defending Rome, and apparently impregnable. Yet on the 29th Mackensen had to tell Kesselring that the 65th Division only had left for tank defence six assault guns, one Tiger tank and a few anti-tank guns.

A house called Villa Crocetta outside Lanuvio was the other great citadel of German resistance. Lanuvio, being on high ground, was more difficult to assault in any case. Truscott was getting impatient with the delay, and told a staff officer to tell General Ryder of the 34th, the 'Red Bulls', to 'crack this Lanuvio, it's holding up the whole thing'.

But Lanuvio was not to be cracked. Stalemate had been reached. There was no progress towards Valmontone. In the last days' fighting virtually all the Allied gains had been in places where the Germans had withdrawn, and this included Ardea in front of the British 5th Division near the coast.

Vaughan-Thomas went to look at the Valmontone gap, where the Hermann Goerings were digging in. There had been a disaster here, when American artillery of the 3rd Infantry had by mistake bombarded positions held by their own men, including a group of a hundred and sixty new recruits, most of whom were killed or hurt. There had been a similar occurrence at Cori when the small town was bombed after American troops had occupied it. On the other hand Task Force Howze had taken advantage of a mistake on the German side, due to a confusion over orders, and had mown down scores of Hermann Goerings in an almost suicidal counterattack. Men in Howze's outposts had thought they must have been Americans. 'Hell, no, shoot them up!' Howze had roared down the phone.

Yet the valley looked lushly rich after the devastated Beachhead. Vaughan-Thomas watched shells dropping on the church at Artena. A pitiful procession of refugees passed him on the tree-lined road – old folk and children, stumbling, bewildered, whimpering when a shell burst too close. He heard an American voice shout: 'Hey, can anyone speak dago around here?'

In another area his Transatlantic colleague Eric Sevareid saw the sprawled figure of a young German soldier. 'Two American soldiers were resting and smoking cigarettes, a few feet away, paying the body no attention. "Oh him?" one of them said in response to a question. "Son of a bitch kept lagging behind the others when we brought them in. We got tired of hurrying him up all the time." Thus casually was murder deliberately announced by boys who a year before had taken no lives but those of squirrel or pheasant.'

Murder in war is not always casual. Pfc Lloyd C. Greer of the 180th Infantry Regiment in 45th Division returned to his unit after escaping from a prison camp. He told how he had been captured in February and taken to a farmhouse where there had been about thirty-five German soldiers. 'On the way to the house we passed two other German soldiers standing over two bodies on the ground. One of the men on the ground

was American. I think the other was too. The former was groaning and
had apparently been badly wounded. The latter may have been dead.
While I watched, one of the German soldiers pulled out a pistol and shot
the wounded man on the ground. I understood that the unit which
captured us was part of the famous Hermann Goering Division.'

And now there was a new cause for friction between Clark and
Alexander. The French Expeditionary Force was poised in the mountains
above Ferentino on Route 6, several miles ahead of the Eighth Army. Juin
proposed, therefore, that he should take Ferentino and then follow on up
Route 6 to Valmontone – something which would greatly assist Clark's
embattled divisions on the other side of the Alban Hills.

At last Clark was appreciating the value of Valmontone. But
Alexander refused to give this permisssion to Juin; he wanted Route 6
clear for the Eighth Army and its armour.

'My French corps is being pinched out,' Clark wrote in his diary. No
doubt his suspicions were aroused further when Alexander said that
without uninterrupted freedom to use Route 6 it would be impossible
to bring the Eighth Army to bear in the battle for Rome. There was
nothing for it but for Clark to persuade the French to continue on
their difficult course through the mountains, with the object of joining up
with the American 3rd Infantry at Artena.

Eventually Alexander – realizing that there was still little hope of the
Canadians and the 78th Division gathering much speed – finally agreed
that if the Fifth Army were to capture Valmontone then it could use
Route 6 for the attack on Rome. The Eighth Army would swing
northwards and thereby bypass the city.

On 30 May Lieutenant Wunn repulsed five attacks. The *Stuetzpunkt* had
been reduced to fifty men. As the chronicler of the 65th Division recalled:
'What the Allies could not achieve by force, they were now trying to
obtain with sweet words.' They promised Wunn 'honourable treatment'
if he surrendered. His answer was probably not understood, *'Goetz von
Berlichingen'*, which, although the title of one of Goethe's early plays, to a
German simply means 'Up your arse'.

'Three more times the enemy attacked Campoleone, but in vain,' the
chronicler continued. 'Wunn eventually had to clear out, to avoid being
encircled. He had thirty-five men left and destroyed all the weapons he
could not take with him.' In due course he was awarded the Knight's
Cross for his bravery, as were Lieutenant Finkbeiner and Corporal Vetter,
both of the 14th Company of the 147th Grenadier Regiment, holding
another point nearby. Between 30 and 31 May seventy Allied tanks had
been destroyed around Campoleone, fourteen personally by Corporal

Vetter. Wunn was later to die of wounds outside Bologna, and Vetter was to be killed by low-flying aircraft outside Rome.

Still there was no sign of the Campoleone-Lanuvio line breaking. The mounting American casualties were becoming alarming, and the casualty clearing stations in the vineyards could at times hardly cope with such a torrent of wounded. Both sides were exhausted. The exploits of Vetter were matched by Captain Galt of the 168th US Infantry Regiment, who single-handed killed forty Germans; he was awarded the Medal of Honor posthumously.

If Clark did not break this position in three or four days, there was a possibility that he would have to wait for the Eighth Army and go in with a co-ordinated attack with both armies. And this, of course, for him would be both humiliating and disastrous.

Nevertheless the turning point in the battle for Rome was about to be reached, and this was due to General Fred Walker, the rugged commander – ex-Ohio farm-boy and now honorary Texan – of the 36th Division. The German command had come to realize that there was a possibly dangerous gap in their defences on the slopes of Monte Artemisio to the east of Velletri, but Mackensen had concluded that the difficult terrain would counterbalance any lack of German strength there. He did not know that patrols of Walker's Texans had been roaming the slopes since 27 May.

The 36th had, frankly, come to be looked down on by the other divisions in the Fifth Army. It was considered not only to be a 'hard luck outfit' but trigger-happy. This made Walker, 'the Old Man', determined to redeem his division's reputation. If his troops could scale Monte Artemisio, then Velletri would be cut off. Both Clark and Truscott realized the potentialities of the idea, but felt it could scarcely be achieved. Clark said to Walker: 'Fred, I can't OK this. If you do it and succeed, we are on our way to Rome; but if you fail you will have to bear the brunt of what comes with the failure, and your action will be without my approval or the approval of Truscott.'

Before midnight on 30 May, by the light of a new moon, the 2nd Battalion of the 142nd Infantry Regiment set out on its arduous climb, with the help of Italian guides. Several German sentries were eliminated deftly and noiselessly on the way, their jugulars cut by wire and knives. The leading squads reached the crest by dawn without meeting opposition, and were not spotted by the enemy until the afternoon. A clever ruse at first light had destroyed the neighbouring German positions. Aircraft had been sent in from the north, and the Germans, thinking that they were their own planes, had sent up Very lights to indicate their positions. The bombs fell right on their targets. So now Velletri was completely

overlooked and there were road-blocks on all but one of the Germans'
escape routes. After so many days of frustration, this news, as Clark said,
'caused us all to turn handsprings'.

Kesselring however was raging. For the third time Mackensen offered
to resign his command, and this time it was accepted. In less than a week
he left for Germany, and his place was taken by General Joachim
Lemelsen.

For some days the 1st SSF had been occupying Artena, still the farthest
point of the II Corps front facing Valmontone. Many fine Forcemen had
been lost, and many stories have survived about this strange, hardboiled
organization where differences in rank hardly mattered except to define
combat duties. Colonel George Walton remembers watching men seeing
their buddies going out on patrol and taking bets on whether they would
return alive or not. Major Jack Sector, a Jewish Canadian, was a Forceman
about whom legends grew. He never carried a weapon, only a swagger-
stick, and would laugh and joke in the toughest spots. Then, at last, he was
mortally hit, by an 88, and his last words were: 'Here, take my watch. I
won't need it.'

The 36th's spectacular achievement on Monte Artemisio and the
imminent fall of Velletri made it imperative that Valmontone should be
captured quickly, and it was at this stage that Alexander agreed that the
French Expeditionary Corps should advance on the town, and that the
rest of Route 6 should be in Fifth Army territory. Juin was told that his
ultimate objective would be to seize a crossing over the Tiber east of
Rome.

The Germans were still fighting back hard, though obviously weakening. Needless to say the French made rapid progress. Keyes' II Corps,
consisting now of the 1st SSF, the Howze Task Force, and the 3rd, 85th
and 88th Divisions, seemed destined to be the first in the race for Rome.
On 1 June a white flag was raised over Valmontone. Iron Mike O'Daniel
ordered his 3rd Division artillery to 'plaster the hell' out of anything that
went along Route 6. 'The important thing is to shoot every goddam
vehicle that comes by there.'

Velletri was entered, at last, on 1 June: a ghost town. The place was
'littered with the bodies of Krauts', and two hundred and fifty prisoners
were taken. The Krauts had also pillaged the fourteenth-century church
of Santa Maria del Trivio and sacked the seminary, though the German
command had obviously later put up an out of bounds notice, threatening
the death penalty for entering or plundering the building. The Cathedral
was half in ruins, and only a third of the Palazzo Comunale remained.
Doors of houses were torn off, windows gaped.

On 31 May the Canadians of the Eighth Army had made a sudden dash forward and had captured the important market town of Frosinone, capital of the province of which Cassino was a part. Kesselring's fear of another Stalingrad for Vietinghoff's Tenth Army thus returned. Units from the coastal area of the Fourteenth Army and whatever reserves were available were rushed to safeguard the right flank of the Tenth in the area of Tivoli. But on 2 June Lanuvio fell: the ancient Lanuvium, where once there had been a temple to Juno, and where once, so Livy said, the statues had shed blood; and where, for good measure, one of the great Italian admirals had been born, Marcantonio Colonna, a victor of Lepanto.

There were insufficient German reserves to plug the gap. Kesselring gave the order for both Armies to withdraw.

Vietinghoff, who had been ill for some while, could carry on no longer and was forced to hand over his command of the Tenth Army. Westphal, Kesselring's chief of staff, collapsed from nervous strain.

Alexander and Clark met on 2 June. It was a difficult encounter once more, though somewhat glossed over in Clark's memoirs, where he speaks of his demand that the French should take over yet more of the territory of the Eighth Army (thus keeping the latter at a safer distance from Rome?). 'I rather expected an argument, but Alexander said that I shouldn't worry; if my attack didn't go through he would bring in the whole Eighth Army to assure success. I replied that our attack was going through.' Clark also says that it was made clear that an eventual communiqué should be released specifically saying that 'Fifth Army troops' had entered Rome.

He did not mention in his memoirs that the future boundaries between the Armies after the fall of Rome were also discussed. Harding, as Alexander's chief of staff, recalls that this was their nearest approach to 'coming to blows' with Clark. And Sidney Mathews, recording his interview with Clark after the war, has said: 'Everybody was anxious to get to Rome or to take part in its capture ... The French Expeditionary Corps, Clark says, wanted to be in on it [as did the Poles] ... When Alexander told Clark he wanted the Eighth Army to take part in its capture, Clark got pretty sore. He told Alexander that if he [Alexander] gave him [Clark] such an order he would refuse to obey it and if the Eighth Army tried to advance on Rome, Clark said he would have his troops fire on the Eighth Army. Alexander did not press the point ...'

Juin also apparently got the message, and kept his men away from Rome.

ROME

The distant menace of heavy guns seemed out of place in such perfect Roman weather. 'Always these guns, always nearer,' wrote Mother Mary St Luke. The incarcerated diplomats in the Vatican watched the dive-bombing on the outskirts of Rome from a hill in the garden. At night there was a constant pulsing glow in the direction of Velletri. History was about to turn another page.

The question at the back of every Roman's mind was, of course, whether or not the Germans would defend the city, and there were clear signs that they intended to do so. But any feeling of dread was, for most people, counteracted by hope. Josette Bruccoleri remembered: 'Everyone seemed to be in possession of a great secret which they did not dare reveal. People hardly spoke to each other and if they did it was only for a moment. I myself felt like a time-bomb ready to explode, but like everybody else I did my best to look as innocent as possible.' The BBC news was saying that it was better to surround Kesselring's Armies than to capture Rome. 'Oh yes, is it?' said Mother Mary. 'We are not strategists, armchair or otherwise, but we have practical knowledge of the urgent need of liberating Rome.'

Old people collapsed from lack of food in the streets. Beggars were everywhere. It gave Mother Mary 'heartache' to see how cadaverous some friends looked. Once again the Allies had turned down a suggestion of a way of feeding Rome, this time again by sea, using Spanish and Irish ships.

The news that yet another revered Benedictine shrine had been bombed by the Allies was seized on gleefully by the Fascist press – the Renaissance cloister at the convent of Santa Scolastica at Subiaco had been damaged, and a workman and a student had been killed. Bombs had also been dropped on the Villa D'Este at Tivoli. The Anglo-Saxon barbarians were coming.

The Fascist police seemed to be possessed by a kind of frenzy, and were horribly successful in capturing key Resistance figures. Among others they caught Generals Oddone and Filippo Caruso, who were sent to Via Tasso. Lieutenant Bill Simpson, a helper in the O'Flaherty-Derry organization, had also been rounded up and was believed to be in the Regina Coeli prison.

Then, suddenly, it was noticed that senior German officers' luggage was being sent north from the Via Veneto hotels. There was a mysterious fire at Koch's torture-house, Pensione Jaccarino. And Monsignor O'Flaherty received a surprising message from Koch himself. Could the Monsignor arrange for Koch's mother and sister to be housed in a convent, and in return Koch would make sure that O'Flaherty's friends in prison would not be deported north? O'Flaherty asked, as an earnest of good intention, for the release of Simpson and a Captain John Armstrong, who was thought to have been in Regina Coeli for nine months; but events were moving too quickly ...

The Allied radio at Anzio broadcast names and addresses of spies and collaborators with the *Nazifascisti*. The OSS man Peter Tompkins was annoyed about this. He had the addresses filed away and was hoping to hand them over to the Allied authorities as soon as Rome was liberated. Now those people were simply fleeing northwards. Mother Mary wrote: 'Two of the informers mentioned yesterday by the Anzio wireless are the porter of a house we know, and his wife. They have specialized in reporting the whereabouts of Jews. This morning they are sitting in their lodge shedding tears; and well they may.' Josette Bruccoleri was told by her porter's wife: '*Signorina*, if Angelo is arrested when the Allies come, I'll put a knife in your mother.'

★   ★   ★   ★

In the Castelli district around the Alban Hills, following the code words *Anna Maria è promossa*, partisans were harassing German supply lines with considerable success. Carla Capponi was slightly wounded by shrapnel in a hit-and-run raid. She and Rosario Bentivegna were summoned back to the Gap headquarters in Rome, but Carla was not well, spitting blood and with a high temperature. She recovered a little, and was sent with Rosario and another Gapist, Fiorentini, on bicycles to Tivoli, to be ready in case of an Allied *lancio* or air-drop.

On 2 June it was the *festa* of Sant'Eugenio, Pius XII's name-day. The Pope's message of warning was broadcast to the world: 'Whoever raises a hand against Rome will be guilty of matricide to the whole civilized world and in the eternal judgement of God.' That evening the codeword *Elefante*, Elephant, came over the air from the South. This meant that the Allies' arrival was imminent.

The Lateran Seminario, packed with what Churchill – who could not be shaken from his fixation against the CLN – was to call 'aged and hungry politicians', began to buzz like an excited beehive.

★   ★   ★   ★

Captain Charlstrom of the US medical corps examined a few of the Caesar Line dugouts. You had to descend twenty steps in some of them, and below were beds, tables, even kitchen stoves. 'Those damned Krauts were living in comfort', while good American blood was flowing outside. Sometimes you realized that women had been kept down there.

And now Anzio Annie, the famed and hated 28 cm railway gun, was captured, hidden in the Nemi tunnel which the 362 Division had also been using as a headquarters. The weight of the gun was 479,600 pounds and its length was 96 feet; its 561-pound shell could be fired thirty-eight miles, and it had required a team of ten men.

On to Lake Nemi: 'navelled in the woody hills', Byron had said. In normal times the towns around this enchanted place, early in June, would be thronged with Romans for the *sagra delle fragole*, the feast of strawberries. When shells dropped on the placid surface, they looked like whale spouts, and masses of silver fish floated on the surface.

The sheds housing Caligula's boats from Lake Nemi had been burnt, with everything in them, by the retreating Germans, so it was said. Others blamed careless refugee families. Whatever the truth, it was a major archaeological tragedy.

The unreality of death lurking in such countryside was like a dream. In the dappled groves and verdurous glooms, with the hot sun above, men were killing one another, shells screaming backwards and forwards, tanks flaming, booby traps exploding. As Sevareid said, 'the air was charged with excitement, savage triumph and obscene defeat'.

Rome was falling ... The horror of bluebottles feasting where a dead German, face downwards, had shat himself.

Lieutenant Harold T. Bond was aide to General Stack, deputy commander of the 36th Division. Near Nemi the general had gone on some urgent business, leaving Bond behind. Bond came across a sergeant whom he knew. The man was badly wounded, his face drained white, and clutching his belly in pain. He recognized Bond and asked to be put on the general's jeep and driven to first aid. 'The request was terrible for me. I wanted very much to do this, but I felt I could not. With a pitched fight in progress here and with the whole division engaged in a fast moving battle the general might return at any moment and move to another part of the battlefield. I had to say no. He didn't reply at all, but just stared at me for a while before closing his eyes in pain. I shall always remember his stare, half incredulous and half contemptuous.'

Rome was falling. Sevareid saw a child kicking a dead German officer, until a woman shoved it aside and removed the man's boots.

Genzano, Albano, Castel Gandolfo fell. Through field-glasses you could see the dome of St Peter's.

Highway 7 climbed uphill. Harmon's 1st Armored was on that road, in the vanguard of VI Corps. 'A hell of a place to put an armored division, on top of these mountains,' he grumbled.

But at present it was II Corps which looked like winning the race, from Valmontone. The spearhead of the Corps was under the 1st SSF's General Frederick, who also had Task Force Howze attached to him. As usual Frederick was always far out ahead. Once when he had been slightly wounded Colonel Akehurst, the Canadian regimental commander, had to tell him: 'Please don't get in front of my regiment again.' The next time this lanky unmilitary-looking general was hurt, he said to Akehurst: 'Jack, I kept my word, I didn't get in front of *your* regiment. This one happened when I was in front of another outfit.'

Perhaps Clark was now taking notice of Ultra. For on 2 June Ultra had decoded Kesselring's request to Hitler for permission to evacuate Rome without fighting in the city, and on 3 June Hitler had agreed. For once Hitler must be accorded some credit; Rome, he said, was a 'place of culture' and must not be a 'scene of combat operations'. Mussolini, on the other hand, is said to have asked that Rome should be defended street by street – 'Why should the citizens of Rome have a better life than those of Cassino?'

It was the last big battle south of Rome, a desperate attempt by the Germans to prevent their two Armies from losing contact. The Fourteenth Army had lost seventy-five per cent of its manpower since 23 May. The paratroopers forcing the British and the Panzer Grenadier regiments north of Lake Albano held on almost to the last round, so that the remainder of the army could withdraw across the plain east of Rome.

The war diary of an artilleryman of the German 65th Division ran: 'The whole day Tommy is attacking. We answer until the gun-barrels are red-hot. At 12.15 groups of enemy tanks are trying to break through at the *Schotterstrasse*. This attack also collapses in our fire. At 1600 Tommy attacks again. Soon after that we receive orders to retreat. Our assembly point is about eighteen kilometres from Rome [at Mussolini's Exhibition buildings].'

It was reckoned that 168 tanks had been destroyed by the 65th in front of the *Schotterstrasse* and Campoleone. In recognition of the achievements of this horse-drawn division, General Helmuth Pfeifer and Colonel Martin Strahammer were later awarded oakleaves to the Knight's Cross.

On the opposing side, the only VC of the British 5th Division was won posthumously by Sergeant Rogers of the Wiltshires.

Two posthumous Medals of Honor went to Private Elden Johnson and Pfc Herbert Christian, both of the 15th Infantry Regiment in the US 3rd Division, in what has been described as 'one of the most stirring tales of courage and self-sacrifice in the annals of United States military history'.

In order to save their comrades' lives both continued to fight on, although mortally wounded; Johnson had been hit in the stomach by a machine-gun, Christian had lost a leg — he crawled onwards on one knee and a bloody stump, 'raking the Kraut with his tommy-gun' until he was shot down and died.

This last episode took place during a German rearguard action near Palestrina, on the other side of the Fifth Army front. The Germans still feared that II Corps would thrust on from Valmontone, past Palestrina to Tivoli, thus not only separating their two Armies but preventing a withdrawal to the important bridges north of Rome, where a new line could be formed. The danger seemed even greater now that the French were also approaching Palestrina on the US 3rd's right. But whatever chances the Americans had of effecting either of these, they were ignored. Rome, at present, was the one and only goal, and the 3rd's positions around Palestrina were handed over to the French. Indeed, from what Gruenther told Clark, it would seem that there could have been very little overall control left at Fifth Army headquarters on the afternoon of 3 June. Such was the excitement and optimism, he said, 'no one is doing any work here ... all semblance of discipline had broken down'. Everyone had his 'pants full of ants'.

With the British Eighth Army on the move, Kesselring was extracting his Tenth Army through the Abruzzi mountains in a masterly manner — all the more impressive now that he had lost his three most important generals. Senger's XIV Panzer Corps was despatched to Tivoli, seven divisions being pulled back through the often precipitous roads in five days, mostly by night. All of which showed that Clark had some justification in saying that there would have still been escape routes for the Germans even if he had driven on to Valmontone on Route 6 in the early days.

As usual Senger, during his withdrawal, had time to appreciate the glories of the 'sacred valley' through which his XIV Corps passed: the rich vegetation and the ilexes, olive groves, throbbing with cicadas and scented with sweet box, and the river dashing wildly below. He has described awakening to find himself in a 'wonderful wood of chestnut trees in a beautiful setting'; he had not, he said, had so refreshing a night's rest for many a month. It was like moving through a landscape by Claude. 'I spent the following night in a castle at Orvinio, which lies at a good elevation. Here, in the deserted but well-furnished bedroom of a young marchesa, I slept in a wonderfully wide bed, with clean linen and a bath provided.'

ROME

During the afternoon of 3 June several prisoners at Regina Coeli were put in lorries and sent north.

A number of other prisoners at Via Tasso were also selected for removal. The first lorry contained fourteen men, including the trades unionist Bruno Buozzi, four of Peter Tompkins' helpers, and Captain John Armstrong, who had recently been transferred from Regina Coeli. At a dreary spot called La Storta, where in *vetturino* days horses had been changed at the last staging post before Rome, all fourteen were taken out and shot, their bodies being left in a schoolhouse.

Rome was falling.

Generals Oddone and Filippo Caruso, the Gapists Salinari and Falcioni, and the Duchessina Mita di Cesarò's fiancé, Uberto Corti, were among those lined up ready for the next load. After a long wait they were told that their lorry had broken down. The noise of bursting shells seemed to be getting louder. The German guards were obviously scared and ordered the prisoners back into their cells.

Padre Pfeiffer, on behalf of the Pope, came to the prison and fetched Giuliano Vassalli, the Socialist for whose release Pius XII had asked General Wolff three weeks before.

Rome was falling.

The Germans were as anxious as the Allies to prevent a mass uprising by the Roman population. The necessary spark, presumably, would happen if it was clear that the city was to be defended. Or would the Germans, as Mother Mary said, cease upon the midnight with no pain – just fold up their tents like Arabs? Kesselring gave orders, to avoid suspicion of immediate withdrawal, that General Maeltzer and other high officials should that evening attend a gala performance of Gigli singing in *Un ballo in maschera*.

The all-important bridges across the Tiber were blocked by machine-gun posts. Thus, for civilians, the city was cut in two.

With a feeling of total uselessness, D'Arcy Osborne listened to the artillery and heavy bombings, quite near, and to 'other indeterminate warlike bonkings'. In that 'heavenly' weather he eased his mind by going for a bicycle ride with the youngest Tittmann, 'Tarzan', in the Vatican gardens. That night he could not sleep. 'An unending and exceedingly noisy stream of German motorized traffic, including heavy tanks, poured north along the branch of Via Aurelia beneath our windows. At 2.30 I went on the roof to look. It was lovely up there, with a bright moon and a lot of red flares in the sky due north.'

During the small hours the Italian generals in Via Tasso were suddenly set free and made their way to the Lateran. There they were taken to Ivanoe Bonomi, as head of the CLN – he was horrified by the sight of Filippo Caruso, swollen and limping from torture, his mouth still bleeding after fourteen teeth had been ripped out.

Caruso's namesake, the Fascist police chief in Rome, Pietro Caruso, left at dawn from the Plaza Hotel in his Alfa Romeo, taking with him a quantity of jewellery, watches, pound notes and *lire*. Near Lake Bracciano a German car crashed into him and his leg was broken. His identity was discovered whilst in hospital at Viterbo, so in due course he found himself sent back to Rome, to a cell in Regina Coeli.

Pietro Koch made the journey northwards unscathed, to carry on his work first in Florence and then in the 'Villa Triste' in Milan, by which time his methods of interrogation had achieved further refinements, and where for some reason he attracted people from the stage as accomplices, including two well-known film stars, Osvaldo Valenti and Luisa Ferida. Both Koch and Pietro Caruso were to be tried in Rome and shot at Forte Bravetta, the scene of so many patriots' executions. Before Caruso died, the Pope sent him a rosary, for which he was much criticized.

Kappler also left in good time. He too was to be arrested and after the war tried in Rome. He was to be condemned to life imprisonment, and was visited in prison at Gaeta by Monsignor O'Flaherty, who converted him to Roman Catholicism.

Celeste Di Porto, the Jewish prostitute known as the Black Panther, had no intention of leaving Rome. She looked forward to new clients among GIs and Tommies.

It was not yet time for Maeltzer to depart. Tompkins heard that he was 'stinking drunk, speaking in lamentable French' and that his headquarters was in complete confusion. Colonel Eugen Dollmann, on the other hand, boldly plunged southwards through the shelling to Frascati to say goodbye to Kesselring. He found the Field-Marshal pale and exhausted. They shook hands and looked forward to meeting again in Florence.

Rome was falling.

Dollmann took a last walk round some favourite spots in the city he had known and loved since 1927. Then he left, as he cynically said, before 'all the Romans, true and otherwise, flung themselves eagerly at the feet of their liberators'.

Early that morning the Allies had dropped leaflets over Rome. They were headlined 'Headquarters of General Alexander' and urged the citizens of Rome, now that liberation was at hand, 'to stand shoulder-to-shoulder to protect the city from destruction and to defeat our common enemies'. Romans should do everything they could to safeguard public services, telephone and telegraph plants, railways. They should remove any barriers or obstructions from streets to leave free passages for military vehicles, so that Allied troops could pass through without hindrance. 'Citizens of Rome, this is not the time for demonstrations. Obey these directions and go on with your regular work. Rome is yours! Your job is to save the city, ours is to destroy the enemy.'

These last words, repeated on the radio, have been misinterpreted by certain writers as a call to rise up, the opposite, of course, being the truth. Togliatti also sent a message instructing the Communists not to attempt any independent action, which in some ways must have been a disappointment to his most ardent supporters. Various other reasons have been given for *la mancata Insurrezione*, the Insurrection that never was, in Rome, a chief one being that the *Nazifascisti* had been so successful in rounding up leaders of the Gaps and the pro-Badoglio Military Front (i.e. Oddone and Filippo Caruso); also the man who, after so much fuss weeks ago, had become head of the Military Front, as being more acceptable to the CLN – old General Bencivegna – was still semi-immobilized with his bad leg in the Lateran. And very little help, if any, could have been expected from partisan bands outside Rome. Finally, when compared with the northern industrial cities, Rome was dominated by the upper, middle and clerical classes.

Exasperated by the sense of paralysis, Peter Tompkins took it upon himself to write an order, on headed OSS paper, to the Italian 'Republican' authorities now nominally in charge of armed forces and police, instructing them to take charge of public order, to prevent sabotage, arrest deserters and prevent civilians from leaving the city.

Suddenly D'Arcy Osborne was sent for by the Vatican Under-Secretaries of State, Tardini and Montini. He heard that the Germans had 'weighed in' with a last-minute proposal to make Rome into an open city. 'It was too late and absurd, particularly since German troops had been pouring through Rome all last night and this morning.' The only effect would be to deny facilities to the Allies. The Germans also suggested that Florence should be designated a hospital city – the ulterior motive was too transparent.

An exciting moment came when Osborne had a telephone call from Castel Gandolfo, and over the crackling line heard the voice of a British liaison officer with the Fifth Army. Derry also spoke to the officer and

answered questions about bridges being still intact and whether there
was any street fighting. 'The Jerries appear to be withdrawing from the
city very nicely,' Derry told him.

★   ★   ★   ★

Vehicle congestion and the problems of logistics necessarily bedevilled the
progress of the Eighth Army. There had been occasions when the
Canadian Westminsters' vehicles had been suspended over cliffs or
jammed nose to tail in sunken narrow roads. 'If only the country were
more open we would make hay of the whole lot,' noted Alexander.

Now the 6th South African Armoured headed the Canadian Corps.
True to Clark's wishes, the Eighth's line of advance kept well to the
notoriously difficult mountainous centre of Italy, with XIII Corps
aiming for Subiaco and X Corps for Avezzano, and the Tactical Air Force
doing its best. Between 12–31 May it claimed 2,556 German motor
vehicles destroyed and 2,236 damaged. Naturally it was disappointing
not to be able to take part in the entry into Rome, but this was
compensated for by the jubilation in each small town or village liberated.

★   ★   ★   ★

'Please take Rome soon,' Clark's mother wrote. 'I can't stand the wait
much longer. I'm all frazzled out.'

The night of 3–4 June had been a confusion of conflicting rumours as
small task forces rushed towards the *Città Eterna*. In the case of the US II
Corps, Task Force Howze and the 1st SSF were still in the lead, each
having battalions attached to them from the 88th Division. But when the
French relieved the Americans around Palestrina, units of the 3rd Division
were freed to join in the race. General Frederick reported that he had
reached the city limits at 6.20 p.m.

Yet there were strong rearguard posts to be dealt with. Only three
miles from the centre of Rome several II Corps tanks were knocked out.
There were also mines and snipers, and a crowd of eager newspaper
correspondents did not help the situation. Clark arrived with Keyes, to
tell Frederick that he wanted the Tiber bridges seized as quickly as
possible. He also wanted to know why there was a hold-up. As the three
generals posed under a sign marked 'Rome' a sniper's bullet pinged past,
and all three dived into a ditch. 'That's what's holding up the 1st Special
Service Force,' said Frederick.

Truscott's VI Corps was also suffering from traffic jams but able to
advance in a less confused manner. 'Ernie and his boys', Harmon's 1st
Armored, still were in the Corps' vanguard along Route 7. The arches of
the Claudian Aqueduct were a foretaste of the architectural splendours
ahead. Among the umbrella pines and the dark malachite-green flickers of

cypresses were ruins of medieval towers; then came that haunted road, the old Appian Way, still with the marks of chariot ruts, and lined with tombs and sarcophagi, all overgrown now with brambles, ivy and rampant pink oleanders.

But the 36th Division was making unexpectedly quick progress. Truscott found Walker and some of his staff bustling about trying to decide what to do next. He told them they should be half a mile further east. There, however, it was discovered that II Corps' 85th was in danger of crossing their boundary. Keyes remembered that the 36th's chief of staff 'began yelling out to ours like a pig caught under a fence'; if the 85th did cross over, 'he intimated they were going to shoot it out with us'.

By about 3 p.m. Allied tanks had broken through near the Exhibition buildings outside Rome. The headquarters of the German 65th Division established there had already been burning papers and blowing up food dumps, soldiers having been told to take whatever they could carry.

So the division was on the move again, through the westerly outskirts of Rome. The roads were completely deserted. Here was the basilica of San Paolo Fuori le Mura, there were the Tre Fontane, there the Pyramid of Cestius and the Protestant Cemetery – but such famous sights were of no interest now. The 'Jabos' and 'Jaks' were dominating the skies, and they were taking a good harvest.

The 4th Parachutes were in charge of covering the retreat. Corporal Joachim Liebschner, no longer a runner, was now with a heavy machine-gun post on the Appian Way. People said he and his team were crazy to hang on. Then the Americans were sighted, advancing as if they were on a Sunday School outing. Liebschner's team opened up when the enemy was a hundred and fifty yards away. The Amis, having no protection, all fell down. Dead silence followed for half an hour, then the Ami artillery really did let fly. All one could do was to crouch in the little bunkers.

Soon the Germans could see the shadows of Americans jumping over the bunkers. They waited, then went up and began firing. In the battle that followed only Liebschner and two others were left alive, and all three were taken prisoner. One German was badly wounded and carried off in a Red Cross jeep, another was shot dead out of hand in the back. Liebschner was kept for questioning, and for three days had nothing to eat or drink, usually under a glaring light; he only gave in after he had been blindfolded and told he was going to be shot. A sergeant said to him: 'You haven't been reported yet as a POW, so if you die nobody will know.' Liebschner was sent to Anzio on burial duties.

Liebschner has said that only then did he realize that the war was lost for Germany. 'I saw vehicles, tanks, jeeps, guns, lorries in long columns, as long as the road stretched and as far as the eye could see. There were even water-lorries sprinkling the roads to keep the dust down. Never had I seen such an array. And this was just the supply route, not even the masses they must have had at the front line. I was used to our lorries sprinting along under shellfire, in ones or twos or threes.'

The bridges south of Rome, not being of historical interest, had already been destroyed, and this meant that many Germans had to swim across the Tiber. North of Rome along the Via Aurelia the Jabos were causing havoc among the convoys. They were like birds of prey wheeling above, Sergeant Zumfelde of the Pioneers has recalled. You were always having to leap into a ditch. All the while civilians were streaming past, carrying bags and equipment obviously looted from a German hospital.

'At about 6 p.m. there was a lull in the dive-bombing,' said another Fourteenth Army man. 'On the roads we had lorries, guns, horse-drawn vehicles, anti-aircraft guns – very often in three columns, side by side, and in among them soldiers from different units. The shambles was grotesque. Columns tried to overtake each other, and the ack-ack attempted to take up firing positions. Officers on motor bikes kept trying to get those columns into order ...'

ROME

In the Vatican the elder Tittmann boy, Haroldino, aged fifteen, wrote in his diary: 'Today we did nothing except watch the Germans retreat. I got the best view of all, as I had gone into the nuns' garden, which overlooks the road on which the Germans were retreating ... They were extensively using horses to draw carriages, waggons and every kind of contraption you could think of. Some were even on bicycles. They had stolen all Rome's horse-drawn cabs. They also used horses to pull their artillery. One felt rather sorry for them; they looked so young. Some were tired and dirty ... There were long columns marching. These were the ones that looked exhausted. Some had to carry machine-guns on their shoulders. They looked terribly depressed. Some stopped right below me and sat on some grass. Others bought some filthy lemonade from a little stand also right below me. I must say that the Romans were very kind to them, although they were immensely relieved to see them leaving. They gave the Germans drinks and cigarettes. It is in the character of the Romans to be kind to everybody in trouble.'

D'Arcy Osborne watched the retreat down the 'rather slummy street' from the roof of the Santa Marta hospice, 'but it became too social up there so I came down and watched dive-bombing behind the radio masts from my room'. As Haroldino added, one could actually see the bombs dropping and little spurts of flame from the machine-guns. 'It was rather sickening to see tired German boys walking past us and then watch them being dive-bombed and strafed.'

From time to time explosions and rifle-fire could be heard. Osborne was told that the latter was due to civilians looting shops. The Germans blew up patrol and ammunition dumps at the Macao barracks and the Verano cemetery. They also succeeded in destroying the Fiat works in Viale Manzoni and three railway yards, but patriots saved many public buildings, in particular the main telephone exchange, by removing detonators from mines. No attempt was made to blow up the main bridges.

A blond German soldier smelling of sweat and fear asked Josette Bruccoleri the way to Florence, and she gave him some cherries. 'I saw young boys of about seventeen and eighteen years old, exhausted and half-starved, hardly able to walk. Some were crying, it was pitiful, others were more courageous, perhaps older, and marched in threes singing.' Vera Cacciatore, the curator of the Keats-Shelley house, saw them going down the Corso, mostly very young and in rags, usually singing and shouting. The Italians stood back – they did not harass them, it would have been like hitting someone who was dying. Once in Piazza di Spagna some Germans fired into a crowd and a man dropped.

Mrs Cacciatore afterwards walked to Piazza del Popolo. It was deserted, except for two people, a beggar and a prostitute under the arch. 'You read about invasions, but it is extraordinary actually to be present when two armies are going through a city. We had no water, gas or electricity, only the telephone. There was a complete breakdown of services, a void, no government at all.'

Campidoglio – St Peter's

Sometimes a Mark IV tank or a scout car would block main highways into Rome, and partisans would then guide the Americans through back alleys. There were some scuffles between civilians and Fascist police, particularly at the War Ministry and in Piazza Farnese. Individual groups of partisans had been allocated the tasks of occupying most of the ministries, public buildings, banks and newspaper offices. Carla Capponi raced to the offices of the paper *Il Tevere*, and from there the first non-clandestine copy of the Communist *L'Unità* was eventually produced.

Major Sam Derry sent his helper Joe Pollak to San Paolo Fuori le Mura in order to liaise with an American advance guard, in point of fact part of the 1st Armored. Miraculously, Pollak had found a motor-bike, and on the way passed lines of weary retreating Germans who had mistaken him for a comrade: '*Heil!*' The Americans, needless to say, were at first suspicious, but Pollak was able to convince them not only of his own good faith but that of people claiming to be partisans, and thus Rome's main gas works, situated close to San Paolo, were saved from being blown up.

During the afternoon of 4 June prisoners at Via Tasso heard cries from below: '*Fratelli, uscite! Non c'è nessuno.* Brothers, come out! There's nobody here.' They emerged, dazzled by the daylight, and local people dashed in to ransack the premises, in the process destroying papers and other material which could have been valuable later as incriminating evidence.

The Rector of the Lateran Seminary, Monsignor Ronca, was urging Bonomi to contact in the name of the CLN whatever Fascist authorities remained (the same authorities, as it happened, to whom Peter Tompkins had written) to make some effort about ensuring public order and handing over the city to the Allies. Bonomi agreed finally, and while discussions began two excited priests rushed into his room with the astounding news that Allied troops were already outside the walls. They went on to the terrace, where they found a small crowd of other eminent sightseers. A tank appeared through the great castellated gateway and halted suddenly in front of the basilica, as if it was stunned by such venerable grandeur. A few civilians came up to it shouting, and someone unfurled the green, white and red Italian flag. Then more tanks arrived. People gathered round Bonomi and shook his hand, hailing him as the country's future leader.

On the northern perimeter companies of Task Force Howze, the 1st SSF and the 88th Division fanned out towards four bridges, including Ponte Milvio, famous for its associations with the Emperor Constantine and with Garibaldi. As darkness fell, two units mistook one another for Germans, and it was then that General Frederick was wounded for the seventh time.

A captain of the 88th resting on the little fountain shaped like a baroque ship in the Piazza di Spagna found the stones still warm from the June sun. In the moonlight he could hear people clapping from upper windows. Two dead Germans lay outside the English church in Via del Babuino.

The Colosseum had been used as a central supply-point by the German Parachutists, since it gave good cover from dive-bombers. Sergeant Hoege of the 4th Paras had the hard task of sending food and arms to outposts – one never knew where they had moved from hour to hour. Eventually he managed to cross Ponte Milvio with the American 88th close on his tail; he had had to leave behind his company commander, who was badly wounded.

At about 8 p.m. Irish Dominicans at San Clemente near the Colosseum heard a commotion like big wheels grinding and went out to investigate. A line of American tanks was drawn up close to the walls of the college. 'Two of the Fathers walked along the tanks, but no soldier spoke or made a noise. Suddenly from the last tank there jumped an officer, who went down on his knees and asked for a blessing ... The people who had gathered in the street joined with us in welcoming the Americans, and in many windows flags appeared. They were indeed amazed to see that sign of religion since posters and leaflets depicted the Allies as savages and murderers.' The Fathers then invited the soldiers into the college for wine and cold showers; as San Clemente was built on an underground river, which emptied into the Cloaca Maxima, it was one of the few places left in Rome with fresh running water.

Private Gerold Guensberg, back from hospital in Naples and late of the US 3rd Division, had been assigned to the 1st SSF. He arrived in a jeep just as the sun was setting. 'A vast crowd had gathered on both sides of the road. They were cheering madly as they held aloft flowers, jugs filled with liquids and other symbols with which to greet victorious armies.

Most men seemed to wear priests' cassocks or monks' cowls.' Only by fits and starts could the jeep advance into Rome until it was finally drowned in a mass of humanity. There was no hope of getting to Ponte Milvio or any other bridge that night. 'Some monk inquired in English why we had waited so many months before coming to Rome. That was the end of any serious philosophical discussions. Hands began to reach out and I found myself following a young signorina into a building nearby ...'

Not that all the Germans had withdrawn by then from Rome. A battalion of General Greiner's 362nd Infantry was wandering around back streets looking for a bridge that had not yet been captured. Sometimes the Romans mistook them for Americans and began pelting them with little pink roses. Sometimes there were bloody collisions with American patrols. Finally an unprotected railway bridge was discovered, and in this way by early morning the approximately one hundred survivors were able to reach new positions on Via Trionfale near Monte Mario.

Some two thousand Germans were trapped by the British 5th Division near the Tiber's mouth and taken prisoner. Three Green Howards officers could not bear the suspense of waiting, and decided to risk being hanged, drawn and quartered by General Clark; they got into a jeep and were thus among the first into Rome. Hence the cry that went round: '*Gli inglesi stanno al Grand Hotel*, the English are at the Grand Hotel.'

During the night elements of the 36th Division reached Piazza Venezia and the 'Wedding Cake', the Victor Emmanuel monument. They crossed by the best known of all Roman bridges, the Sant'Angelo, lined with its statues of angels, and saw the bronze quadriga on the round castle silhouetted in black against the parachute flares. Perhaps the ghosts of the Emperor Hadrian, of Beatrice Cenci, of the Borgia Pope Alexander VI and of Tosca looked down as the legionnaires from Texas swung leftwards into the Via della Conciliazione, to be faced by the immensity of St Peter's in the dawn. 'We can't go in there!' General Stack cried, pointing at the Vatican. 'We'll create an international incident.' After much gesticulating with the Italian guides, he ordered the column to plunge off to the right, the wrong direction, where everything was soon snarled up by the crowds of cheering Romans just risen from bed.

In spite of the *inglesi* inside the hotel, a German sniper remained for quite a while on the roof of the Grand, terrorizing the neighbourhood until captured. All credit, therefore, to Mrs Kiernan, wife of the Irish Minister, when in the morning she risked being sniped and ventured out to the nearby railway station. She saw a lot of lads lying about on the pavement and presumed they were Germans. Then one sat up and said in an American accent: 'Say, sister. Come and park your ass near me.' She knew that she had been liberated.

The 1st Armored crossed at the island in the Tiber, close to where Horatius had made his renowned stand, and swept past the Regina Coeli prison. D'Arcy Osborne saw some of their tanks on Via Aurelia early that morning; and they advanced so quickly that Sergeant Hoege of the German Paras had to leave his breakfast behind.

With daylight the American dive-bombing began again. Near Lake Bracciano Hoege saw horse-drawn German vehicles coming up at the gallop; there were shouts that American tanks were only three kilometres away.

Mark Clark arrived in Rome at 8 a.m. with his entourage of staff officers. He drove first in his jeep to St Peter's, and there posed for what is now a familiar photograph with a priest, who was none other than O'Flaherty. Clark tells us that this priest said: 'Welcome to Rome. Is there anything I can do for you?' On Clark saying that he wanted to go to the Campidoglio on the Capitoline Hill, the priest arranged for a youth on a bicycle to guide him there through the crowds.

Bells were ringing. Clark climbed the great stairway built for the Holy Roman Emperor Charles V in 1536. Here Cola di Rienzo had been mortally stabbed. On the right was the Tarpeian Rock, on the left the Aracoeli church. He was approaching one of the most beautiful and majestic places in the world, the centre of civilization. He was the conqueror. He had a right to be proud.

The statue of Marcus Aurelius had been taken away to safety. On this spot Brutus had harangued the people after Caesar's murder. Here, in 1764, Gibbon had been inspired to write the *Decline and Fall*. Behind Michelangelo's Senate House lay the colonnaded temples and basilicas of the Forum, and above them were the ilexes half concealing the ruins of the Palatine.

Ave Roma Immortalis.

Another well-known photograph shows Clark, his elation hardly suppressed, climbing the Senate House steps. With him are his two Corps commanders Keyes and Truscott, the latter looking grubby still from battle – and a little embarrassed.

Correspondents, newsreel men and photographers had been summoned. Juin was allowed to be there, and in due course General Bencivegna arrived from the Lateran. Eric Sevareid found General Clark lounging on a balustrade, modestly surprised that this discussion with his Corps commanders had turned into a press conference. After the photographers had finished, Clark made a short speech: 'This is a great day for the Fifth Army and for the French, British, and American troops of the Fifth who have made this victory possible.' As Truscott was to say: 'I reckon it was, but I was anxious to get out of this posturing and on with the business of war.' Sevareid was disgusted: 'It was not, apparently, a great day for the world, for the Allies, for all the suffering people who had desperately looked toward the time of peace.' It was not even a great day for the Eighth Army.

In the three and a half weeks since Diadem started, American casualties had been some 18,000, British Commonwealth and Poles 15,000, French (proportionately the largest) nearly 11,000, while total German casualties have been estimated at over 38,000. 82,000 altogether.

One of Sevareid's colleagues said: 'On this historic day I feel like vomiting.'

During the afternoon placards appeared everywhere in Italian: 'Come to St Peter's at six o'clock to thank the Pope.'

Mother Mary St Luke was in the huge crowd that packed the Piazza. 'The afternoon light slanted across the roof of the Basilica, spilling torrents of golden light on the sea of colour below. With the flags and banners, it looked like a herbaceous border in full bloom. Soldiers in battle-dress provided an olive-drab background.' Ceremonial draping was thrown over the parapet of the central balcony and the great bell ceased to toll. Then the slender white figure of the Pontiff appeared and raised his hand for silence. He seemed to shimmer. Every phrase in his short speech over the microphone brought a crash of applause.

From that balcony one looks across the Tiber, across ochre and amber roofs, to the Quirinale palace and the Campidoglio, and to the starkly white Victor Emmanuel monument, symbol of the unification of Italy and the overthrow of Papal temporal power. On this historic day, 5 June 1944, Romans in their hundreds of thousands knelt before not only the Vicar of Christ but the personification of deliverance from tyranny and of a new Risorgimento.

Denis Johnston of the BBC saw the scene as a foreigner and watched while the Pope 'gave thanks to supernatural agencies, for all the blessings that so clearly had flown from himself'.

Alexander toured Rome quietly by jeep. At least the Commander-in-Chief was accorded this privilege. Elsewhere, as bridges east of Rome had been demolished, a staff officer of the 6th South African Armoured Division tried to obtain permission for passage over one of the city's bridges. He was held back at gunpoint by a white-helmeted military policeman, as was Major Sidney VC.

D'Arcy Osborne was photographed by a New Zealand press photographer and met Harold Caccia, British representative of the Control

Commission, and his American opposite number Sam Reber. Harold Caccia asked if he could have a bath. General Freyberg, in the South, sent a car for his son. Prince Filippo Doria became Mayor of Rome. Princess Pallavicini found that Dollmann had been occupying a house she owned at Porta Latina.

The Duchess of Sermoneta got her silver tea set out of the bank, in readiness for British friends in the Brigade of Guards. The Black Panther was put in Regina Coeli but escaped and hitch-hiked to Naples in an American jeep. Windows of shops owned by Fascists were stoned and smashed. Sevareid saw terrified owners running and stumbling, blood down their faces. The rat-hunt was on.

The Allied S-Force managed to round up forty-seven German agents and seventeen radio sets. According to Osborne, the Communist headquarters was also 'raided', to bring the Communists 'into line' about disbanding their forces. Princes Francesco Ruspoli, Pignatelli, Massimo and Tasca di Cutò and Duke Andrea Caraffa were among those arrested and sent to a high-class detention centre near Salerno at Padula, eventually to house eighteen hundred people. The Excelsior Hotel that night was like a roaring brothel.

It was quieter up on the Janiculum where Lieutenant Harold Bond was quartered with the headquarters of the 36th Division in a 'Renaissance mansion', perhaps Palazzo Corsini where Queen Christina had lived, close to the Vascello so gloriously defended in June 1848 by Garibaldi. Among flowering hedges, pools and cypresses he looked down upon that superb and famous view of Rome. Lights came on below and he heard laughter. Rome was being rejuvenated — as she had been so many times before.

At Ravello the king of Italy made one last attempt to assert himself, demanding that he should be allowed to go to Rome where he would hand over his powers to his son, Crown Prince Umberto. Then the Action Party representatives in the Salerno government began saying that anyway they now considered Umberto unacceptable, partly because of an indiscreet interview he had given to *The Times* a month before. 'Always that brainless Action Party,' wrote Benedetto Croce crossly in his diary. 'Are we to send everything sky-high?' It was absurd to do this at the very last minute.

However, General Mason-MacFarlane, as head of the Allied Control Commission, called on the king and got him to transfer his powers forthwith to Umberto, who now became *Luogotenente* or Lieutenant-General of the Realm. The king also said that he would now completely disappear from the political scene. Badoglio handed in his resignation.

On 8 June the *Luogotenente* flew to Rome, as did Badoglio, Sforza,

Croce, Togliatti and other politicians from the South. Badoglio had already said that he did not wish to take part in any new government, negotiations for which were conducted under the auspices of Mason-MacFarlane but without reference to the Allied Combined Chiefs of Staff. So Bonomi was elected Prime Minister. This *fait accompli* aroused Churchill's utmost ire: 'I am surprised and shocked about Badoglio being replaced by this wretched old Bonomi [the same age as himself]. We have lost the only competent Italian with whom we could deal.' Churchill also told Roosevelt that the change was a disaster; he had thought Badoglio would 'go on' until 'we could bring the democratic North in'. A similar telegram about these 'non-elected come-backs' was sent to Stalin. The situation was further complicated by 'Mason-Mac' tactlessly telling Bonomi without authority that the Allies would not tolerate Sforza as Foreign Minister.

Osborne saw Sforza, Croce and others and thought them 'far too old to form a Ministry'. For their part the politicians from the South, as Croce said, felt that they were being received coldly and with diffidence by the Rome CLN, 'as though we had travelled away from the straight road of which they alone possessed the key and knew the direction'. In the end, Croce, Sforza, Togliatti, Saragat for the Socialists, and De Gasperi for the Christian Democrats, were made ministers without portfolio and Bonomi took on foreign affairs himself. In the end, too, Churchill had to calm himself, especially as the Bonomi government undertook to accept all obligations entered into by Badoglio.

On 6 June Bogomolov, the Russian representative on the Allied Commission, asked to see the Pope. According to his American counterpart, Robert Murphy, the Pope said: 'That can wait. I want deeds not words. Where are the churches, where are the priests in the Soviet Union?'

On 7 June British troops began to appear in Rome, and bagpipes were played in Piazza Venezia. On that same day the Pope consented to meet the Allied pressmen. No black veils or black dresses now for the ladies; Osborne heard that a woman correspondent went to the audience in pants and a forage cap. 'Photographers were incessantly interrupting His Holiness with flashlight effects and cries of "Hold it Pope" and "Attaboy".' He added: 'H.H. has suffered greatly by his visit to the US and is poisoned by the Hollywood publicity bug. But you can't do that if you are Pope without hopelessly cheapening and vulgarizing your Office. It makes me sick when I think of Pius XI. You can't compensate for ... well, never mind. Better not said.'

Denis Johnston saw a correspondent called Yehudi first in line to receive rosary beads and blessings. Then this Yehudi dashed to the end of the queue and started again, to receive yet another string. As he was about to try once more, a colleague said: 'What's the idea, Yehudi? You're not one of the Faithful, surely?' To which Yehudi replied: 'These are good. You can lay any chambermaid in Montreal with one of these.' Attaboy!

About this time Evelina Weiss, an Austrian, was executed for high treason by a German firing-squad at Orbetello, ninety miles north of Rome. She had been an interpreter for Kappler at Via Tasso, and it had only just been discovered that she had been passing on lists of suspects, including Jews.

She had been working in collusion with Donato Carretta, director of Regina Coeli. Carretta had also saved many lives and had connections with the CLN throughout the Occupation. He was the chief witness at the trial of the police chief Pietro Caruso. Spotted in the hall of the Palazzo di Giustizia by a crowd screaming for Caruso's blood, he was immediately identified in the minds of widows and mothers of men who had died or had suffered under the *Nazifascisti* as the personification of official collaboration with the Germans. He was thereupon seized, as if by maenads, beaten and trampled on, the numerous police hardly attempting to intervene. Next he was dragged half-naked in front of a tram, the driver of which refused to run over him. So he was thrown into the Tiber and youths bashed him with oars until he died. His body, followed by at least ten thousand people, was hauled by the legs to Regina Coeli and hung by the head from the bars of a window.

Oh, Tiber! Father Tiber! Friends, Romans, countrymen.

Celeste Di Porto was more fortunate. She operated as a prostitute in Naples until May 1945, when she was visited by three clients who were Roman Jews. She was arrested, and in 1947 sentenced to twelve years' imprisonment. Not long afterwards she was released in order to become a nun, but after a year was dismissed from her convent. Foolishly she returned to Rome, where she was nearly lynched after a chase. In her fifties, she is believed to be still working as a prostitute in Milan.

June was the month in which partisan activity began to be a real menace to the German army. As Kesselring was to say at his trial, an irregular battle of unleashed passions was about to begin. The attitude of his troops, withdrawing northwards in that Italian summer, and strafed continually even at nights under the bright moon, turned at times to fury when confronted by ambushes or fired at suddenly from houses. That fury was reciprocated.

At San Polo outside Arezzo partisans were beaten and shot. The regimental commander of the 94th Infantry Division decided to blow up their graves so that no trace of maltreatment would be discovered. On 6 July women and children died at San Giustino di Valdarno when houses used as strongpoints were blasted by LXXVI Panzer Corps. Far worse was to happen, especially above Carrara and in the mountains south of Bologna. On 20 August at San Terenzo-Bandine a hundred and five people were shot, not more than seven being adult males, and mostly with hands tied behind their backs with barbed wire, after seventeen SS had been killed by partisans. Hundreds were massacred in the region of Monte Sole and Marzabotto where the Stella Rossa band, one thousand strong, was operating with the support of SOE.

These were among the extreme cases. Kesselring had to form special units to combat the partisans. 'Unless one intended to commit suicide,' he said, 'guerrilla warfare required a complete moral readjustment which in itself concealed dangers. These could, however, be avoided only by committing well-disciplined troops under a rigid command.' He tried to take precautions against 'unreasonable measures' by individual commanders. But some human beings he found were corruptible.

'My soldiers,' he also said, 'were ambushed; they were hunted; they were burned – the wounded soldiers in the Red Cross ambulances were burned; their bodies were nailed to window frames, their eyes struck out, their noses and ears were cut off, also their sexual organs; they were put into barrels which were filled with water and afterwards machine-gunned, and, last but not least, in Pisa as a sign of gratitude that we supplied the children with milk, the wells were poisoned.'

Blow, bugle, blow on Monte Sole. Set the wild echoes flying about the Leaning Tower. Blow, bugle ...

The war was by no means over. At least Rome had been spared.

At Cuneo in Piemonte, after the war, a marble slab was erected with a long inscription written by the well-known jurist Piero Calamandrei, rector of Florence University, and addressed to 'Comrade Kesselring'. Free men, Calamandrei's inscription ended, would gather in dignity rather than in hatred 'to redeem the shame and terror' of Kesselring's world.

The trial of Field-Marshal Albert Kesselring by a British military tribunal in Venice began in February 1947 and lasted over three months. He was charged with having been concerned in the Ardeatine Caves massacre, and with inciting forces under his command to kill Italian civilians as reprisals between June and August 1944. A few months earlier, in a trial of only eleven days in Rome, Generals Maeltzer and Mackensen had been sentenced to death by another British court for their part in the Ardeatine Caves affair.

Maeltzer, that once 'rubicund clown', looked drawn and defeated at the trial. A Jesuit priest, German, testified to Maeltzer's deep religious convictions and 'outspoken admiration for Pope Pius XII'. Mackensen, on hearing that he was to be tried, is reported to have said: 'Thank God my father is not alive.' He also said to Colonel Tomlin, the British commander of the Rome area, who had visited him in his cell, 'If I am to be shot, will you please record my request that I do not wish to be blindfolded.' And Kesselring said at that trial: 'If General von Mackensen is found guilty, then I am guilty too.'

Kesselring's dignity at his own trial greatly impressed many onlookers, though on occasions he lost his temper because he felt he was not being treated in accordance with his rank. He was found guilty and sentenced to be shot. But there were those, like one of the witnesses, Colonel Scotland, who thought the trial had been 'tortuous, ill-informed and rambling' and were appalled by the verdict. In particular they considered that the court had seemed unable to grasp the fact that Kesselring's military authority in Italy had been independent and separate from the Gestapo-SD. At least nobody could deny that he had been one of the most brilliant strategists of the war, on either side. As a member of the court admitted later: 'He was a soldier's soldier through and through.' Kesselring certainly did not look like an ogre.

Churchill, no longer Prime Minister, cabled Alexander, who was by then Governor-General in Canada: 'Am concerned about Kesselring's death sentence, and propose to raise question in Parliament.' Alexander cabled back that he too was concerned and asked Churchill what he suggested. Churchill said that he should make his views known to Attlee, so Alexander cabled to the Prime Minister: 'I am unhappy about Kesselring's sentence. I hope it will be commuted. Personally, as his old opponent on the battlefield, I have no complaint against him. Kesselring and his soldiers fought hard and clean.'

Kappler was sentenced in July 1948, not only because of the Ardeatine Caves but also because in September 1943 he had extorted the fifty kilograms of gold in place of two hundred Roman Jews who would otherwise have been deported to Germany. By a complication in Italian law he could not be sentenced to death. Inevitably, therefore, and as a result of Alexander's intervention, the sentences on Kesselring, Maeltzer and Mackensen came to be commuted to imprisonment of twenty years each. Maeltzer died in prison, but Kesselring and Mackensen were released in 1952. Kesselring died in 1960 and Mackensen in 1969.

In the mid-1970s it was diagnosed that Kappler had cancer, so he was transferred to Rome for treatment. In 1977 his wife smuggled him out of hospital and took him to Germany, where he died the following year.

After the fall of Florence in August 1944 an Italian priest asked the Irish

Abbot of San Clemente in Rome, Father Dowdall, to apply to a Father Cahill, who was liaison officer between the American Army and the Vatican, for a permit to go up there on business. Father Cahill eventually agreed, and scrawled on a piece of paper 'Give this guy a break', just signing it 'Cahill'. The priest was worried and asked the Abbot what 'guy' and 'break' meant. It was explained that the former was American for gentleman or nobleman, and that 'break' meant removing a barrier. Strange to say, two months later the priest returned happily to San Clemente in order to thank the Abbot, and to say that whenever he had shown this paper to a soldier or guard he had been let through at once.

The task of exhuming the 335 bodies in the Ardeatine Caves had also begun by August 1944. Vera Simoni, still hoping against hope that her father had not died but had been sent to Frankfurt, nevertheless went daily to watch the work. Anything that might identify a victim was put into an envelope – a piece of paper, hair, rag – with a number corresponding to a coffin. One day she looked at the contents of envelope 44. 'It was a knife in my heart. I saw my father's denture.' That was not something which in his lifetime she normally would have seen, but she had happened once to go to the dentist to fetch her father and had then noticed the denture on a table by the chair. She did not tell her mother about it, but suggested she might come with her to look in coffin 44. 'Well it was him. We could not recognize his face, but we knew his clothes. We took the cords that had bound his feet and hands. I have them still.'

Sorrento – Castiglione Fiorentino

Whilst convalescing at Sorrento I found that Benedetto Croce's family was living in Villa Tritone, next to the Hotel Tramontano, and I soon became friendly with his four daughters. Croce himself I found rather alarming, red-faced and delicate-looking, fussed over by a retinue of females as if he were a precious fruit in cotton wool.

On 6 June I heard the news: the Second Front (Overlord) had started in Normandy, the moment we had longed for all those months. By this time I was living in the annexe of the hotel, a villa among olive groves that was in an even more wonderful position, with a view of Capri and amazingly transparent sapphire water to bathe in. All of us in the villa went wild and could hardly eat breakfast. People were whistling, singing, laughing. The Liberation of Rome had definitely now been outshone.

Later in the day I took three of the Croce daughters out in a boat. I made some probably banal remark about the peacefulness of the bay compared to what must be going on in Normandy. At which the eldest, Elena, shrieked at me: 'My goodness, do you mean you've been sitting here all the time and haven't told us that the Second Front has started? Now I know that you are an Englishman!' For the news had not penetrated Villa Tritone. So we rowed back madly to the house, and interrupted the old man, who was waiting for his summons to Rome and who, as I now see from his published diary, was in the throes of reading the manuscript of 'noteworthy essays' on history and philosophy by a young soldier.

Soon I was called to the front again, and I was delighted to be joined by Timmy Lloyd – our great hope was that it would mean that, at last, we would see Rome, if only for a few hours on our way north. But that was not to be the case. The battle for Florence was about to begin, and Alexander was apparently concentrating on the capture of Arezzo. Reinforcements were needed urgently.

6 July was my twenty-first birthday. On that day, my first back in

the line, I found myself in a shallow trench scraped out of some scree, on a mountain high above a walled town which I was told was Castiglione Fiorentino. Then I heard that at 2330 hours I would have to take out a small patrol, perhaps myself and one man only, to see whether a place known as Spandau Ridge was still occupied by the enemy or not. The ground was completely open. There was no cover, and there would be a full moon. My sergeant muttered 'Suicide!' There could be no chance of the patrol surviving if the Germans were still on that ridge.

So I was going to die. My mind was numb. I could not even think of home. The sergeant suggested I should meanwhile try to sleep and I did sleep, deeply.

I was awoken by schmeisser fire and grenades. It was a German counter-attack, and this in a sense had saved me. We saw we were about to be overrun, and I had to withdraw the platoon a hundred yards downhill.

After a while it was quiet, and I decided to find our company headquarters. I climbed up the mountain again, only to find the headquarters trenches empty. Almost at that same moment I heard mortar fire from our own lines, down in the valley, and shells came dropping down all round me. I realized immediately that the entire company must have moved out, and that now our people were shelling the positions in case the Germans had taken over.

During a lull I jumped up, and as I took my first step the whole world cracked open in a sheet of flames. There was a noise like a dinner gong in my head. My face was all sticky, and hot liquid streamed into my eyes. I knew I had been hit, and vaguely I heard German voices crying out quite near. I managed to keep walking towards the valley, my arm was limp, my thigh was stinging. I kept thinking of a man in my platoon who had been hit by a shell that morning and whom we had had to leave, to die alone. Whenever I stopped walking, I began to lose consciousness. I had to keep going. I did not want to die alone.

A long while afterwards I awoke to find myself in a field hospital near Perugia. Before the clouds of morphia enveloped me again I tried to write a reassuring letter to my parents. I also remember thinking: 'Now at last I shall see Rome.' Timmy never saw Rome, though. He was killed on the night of 26 July. Whilst on patrol he had come face to face with a figure, and had realized too late that it was a German's.

Events in 1943

14–24 Jan.:	Casablanca Conference. Principle of unconditional surrender announced.
2 Feb.:	German resistance ends in Stalingrad. Turning point of war in Russia.
13 May:	Axis forces defeated in North Africa.
10 July:	Allies land in Sicily.
19 July:	Mussolini meets Hitler. German help for Italy refused. First Allied bombing of Rome.
25 July:	Mussolini arrested. Marshal Badoglio chief of Italian government.
13 Aug.:	Second Allied bombing of Rome. Political prisoners being released in Italy.
14 Aug.:	Badoglio declares Rome an open city.
15 Aug.:	Secret discussions in Madrid about Italian collaboration with Allies.
17 Aug.:	All Sicily in Allied hands.
17–24 Aug.:	Quebec Conference. Eisenhower to maintain 'unrelenting pressure' in Italy. 1 May 1944 target date for cross-Channel invasion (Operation Overlord).
23 Aug.:	Russians advancing. Kharkov recaptured.
3 Sept.:	British Eighth Army crosses Straits of Messina unopposed. Italian Armistice signed in secret.
8 Sept.:	6.30 p.m. Eisenhower announces Armistice, though not expected by Badoglio until 12 Sept. No Allied air drops in vicinity of Rome as hoped for by Badoglio.
9 Sept.:	US Fifth Army lands at Salerno. 8th Army lands at Taranto. Royal family, Badoglio flee Rome. Fierce German reprisals against Italian garrisons in Yugoslavia, etc. Italian fleet sails to Malta. The CLN (Committee of National Liberation), anti-Badoglio coalition of left

and right parties, formed in Rome under Ivanoe Bonomi. German shells land in centre of Rome.

10 Sept.: Hitler announces 'very hard measures' against Italy, which must be a 'lesson for all'. Germans crush resistance and enter Rome. CLN goes underground. King's son-in-law, Calvi di Bergolo, military governor of Rome.

11 Sept.: Germans confirm Rome's open city status, not acknowledged by Allies.

12 Sept.: Mussolini rescued by Skorzeny and flown to Munich. Strict martial law in Rome. Curfew. Food situation deteriorating.

13–17 Sept.: British landings in Aegean Islands.

16 Sept.: Fifth and Eighth Armies link up near Salerno.

23 Sept.: Calvi di Bergolo arrested. Mussolini's Social Republic ('Government of Salò') proclaimed in North. Clandestine Military Front, pro-Badoglio, formed in Rome under Colonel Montezemolo.

26 Sept.: Colonel Kappler of SS demands 200 hostages or 50 kgs of gold from Roman Jews – paid on 28 Sept.

1 Oct.: Allies enter Naples, after four days' popular uprising.

3 Oct.: Last Germans withdraw from Sardinia and Corsica.

4 Oct.: Hitler orders stand in Italy, from Gaeta to Ortona (Bernhard and Gustav Lines).

7 Oct.: Nazi round-up of Roman Carabinieri.

9 Oct.: Man-hunts for forced labour begin in Rome.

11 Oct.: Nazi sequestration of Roman Jewish Community's library and ancient documents.

13 Oct.: Badoglio government declares war on Germany and accepted as 'co-belligerent' by Allies.

16 Oct.: Mass round-up of Roman Jews and deportations to death-camps in Germany.

18 Oct.: First Communist partisan attack on German troops in Rome.

19 Oct.: Allied Foreign Ministers meet in Moscow.

23 Oct.: Red Army breaks through on lower Dnieper.

24 Oct.: Eisenhower requests retention of landing-craft, pending plans for new amphibious landing in Italy.

1 Nov.: Germans in Crimea cut off.

2 Nov.: Fifth Army reaches River Garigliano.

5 Nov.: Vatican bombed by unknown aircraft.

5–7 Nov.: Secret Allied talks with Turks in Cairo.

6 Nov.: Hitler orders Kesselring to take over all Italian theatre. Rommel transferred to N-W Europe.

8 Nov.:	Eighth Army reaches River Sangro. Fifth Army draws up outline for landing near Rome ('Operation Shingle').
13 Nov.:	British evacuate Aegean Islands.
22–25 Nov.:	Cairo Conference: Churchill, Roosevelt. Churchill advocates taking Rome in January. British favour 'war of attrition' in Mediterranean versus American desire for strong decisive thrusts in N. France and Burma.
27 Nov.:	New Allied attack in Italy, impeded by bad weather.
28 Nov.:	Teheran Conference: Roosevelt, Stalin, Churchill. Over-
1 Dec.:	lord postponed until end May; possibly simultaneous landing in S. France ('Operation Anvil'). Winter offensive in Italy to continue, at Churchill's insistence.
2 Dec.:	German air-raid on Bari. 17 ships sunk.
4–6 Dec.:	Cairo Conference resumed: Churchill, Roosevelt. Overlord and Anvil to be supreme operations for 1944. Eisenhower to return to Britain as Overlord commander.
5 Dec.:	Fifth Army capture Monte Camino, south of Cassino.
10 Dec.:	Communist partisan bombs at Hotel Flora, German HQ in Rome. Original plan for Shingle now considered impractical. Strikes and rioting in Turin factories following Allied air-raids.
11 Dec.:	Churchill with pneumonia in Tunis.
18 Dec.:	Eisenhower to be Supreme Commander, Overlord.
21 Dec.:	Strikes and riots in N. Italian factories.
24–25 Dec.:	Churchill holds conference in Carthage for revival of Shingle.
28 Dec.:	Roosevelt cables agreement to release of 56 landing-craft.

Events in 1944: January–July

7–8 Jan.:	Churchill holds conference at Marrakech. Further landing-craft authorized. Go-ahead for Shingle.
16 Jan.:	French capture Monte Trocchio facing Cassino.
17 Jan.:	British X Corps capture Minturno.
20 Jan.:	US 36 Div. attacks across River Rapido.
22 Jan.:	Shingle: Allies land at Anzio and Nettuno. Second attempt across Rapido.
25 Jan.:	Montezemolo arrested.
27 Jan.:	German blockade of Leningrad lifted.
28 Jan.:	CLN congress in Bari.
30 Jan.:	Rangers' attack on Cisterna.
31 Jan.:	British 1st Div. at nearest point to Campoleone.
1 Feb.:	Nazis round up about 2,000 Romans in Via Nazionale.
3 Feb.:	Fascist police raid St Paul's basilica.
4 Feb.:	British pull back from Campoleone to Aprilia.
9 Feb.:	Germans capture Aprilia.
10 Feb.:	Allies bomb Castel Gandolfo: 500 casualties.
15 Feb.:	Bombing of Monte Cassino monastery.
16–17 Feb.:	Heavy Allied air-raids on Rome.
16–19 Feb.:	German Fourteenth Army all-out attack on Beachhead.
22 Feb.:	General Lucas replaced at Anzio by General Truscott.
23 Feb.:	Eisenhower and British Chiefs of Staff recommend first priority for Italian campaign; approved by CCS on 25 Feb.
1 Mar.:	Bombs drop close to Vatican, causing damage to Papal buildings.
2 Mar.:	Death of Teresa Gullace.
3 Mar.:	Allied raid on Rome: many casualties.
10 Mar.:	Gap attack on Fascist procession in Via Tomacelli.
12 Mar.:	Pope's concourse in St Peter's Square.

15 Mar.:	Allies' concentrated bombardment of Cassino town.
18 Mar.:	Germans enter Hungary.
19 Mar.:	Allied raid on Rome: many casualties.
23 Mar.:	Alexander halts attack on Cassino. Bonomi resigns as head of CLN. Gapists explode bomb in Via Rasella, killing 33 German military police.
24 Mar.:	Nazi reprisal for Via Rasella: 335 Italians executed in the Ardeatine Caves. Allied CCS agree to postpone Operation Anvil, target date 10 July.
End Mar.:	Arrival of Palmiro Togliatti ('Ercole'), head of Italian Communist party, from Moscow.
3 Apr.:	*Pravda* announces Togliatti's decree that Communists must collaborate with Badoglio and king. Execution of Padre Morosini.
10 Apr.:	Russians capture Odessa.
11 Apr.:	Russians enter Crimea. Round-up of 800 in Quadraro district of Rome.
21 Apr.:	Badoglio reconstitutes his Cabinet on all-party basis.
5 May:	Roman CLN recognizes Badoglio's government. Bonomi back as head of Rome CLN.
9 May:	Russians capture Sebastopol.
10 May:	Secret meeting between Pius XII and General Wolff of SS.
11 May:	Operation Diadem: Allied offensive against Gustav and Hitler Lines.
13 May:	French capture Monte Maio.
14 May:	Beginning of deportations of Hungarian Jews to Auschwitz.
18 May:	Poles capture Monte Cassino. US II Corps capture Formia.
23 May:	VI Corps break out of Anzio Beachhead. Canadians pierce Hitler Line.
25 May:	Fall of Cisterna. Link-up between Beachhead forces and US II Corps.
28 May:	Germans withdraw from Aprilia.
1 June:	Fifth Army enters Velletri.
4 June:	Fifth Army enters Rome.
5 June:	King Victor Emmanuel signs decree creating Prince Umberto Lieutenant-General of the Realm.
6 June:	Overlord: Allies land in Normandy.
8 June:	Badoglio resigns.
9 June:	New Italian six-party government formed in Rome under Bonomi.

13 June:	First V-1 lands in England.
14 June:	South Africans enter Orvieto.
Midsummer:	End of Japanese threat to India. Russians clear Crimea and Ukraine, attack in Finland and S. Poland.
3 July:	French enter Siena.
4 July:	Eighth Army captures Castiglione Fiorentino.
20 July:	Attempt on Hitler's life fails.

Acknowledgements, Sources and Notes

The following were among those who kindly let me interview them: Federico Alessandrini, Aileen Armellini, Luisa Arpini Collinson, Sandro Ballio, Sergeant Richard Bates, Riccardo Bauer, Captain Mieczyslaw Bialkiewicz, the late Prince Stefano Borghese, Monsignor Byrnes, Vera Cacciatore, Bruno Cagli, Antonio Call, On. Carla Capponi, Tom Carini, Sofia Cavaletti, Mrs Nathan Ciucci, Mary Corell, Baronessa Diana Corsi, Contessa Mita Corti di Cesarò, Raimondo Craveri, Piero Della Seta, Rt Hon. Viscount De L'Isle VC, KG, Lt-Colonel Sam Derry, Donald Downes, Raoul Falcioni, Mario Forti, Carlo Alberto Gentiloni Silverj, Marisa Giuliani, Rt Hon. Lord Glendevon, Renato Guttuso, Field-Marshal Lord Harding of Petherton, Colonel Dick Hewitt, Commander Gerard Holdsworth, Laura Ingrao Lombardo Radice, Major-General H. A. Lascelles, Furio Lauri, 'Lorenzo', Monsignor Loreti, Falcone Lucifero, W. McCall, A. G. Mack, Monsignor McDaid, Charles Mackintosh, Rt Hon. Harold Macmillan, Sir Henry Marking, Lily Marx, John Miller, Archbishop Andrea Di Montezemolo, Conte Umberto Morra, Marchese Michele Multedo, Malcolm Munthe, Marisa Musu, Elio Nissim, Principessa Nini Pallavicini, the late Marchesa Claudia Patrizi, Principessa Enza Pignatelli Aragona, Donna Orietta Pogson Doria Pamphilj, Joe Pollak, Brigadier Geoffrey Rimbault, Goffredo Roccas, Principe Francesco Ruspoli, Josette Scarisbrick Bruccoleri, Major-General James Scott-Elliot, Derrick Scott-Job, Vera Simoni-Tham, Major-General Naranjin Singh, the late Field-Marshal Sir Gerald Templer KG, Lady Thorneycroft, Brigadier G. E. Thubron, Colonel S. C. Tomlin, On. Antonello Trombadori, Peter Tumiati, Peter Tunnard, Monsignor Elio Venier, Fernando Vitagliano, Claudia Vinciguerra, Hon. Mrs Douglas Woodruff, Peppino Zamboni.

B. S. Cortis, late of the London Irish, also introduced me to several ex-comrades-in-arms, including Sergeants Evans and Jones, and provided me with the reminiscences of Sergeant Folkerd.

My gratitude also goes to the following for assistance in a variety of ways, including written or taped reminiscences, and in addition to those people specially mentioned in the Prologue: Zara Olivia Algardi, Martin Blumenson, Liana Burgess, Robin Campbell, R. P. M. Child, Frank D. Cooper, Nicoletta Coppini, Elena Croce, Sir Douglas Dodds-Parker, F. O. Fingel, Ernest F. Fisher Jr, Edward Fuller, Mrs Aubrey Gibbon, R. A. Gristwood, Gerold Guensberg, W. S. Hall, Mark Hamilton, Lord Hardinge of Penshurst, A. C. Lefeiste, John Letts, Vera Lombardi, George Low, Dr W. Macleod, Lady McEwen, John McNab, Barbara Milne, Peter O. Montgomery, Bill Neill-Hall, Gabriele Pantucci, Ken Peterson, Gordon M. Quarnstrom, Josephine Reid, Anthony Rhodes, Conte Alvise Savorgan di Brazzà, Charles A. Shaugnessy, Connie Sherley, Ingo Spaeing, Mark Steinitz, Dr Barbara Stimson, Scott Supplee, Ronald E. Swerczek, John E. Taylor, Nan Taylor, the Tittmann family, Alan D. Williams, Robert Wolfe, Weiner Ziesche, Steve Cox, Piero Pantucci, Antonio Sannino, Ilsa Yardley, and for the index, Tony Raven.

The diaries, etc., sent to me by Wilhelm Velten from his personal archives included those by Hackenback, Luy, Schaller, Weber, Wessell, Zumfelde, and at Cassino Austermann and Schmitz. As already recorded, Major-General Walther Gericke sent me his Anzio war diary. Georg Schmitz also sent me his *Dokumentation Fotos-Berichte* for the International Peace Meeting at Cassino in 1974; his story of the Cassino bombing appeared in *Fallschirmjaeger Fallschirmspringer* (1971). Joachim Liebschner also obtained articles by Gericke (1954), Hermann (1959) and Hoege (1965) from *Der Deutsche Fallschirmjaeger*, and by Oehler (1962) from *Alte Kameraden*.

For permission to quote from Sir D'Arcy Osborne's diary I am grateful to Robin Campbell; from Nick Mansell's diary to the executor of Ben Smith; from Tina and Delia Whitaker's diaries to Tony Whitaker; from Mother Mary St Luke's diary to Mrs Daniel M. McKeon and Robert L. Hoguet; from his own diary to Harold H. Tittmann 3rd.

Many articles on Roman clergy during the war have been published by Monsignor Venier in *Rivista Diocesana di Roma*. The articles on Jews from the Pacifici archives mostly appeared in *Il Giornale d'Italia* (1945), *L'Espresso* (April 1960) and *Shalom* (various). Gianni Bisiac's TV Documentary film *Testimoni Oculari* was produced for RAI, Rome, in 1979.

I am greatly indebted to the staff of ANPI (*Associazione Nazionale Partigiani Italiani*), Rome, for guiding me to many articles and books concerning the Resistance, and similarly to the staff of the Imperial War Museum library for showing me articles on Anzio and Cassino in various

British regimental magazines and histories, in particular *The London Scottish Regimental Gazette, The Magazine of the Royal Ulster Rifles, The KSLI Journal, The Reconnaissance Journal,* as well as the Tuker and Royle MSS, and a microfilm of Corporal R. H. Turner's diary (not quoted).

The transcripts I received from Carlisle Barracks, Pa., in addition to General Lucas' diary and the Clark interviews with Mathews and Rittgers, were interviews with Charlstrom, Howze, Norris, Yarborough and some others not quoted in this book. Peter Tompkins generously sent me copies of many of his secret radio messages and other documents.

In the following sources listed chapter by chapter I have included books that I consider to be essential as background reading. I have assumed, after a book has been first mentioned, that in subsequent chapters any further reference to it will be self-evident to the reader.

JANUARY

Rome
The main files at the Public Record Office, Kew, that I have used as a basis of research in all the chapters on Rome and the Vatican are FO371/37254–5, 37334, 43869–77, 44213–27, 50084; PREM3/243–9; WO16/3926,3941,4038. Files that concern escaped POWs include FO381/87–9, FO916/693 and WO204/1012 (Report on the Rome Organization). The FO898 files deal with underground propaganda, and WO204/943 with 'S' Force. Vatican papers on '*Victimes de la Guerre*', Jan. 1944–July 1945, were published in 1980: *Actes et Documents du Saint Siège relatifs à la Seconde Guerre Mondiale,* vol. 10, edited by Pierre Blet, Robert A. Graham, Angelo Martini, Burkhardt Schneider; vol. 9, dealing with 1943, was published in 1975.

Two Italian histories of Rome during the German occupation that I have found essential are *La resistenza in Roma* in 2 volumes by Renato Perrone Capano (Naples 1963) and *Storia della resistenza romana* by Enzo Piscitelli (Rome 1965). *Storia dell'Italia partigiana* by Giorgio Bocca was also a help. *The Story of the Italian Resistance* by Roberto Battaglia (London 1956) is useful but brief on Rome. Paolo Monelli's *Roma 1943* (Pescara 1959) carries the story into 1944. Robert Katz's *Black Sabbath* (London 1969) is regarded as the standard work on the October 1943 deportation of Roman Jews. Dan Kurzman's *The Race for Rome* (New York 1975) is a popular account of the period, political and military, with much original research.

Books of published memoirs, diaries, etc., have been supplemented by personal interviews and other documents. Mother Mary St Luke's diary was published as *Inside Rome with the Germans* by Jane Scrivener

(New York 1954). Vittoria Sermoneta's memoirs were entitled *Sparkle Distant Worlds* (London 1947). Eugen Dollmann is the author of *Roma Nazista* (Milan 1949), *Call me Coward* (London 1956) and *The Interpreter* (London 1967). For Ivanoe Bonomi's diary *Diario di un anno* (Milan 1947). Sam Derry's adventures are recounted in his *Rome Escape Line* (London 1960), Peter Tompkins' in *A Spy in Rome* (London 1962); further exploits of the OSS appear in the *War Report of the Strategic Services* (Washington 1949), R. Harris Smith's *OSS* (Berkeley 1972) and Anthony Cave Brown's *The Secret War Report of the OSS* (New York 1976). In addition, there are many OSS files available at the Modern Military Branch, Military Archives Division, Washington DC. According-ing to Harris Smith, on Christmas Eve 1943 SOE was ordered not to have any direct dealings with the Roman underground, but this has yet to be confirmed. Ernst von Weizsaecker's *Memoirs* were published in London in 1951. *Scarlet Pimpernel of the Vatican* by J. P. Gallagher (London 1967) is a biography of Monsignor O'Flaherty. Before the arrival of Major Derry in Rome the Escape Organization had been run by a 'Council of Three': O'Flaherty, Mrs Henrietta Chevalier (Maltese) and Count Sarsfield Salazar of the Swiss Legation. A biography of Padre Benedetto has appeared as *The Incredible Mission of Father Benoît* by Fernande Leboucher (London 1970). Among the attacks on the Pope's attitude towards the Jews the best known are *The Representative* by Rolf Hochhuth (London 1964) and *Pius XII and the Third Reich* by Saul Fried-laender (New York 1966); counterblasts have appeared in the intro-duction to *Actes et Documents* vol. 10 and in books such as Anthony Rhodes' *The Vatican in the Age of the Dictators* (London 1973) and *Il Vaticano e il Nazismo* by Robert A. Graham (Rome 1975). Zolli's apologia was published as *Before the Dawn* (New York 1954) under the name of Eugenio Zolli. Weizsaecker and his aide Kessel claimed that, in the matter of Jewish deportations, they had done all they could to warn the Vatican, the Curia and the Pope against 'rash utterances'. Kessel said later that he was convinced that the Pope almost broke down under 'conflicts of conscience' while he struggled to find the right answer, and that this 'agony of spirit' was shared by Montini. In point of fact 8,000 Jews had originally been marked for elimination. The Cardinal's prompt protest to Weizsaecker, on the Pope's order, and another by Monsignor Aloys Hudal, Rector of the German Church, Santa Maria dell'Anima, to the German military commander of Rome, obviously were instrumental in alerting Berlin and Hitler to the possibility of a disastrous break with the Vatican, and the round-up of Jews was halted. In the event the Pope kept his silence, except for elliptical communiqués in *L'Osservatore Romano*.

The Whitakers also feature in my *Princes Under the Volcano* (London

1972). *From the Ashes of Disgrace* by Frank Maugeri was published in New York in 1948.

Carthage – Marrakech – Caserta

The 'Shingle' papers at the PRO are in PREM/248/1–7. Churchill's vol. 5 of his war memoirs, *Closing the Ring* (London 1952), is vital to any account of the preparations for the Anzio landings. See also John Ehrman's *Grand Strategy*, vol. 5 in the *History of the Second World War, UK Military Series* (London 1956) and Arthur Bryant's *Triumph in the West* (Alanbrooke's diaries, London 1959), Albert C. Wedemeyer's *Wedemeyer Reports!* (New York 1958), Robert E. Sherwood's *Roosevelt and Hopkins* (New York 1950), *On Active Service in Peace and War* by Henry L. Stimson and McGeorge Bundy (London 1959), *The Mediterranean Strategy in the Second World War* by Michael Howard (London 1968), and *The Struggle for the Mediterranean* by Raymond de Belot (Princeton 1951). The two important official histories of the Italian campaign up to the end of March 1944 are *Salerno to Cassino* by Martin Blumenson (*US Army in World War II*, Washington 1969) and *The Mediterranean and the Middle East* by C. J. V. Molony and others (*UK Military Series*, vol. 5, London 1973). The quotation likening Wilson to cheese and beer is from Kenneth Strong's *Intelligence at the Top* (London 1966). Clark's opinion of Alexander is from the Rittgers interview (*supra*); all remarks by Clark quoted in this book are from Rittgers unless otherwise stated.

Brindisi

The 'Abdication Issue' is covered at the PRO by FO371/43909–12, Badoglio by PREM3/24312 and Sforza by FO371/43899. Various political matters are in PREM3/241–7, 243/8, 250/3 (PREM/249/3B 'Negotiations for Surrender' is closed for 75 years!); FO371/43814, 43837–8; WO204/3833. At the Franklin D. Roosevelt Library, Hyde Park, NY, PSF Box 57 Italy 1943–5 has papers on Badoglio, Bonomi and Sforza; Box 71 has wartime Vatican correspondence. Several of these documents have been printed in *Foreign Relations of the United States, Diplomatic Papers 1944, vol. III The British Commonwealth and Europe* (Washington 1965). Harold Macmillan's characteristically urbane *The Blast of War* (London 1967) and Robert Murphy's *Diplomat among Warriors* (London 1964) are also important sources. Much original research among British and US official papers has been synthesized in David W. Ellwood's *L'alleato nemico* (Milan 1977). See also *Allied Military Administration of Italy 1943–1945* by C. R. S. Harris in the *UK Military Series* (London 1957) and Elizabeth Barker's *Churchill and Eden at War* (London 1978). The Salò government has been the subject of two major works: *The*

Brutal Friendship by F. W. Deakin (London 1962) and *Salò* by Silvio Bertoldi (Milan 1976). A vivid description of liberated Naples, including prostitution, is given in Norman Lewis' *Naples '44* (London 1978).

Anzio

The first narrative books of importance to be published on the Anzio fighting were Wynford Vaughan-Thomas' *Anzio* (London 1961) and Martin Blumenson's *Anzio: The Gamble that Failed* (London 1963). Christopher Hibbert's *Anzio: Bid for Rome* (London 1970) is an excellent summary. Peter Verney's *Anzio: An Unexpected Fury* (London 1978) retells the story from the British viewpoint, with clear maps, and is based in part on interviews with generals, etc. Two standard works are *The Anzio Beachhead* by John Bowditch 3rd (*American Forces in Action Series*, Washington 1947) and *Sicily–Salerno–Anzio* by Samuel Eliot Morison (Boston 1954). *Command Missions* by Lucian K. Truscott (New York 1954) contains Hong's story and is essential reading generally; it is strange that neither this nor Fred Sheehan's *Anzio: Epic of Bravery* (Norman, Oklahoma 1964) were published in Britain. I have quoted from *Red Shingle: US Naval Proceedings* vol. 73 no. 534 by Theodore Wyman (Washington 1947). The Silvestris' story and the finding of Angelita are recounted in the privately printed *Dove è Max (Angelita di Anzio)* by Ennio Silvestri, who also has a file of newspaper reports on Fusilier Hayes and Angelita. The many Ultra files at the PRO are in DEFE3; see also *Ultra Goes to War* by Ronald Lewin (London 1978) and *The Ultra Secret* by F. W. Winterbotham (London 1974), the latter especially for the later advance on Rome. For the campaign in general see *Fifth Army History* published by the Fifth Army Historical Section Italy 1945, *The Italian Campaign 1943–45* by G. A. Shepperd (London 1968), *From Salerno to the Alps: A History of the Fifth Army* by Chester G. Starr (Washington 1948) and *The Battle for Italy* by W. G. F. Jackson (London 1967). A theory about the name 'Angelita' instead of Angelina is that it was merely a mistake by Hayes, and that she could have been the abandoned child of shepherds down for the winter from the Abruzzi mountains. Dollmann's statement comes from *Testimoni Oculari (op cit)*.

Monte Soratte – Albano

Key books concerning the German aspect at Anzio – apart from Molony and Blumenson (*op cit*) – are *A Soldier's Story* by Albert Kesselring (London 1953), Walter Warlimont's *Inside Hitler's Headquarters* (London 1964) and Siegfried Westphal's *The German Army in the West* (London 1951). The Modern Military Branch, Military Archives, Washington DC, has invaluable German material, in particular transcripts by Kesselring and Westphal (B-270), Mackensen (C-061), Fries (D-141), Maeltzer

(D-314), Senger (C-095), and comments (C-097) by Kesselring, Senger, Vietinghoff and Warlimont on *The Drive on Rome* by Britt Bailey (R-50); see also *The Campaign in Italy* ch. 12 by Hauser (T-1a). Wilhelm Velten's history of the 65th Division is entitled *Vom Kugelbaum zur Handgranate* (Neckargemuend 1974). *Anzio-Nettuno* by Joerg Staiger (Neckargemuend 1962) is a succinct account with interesting maps.

Rome

The activities of the O'Flaherty-Derry organization are further described in *Be Not Fearful* by John Furman (London 1959). There is a story that Colin Lesslie, before the landings at Anzio, planned an escape through the German lines by hiding in a coffin. Ultimately there were 3,925 names of ex-POWs throughout Italy on Derry's list, including 185 Americans, 429 Russians and various other nationalities. *Lettere a Milano* by Giorgio Amendola (Rome 1973) is essential for the Communist background. Antonello Trombadori gives details of Gap formations and attacks in *Formazioni partigiane del PCI*, as well as an account of the role of Communist women, in *Quaderni della resistenza laziale* (Rome 1975). Until the publication of the *Actes et Documents* volumes, Alberto Giovannetti's *Roma città aperta* (Milan 1962) was regarded as a main book on the Vatican attitude towards the bombing of Rome. The ordeal of Montezemolo is described by his cousin Fulvia Ripa di Meana in *Roma clandestina* (Rome 1945) and in Gabrio Lombardi's *Montezemolo* (Rome 1972), a companion volume to Guido Stendardo's *Via Tasso* (Rome 1965). For partisan warfare in the Alban Hills see *Guerriglia nei castelli romani* by Pino Levi Cavaglione (Rome 1945) and *I partigiani sovietici nella resistenza italiana* by Mauro Galleri (Rome 1967). After her escape Princess Pallavicini was told that the Germans, bemused by the splendour of her palace, had said: 'We'll come back tomorrow and take everything away.' So for the rest of the night the servants were busy removing the remainder of the pictures and the best furniture to safety. A price of ten million *lire* was put on the princess' head.

Anzio

For a full account of the disastrous Rapido crossing on 20 January see Martin Blumenson's *Bloody River* (London 1970), and for an examination of Lucas' predicament see Blumenson's contribution in Kent Roberts Greenfield's *Command Decisions* (London 1969). The following have many vivid stories of exploits in battle, some quoted or referred to by me: Nigel Nicolson's *The Grenadier Guards in the War 1939–1945* vol. 2 (Aldershot 1949), David Erskine's *The Scots Guards 1919–1955* (London 1956), D. J. L. FitzGerald's *History of the Irish Guards in the Second World War* (Aldershot 1949). Nigel Nicolson is also the author of *Alex* (London

1973); see also Alexander's autobiography, edited by John North, *The Alexander Memoirs* (London 1962) and *Alexander of Tunis as Military Commander* by W. G. F. Jackson (London 1971). The Rangers' stories are told in James J. Altieri's *The Spearheaders* (Indianapolis 1960). Robert H. Adleman and George Walton are the authors of the racy history of the 1st Special Service Force, *The Devil's Brigade* (Philadelphia 1966), to which I am indebted for various anecdotes about Forcemen throughout this book. The SOE group's sad experience at Anzio is chronicled in Malcolm Munthe's *Sweet is War* (London 1954), Max Salvadori's *The Labour and the Wounds* (London 1958) and Alberto Tarchiani's *Il mio diario di Anzio* (Milan 1947). General Ernie Harmon's autobiography is entitled *Combat Commander* (Englewood Cliffs 1970). The plight of civilian refugees near Anzio is well illustrated in *I giorni della guerra in provincia di Littoria* by Pier Giacomo Sottoriva (Latina 1974). The description of Harmon was given to me verbally by Sir Gerald Templer.

FEBRUARY

Rome

Moravia's telephone call appears in his Foreword to *16 ottobre 1943: otto ebrei* by Giacomo Debenedetti (Milan 1959). Other books concerning Roman Jews include *La comunità di Roma sotto l'incubo della Svastica* by Michael Tagliacozzo (Milan 1963) and *Mussolini and the Jews* by Meir Michaelis (Oxford 1978). Kappler had demanded that the fifty kilograms of gold should be handed over within thirty-six hours. Zolli had received the Pope's promise of a loan of fifteen kilograms, but this turned out to be unnecessary. Immediately after the payment had been made in full, the Gestapo raided the Synagogue, a preliminary to the seizure of books, manuscripts, etc. General Raffaele Cadorna was one of those sheltered by Padre Barbieri (*La riscossa*, Milan 1948). Some other source books on the Occupation of Rome include *La prigionia di Roma* by Carlo Trabucco (Rome 1945), *Roma sotto il terrore* by A. Troisio (Rome 1944), *Rome under the Terror* by M. de Wyss (London 1945), *Occasione mancate* by Jo Di Benigno (Rome 1945), *Caccia all'Uomo* by Luciana Morpurgo (Rome 1946), *Italy Speaks* by Barbara Carter (London 1947), *Il sole è sorto a Roma* by Lorenzo D'Agostini and Roberto Forti (Rome 1965), *Quegli anni* by Claudia Patrizi (Vicenza 1973), and an escape story *Single to Rome* by E. Garrad-Cole (London 1955). Eitel Moellhausen's memoirs were published as *La carta perdente* (Rome 1948). Weizsaecker was attacked by Sir Lewis Namier in *In the Nazi Era* (London 1952). Kessel's reference to Hitler like a trapped beast, etc., comes from *Der Papst und die Juden* in *Die Welt* 6 April 1962. On the subject of Pius XII's supposed bias in favour of the German people, it is worth recording that D'Arcy Osborne in his diary of 28 December 1940 said that the Pope had expressed to him his 'unstinted admiration for British resistance, which he said was almost superhuman'.

Princess Doria had refused to be one of the 'Mothers of Italy' (in Mussolini's words) who gave up their wedding rings for the Cause, the invasion of Abyssinia. On the great day the people had lined up to drop their rings into an urn on the Victor Emmanuel monument. It was noticed that Palazzo Doria was the only building in the Corso without a flag; a mob broke in and came up the staircase, six abreast. At the top they were met by the princess, who had been making scones and was in an apron covered with flour. 'The prince is out,' she said. Assuming she was the cook, they merely smashed up some furniture, hung out their own flag and went away.

Cassino

For a general history of Cassino see *Cassino dall'ottocento al novecento* (Rome 1977), and of the monastery *Monte Cassino: la vita, l'irradazione* by Tomaso Leccisotti (Montecassino 1971). The bitter monks' booklet is entitled *The Bombardment of Monte Cassino* by Herbert Bloch (Montecassino 1976, originally printed in *Benedictina* XX, in time for the International Peace Meeting at Cassino in 1974). Tancredi Grossi's *Il calvario di Cassino* was published at Cassino in 1946 and reissued in 1977. A famous account of the Cassino battles is Fred Majdalany's *Cassino: Portrait of a Battle* (London 1957). *Incontro a Cassino* edited by Lilya A. Alecchi (Rome 1970) contains many useful articles by different nationalities. Rudolf Boehmler's *Monte Cassino* (London 1964) and Frido von Senger und Etterlin's *Neither Fear nor Hope* (London 1960) are chief source-books for anyone writing about the German side; the description of the bombed Loggia is from Boehmler. The destruction of Naples university is described in *L'Università di Napoli incendiata dai tedeschi* (Naples 1944). Harold Nicolson's remark comes from his *Letters and Diaries* (London 1968). Harold L. Bond is the author of *Return to Cassino* (London 1964). The histories of *Fourth Indian Division* (London 1949) and *The 9th Gurkha Rifles* (London 1953) are by G. R. Stevens; see also *The Campaign in Italy 1943–1945* by Dharm Pal (New Delhi 1960). A biography of Freyberg, *General Lord Freyberg V.C.*, was written by Peter Singleton-Gates (London 1963). N. C. Phillips is the author of *Sangro to Cassino: New Zealand in the Second World War* (Wellington 1957), another essential source-book. The extract from Kippenberger's diary is in *Infantry Brigadier* by Howard Kippenberger (London 1961). The novel by Sven Hassel is entitled *Monte Cassino* (London 1969). Freyberg's 'key words' to Gruenther on the bombing are in a memo signed 'Gruenther' in *Monte Cassino bombing, Feb 12 1944, Fifth Army Rpt of Monte Cassino bombing* (*cf.* Blumenson, *Salerno to Cassino*).

Anzio – Carroceto, Anzio – Fischfang

For background to these chapters, in addition to other works cited above, see *Staff Officer with the Fifth Army* by Edmund F. Ball (New York 1958) and *La battaglia di Anzio* by T. R. Fehrenbach (Milan 1962). *The History of the Third Infantry Division* by Donald G. Taggart (Washington 1947), *The Fighting Forty-Fifth* by Leo V. Bishop (Baton Rouge 1946) and *The Battle History of the 1st Armored Division* by George F. Howe (Washington 1954) are all important sources whenever I refer to these divisions – here the description of the 157th at the caves comes from Bishop; and see *The Caves of Anzio* by Edward A. Raymond in the *US Field Artillery Journal* vol. 34 no. 12, December 1944. The Mueller, Johnston, Biggars stories can be found in Sheehan's *Anzio* (*op cit*). Besides British regimental histories already mentioned, the following have been used for reference in particular: *History of the 2/7th Bn. The Queen's Royal Regiment 1939–1946* by Roy E. Bullen (Exeter 1958), *The Loyal Regiment* by C. G. T. Dean (Preston 1955), *6th Gordons 1939–1945* (Aberdeen 1946), *The Story of the 2nd Battalion the Sherwood Foresters* by John U. A. Masters (Aldershot 1946), *The London Irish at War* (Chelsea n.d.). J. A. Rose's account, *With a Casualty Clearing Station at Anzio*, was republished in *The KSLI Journal* vol. 16 from *Blackwood's Magazine* (1946).

MARCH

Rome

There is a fascinating but grim feature on the German occupation of Rome, with reproductions of original 1944 sketches by R. Pullini, in the *Time-Life* book *The Italian Campaign* by Robert Wallace (Alexandria Va. 1978), which also includes many outstanding photographs of battles, etc., throughout the campaign. A version of the Florentine lady story appears in *Rumour and Reflection* by Bernard Berenson (London 1962).

Cassino – Anzio

For the struggle over 'Anvil' see Maurice Matloff's chapter in *Command Decisions*, ed. Greenfield (*op cit*). *The British Fifth Division 1939–1945* by George Aris and C. S. Dartnell was published in London in 1959, and *The Story of the Green Howards* by W. A. T. Synge was published at Richmond, Yorks., in 1952.

Cassino

Christopher Buckley's *Road to Rome* and Denis Johnston's *Nine Rivers from Jordan*, both exceptional books, were published in 1945 and 1953 respectively. *La Campagne d'Italie* by Alphonse Juin was published in Paris in 1952. The quotation from a German machine-gunner's letter comes from Majdalany's *Cassino* (*op cit*).

Rome

The most detailed though controversial book on Via Rasella and the Ardeatine Caves is Robert Katz's *Death in Rome* (New York 1967). It was filmed by Carlo Ponti and Georges Cosmatos, with Richard Burton as Kappler and Marcello Mastroianni as a priest who sacrifices himself in the Caves. Katz, Ponti and Cosmatos were sued by Pius XII's niece and sister for defaming the memory of the late Pontiff. They lost the case but appealed; the result was inconclusive – 'History will judge'. However the Supreme Court (1981) has ordered the case to be reopened. The closing speeches of counsels for defence and opposition in the second trial were published in *Gli oratori del giorno* (Rome 1976). The revised version of Attilio Ascarelli's *Le Fosse Ardeatine* (Bologna 1965) gives many original documentary sources verbatim, including the full text of the sentence on Kappler. Under the thirty years' rule the trials of Kesselring, Maeltzer and Mackensen are now available at the PRO, and I have had recourse to these, especially when quoting Kesselring's views on partisans; Kesselring's trial is in WO366–77, Maeltzer and Mackensen in WO235/438–9. The publication of *Actes et Documents* vol. 10 (*op cit*) has also been important as giving the Vatican's stance, though revealing a lack of documentary evidence in its archives; vol. 9 (1975) is also useful in relation to the Pope's attitude towards the persecution of Jews in general in 1943. Also in the archives there is a note by Montini, dated 19–20 March, briefly recording the visit by Marchesa Ripa di Meana on behalf of Montezemolo, and there is another about it on 25 March. An undated comment by Montini runs: 'Suspend; it seems he has been killed as a result of the events at Via Rasella.' Dollmann's reaction to Via Rasella comes from his interview in *Testimoni Oculari* (*op cit*). See also *Poi ce ne andammo insieme* by Guglielmo Morandi (Rome 1944), and *Cattolici nella resistenza romana* by Giuseppe Intersimone (Rome 1976); and for Kessel telephoning the Vatican *The Race for Rome* (*op cit*), and for Capponi and Bentivegna reacting to news of the reprisals *Death in Rome* (*op cit*). Somewhat ironically, in view of the German communiqué about the 'open city', on 25 March a secret appreciation was issued at the Allied headquarters at Caserta by a Colonel Lundquist of G.3 Plans. He had decided that the part of Rome west of the Tiber, including the

Vatican, was 'admirably suited for defence'. 'The Hun,' he said, 'may put us in the position of having to shoot or bomb him out of Vatican City ... If the enemy chooses to fight in the city we may conclude that it will take considerable time to oust him.'

APRIL – JUNE

Anzio

The other towns in Eaker's third group were Modena, Pisa, Padua, Pistoia, Brescia, Cremona, Verona, Cortona, Piacenza, Lucca, Bologna, Arezzo, Ferrara, Vicenza, Prato, Viterbo, Ancona, Bracciano, Frascati and Rimini. The Anzio Derby, along with other 'Quiet Period' anecdotes not mentioned here, appears in *Combat Boots* by Bill Harr (New York 1952). Colonel Spears' story comes from *Anzio* (*op cit*) by Sheehan, who adds that on passing through Normandy Spears met his old friend Patton, who kindly set up another 'sniping stint' for him. For Clark's confrontation with Alexander: *Calculated Risk* and Rittgers interview (*op cit*). I cannot resist a footnote about Prince Bassiano, who was the brother-in-law of Vittoria Sermoneta and husband of Marguerite Caetani, to become the celebrated editor of the literary magazine *Botteghe Oscure*. He was the owner of an original manuscript of *The Divine Comedy*. When he had originally left Rome he had hidden it among his shirts. On his return it had gone, and it was only rediscovered after his death. His heirs assumed that a servant had stolen it for selling to the Germans but had been unable to find a buyer.

Rome

For more about Radio Bari and Radio Londra see papers by Ian Greenlees and Uberto Limantini printed in the *Atti di Convegno* of the Bagni di Lucca Congress for 1972, *Inghilterra e Italia nel '900* (Florence 1973). This book and its sequel on the Congress of 1975, *Italia e Gran Bretagna nella Lotta di Liberazione* (Florence 1977) contain other useful papers on Fascism, PWB, MMIA and the PWB Resistance. See also *Radio Londra 1940–1945* vol. 2 by Maura Piccialuti Caprioli (Rome 1976). In addition to 'Colonello Buonasera' (Col. Stevens) popular features on Radio London were commentaries by Paolo Treves, 'Candidus' (John Marus) and *L'Uomo Qualunque* (Elio Nissim). George Weidenfeld, future publisher, did a regular comic turn as an obtuse Austrian businessman. The main organizers of Radio London were John Shepley, Tony Lawrence and Stuart Hood. *La Resistenze e gli Alleati* by Pietro Secchia and Filippo Frassati (Milan 1962) mostly covers the Resistance in the North, but caused some official consternation at the time by publishing in English the whole text of a secret document, *Report on No. 1 Special Force Activities during April 1945*. Vincenzo Florio's story is told in *Quattro giorni a Via Tasso* (Palermo 1947). There is more about Carini in *Il violino della Quinta Armata* by Gino de Sanctis (Milan 1961). The Allied literature on missions to partisans in the North is still at present sparse, except for general histories such as *Britain and the European Resistance* by David Stafford (Oxford 1980). The Centro Studi Formazioni Autonome di Piemonte has, however, produced an excellent and detailed work, *Le missioni alleate e le formazioni dei partigiani autonomi nella resistenza piemontese* (Cuneo 1980).

Cassino – Anzio

In the *US Army in World War II* series Ernest J. Fisher Jr takes over from Martin Blumenson with *Cassino to the Alps* (Washington 1977), again an important source book for facts and anecdotes. The course of Operation Diadem is followed in *Alexander's Generals* (London 1979) and *The Battle for Rome* by W. G. F. Jackson (London 1969). See also *Les Forces Alliés en Italie* by Marcel Carpentier (Paris 1949) and *Cassino* by Jacques Mordal (Paris 1952). General Anders' own book is entitled *An Army in Exile* (London 1949). Expanded versions of Polish accounts given by me, along with many other first-hand stories, are in *Trzecia Dywizja Strzelcow Karpackich 1942–1947* edited by Mieczslaw Mlotek (London 1978). *Monte Cassino* by Charles Connell (London 1963) is told largely from the Polish point of view, as in *Cassino – Anatomy of a Battle* by Janusz Piekalkiewicz (London 1980). Will Lang's account of the French near Esperia comes from the *Time-Life* book *The Italian Campaign* (*op cit*). To Allied troops all Moroccans were colloquially known as Goums, though the word Goum meant in fact the equivalent of a company in the 2nd Moroccan Division.

'Stalingrad' – Valmontone, 'Stalingrad' – Rome

In *Command Decisions* (*op cit*) the essay on *General Clark's Decision to Drive on Rome* is by Sidney T. Mathews, who in his 1948 interview recorded Clark's remark about an 'easy victory' for the Eighth Army. 'Throwing the British a rope' is from the Rittgers interview. *The Canadians in Italy 1943–1945* by G. W. L. Nicholson (Ottawa 1957) is also useful as a detailed account of the campaign. For Walker and Clark, Walker and Keyes, Clark's mother, see *Rome Fell Today* by Robert H. Adleman and George Walton (Boston 1968), for 1st SSF again *The Devil's Brigade* (*op cit*), for some individual 3rd Division exploits again *The History of the Third Infantry Division* (*op cit*). Eric Sevareid's fine book is *Not So Wild A Dream* (New York 1962); Harold L. Bond's is *Return to Cassino* (London 1964). See also for this period *But for the Grace of*

God by J. Patrick Carroll-Abbing (New York 1965). Filippo Caruso is the author of *L'arma dei carabinieri in Roma durante l'occupazione tedesca* (Rome 1949).

Campidoglio – St Peter's, Sorrento

For General Stack at St Peter's see Bond's *Return to Cassino* (*op cit*), and for Mrs Kiernan at the railway station Johnston's *Nine Rivers from Jordan* (*op cit*). In *Calculated Risk* Clark says that the priest (O'Flaherty) he encountered at St Peter's was 'from Detroit'. Michael Stern has an account of the entry into Rome in *An American in Rome* (New York 1964). Father Raymund M. Dowdall OP, then Abbot of San Clemente, is the author of *Memories of Italy* (Athlone 1972). Photographs show that the Pope gave souvenir cards not rosaries (*pace* Johnston) to the war correspondents. The trial of Pietro Caruso and the lynching of Carretta are described in detail in *Processi ai fascisti* by Zara Algardi (Florence 1958). The massacre on Monte Sole is the subject of *Silence on Monte Sole* by Jack Olsen (London 1968), and Colonel A. P. Scotland writes in defence of Kesselring in *The London Cage* (London 1957) and *Der Fall Kesselring* (Bonn 1952). Nigel Nicolson writes of Alexander's intervention about Kesselring's sentence in *Alex* (*op cit*). For his part, Kesselring said of the Allied troops at Anzio: 'We felt we were opposed by equals. Our enemy was of the highest quality.' There is an unsubstantiated but feasible rumour that after the Allied entry into Rome O'Flaherty helped Germans in hiding. O'Flaherty's helper on Vatican Radio, Father Owen Snedden, later became a bishop in New Zealand; he had been giving his food rations to the poor, so that by the liberation he weighed only seven stone. Benedetto Croce's diary was translated as *Croce, the King and the Allies* (London 1950).

Appendix

This poem was published in *Staff Officer with the Fifth Army* by Edmund F. Ball. He says that it was written by six men in the American armed forces in Italy and published in *Army Literature*. Three of the authors lost their lives in battle and three were captured and became prisoners of war – their names now unknown. As he also rightly says, the poem is far from being great poetry, just a jingle in fact, but it is extraordinarily vivid as showing the Serviceman's view of the pathos and degradation of Southern Italy – the Naples area really – during the winter of 1943–4. I do not, however, agree with all of the last lines. I was one of those who grew to love the South, in spite of the wretchedness, and am always ready to return.

Panorama of Italy

If I were an artist with nothing to do
I'd paint a picture, a composite view
Of historic Italy in which I'd show
Visions of contrasts, the high and the low.

There'd be towering mountains and deep blue sea;
Filthy brats yelling 'Caramella' at me;
High-plumed horses and colourful carts,
Two-toned tresses on bustling tarts.

I'd show Napoleonic caps, on carabinieri;
Dejected old women with too much to carry;
A dignified gentleman with a Balbo beard;
Bare-bottomed bambinos with both ends smeared.

Castle and palace, opera house too,
Hotel on a mountain, marvellous view,
Homes made of weeds, stone and mud,
People covered with scabs, scurvy and mud.

Chapels and churches, great to behold,
Each a king's ransom in glittering gold;
Poverty and want, men craving for food,
Picking thro' garbage, practically nude.

Stately cathedrals, with high-toned bells;
Ricouvre shelters, with horrible smells;
Moulding catacombs, a place for the dead,
Noisy civilians clamouring for bread.

Palatial villas with palm trees tall,
Stinking hovel, mere hole in the wall;
Tree fringed lawns, swept up by the breeze,
Goats wading in filth, up to their knees.

Revealing statues, all details complete,
A sensual lass with scars on her feet,
Big-breasted damsels, but never a bra,
Bumping against you – there should be a law.

Creeping boulevards, a spangled team,
Alleys that wind like a dope fiend's dream,
Flowers blooming on the side of a hill,
A sidewalk latrine, privacy nil.

Two-by-four shops with shelving all bare,
Gesturing merchants, arms flailing the air,
Narrow gauge sidewalks, more like a shelf,
Butt-puffing youngster scratching himself.

Lumbering carts hogging the road,
Nondescript truck, frequently towed;
Diminutive donkeys, loaded for bear,
Horse-drawn taxis seeking a fare.

Determined pedestrians courting disaster,
Walking in the gutter, where movement is faster;
Italian drivers all accident bound,
Weaving and twisting to cover the ground.

Home-made brooms, weeds tied to a stick,
Used on the street, to clean off the brick,
Bicycles and push-carts, blocking your path,
Street corner politicos needing a bath.

Barbers galore with manners mild,
Prolific women all heavy with child,
Il Duce's secret weapon, kids by the score,
Caused by his bonus, which is no more.

Arrogant wretches picking up snipes,
Miniature Fiats, various types;
Young street-singer, hand-organ tune,
Shoe shining boys, sidewalk saloon.

A beauteous maiden, a smile on her face,
With a breath of garlic, fouling the place;
Listless housewife, no shoes on her feet,
Washing and cooking out on the street.

The family wash of tattle-tale grey,
Hung from the balcony, blocking the way;
Native coffee, God! what a mixture,
Tiled bathrooms, with one extra fixture.

Families dining from one common bowl,
Next to a fish-shop, a terrible hole;
Italian zoot-suiters, flashily dressed,
Bare-footed beggars looking depressed.

Mud-smeared children, clustering about,
Filling their jars from a community spout;
A dutiful mother, with a look of despair,
Picking the lice from her small daughter's hair.

Capable craftsmen skilled at their art,
Decrepit old shacks, falling apart;
Intricate needle-work out on display,
Surrounded by filth, rot and decay.

Elegant caskets, carved out by hand,
Odorous factories, where leather is tanned;
A shoe-maker's shop, a black-market store,
Crawling with vermin, no screen on the door.

I've tried to describe the things I have seen,
Panorama of Italy, the brown and the green,
I've neglected the war scars, visible yet,
But those are things we want to forget.

I'm glad that I came, and damned anxious to go,
Give it back to the natives, I'm ready to blow.

Index

Genzano, 66, 306

Gericke, Major Walther, Battle Group Gericke, 52–3, 90, 148, 151, 152, 162, 242

German armed forces:
 Tenth Army, 51, 244–5, 281, 303, 308
 Fourteenth Army, 51, 53, 89, 289, 303, 307
 XIV Panzer Corps, 126, 308
 LXXVI Panzer Corps, 324
 1 Parachute Corps, 51, 55, 89
 Battle Groups, 52, 90
 Hermann Goering Panzer Division, 53, 54, 55, 71, 78, 90, 128, 154, 161, 282, 289, 290, 299
 65th Infantry Division, 55, 90, 91, 170–1, 195, 285, 293, 298, 307, 313
 71st Infantry Division, 90
 94th Infantry Division, 271, 323–4
 334th Infantry Division, 282
 362nd Infantry Division, 244, 284, 318
 715th Infantry Division, 284, 285, 288, 290
 26th Panzer Division, 163, 282
 3rd Panzer Grenadier Division, 90, 91, 160
 29th Panzer Grenadier Division, 51, 163, 194, 243, 276, 282, 284
 90th Panzer Grenadier Division, 51, 138, 140, 187
 1st Parachute Division, 90, 138, 187, 188, 206, 269, 274
 4th Parachute Division, 52, 90, 155, 161, 242, 285, 293, 313
 165th Artillery Regiment, 92
 145th Grenadier Regiment, 93–4, 149–150, 240
 147th Grenadier Regiment, 146, 150, 298, 300
 Infantry Lehr Regiment, 94, 145, 154, 160–1
 9th Panzer Grenadier Regiment, 171
 200th Panzer Grenadier Regiment, 52
 3rd Parachute Regiment, 188, 198, 200, 208, 270
 11th Parachute Regiment, 197
 7th Battalion zbV, 244

Gerratana, Valentino, 19, 20

Gesmundo, Professor Gioacchino, 101, 220, 257

Gestapo: 12, 16, 17, 101, 342; interrogation centre, see Tasso, Via

Gigli, Beniamino, 178, 309

Giglio, Lieutenant Maurizio ('Cervo'), 23, 60–1, 106–7, 108, 115, 218, 218–19, 230

Ginzburg, Leone, 101

Giuseppe (police spy), 253

Goebbels, Joseph Paul, 134, 137

Goering, Hermann, 51, 120, 256

Goliath (miniature tank), 94, 164

Goums, see French armed forces, Moroccan troops

Graeser, Lieutenant-General Fritz-Hubert, Battle Group Graeser, 90, 91, 92, 94, 148, 151, 152

Graziani, Marshal Rodolfo, 51, 107

Greer, Private 1st Class Lloyd C., 299–300

Gregson-Ellis, Major-General P. G. S., 194, 234

Greiner, Lieutenant-General Heinz, 244

Grossi, Tancredi, 123–4, 198

Grottaferrata, 52

Gruenther, Major-General Alfred M., 131, 291–2, 308

Gruppi di Azione Patriottica, see GAPs

Gubbins, General Sir Colin, 81

Gubbins, Captain Michael, 81, 82, 148–9

Guensberg, Private 1st Class Gerold, 282–283, 284, 317–18

Gullace, Teresa, 175–6

'Gully', The, Anzio, 146–7, 150, 154

Gurbiel, Lieutenant Casimir, 274

Gustav Line, 31, 33, 40, 51, 53, 71, 89–90, 123, 139, 266

'Gusville', Anzio, 234

Guttuso, Renato, 114

Hackenbeck, Private Heinz, 92–3

'Hangman's Hill', Cassino, see Point 435

Harding, Lieutenant-General Sir John, 131–2, 266, 303

Hargreaves, Lieutenant J. M., 70

Harmon, Major-General Ernest W., 73, 77, 157, 166–7, 234, 282, 291, 306–7, 312

Harriman, Averell, 181

Hartnell, Brigadier S. F., 142

Hassel, Sven, 138

Hauber, Captain Friedrich, Battalion Hauber, 52, 53, 91

Hauser, Major-General W.-R., 163, 221

Hayes, Fusilier Christopher, 48–9, 82–3

Healey, Major Denis, 43

Heidrich, Lieutenant-General Richard, 188, 202, 205–6

Heilman, Lieutenant Gus, 234

Heilmann, Colonel Ludwig, 188, 202, 206

READ MORE IN PIMLICO MILITARY CLASSICS

John Keegan

The Face of Battle:
A Study of Agincourt, Waterloo and the Somme

'This without any doubt is one of the half-dozen best books on warfare to appear in the English language since the end of the Second World War.' Michael Howard, *Sunday Times*

The Face of Battle is military history from the battlefield: a look at the direct experience of individuals at 'the point of maximum danger'. It examines the physical conditions of fighting, the particular emotions and behaviour generated by battle, as well as the motives that impel soldiers to stand and fight rather than run away. And in his scrupulous reassessment of three battles, John Keegan vividly conveys their reality for the participants, whether facing the arrow cloud of Agincourt, the levelled muskets of Waterloo or the steel rain of the Somme.

'In this book, which is so creative, so original, one learns as much about the nature of man as of battle.' J. H. Plumb, *New York Times Book Review*

'The most brilliant evocation of military experience in our time.' C.P. Snow

£ 10.00   0712650903

John Keegan

A History of Warfare

WINNER OF THE DUFF COOPER PRIZE

£ 9.99   0712698507

John Keegan

The Mask of Command: A Study of Generalship

'The brilliant, vivid pictures of each subject are interspersed with reflections on the relation between society and the use of force. The framework of four masks gives the author the opportunity to display not only his encyclopaedic knowledge of military history, but also his sparkling literary skill.' Field Marshal Lord Carver, *Sunday Telegraph*

The Mask of Command is about generals: who they are, what they do and how they affect the world we live in. Most studies of generalship have focused on individual character and behaviour. While these are not neglected in this remarkable book, its central argument is that, like warfare itself, generalship is a cultural enterprise, providing a key to understanding a particular era or place, as much as it is an exercise in power or military skill. Through portraits of four generals – archetypal hero Alexander the Great, anti-hero Wellington, the unheroic Ulysses S. Grant and the false heroic of Hitler – John Keegan propounds the view of heroism in warfare as inextricable linked with the political imperative of the age and place. He demonstrates how the role of the general alters with the ethos of the society that creates him and concludes that there is no place for heroism in a nuclear world. *The Mask of Command* is a companion volume to John Keegan's classic study of the individual soldier, *The Face of Battle*: together they form a masterpiece of military and human history.

'As well as being a rare military historian who can also write gracefully, John Keegan has a distinguished capacity for peering behind the conventional view of events.' Alistair Horne, *Sunday Times*

£ 8.99   1844137384

John Keegan

Six Armies in Normandy:
From D-Day to the Liberation of Paris

'An unsurpassed account of the Allied invasion of France from D-Day to the liberation of Paris. As a military historian John Keegan has the qualities of the best commanders, broad strategic grasp combined with insight into the human fibre of the battlefield, and an eye to what the lessons portend.' *Observer*

The Allied assault on Normandy beaches was an almost flawless success, but it was to take three months of bitter fighting before the German defence of Normandy finally collapsed and Paris was liberated.

In this masterly and highly individual account of that struggle, the reader is subjected to the gruelling ordeals confronted by the combatants – each encounter related from the point of view of a different nationality. In this was we learn precisely what it was like to take part in the American airborne landings, move up the Canadian beachhead under a blistering hail of fire, attack on foot across country with Scottish infantry, engage the enemy from a British tank, move into the German counter-attack at Morain, close the Falaise Pocket under Polish command and liberate Paris as a Free Frenchman.

Six Armies in Normandy transcends conventional military history while providing an intensely vivid picture of one of the Second World War's most crucial campaigns.

£ 8.99   1844137392

John Keegan

The Battle for History: Re-Fighting World War II

'John Keegan is at once the most readable and the most original of living military historians.' *New York Times Book Review*

This is the definitive history of World War II. Existing histories of the conflict have raised as many questions as they answer: Did President Roosevelt have foreknowledge of the attack on Pearl Harbor? Could the Allies have invaded France before 1944?

Here John Keegan assesses the literature that has emerged from World War II – and the controversies that have arisen from that literature. He examines general histories and biographies, accounts of individual campaigns, and studies of espionage and resistance. This is the story of the ways in which the War has been refought by two generations of its chroniclers, as told by one of the greatest of them all.

'This slim volume contains great erudition and a fund of commonsense.' *The Times*

'An invaluable review of the literature and the continuing arguments...Anyone curious about the War needs to read Mr Keegan.' *Spectator*

£10.00   0712673601

John Keegan

Warpaths:
Travels of a Military history in North America

'He writes better on war than anyone else in the English-speaking world...A delight.' *Sunday Telegraph*

Military history and geography explain each other in North America as nowhere else in the world. Award-winning historian John Keegan explores their relationship and examines the battles fought over three centuries between Frenchman and Indian, Royalist and colonist, Union and Confederacy.

'Keegan visits all the battle sites in turn and brings them to life with the evocative prose that his admirers will remember from *The Face of Battle*...This opus is a labour of love.' *Mail on Sunday*

'He combines personal experiences with professional observations in a way that makes this sterling book an engrossing blend of anecdotal reminiscence and analytical reflection...Like all good writers of good history, Keegan distils the complex into the essence. He describes the contours of the American land which caused one force to succeed and the other to succumb. And he profiles the leaders who hesitated fatally. And all the while, he chats about the nature of war, casually passing on one arresting observation after another. ' *Daily Telegraph*

'Arresting.' *Daily Telegraph*

£ 9.99   0712673261

John Keegan

The Second World War

An outstanding history of the Second World War by one of our most distinguished historians.

In this comprehensive history, John Keegan explores both the technical and the human impact of the greatest war of all time. He focuses on five crucial battles and offers new insights into the distinctive methods and motivations of modern warfare. In knowledgeable, perceptive analysis of the airborne battle of Crete, the carrier battle of Midway, the tank battle of Falaise, the city battle of Berlin, and the amphibious battle of Okinawa, Keegan illuminates the strategic dilemmas faced by the leaders and the consequences of their decisions on the fighting men and the course of the war as a whole.

'In this magnificently illustrated volume, our most original military historian gives the whys and wherefores of war as well as the blood and guts.' *Mail on Sunday*

'John Keegan's history of World War II stands above the competition.' *Preview*

'As a military historian [John Keegan] has a remarkable capacity to appreciate both the political context of the war and its immediate meaning for those caught in the heat of battle…The war is divided into three theatres – Western and Eastern Europe and the Pacific – up to 1943, and from 1943 to 1945. In each theatre and at each stage he opens with the strategic dilemmas confronting one of the key actors and then takes a particular battle to illustrate the changing character of warfare…Lucid, informed and authoritative.' *Sunday Times*

£15.00   0712673482

Order more Pimlico titles from your local bookshop, or have them delivered direct to your door by
BOOKPOST

• John Keegan, *The Face of Battle*	£10.00	0712650903
• John Keegan, *A History of Warfare*	£9.99	0712698507
• John Keegan, *The Mask of Command*	£8.99	1844137384
• John Keegan, *Six Armies in Normandy*	£8.99	1844137392
• John Keegan, *The Battle for History*	£10.00	0712673601
• John Keegan, *Warpaths*	£9.99	0712673261
• John Keegan, *The Second World War*	£15.00	0712673482

FREE POST AND PACKING

Overseas customers allow £2 per paperback

PHONE: 01624 677237

POST: Random House Books
C/o Bookpost, PO Box 29, Douglas
Isle of Man, IM99 1BQ

FAX: 01624 670923

EMAIL: bookshop@enterprise.net

Cheques and credit cards accepted

Prices and availability subject to change without notice.
Allow 28 days for delivery

www.randomhouse.co.uk/pimlico